ABORIGINAL FIELDS OF PRACTICE

ABORIGINAL FIELDS OF PRACTICE

Edited By

BINDI BENNETT

First published 2021 by
RED GLOBE PRESS

Red Globe Press in the UK is an imprint of Macmillan Education Limited, registered in England, company number 01755588, of 4 Crinan Street, London, N1 9XW.

Red Globe Press® is a registered trademark in the United States, the United Kingdom, Europe and other countries.

ISBN 978-1-352-01233-0 hardback
ISBN 978-1-352-01228-6 paperback

This book is printed on paper suitable for recycling and made from fully managed and sustained forest sources. Logging, pulping and manufacturing processes are expected to conform to the environmental regulations of the country of origin.

A catalogue record for this book is available from the British Library.

A catalog record for this book is available from the Library of Congress.

Publisher responsible for the title: Helen Caunce, Peter Hooper
Assistant Editor: Verity Rimmer
Cover Designer: Laura de Grasse
Production Editor: Elizabeth Holmes
Marketing Manager: Fiona McNeill (Australia and NZ) and Amy Suratia

CONTENTS

Contents

Contents

Contents

LIST OF FIGURES

Figures

ACKNOWLEDGEMENTS

The authors wish to acknowledge the Traditional custodians of this sovereign and unceded land, now named Australia. We wish to acknowledge our Elders past and present and thank them for continuing to guide us in their wisdom.

We thank all of the contributors for sharing their knowledge, skills and wisdom with us in this book and for all the hard work and energy put into creating this book for social workers.

On a personal note, Bindi would like to thank her family, friends and animals for their continued support in her endeavors and for loving her just as she is.

Amy Kennedy wishes to acknowledge the perpetual strength, survival, resistance and resilience of all First Nations people. She wishes to acknowledge her Ancestors who, through the ongoing trauma, passed on the sacred knowledge of resilience and healing through culture. She dedicates her chapter to her family's first wanggaay (baby) Shelby Jean; and to her family of strong Wiradjuri descendants.

Bindi would like to acknowledge all of the authors in Alston, M., & McKinnon, J. (Eds.). (2005). *Social work: Fields of practice*. Oxford University Press, USA. as her inspiration for this book.

WORKING WITH PARTICULAR INTEREST

1 The Intersectionality of Indigeneity and Gender in Australian Social Work

Jacob Prehn, Jaycynta Krakouer, and Todd J. Fernando

This chapter explores the intersection of gender and ethnicity/race for social work practice with Aboriginal and Torres Strait Islander[1] peoples in Australia. We argue that successfully navigating the intersection of these identities are paramount to effective social work practice with Indigenous Australians. To articulate this, we begin by challenging the dominant gender binary narrative. This social construction has dramatically shaped the provision of gendered services, which are often inadequate for meeting the needs of Indigenous peoples, let alone those further marginalised in specific ways by their intersecting gendered identity. We suggest that a means of alleviating these structural issues is through understanding, reflecting, and employing an intersectional practice framework within the client–worker relationship as it relates to Aboriginal and Torres Strait Islander peoples. Although this intersectional practice framework lightens the inadequate provision of services for Aboriginal and Torres Strait Islander peoples and their gendered requirements, structural change, inclusive of intersectional considerations, is ultimately needed.

Standpoint This chapter uses Indigenous standpoint theory to frame our approach to the topic of Indigeneity and gender, their intersection, and social work in Australia. Standpoint is theoretically summarised as the way in which social positioning, epistemology, axiology, and ontology guides the research process (Walter, 2013). The theory of standpoint helps us to acknowledge the world around us, our social positioning in it, and how this positioning relates to others and society. All three authors of this chapter are Aboriginal, and each identifies with a different Aboriginal nation across Australia.[2] We each identify with different gendered identities, male, female, and queer. Additionally, we are all either employed or studying in a tertiary educational institution, and two of us are qualified social workers. We argue these social contexts are central in shaping our held worldview and influence the way we have conceptualised, written, and disseminated the chapter.

Introduction

According to the World Health Organisation (2019), gender is commonly referred to as the socially constructed characteristics of women and men, inclusive of associated gender norms, roles, and relationships. However, this very definition, by one of the leading international health organisations, is grounded in Western settler-colonial gender binaries (Smith, 2010). This classification overlooks gendered identities situated outside the traditional Western settler binary of male or female. We advocate the conceptualisation of gender outside this dualistic framework, to instead be inclusive of additional identities such as non-binary, queer, or culturally specific genders like Fa'afāfine (Schmidt, 2016), Two-spirit (Jacobs, Thomas, & Lang, 1997), and Sistergirl/Brotherboy (Kerry, 2014).

Within both Aboriginal and Torres Strait Islander and Western societies, gender is a central social category that shapes identity, rules, and norms. Although sex and gender are different entities, both Indigenous and Western societies place gendered constraints, rules, and expectations on people, often based on their assigned sex at birth (Prince, 2005; Veenstra, 2011). These societal expectations and customs result in gender stereotypes and normativity that operate differently in Western and Indigenous societies. For example, in Western society, men are expected to conform to a rigid set of constraints to exhibit signs of strength and (cis heterosexual) masculinity (RW Connell, 2005b; Ford, 2018). These expectations result in unwritten societal rules for men – such as *'boys don't cry'* and *'toughen up and be a man'* – that can create environments of toxic masculinity (Ford, 2018). Conversely, the notion of *'holding men'* is one Aboriginal cultural practice which encourages males to deeply caring for fellow males (McCoy, 2008), a phenomenon which would likely be marginalised by Western masculinity. Because of gender's significance in shaping people's lives, a gendered approach to health and wellbeing has been suggested as advantageous (see for example Bates, Hankivsky, and Springer (2009) and Verbrugge (1985)).

Gender can significantly influence individual and collective health and wellbeing experiences. Previous research regarding this has explored the meaning of gendered experiences of health, such as accessing health services (Browne et al., 2011; Canuto, Wittert, Harfield, & Brown, 2018; Lachapelle, Dunnagan, & Bird, 2011), and the understanding of disease and illness (Australian Bureau of Statistics, 2013; Kidd, Gibbons, Kara, Blundell, & Berryman, 2013). The notion of gendered health and wellbeing approaches is further complicated when considering intersecting identities. As Bates et al. (2009, p. 1003) argue, for Aboriginal and Torres Strait Islander peoples *'a focus on only the gendered status of women, or differences between "men" and "women," without attention to concurrent intersecting statuses can, therefore, obscure important heterogeneity'*. Other academics and writers such as Croll, Neumark-Sztainer, Story, and Ireland (2002), and Krieger, Chen, Waterman, Rehkopf, and Subramanian (2003) have also explored the intersection of gender and ethnicity in health contexts. They too promote a gendered approach to health and wellbeing while being cognisant of the role of ethnicity in further shaping health and wellbeing experiences. The significance of gender in shaping and ordering Aboriginal and Torres Strait Islander, and non-Indigenous societies, means that, for effective practice, social workers need to feel confident to navigate the intersection of gender and Indigeneity, as well as any other relevant social contexts which may be operating (Prehn, 2019).

This chapter explores the intersectionality of gender and ethnicity in social work practice with Aboriginal and Torres Strait Islander peoples. We argue that understanding the diverse dynamics of gender, as a social worker, is a central component to effectively attain best practice outcomes with Indigenous peoples. To achieve this, we explore the construction of gender and the role of power within Aboriginal and Torres Strait Islander and Western societies. We then discuss policy and direct practice, the centrality of the client–worker relationship, and Indigenous community protocols as components of successfully working with Aboriginal and Torres Strait Islander peoples. Overall, we advocate for the utilisation of an intersectional practice framework, coupled with advocacy for appropriate structural change that rejects gender normativity.

Gender

Gender is a social construct that shapes and influences individual and collective societal experiences. Social workers should recognise that 'sex and gender are not the same thing' (Prince, 2005, p. 29). Sex is an individual's biological makeup that develops before birth and depends on a variety of factors. These components include:

> Gonads (ovary or testes).
> Sex hormones (estrogen or testosterone).
> Reproductive anatomy (uterus or prostate gland).
> External genitalia (vulva or penis). And,
> The presence of a Y chromosome.
> (Daly & Wilson, 1983; Stoller, 2020)

The binary of being categorised as male or female is not as simple as traditional definitions of sex suggest. If all five of these components are not simultaneously aligned, then an individual's assigned sex at birth may not reflect their physical body (Daly & Wilson, 1983; Stoller, 2020). This complexity can be further compounded if the prescribed gender does not align with societal sex and gendered norms (Beemyn & Rankin, 2011). Moving away from traditional Western sex and gender binaries is important to be inclusive of those who sit outside these categories.

From a Western perspective, the term gender can be traced back to ancient Greece, where its early development has been attributed to the work of Protagoras (Roberts, 2013). However, it was not until more recent times in the 1950s and 1960s that the conceptualisation of gender progressed into a malleable and workable social term (Holmes, 2012). Gender became particularly prominent with the work of early feminists (Freedman, 2007) who aimed to challenge patriarchal power.[3] Since then, gender has become one of the key social categories widely discussed within social work literature (Adams, 2015; Burdge, 2007; Orme, 2002) and the academy more broadly (Aboriginal Health Council of South Australia, 2019; Connell, 2005b; Fredericks et al., 2017; Pease, 2002). Understanding gender, and gender differences, is historically rooted in and confined to a male/female paradigm (Robbins & McGowan, 2016). This is the case in both Western and Indigenous Australian societies. However, the history of the feminist movement (including feminist standpoint theory) became a catalyst for researchers to consider the multifaceted experiences and standpoints of gender and its associated identities (Harding, 2004). This new lens – which is now playing out in Indigenous Australian societies – captured the growing ways in which gender identity challenged the male/female paradigm in recent times.

The diversity of gender is recognised within Aboriginal societies insofar as terms such as Brotherboy and Sistergirl are used to describe the experience of Aboriginal transgender people (Farrell, 2017). Beyond the use of Brotherboy and Sistergirl, no term exists or is widely accepted to represent Lesbian, Gay, Bisexual, Transgender, Intersex or Queer Aboriginal and Torres Strait Islander peoples. As a result, limitations and certain complications arise to describe people identifying as such, without inference to the Western concept of the LGBTIQ umbrella and its associated identities' values and ways of being. This is also the case for defining Aboriginal and Torres Strait Islander peoples who view their gender as being separate from the Western binary of male or female.

Men's business and women's business

From an Aboriginal and Torres Strait Islander perspective, gender plays a significant role across various cultural, health, and wellbeing domains. These include cultural practices (McCoy, 2008), lived experiences (Aboriginal Health Council of South Australia, 2019; Connell, 2005a; Fredericks et al., 2017), and health outcomes (Australian Department of Health and Ageing, 2013; McCalman et al., 2010; Tsey et al., 2007). Gender shapes particular roles held by both males and females within Aboriginal and Torres Strait Islander societies (Aboriginal Health Council of South Australia, 2019; Fredericks, Adams, & Best, 2014; Fredericks et al., 2017). Historically, and through to contemporary times, gender outlines specific cultural processes – such as participation in lore and undertaking of ceremony and cultural practices – for men and women. Often referred to as men's or women's business (Fredericks et al., 2014; McCoy, 2008), this gender-specific business is passed from Elders of the same gender, at particular times, to youth or adults in a specific Aboriginal or Torres Strait Islander community. An example of gender operating in Aboriginal society is the playing of the yidaki (colloquially known as the didgeridoo). Playing of the yidaki is a strictly male activity; if females play the instrument it is believed to result in infertility (Newcastle, 2017). Men's and women's business is diverse throughout the continent, with specific processes varying by the community. While men's and women's business fosters cultural continuity (via enabling cultural knowledge to be passed from one generation to the next), it can also serve to create gendered norms and expectations that exclude some Indigenous peoples. This exclusion – by way of gender normativity – will be discussed later in the 'gender and power' section of this chapter.

In Aboriginal and Torres Strait Islander society, there is significant cultural and gender diversity that exists across nations, mobs, and clan groups. This multiplicity is further impacted and shaped by the process of colonisation, with invasion occurring at different times throughout the continent (Dudgeon, Wright, Paradies, Garvey, & Walker, 2014). An example of cultural and gendered diversity is the male cultural practice of '*holding*' specific to Putu people in Western Australia (McCoy, 2008). The notion of holding can be translated to caring deeply for another male and being there for them, particularly in times of need. From a Western perspective of masculinity, this could be interpreted as feminine and not 'manly behaviour', conflicting with constructs of hegemonic masculinity (Connell, 1995, 2005a).

The process of colonisation aimed not only to remove Aboriginal people from the land for economic purposes (Watson, 2009), but also to colonise and shape their lives. The British '*believed that the introduction of Western education and Christianity would transform a morally decedent society*' (Tharoor, 2018, p. 201). Colonisation intended to breakdown and re-mould Aboriginal gender roles and identities to match those of settler-colonial society and the metropole (Connell, 2007; Wolfe, 1999, 2006). Of the available historical records, these accounts are often from the epistemological positioning of Europeans, from eyewitness accounts left by settlers, government employees, and religious figures (Ganter, 1999). The effect of gender colonisation was experienced in other parts of the world too, for example, by the Bengal in India (Sinha, 1995), whose males were considered 'too feminine' by British standards of masculinity. In Southern Africa, men sought to model their masculinity on traits exerted by the colonisers to gain favour (Morrell, 1998). In the Americas, two-spirit people were considered a third gender identity that held a prominent role in society and ceremony (Hardin, 2002). However, because this gender construct was at odds with the beliefs of the Spanish Conquistadors, particularly brutal and violent acts were inflicted upon the two-spirit people. The origins of the notion of machismo, a form of hyper-masculinity, can be traced back to this treatment of two-spirit people in the Americas (Driskill, 2011).

Ultimately, gender is a social construct that, for Black, Brown, and Indigenous peoples worldwide, has been shaped through contact with

Western, colonial societies. Unlike those who occupy a dominant position in Australian settler-colonial society, Indigenous Australians' experiences of gender have been shaped by violent conflict, warfare, and genocide. Power, consequently, intersects with Indigenous people's experiences of gender normativity in Western society.

Power and gender

Power is an important consideration in understanding the intersection of gender and Indigeneity. Power refers to the ability of an individual, or a collective group, to exert their own free will within the context of social relationships, even in the face of resistance (Wallimann, Tatsis, & Zito, 1977). Historically, Aboriginal and Torres Strait Islander peoples have been subjected to horrific violence, genocide, forcible dislocation from their lands, and systemic denial of the agency at the hands of the coloniser (Bringing Them Home, 1997; Reynolds, 2006). However, power continues to elude Aboriginal Australians; in some instances, Aboriginal and Islander peoples are treated as subordinate and childlike in comparison with white Australians (Nakata, 2018). It is well documented that Aboriginal and Torres Strait Islander peoples experience oppression and marginalisation within Australian settler-colonial society (Habibis, Taylor, Walter, & Elder, 2016). However, at the intersection of gender and Indigeneity, a further layer of oppression is experienced by Indigenous women and gender-diverse peoples.

Aboriginal and Torres Strait Islander males experience both privilege and oppression within Australian settler-colonial society, which, like other Western countries, is patriarchal in its orientation (Connell, 2005b). Aboriginal men experience privilege over Indigenous women and other gendered identities across various socioeconomic domains (such as employment, income, household labour, and childrearing expectations; see, for example, Biddle, Howlett, Hunter, and Paradies (2013), Coston and Kimmel (2012), and Shields (2008)). However, comparatively with white males in Australian settler society, Aboriginal and Torres Strait Islander men do not have the same access to privilege, evidenced by experiences of interpersonal and systemic racism (Mukandi et al., 2019; Paradies, 2006; Paradies et al., 2015). Similarly, Aboriginal women, children, and non-binary persons experience privilege and oppression differently compared with their non-Indigenous counterparts as a result of their Indigeneity (McGlade, 2012; Moreton-Robinson, 2000).

In response to Aboriginal women's experiences of patriarchy, as distinct from non-Aboriginal women's experiences of patriarchy, Aboriginal feminist scholarship tackles the intersection of race and gender. Aboriginal feminist and law scholar, Hannah McGlade (2012, p. 67) articulates that

> ... Aboriginal feminism utilises the critique of feminism along with anti-colonialism to show how Aboriginal people, in particular women, are affected by colonialism and patriarchy. Aboriginal feminism takes account of both racism and sexism, and Aboriginal feminists are the clearest in linking sex and race oppression. Aboriginal feminists are therefore identified as political adversaries not only by colonial society but also by Indigenous male elites whose power they challenge.

Power in this context is inextricably linked to patriarchy, a structure within male-oriented societies whereby the oppression of women (as well as non-binary persons) is perpetuated by men (Breckenridge & Carmody, 1992). However, at the intersection of gender and Aboriginality, issues of race and racism have taken precedence over experiences of sexism. Aboriginal legal scholar Larissa Behrendt (1993, p. 34) has articulated how racism is experienced as the primary form of discrimination for Aboriginal women, noting that '*For white women, sexism is the enemy. For black women, racism is just as insidious*'. Behrendt (1993) highlights the conflict of diversity between Aboriginal and white women's experiences of patriarchy. This feminist conflict at the intersection of race is explored in Aileen Moreton-Robinson's seminal work, *Talkin' Up to the White Woman*, whereby Moreton-Robinson (2000) identifies white women as Aboriginal women's oppressors. An added dimension of complexity concerns normative gender ideals, with gender norms further oppressing Aboriginal peoples who do not conform to Western gender stereotypes.

Earlier in the chapter, men's and women's business were discussed as gendered cultural protocols that enable cultural continuity and the transmission of cultural knowledge from one generation to the next. Traditionally, and in some contemporary contexts, First Nations lore (which consists of knowledge, beliefs, rules, and customs) governs Aboriginal and Torres Strait Islander societies. Certain lore may belong exclusively to men or women, thus giving rise to the distinction between men's and women's business. Men's and women's business have an important place in Aboriginal and Torres Strait Islander societies: they enable cultural transmission, keep culture alive, and in some cases, can enable healing[4] and wellbeing (Healing Foundation, 2020). However, men's and women's business can also create gender norms that exclude some Aboriginal and Torres Strait Islander peoples.

For Aboriginal and Torres Strait Islander peoples, gender normativity operates through men's and women's business. Men may be expected to only discuss health issues with other men, and vice versa for women. However, First Nations peoples who do not subscribe to male/female gender binaries and/or expressions are excluded from participation in men's and women's business. Similarly, First Nations peoples who do not have access to gendered cultural knowledge (as a result of cultural disconnection) are also excluded from men's and women's business. Depending on the community, men's and women's business may be more or less paramount in shaping day-to-day life. The purpose here is not to reject men's and women's business altogether. Rather, we wish to highlight that gender normativity operates in Aboriginal and Torres Strait Islander societies via men's and women's business that are exclusive by nature. Social workers need to be cognisant of this exclusion and the need to avoid gendered cultural assumptions.

Sexuality

Related to gender normativity, heteronormativity is the idea that being straight is to be normal, and to be anything else is 'not normal' (Schilt & Westbrook, 2009). Many of the terms and definitions used to describe sex, sexuality, and gender diversity in Western society often occur outside of heteronormative binary systems. This means that for the most part, queer people have rejected the labels and definitions straight people have determined. In doing so, queer people have rebuilt a lexicon to describe a range of sexuality and gender experiences. As revolutionary as this sounds, it is crucial to recognise that LGBTIQ terminology – Lesbian, Gay, Bisexual, Transgender, Intersex, and Queer – are inherent, though not exclusively, Western concepts. Some scholars, such as Clark (2015) and Smith (2010), argue that these terms, and their definitions, do not necessarily provide an adequate understanding of the range of gender and sexual diversity (including experiences) within non-white populations (Da Silva, 2007). This is an important distinction to make because many of the countries in which these terms and definitions were formulated are largely multicultural societies.

The terms that promote the diversity of gender and sexuality have historically connected themselves to whiteness, and consequently have mostly ignored the cultural histories of gender and sexuality produced throughout the world. It has cultivated a gender and queer-normativity that is underpinned mainly by white experiences. This history is essential to understand when considering the successful design of policy and programs within social work that target gendered identities within different cultural groups. It is also necessary to understand the historical and cultural experiences of non-white populations and their concepts and ideas around gender and sexuality. A failure to learn or recognise these experiences puts us all at risk of promoting assimilation within policy, program, and practice, especially in the field of social work. Australian history shows how devastating assimilation can be for existing cultures: it is a path we cannot trek again.

Heteronormativity

Often, the term assimilation is used in a language that underpins discourses about race in society. Assimilation, however, is a vastly complex process and when woven into the thread of sexuality, the concept of assimilation becomes multifaceted. As such, the defining themes of sexuality – as enforced by Western schools of thought – depend profoundly on a homosexual/heterosexual paradigm to successfully compartmentalise an ideal order of Western society. We see this methodology also being played out in race, class, education, and gender.

The power and role that religion has and continues to play in our societies provide a foundation to enforce the claim that any system of sexuality or gender outside the Western sphere could be easily demarcated as an undesirable falsehood. When we prod a little deeper into differing narratives, we find that, globally, concepts of gender and sexuality are considerably complex.

The diversity of language to describe gender is recognised within Indigenous Australians societies, insofar as terms Brotherboy and Sistergirl are used to describe the cultural practices and realities of Indigenous Australian transgender people. Internationally, Maori use the term Takatāpui to describe cultural practices for people who identify as both gay and Maori (Murray, 2003). In 1990, Native American populations (and, to an extent, Canadian First Nations) moved to restore a more inclusive historical term, Two-Spirit.[5] In Indian society, the term Hijra[6] is employed to identify a population that are considered neither man nor woman – but instead, Hijras choose to enjoy the femininity of the world (Hall & O'Donovan, 2014). Within the Samoan and Polynesian diasporas, Fa'afafine[7] are people who identify themselves as a third-gender or non-binary (Schmidt, 2016).

There are many more examples of gender and sexuality variations from the African diaspora, South America, parts of Europe, across the Middle East, and even throughout Asia. What these examples tell us is that societies and cultures across the globe have used diverse gender and sexuality concepts for many thousands of years and that for Indigenous peoples, the intersection of Indigeneity, gender, and power hold considerable complexity. Social work practitioners need to take these intersections into account to practice cultural humility[8] with Indigenous Australian service users.

Policy and practice context

A nuanced understanding of the policy and practice context that impacts service delivery is critical for social workers. Underpinned by an ideology of 'individual responsibility' for welfare in contemporary times, at a policy level, neoliberalism has resulted in funding cuts to social work services and the transformation of service delivery in some sectors (e.g. the National Disability Insurance Scheme (NDIS) is an example of market-driven service provision) (Marston, Cowling, & Bielefeld, 2016; Walter, 2010). While it is beyond the scope of this chapter to go into depth about neoliberalism, social workers must understand its impact on service delivery.

Neoliberalism is a political ideology that espouses the importance of the free market, deregulation, privatisation, and individual responsibility (Jamrozik, 2009; Mendes, 2017). It should not be mistaken for capitalism; instead, neoliberalism dictates how capitalism should be operationalised (Venugopal, 2015). Neoliberalism is an ideology that is not concerned with the wellbeing of communities, but rather with the wellbeing of the market. One of the central tenets underpinning neoliberalism is that, without interference, the market will provide for citizens – via 'trickle-down economics' – who take advantage of market opportunities (such as employment, housing, and other economic opportunities) (Jamrozik, 2009; Mendes, 2017). Individuals are responsible for their wellbeing, with their wellbeing best assured via deregulated market forces.

Conversely, those who rely on state-sanctioned welfare interfere with market forces, which creates further problems, both for the economy and themselves (Jamrozik, 2009). 'Dependence' on government welfare is thus discouraged, and 'disincentives' for accessing government-funded support are put in place by governments (Venugopal, 2015; Walter, 2010). At this intersection, social work services – who are often funded by governments – are subject to funding restrictions, increased competition with other service providers for funding, increased accountability to governments for services provided, and in some cases, surveillance of their clients (i.e. most common in Centrelink (now known as Services Australia) or job-seeker support services) (Bielefeld, 2018). A discussion of the political ideology that underpins contemporary social work services in Australia is necessary to shift the focus away from the individual characteristics of service users, to the broader macro-environment. At the macro level, the impact of systemic racism, growing inequality in society, and gender normativity can be taken into account. Without a focus on societal and systemic issues at the macro level, there can be a tendency to focus on individual pathology or 'dysfunction', which is not helpful to a discussion about Indigeneity, gender, and power.

At the practice level, social work services in Australia are typically offered within specific contexts or 'fields' of practice (such as hospitals, alcohol and other drug (AOD) services, or child and family welfare). These are frequently dependent on local, state, and/or federal government funding. Services are typically delivered based on a single presenting need, with few social work services addressing dual or multiple needs (such as AOD, domestic family violence, and child and family welfare). Furthermore, service delivery is rarely offered based on gender (one exception to this is domestic family violence (DFV) services, where service delivery may be underpinned by feminist frameworks for practice) (Neave, Faulkner, & Nicholson, 2016). Conversely, Aboriginal Community-Controlled Organisations (ACCOs) do deliver social work services based on Aboriginality within certain fields of practice, such as health and child and family welfare. For example, in Victoria, the Victorian Aboriginal Child Care Agency (VACCA) offers a host of child and family welfare services – from early intervention family support, through to foster care services – to children and families who identify as Aboriginal and/or Torres Strait Islander (VACCA, 2018).

While there are some social work services delivered to Aboriginal and Torres Strait Islander peoples on the basis of Aboriginality, these services do not always respond to the intersection of Aboriginality and gender. Instead, Aboriginality tends to take precedence over gender in service delivery, without an appreciation of the various intersections of people's identities (Crenshaw, 1991). This particular service delivery practised by the Aboriginal community-controlled health sector reveals a failure to extend the principles of cultural safety for those Indigenous patients who identify their gender outside the heteronormative binary of male or female (Canuto et al., 2018). The lack of cultural safety of services to provide appropriate gendered-specific services is a major shortcoming for best practice of service delivery; cultural safety is one of the critical components of the cultural and social determinants of health (Connell, 2012).

Therefore, we argue that intersectionality, as a framework for practice, enables an appreciation of how Aboriginal people's social and political identities – which encompass gender identity, race, class, sexuality, religion, (dis)ability as well as other identity markers – intersect with one another to create uniqueness, at both an individual level and a collective level (Christie, 2006; Ferlatte et al., 2018; McCall, 2005). Discrimination and oppression operate differently depending on Indigenous people's intersecting identities. The importance of intersectionality as a framework to support the individual client–worker relationship is discussed below.

Client–worker relationship

Entire units are taught at Australian universities[9] on social work practice with Indigenous Australians. We do not intend to go into depth in this chapter, but instead, to base our practice-based suggestions specifically around the intersection of Indigeneity and gender. We advocate that, for social workers to effectively practice with Indigenous Australians at the intersection of gender, social workers must:

1. Understand Australia's First Nations history.

2. Be aware of diversity (intersectionality as a framework).

3. Reflect on their ethnocentrism and other intersecting identities.

4. Be aware of local First Nations community contexts.

Understand Australia's First Nations history

When social workers are practicing with Aboriginal and Torres Strait Islander peoples, the nurturing of this relationship is a central pillar in the facilitation of achieving meaningful empowerment, growth, and lasting change. First and foremost, a legacy of distrust exists between Aboriginal and Torres Strait Islander communities and social workers (Bennett, Zubrzycki, & Bacon, 2011). Social workers were complicit in removing Aboriginal and Torres Strait Islander children from their families throughout the Stolen Generations (Van Krieken, 1999; Zuchowski, Savage, Miles, & Gair, 2013), which has had profound impacts on Aboriginal and Torres Strait Islander peoples and their perception of the social work profession (Australian Association of Social Workers, 2010; Dudgeon et al., 2014; Harms et al., 2011). Acknowledging this, and being aware of its influence, is a critical component to nurturing successful client–worker relationships, as highlighted by Harms et al. (2011, pp. 160–161) in a paper examining Aboriginal and Torres Strait Islander perspectives of social workers:

> Community members reported a variety of positive and negative experiences with social workers. They identified attentiveness, availability, and practical involvement as central to effective social work practice. Core to the success of the relationship was respect for the client and honesty in the relationship. They wanted workers to use everyday language, provide practical assistance, make the time to listen, understand family and community structures, and involve the client in the process.

In the same way, social workers practice with other marginalised groups, we suggest a healthy client–worker relationship is built upon the social work profession's foundational concepts: trust, respect, self-determination, and accountability (Australian Association of Social Workers, 2013). Taking the necessary time to facilitate a relationship grounded in trust, respect, self-determination, and accountability is paramount. This should be the first step to creating an effective client–worker relationship.

Intersectional framework

In regard to gender and social work practice with Aboriginal and Torres Strait Islander peoples, we suggest utilising an intersectional framework for practice (Crenshaw, 1991). Intersectionality, as a practice framework, enables the consideration of multiple, intersecting identities, such as Indigeneity, gender identity, class, sexuality, and (dis)ability, in social work practice (Crenshaw, 1991). This multifaceted intersectional framework allows for different social contexts to be addressed simultaneously (Bastos, Harnois, & Paradies, 2017). For example, Aboriginality and non-binary gender identity may both marginalise a person accessing mental health services, yet coupled together, experiences of marginalisation may be further compounded. Via intersectionality as a framework for practice, additional frontiers of oppression or privilege can be identified, appropriately understood, and addressed.

Aboriginal and Torres Strait Islander peoples – as individuals and as a group – experience various degrees of oppression and privilege in nuanced ways that need to be considered and understood.

Ethnocentrism

Intersectional practice also enables a review of ethnocentrism and our own intersecting identities as practitioners. For effective practice with Aboriginal and Torres Strait Islanders, we ask practitioners to reflect on their social positioning and ethnocentrism. Walter, Taylor, and Habibis (2011) have highlighted that the majority of Australian social workers are white and that this whiteness is privileged throughout settler-colonial society. Whiteness – as a structure that privileges white identity and Western ways of doing, subsequently producing white privilege – permeates many aspects of the social work profession in Australia, such as education, policy, institutions, and direct practice. Reflecting on how whiteness and other identities – such as able-bodied or cis-heterosexual – may be operating in the client–worker relationship – and in what ways this power dynamic may be influencing direct practice – is a fruitful endeavour that will ultimately strengthen the client–worker relationship. Awareness of the systems and structures that perpetuate whiteness and white privilege is crucial. It is also paramount to be aware of local Aboriginal and Torres Strait Islander contexts, and community protocols to strengthen the client–worker relationship.

Aboriginal and Torres Strait Islander community protocols

The fourth component we advocate to improve the client–worker relationship is an awareness of the local context. There are a variety of similarities and differences amongst Aboriginal and Torres Strait Islander peoples and communities throughout Australia, with social workers needing to be cognisant of this diversity. Aboriginal and Torres Strait Islander people are not an homogenous group; there are over 500 different communities, each with their protocols (Dudgeon et al., 2014). As such, gendered community conventions will vary. For social workers, understanding local Aboriginal and Torres Strait Islander community protocols are an essential component to achieve best practice outcomes, meet practice standards (Australian Association of Social Workers, 2013), and ensure cultural competence (Harms et al., 2011; Walker, 2014).

When practicing as a social worker with Aboriginal and Torres Strait Islander peoples, community protocols can shape appropriate processes (Harms et al., 2011). For example, '*Alcohol can be sensitive to discuss due to cultural protocols such as kinship/family systems, gender or age, shame (embarrassment) or community and social acceptance of alcohol*' (Harrison et al., 2019, p. 6). Understanding relevant Indigenous community protocols is an important component of effective social work practice.

When practising in a mental health context, social workers are one of five professions required to abide by the National Standards for the Mental Health Workforce Guidelines 2013 (Victorian Government Department of Health, 2013). These practice standards highlight the significance of understanding and following local community protocols when working with Australia's First Nations peoples. This is discussed in Standard 4: Working with Aboriginal and Torres Strait Islander people, families and communities: Subsection 7 *'Seeks to understand and work within local cultural protocols and kinship structures of Aboriginal and Torres Strait Islander communities'* and subsection 8 *'Respectfully follow Indigenous protocols in community contexts, such as the process of vouching in which one or some of the community members attest to the person wishing to enter the community'* (Victorian Government Department of Health, 2013, p. 14).

Developing relationships and collaborating with Aboriginal and Torres Strait Islander Aboriginal Health Workers (ATSIHW) and Health Practitioners (ATSIHP) are a fruitful means of understanding local community protocols regarding gender in health contexts. ATSIHW/HPs are a key allied health profession in the Indigenous health sphere (Health Workforce Australia, 2011). Generally, they have an in-depth understanding of the Aboriginal or Torres Strait Islander community in which they work. Working in partnership with them can improve social work practice by utilising their in-depth understanding of their local First Nations community. This is one example regarding strengthening social work practice in health contexts; outside of health contexts, social workers need to build relationships with the local community, taking the advice of those who have seniority in the community.

Future Research

There is limited research regarding the role played by gender within Aboriginal and Torres Strait Islander communities across Australia. Gender is a key social phenomenon that shapes individual and collective experiences, therefore having a greater understanding of its functioning is needed to achieve high-quality social work practice outcomes. Of the research available, historically it has been from a Western standpoint as an anthropological phenomenon, rather than an Indigenous lived experience (Baskin, 2005; Ganter, 1999; Smith, 1999). Further, there is significantly less research regarding Indigenous peoples in Australia and non-binary gender identities, and how this impacts social work practice and health outcomes.

The Aboriginal Health Council of South Australia (2019, p. 1) made a similar suggestion regarding Aboriginal and Torres Strait Islander LGBTIQ peoples. *'Further research is required to raise awareness of the experiences and needs of LGBT[I]Q peoples, and their contribution to culture and community'*. However, getting accurate data to explore the needs of stigmatised minorities can be difficult. As discussed by the Australian Bureau of Statistics (2018, p. 1):

> Collecting accurate information on either sex or gender in the Australian Census has many challenges. Most households complete the Census without contact with an interviewer or any interaction with ABS [Australian Bureau of Statistics] staff. This means that the ABS cannot answer any questions from the respondent or explain any of the Census questions – for example, explaining the difference between sex and gender.

In the 2016 Australian Census, 5.4 per 100,000 people provided a valid and intentional sex/gender diverse response. Because of the Census limitations, when an alternative pilot test was conducted, the response rate grew to 257 per 100,000 (Australian Bureau of Statistics, 2018). These significant variations highlight the need for studies to include LGBTIQ peoples in their conceptualisation. The lack of research regarding First Nations people and intersecting gendered identifies (particularly non-binary genders) presents an exciting and meaningful but also challenging opportunity for future investigating. However, we advocate for the usage of Indigenous Data Sovereignty principles in studies involving Aboriginal and Torres Strait Islander people (Maiam nayri Wingara, 2018; Walter & Suina, 2019). Further, we suggest research on the topic of Indigeneity and gendered intersections should be led by those with lived experience of that intersecting identity. For example, research about queer Aboriginal people is led by a queer Aboriginal person, this recognises the challenges of a person with a different social positioning and held worldview to appropriately comprehend and accurately articulate these complex identities.

Conclusion

This chapter has argued for the usage of an intersectional practice framework to successfully navigate the intersection of gender and Indigeneity when working with Aboriginal and Torres Strait Islander peoples. Gender is a dominant feature of Indigenous and non-Indigenous society, shaping and determining behaviours, processes, norms, and cultural practices. However, the progression of settler-colonialism has impacted and shaped Aboriginal and Torres Strait Islander gender roles, pressuring the adoption of traditional Western binary gender characterisations which further marginalise and disempower those who lay outside these binaries.

To effectively navigate the dual frontiers of Indigeneity and gender, we advocate for the utilisation of an intersectional practice framework. The application of this framework is fruitful for effective social work practice, inclusive of policy, and the direct client–worker relationship. This intersectional approach allows for additional social phenomena such as class, sexuality, age, and (dis)ability to be considered and incorporated into direct practice considerations. However, the ultimate goal should always be working towards structural change; the dismantling of gender binaries and the decolonisation of current settler-colonial structures must be a priority for social work with Indigenous Australians.

Notes

1. Various terms, including Indigenous Australians, Indigenous, Aboriginal, and Aboriginal and Torres Strait Islander, are deliberately used throughout this chapter to refer to Australia's First Nations peoples. The use of diverse terms reflects the diversity within Australia's First Nations peoples, including diverse preferences for terms of address.

2. Please see the author biographies section of this book for specific Aboriginal identity.

3. It is beyond the scope of this chapter to describe and define patriarchy and patriarchal power. Readers interested in this topic may like to read seminal works by Gerda Lerner (*The Creation of Patriarchy*, 1987; *The Creation of Feminist Consciousness*, 1994) and Raewyn Connell (*Masculinities*, 2005). Seminal works by Angela Y. Davis (*Women, Race, & Class*, 1983), Patricia Hill Collins (*Black Feminist Thought*, 2000) and Aileen Moreton-Robinson (*Talkin' Up to the White Woman*, 2000) provide critiques on Western 'white' versions of feminism.

4. The Healing Foundation discuss men's and women's healing on their website as important methods for recovery from intergenerational trauma and strengthening community. See https://healingfoundation.org.au for further information.

5. This term opposed the use of the imposed anthropological term 'berdache' and has come to refer to contemporary native identities and roles, past and present, including individuals who identify as gay or lesbian or prescribe to non-conforming gender roles (Jacobs et al., 1997).

6. Hijra's are considered demi-gods and have the power to bless or to curse (Hall & O'Donovan, 2014).

7. Fa'afafine is recognised and plays an integral role in traditional and contemporary Polynesian society and culture. Fa'afafine is assigned male at birth but is raised mainly as female and explicitly embodies both masculine and feminine gender traits. Their behaviour typically ranges from extravagantly feminine to conventionally masculine.

8. Tervalon and Murray-Garcia (1998, p. 117) define 'cultural humility' as 'a more suitable goal in multicultural medical education. Cultural humility incorporates a lifelong commitment to self-evaluation and self-critique, to redressing the power imbalances in the patient-physician dynamic, and to developing' mutually beneficial and non-paternalistic clinical and advocacy partnerships with communities on behalf of individuals and defined populations.

9. For example, see the course structure for the Master of Social Work offered at The University of Melbourne, https://study.unimelb.edu.au/find/courses/graduate/master-of-social-work/what-will-i-study/

References

Aboriginal Health Council of South Australia. (2019). *The Aboriginal gender study*. Aboriginal Health Council of South Australia. Retrieved from https://aboriginalgenderstudy.ahcsa.org.au/

Adams, M. (2015). Utilising appropriate methodology and social work practices: Consulting with Aboriginal and Torres Strait Islander males. In C. Fejo-King & J. Poona (Ed.), *Emerging from the margins: First Australians' perspectives of social work*. Canberra, ACT: Magpie Goose Publishing.

Australian Association of Social Workers. (2010). *AASW: Code of Ethics*. Canberra, ACT: Australian Association of Social Workers.

Australian Association of Social Workers. (2013). *AASW: Practice Standards 2013*. Canberra, ACT: Australian Association of Social Workers.

Australian Bureau of Statistics. (2013). *4727.0.55.001 – Australian Aboriginal and Torres Strait Islander Health Survey: First results, Australia, 2012–13*.

Australian Bureau of Statistics. (2018). *2071.0 – Census of population and housing: Reflecting Australia – Stories from the census, 2016*.

Australian Department of Health and Ageing. (2013). *National Aboriginal and Torres Strait Islander Health Plan 2013–2023*. Australian Department of Health and Ageing. Retrieved from https://www.health.gov.au/internet/main/publishing.nsf/content/B92E980680486C3BCA257BF0001BAF01/$File/health-plan.pdf

Baskin, C. (2005). Centring Aboriginal worldviews in social work education. *The Australian Journal of Indigenous Education, 96*. Retrieved from https://login.ezproxy.utas.edu.au/login?url=http://search.ebscohost.com/login.aspx?direct=true&db=edsind&AN=edsind.146512034617247&site=eds-live

Bastos, J. L., Harnois, C. E., & Paradies, Y. C. (2017). Health care barriers, racism, and intersectionality in Australia. *Social Science & Medicine*. doi:https://doi.org/10.1016/j.socscimed.2017.05.010.

Bates, L. M., Hankivsky, O., & Springer, K. W. (2009). Gender and health inequities: A comment on the final report of the WHO commission on the social determinants of health. *Social Science & Medicine, 69*(7), 1002–1004.

Beemyn, G., & Rankin, S. (2011). *The lives of transgender people*. New York, NY: Columbia University Press.

Behrendt, L. (1993). Aboriginal women and the white lies of the feminist movement: Implications for Aboriginal women in rights discourse. *Australian Feminist Law Journal, 1*(1), 27–44.

Bennett, B., Zubrzycki, J., & Bacon, V. (2011). What do we know? The experiences of social workers working alongside Aboriginal people. *Australian Social Work, 64*(1), 20–37.

Biddle, N., Howlett, M., Hunter, B., & Paradies, Y. (2013). Labour market and other discrimination facing Indigenous Australian. *Australian Journal of Labour Economics, 16*(1), 91.

Bielefeld, S. (2018). Indigenous Peoples, neoliberalism and the state: A retreat from rights to 'responsibilisation' via the cashless welfare card. In *The neoliberal state, recognition and Indigenous rights* (pp. 18–21). Canberra, NSW: Australian National University Press.

Breckenridge, J., & Carmody, M. (1992). *Crimes of violence: Australian responses to rape and child sexual assault*. Sydney, NSW: Allen & Unwin.

Bringing Them Home. (1997). *Report of the National Inquiry into the separation of Aboriginal and Torres Strait Islander children from their families*. Sydney, NSW: Human Rights and Equal Opportunity Commission.

Browne, A. J., Smye, V. L., Rodney, P., Tang, S. Y., Mussell, B., & O'Neil, J. (2011). Access to primary care from the perspective of Aboriginal patients at an urban emergency department. *Qualitative Health Research, 21*(3), 333–348.

Burdge, B. J. (2007). Bending gender, ending gender: Theoretical foundations for social work practice with the transgender community. *Social Work, 52*(3), 243–250.

Canuto, K., Wittert, G., Harfield, S., & Brown, A. (2018). "I feel more comfortable speaking to a male": Aboriginal and Torres Strait Islander men's discourse on utilizing primary health care services. *International Journal for Equity in Health, 17*(1), 185. doi:https://doi.org/10.1186/s12939-018-0902-1.

Christie, A. (2006). Negotiating the uncomfortable intersections between gender and professional identities in social work. *Critical Social Policy, 26*(2), 390–411.

Clark, M. (2015). Indigenous subjectivity in Australia: Are we queer? *Journal of Global Indigeneity, 1*(1), 7.

Connell, R. (2005a). Change among the gatekeepers: Men, masculinities, and gender equality in the global arena. *Signs: Journal of Women in Culture and Society, 30*(3), 1801–1825.

Connell, R. (2005b). *Masculinities*. Cambridge: Polity.

Connell, R. (2007). *Southern theory: The global dynamics of knowledge in social science*. Crows Nest, NSW: Allen & Unwin.

Connell, R. (2012). Gender, health and theory: Conceptualizing the issue, in local and world perspective. *Social Science & Medicine, 74*(11), 1675–1683.

Connell, R. W. (1995). *Masculinities*. Berkeley, CA: University of California Press.

Coston, B. M., & Kimmel, M. (2012). Seeing privilege where it isn't: Marginalized masculinities and the intersectionality of privilege. *Journal of Social Issues, 68*(1), 97–111.

Crenshaw, K. (1991). Mapping the margins: Intersectionality, identity politics, and violence against women of color. *Stanford Law Review, 43*(6), 1241–1299.

Croll, J., Neumark-Sztainer, D., Story, M., & Ireland, M. (2002). Prevalence and risk and protective factors related to disordered eating behaviors among adolescents: Relationship to gender and ethnicity. *Journal of Adolescent Health, 31*(2), 166–175.

Da Silva, D. F. (2007). *Toward a global idea of race*. Minneapolis, MN: University of Minnesota Press.

Daly, M., & Wilson, M. (1983). *Sex, evolution, and behavior*. Boston, MA: Willard Grant Press.

Driskill, Q.-L. (2011). *Queer Indigenous studies: Critical interventions in theory, politics, and literature*. Tucson, AZ: University of Arizona Press.

Dudgeon, P., Wright, M., Paradies, Y., Garvey, D., & Walker, I. (2014). Aboriginal social, cultural and historical contexts. In *Working together Aboriginal and*

Torres Strait Islander mental health and wellbeing principles and practice. (pp. 3–24). Canberra, ACT: Australian Government.

Farrell, A. (2017). Archiving the Aboriginal rainbow: Building an Aboriginal LGBTIQ portal. *Australasian Journal of Information Systems, 21.*

Ferlatte, O., Salway, T., Hankivsky, O., Trussler, T., Oliffe, J. L., & Marchand, R. (2018). Recent suicide attempts across multiple social identities among gay and bisexual men: An intersectionality analysis. *Journal of homosexuality, 65*(11), 1507–1526.

Ford, C. (2018). *Boys will be boys: Power, patriarchy and the toxic bonds of mateship.* Crows Nest, NSW: Allen & Unwin.

Fredericks, B., Adams, M., & Best, O. (2014). Indigenous gendered health perspectives. In *Yatdjuligin: Aboriginal and Torres Strait Islander nursing and midwifery care* (pp. 74–86). Cambridge: University Press.

Fredericks, B., Daniels, C., Judd, J., Bainbridge, R., Clapham, K., Longbottom, M., ... & Ball, R. (2017). Gendered Indigenous health and wellbeing within the Australian Health System: a review of the literature.

Freedman, E. (2007). *No turning back: The history of feminism and the future of women.* New York, NY, Ballantine Books.

Ganter, R. (1999). Letters from Mapoon: Colonising Aboriginal gender. *Australian Historical Studies, 29*(113), 267–285. doi:https://doi.org/10.1080/10314619908596102.

Habibis, D., Taylor, P., Walter, M., & Elder, C. (2016). Repositioning the racial gaze: Aboriginal perspectives on race, race relations and governance. *Social Inclusion, 4*(1), 57–67.

Hall, K., & O'Donovan, V. (2014). Shifting gender positions among Hindi-speaking hijras. In V. Bergvall, J. Bind, & A. Freed (Eds.), *Rethinking language and gender research: Theory and practice.* London: Longman.

Hardin, M. (2002). Altering masculinities: The Spanish conquest and the evolution of the Latin American machismo. *International Journal of Sexuality and Gender Studies, 7*(1), 1–22.

Harding, S. G. (2004). *The feminist standpoint theory reader: Intellectual and political controversies.* Hove: Psychology Press.

Harms, L., Middleton, J., Whyte, J., Anderson, I., Clarke, A., Sloan, J., ... Smith, M. (2011). Social work with Aboriginal clients: Perspectives on educational preparation and practice. *Australian Social Work, 64*(2), 156–168. doi:https://doi.org/10.1080/0312407X.2011.577184.

Harrison, K. H., Lee, K. K., Dobbins, T., Wilson, S., Hayman, N., Ivers, R., ... Conigrave, K. (2019). Supporting Aboriginal community controlled health services to deliver alcohol care: Protocol for a cluster randomised controlled trial. *BMJ Open, 9*(11), e030909. doi:https://doi.org/10.1136/bmjopen-2019-030909.

Healing Foundation. (2020). Healing Foundation. Retrieved from https://healingfoundation.org.au/

Health Workforce Australia. (2011). *Aboriginal and Torres Strait Islander health worker project: Environmental scan.* Adelaide, SA: Health Workforce Australia.

Holmes, B. (2012). *Gender: Antiquity and its legacy.* London: Bloomsbury.

Jacobs, S.-E., Thomas, W., & Lang, S. (1997). *Two-spirit people: Native American gender identity, sexuality, and spirituality*. Champaign, IL: University of Illinois Press.

Jamrozik, A. W. (2009). *Social policy in the post-welfare state: Australian society in a changing world*. London: Pearson Education Limited.

Kerry, S. C. (2014). Sistergirls/brotherboys: The status of Indigenous transgender Australians. *International Journal of Transgenderism, 15*(3–4), 173–186. doi:https://doi.org/10.1080/15532739.2014.995262.

Kidd, J., Gibbons, V., Kara, E., Blundell, R., & Berryman, K. (2013). A Whānau Ora journey of Māori men with chronic illness: A Te Korowai analysis. *AlterNative: An International Journal of Indigenous Peoples, 9*(2), 125–141.

Krieger, N., Chen, J. T., Waterman, P. D., Rehkopf, D. H., & Subramanian, S. (2003). Race/ethnicity, gender, and monitoring socioeconomic gradients in health: A comparison of area-based socioeconomic measures – The public health disparities geocoding project. *American Journal of Public Health, 93*(10), 1655–1671.

Lachapelle, P. R., Dunnagan, T., & Bird, J. R. (2011). Applying innovative approaches to address health disparities in native populations: An assessment of the Crow Men's Health Project. *Community Development: Journal of the Community Development Society, 2*, 240.

Maiam nayri Wingara. (2018). An introduction to indigenous data sovereignty. Indigenous data sovereignty communique: Indignous Data Sovereignty Summit, 20 June 2018. Maiam nayri Wingara, Australian Indigenous Governance Institute. *Key Principles*. Retrieved from https://static1. squarespace.com/static/5b3043afb40b9d20411f3512/t/5b6c0f9a0e2e7 25e9cabf4a6/1533808545167/Communique%2B-%2BIndigenous%2BDa ta%2BSovereignty%2BSummit.pdf

Marston, G., Cowling, S., & Bielefeld, S. (2016). Tensions and contradictions in Australian social policy reform: Compulsory income management and the National Disability Insurance Scheme. *Australian Journal of Social Issues, 51*(4), 399–417.

McCall, L. (2005). The complexity of intersectionality. *Signs: Journal of Women in Culture and Society, 30*(3), 1771–1800.

McCalman, J., Tsey, K., Wenitong, M., Wilson, A., McEwan, A., James, Y. C., & Whiteside, M. (2010). Indigenous men's support groups and social and emotional wellbeing: A meta-synthesis of the evidence. *Australian Journal of Primary Health, 16*(2), 159–166.

McCoy, B. F. (2008). *Holding men: Kanyirninpa and the health of Aboriginal men*. Canberra, ACT: Aboriginal Studies Press.

McGlade, H. (2012). *Our greatest challenge: Aboriginal children and human rights*. Canberra, ACT: Aboriginal Studies Press.

Mendes, P. (2017). Australia's welfare wars: The players, the politics and the ideologies. *Aotearoa New Zealand Social Work, 29*(2), 145–148.

Moreton-Robinson, A. (2000). *Talkin'up to the white woman: Aboriginal women and feminism*. Brisbane, QLD: Universty of Queensland Press.

Morrell, R. (1998). Of boys and men: Masculinity and gender in Southern African studies. *Journal of Southern African Studies, 24*(4), 605–630.

Mukandi, B., Singh, D., Brady, K., Willis, J., Sinha, T., Askew, D., & Bond, C. (2019). "So we tell them": Articulating strong Black masculinities in an urban Indigenous community. *AlterNative: An International Journal of Indigenous Peoples, 15*(3), 253–260.

Murray, D. A. (2003). Who is Takatāpui? Māori language, sexuality and identity in Aotearoa/New Zealand. *Anthropologica, 5*, 233–244.

Nakata, S. (2018). The infantilisation of indigenous Australians: A problem for democracy. Griffith Review, (60), 104. Retrieved from www.griffithreview.com/.

Neave, M., Faulkner, P., & Nicholson, T. (2016). Royal Commission into Family Violence: Summary and recommendations. Retrieved from https://www.parliament.vic.gov.au/file_uploads/1a_RFV_112ppA4_SummaryRecommendations.WEB_DXQyLhqv.pdf

Newcastle, A. (2017). *Didgeri: Local collective response*. Retrieved from https://dulwichcentre.com.au/didgeri-local-collective-response-by-anthony-newcastle/

Orme, J. (2002). Social work: Gender, care and justice. *British Journal of Social Work, 32*(6), 799–814.

Paradies, Y. (2006). A systematic review of empirical research on self-reported racism and health. *International Journal of Epidemiology, 35*(4), 888–901.

Paradies, Y., Ben, J., Denson, N., Elias, A., Priest, N., Pieterse, A., ... Gee, G. (2015). Racism as a determinant of health: A systematic review and meta-analysis. *PloS one, 10*(9), e0138511.

Pease, B. (2002). *Men and gender relations*. Croydon: Tertiary Press.

Prehn, J. (2019). How social work can improve the health and wellbeing of Aboriginal men. In B. Bennett & S. Green (Eds.), *Our voices: Aboriginal and Torres Strait Islander social work* (2nd ed., pp. 157–174). London: Red Globe Press.

Prince, V. (2005). Sex vs. gender. *International Journal of Transgenderism, 8*(4), 29–32.

Reynolds, H. (2006). *The other side of the frontier: Aboriginal resistance to the European invasion of Australia*. Sydney, NSW: UNSW Press.

Robbins, C. K., & McGowan, B. L. (2016). Intersectional perspectives on gender and gender identity development. *New Directions for Student Services, 154*(2016), 71–83.

Roberts, W. R. (2013). *Rhetoric*. New York, NY: Start Publishing LLC.

Schilt, K., & Westbrook, L. (2009). Doing gender, doing heteronormativity: "Gender normals," transgender people, and the social maintenance of heterosexuality. *Gender & Society, 23*(4), 440–464.

Schmidt, J. (2016). Being 'like a woman': Fa'afāfine and Samoan masculinity. *The Asia Pacific Journal of Anthropology, 17*(3–4), 287–304. doi:https://doi.org/10.1080/14442213.2016.1182208.

Shields, S. A. (2008). Gender: An intersectionality perspective. *Sex Roles, 59*, 301–311.

Sinha, M. (1995). *Colonial masculinity: The 'manly Englishman' and the 'effeminate Bengali' in the late nineteenth century*. Manchester: Manchester University Press.

Smith, A. (2010). Queer theory and native studies: The heteronormativity of settler colonialism. *GLQ: A Journal of Lesbian and Gay Studies, 16*(1–2), 41–68.

Smith, L. T. (1999). *Decolonising methodologies: Research and Indigenous peoples*. London: Zed Books Ltd.

Stoller, R. J. (2020). *Sex and gender: The development of masculinity and femininity*. London: Routledge.

Tharoor, S. (2018). *Inglorious Empire: What the British did to India*. London: Penguin.

Tervalon, M., & Murray-Garcia, J. (1998). Cultural humility versus cultural competence: A critical distinction in defining physician training outcomes in multicultural education. *Journal of Health Care for the Poor and Underserved, 9*(2), 117–125.

Tsey, K., Wilson, A., Haswell-Elkins, M., Whiteside, M., McCalman, J., Cadet-James, Y., & Wenitong, M. (2007). Empowerment-based research methods: A 10-year approach to enhancing Indigenous social and emotional wellbeing. *Australasian Psychiatry, 15*(1), S34–S38.

VACCA. (2018). *VACCA: Children and families*. Retrieved from https://www.vacca.org/page/services/children-and-families

Van Krieken, R. (1999). The barbarism of civilization: Cultural genocide and the 'stolen generations' 1. *The British Journal of Sociology, 50*(2), 297–315.

Veenstra, G. (2011). Race, gender, class, and sexual orientation: Intersecting axes of inequality and self-rated health in Canada. *International Journal for Equity in Health, 10*(1), 3.

Venugopal, R. (2015). Neoliberalism as concept. *Economy and Society, 44*(2), 165–187. doi:https://doi.org/10.1080/03085147.2015.1013356.

Verbrugge, L. M. (1985). Gender and health: An update on hypotheses and evidence. *Journal of Health and Social Behavior, 26*(3), 156–182. doi:https://doi.org/10.2307/2136750.

Victorian Government Department of Health. (2013). *National Practice Standards for the Mental Health Workforce 2013*. Retrieved from https://www1.health.gov.au/internet/main/publishing.nsf/Content/5D7909E82304E6D2CA257C430004E877/$File/wkstd13.pdf

Walker, R. (2014). Introduction to national standards for the mental health workforce. In *Working together: Aboriginal and Torres Strait Islander mental health and wellbeing principles and practice* (pp. 181–194). Canberra, ACT: Commonwealth of Australia.

Wallimann, I., Tatsis, N. C., & Zito, G. V. (1977). On Max Weber's definition of power. *The Australian and New Zealand Journal of Sociology, 13*(3), 231–235.

Walter, M. (2010). Market forces and Indigenous resistance paradigms. *Social Movement Studies, 9*(2), 121–137.

Walter, M. (2013). The nature of social science research. In M. Walter (Ed.), *Social research methods* (3rd ed.). South Melbourne, VIC: Oxford University Press.

Walter, M., & Suina, M. (2019). Indigenous data, Indigenous methodologies and Indigenous data sovereignty. *International Journal of Social Research Methodology, 22*(3), 233–243. doi:https://doi.org/10.1080/13645579.2018.1531228.

Walter, M., Taylor, S., & Habibis, D. (2011). How white is social work in Australia? *Australian Social Work, 64*(1), 6–19.

Watson, I. (2009). In the Northern Territory Intervention, what is saved or rescued and at what cost? *Cultural Studies Review, 15*(2), 45–60.

Wolfe, P. (1999). *Settler colonialism*. London: A&C Black.

Wolfe, P. (2006). Settler colonialism and the elimination of the native. *Journal of Genocide Research, 8*(4), 387–409. doi:https://doi.org/10.1080/14623520601056240.

World Health Organisation. (2019). *Gender, equity and human rights*. World Health Organisation. Retrieved from https://www.who.int/gender-equity-rights/understanding/gender-definition/en/

Zuchowski, I., Savage, D., Miles, D., & Gair, S. (2013). Decolonising field education – Challenging Australian social work praxis. *Advances in Social Work and Welfare Education, 1*, 48.

2 Working with Aboriginal LGBTIQ+ People

Péta Phelan

Frameworks of practice

Social workers, therapists and mental health professionals endeavour to provide competent and safe approaches to increasingly diverse populations, yet can have difficulty in effectively engaging with clients from different cultural backgrounds.

The term 'culture' is a complex term to define and is most often understood broadly to mean the knowledges, practices, and experiences of racial, ethnic, or religious groups; however, *culture* extends beyond such a limited definition. In 1952, Kroeber and Kluckhohn (1952), two American anthropologists, critically reviewed concepts and definitions of the term culture and compiled a significant list of 164 different definitions (Spencer-Oatey, 2012). According to Samovar and Porter (1994), culture refers to the cumulative deposit of knowledge, experience, beliefs, values, attitudes, meanings, hierarchies, religion, notions of time, roles, spatial relations, concepts of the universe, and material objects and possessions acquired by a group of people in the course of generations through individual and group striving. Culture from this frame extends well beyond the commonly understood definition to include elements such as sexual orientation, gender, generation, social class, occupational group, and a range of other factors (Hofstede, 1994). For the context of this chapter, 'Working with Aboriginal LGBTIQ+ People', it is important to understand that there is significant diversity across the relevant cultural groups, both under the terms and the identity definitions of 'Aboriginal' and 'LGBTIQ+'.

Before the arrival of British colonisers in 1788, Australia was inhabited by the Indigenous peoples – Aboriginal and Torres Strait Islander People, sometimes referred to as the First Australians. Aboriginal people inhabited the whole of the Australian continent and Torres Strait Islander People lived on the islands between Australia and Papua New Guinea, in what is now called the Torres Strait. At the time of colonisation, there were over 500 different clan groups or 'nations' around the continent, many with distinctive cultures, beliefs, and languages (Australian Government, 2020). Today, Indigenous people make up approximately 3.3% of the total Australian population (about 800,000 out of 24 million people (Australian Bureau of Statistics, 2018)). Today, Australia's Indigenous peoples, the Aboriginal people and the Torres Strait Islander people, are two distinct cultural groups with great diversity evident within these two broadly described groups, exemplified by the more than 250 different language groups spread across the nation. They are the holders of unique languages, knowledge systems, and beliefs, possess invaluable traditional knowledge for the sustainable management of natural resources, and have a special relation to and use of their traditional and ancestral lands, waters, or territories, which are of fundamental importance for their physical and cultural survival as peoples (AIATSIS, 2018).

Likewise, LGBTIQ+ is a collective term that refers to people who exist beyond limited heteronormative and binary gender constructs. Lesbian, gay, bisexual, transgender, intersex, and queer (or questioning) persons, although lumped together via the acronym as sexuality and gender minorities (outsiders, deviants, refusers, and radicals), are distinct cultural groups, each of which contains a subset of categorisation and varying subcultures. For example, femme lesbians may share the same sexual orientation as diesel dykes, that is that both subsets identify as lesbians; however, the 'ways of doing and being', the clothing styles, vernacular, knowledge, experiences, beliefs, values, attitudes, meanings, hierarchies, roles, spatial relations, concepts of the universe, and material objects and possessions may differ greatly. Gay men, bisexual people, transgender, non-binary people, intersex people, and those who identify as *queer* will each have their subtypes and subcultures, unique to their umbrella identifier. Conceptualising LGBTIQ+ identities as culture challenges the assumption that sexual orientation is just about who one has intimate relationships and/or sex with, and that gender identity is just about what one wears or how one expresses themselves. Sexuality and gender permeate almost every aspect of our lives, and this continues across the entirety of the life span (Crameri, Barrett, Latham, & Whyte, 2015).

Working with cultural humility

Every person needs to feel that their sense of self and identity is valued in some way by the people and environments that surround them, that regardless of differences one can feel deeply respected and culturally safe. An essential need of all people is to have within them a deep sense of meaning as they live their lives – the perception of the self in relationship to others and the external world significantly impacts human wellbeing and health (Australian Human Rights Commission, 2011).

Curtis et al. (2019) state that 'eliminating Indigenous and ethnic health inequities requires addressing the determinants of health inequities which includes institutionalised racism, and ensuring a health care system that delivers appropriate and equitable care'. Frankland, Bamblett, and Lewis (2011) state that, in regard to Aboriginal peoples, 'culture is essential for the spiritual, emotional, and social growth and maintenance of all peoples… that culture is their spear and shield; their resistance and their resilience. A key challenge is to address the partial removal of traditional culturally-based forms of identity, belonging, stability and protection within Aboriginal communities, in addition to addressing the processes which disempower Aboriginal peoples and disable their voice and ability to practice self-determination.'

Likewise, working with LGBTIQ+ people is similar to working with clients from any cultural group; like other cultural minorities, LGBTIQ+ people have a series of particular experiences and stresses in their lives that can impact on their health and wellbeing outcomes (BeyondBlue, 2014), such as discrimination, marginalisation, oppression, targeted psychological and physical violence, and pervasive heterosexism (BeyondBlue, 2020; Higa et al., 2014). The importance of cultural safety has been recognised in the development of the National Standards for LGBTIQ+ Inclusive Practice in Australia (Gay and Lesbian Health Victoria, 2013) progressing steps to ensure that cultural safety is a fundamental aspect of LGBTIQ+-inclusive practice.

There are a range of terms utilised by professionals, organisations and governments to indicate a level of knowledge and skill acquisition (and commitment to 'diversity practice') when working with communities of people who are othered by the dominant culture, and whose identities and cultures exist outside that which is considered the *norm* or mainstream. These terms are often used interchangeably (and often incorrectly) by those with limited understanding of them, with each of the terms defined differently in both their theoretical underpinnings and, in their practical application.

These terms are:

- Cultural awareness and sensitivity;
- Cultural competence;
- Cultural safety;
- Cultural humility.

Each of these terms indicates a specific level of cultural understanding, with each sequential term encompassing and building upon the knowledge and practice implications of the previous one. Cultural safety builds on the concepts and practices of cultural awareness and cultural sensitivity (Nursing Council of New Zealand, 2011). For example:

Cultural awareness involves education to ensure an understanding of the histories that impact health, well-being and care needs. Cultural sensitivity then expands awareness education to an understanding of power imbalances, particularly between service providers and consumers. Cultural safety then builds on awareness and sensitivity and is characterised by individual staff reflecting on their own values and beliefs and the services they provide. (Crameri et al., 2015)

Cultural awareness & cultural sensitivity

Cultural awareness and sensitivity is defined as the process of conducting a self-examination of one's assumptions and biases (both conscious and unconscious) towards other cultures and the in-depth exploration of one's cultural and professional background. It involves being aware of the existence of discrimination, prejudice, and exclusionary practices in healthcare delivery.

Cultural competence

Cultural competence is defined as a set of congruent values, attitudes, motivations, behaviours, and policies that come together in a system, agency, or among professionals that enables effective work in cross-cultural situations. It also implies having the capacity to function effectively as an individual or an organisation, within the context of the cultural values, beliefs, behaviours, and needs presented by individual consumers and their communities (National Prevention Information Network, 2020), and ultimately creating and fostering an atmosphere of non-discrimination.

The universal approach to training proposes that cultural competence can be taught through reflective awareness, empathy, active listening techniques, and the cognitive mechanisms contributing to cultural insensitivity or blindness, such as implicit biases or stereotyped threats (Agency for Healthcare Research and Quality, 2014).

Cultural competence is a set of congruent behaviours, attitudes and policies that come together in a system, agency or among professionals; enabling that system, agency or those professionals to work effectively in cross-cultural situations. (Cross, Bazron, Dennis, & Isaacs, 1989)

There is growing recognition of the importance of cultural competency and cultural safety at both individual health practitioners and organisational levels to achieve equitable health care. Since the genesis of the term and implementation of practice approaches a number of decades ago, cultural

Box 2.1 The Stages of Cultural Awareness

There are four stages of cultural awareness that reflect a person's progression towards recognising and accepting cultural difference:

Stage 1: Parochial stage. People are all the same.

- The conviction that all people, deep down, hold the same values and beliefs.
- People are aware of their own way of doing things and think that their way is the only way.
- Any cultural differences are neglected.
- People have very limited perspective most often due to a lack of experience with difference.

Stage 2: Ethnocentric stage. Cultural differences exist, but mine is best.

- A realisation that differences in cultural norms, values, customs and beliefs exist; however, 'other' values are seen as less desirable than our own.
- People are aware of some other ways of doing things, but still consider their ways are the best of all.
- People consider the effect of cultural differences to be problematic or even threatening, so its importance is reduced.
- People hold the desire to both defend one's own culture and minimise others.

Stage 3: Synergistic stage. Other cultures have value – I can learn from them.

- Recognition of the complexity and wealth of other people's cultures.
- People observe and accept the potential benefits of other cultures' values and beliefs, and are aware of both their way and other peoples' ways of doing things. Thus, they choose the best way depending on the circumstances.
- People understand that cultural differences can be both problematic and beneficial, but they are open to using them for opening new alternatives/solutions.

Stage 4: Participatory Third Culture stage. More than one cultural frame of reference exists.

- People become aware of their own cultural filters and begin to adapt their perceptions and behaviours.
- Through repeated exposure to or education about other cultures, people develop a deeper understanding of a culture's unique traits, values and norms.
- People shift communication style and behaviours to effectively and appropriately interact with diverse cultures, bringing together people from different cultural backgrounds to derive a culture with a shared context of meanings.

Source: Belyh (2017), Crosby Kile (2018), and Murden et al. (2008)

competence has commanded significant attention, being viewed as the ultimate foundation for fostering cross-cultural communication, reducing health disparities, improving access to better care, increasing health literacy, and promoting health equity (Campinha-Bacote, 2019).

Box 2.2 The Process of Cultural Competence in the Delivery of Healthcare Services: A Model of Care

According to this model, cultural competence is a process of *becoming* competent, not *being* competent. This model views cultural knowledge, cultural skill, cultural encounters, and cultural desire as the five constructs of cultural competence.

- **Cultural knowledge**
  The process in which the healthcare professional seeks to, and obtains, a robust educational foundation regarding culturally diverse groups. The emphasis of knowledge acquisition in this realm must be on the integration of health-related beliefs practices and cultural values, disease incidence and prevalence, and treatment efficacy (Lavizzo-Mourey & Mackenzie, 1996).

- **Cultural skill**
  The ability to conduct a cultural assessment to collect relevant cultural data in an accurate manner regarding the client's presenting problem.

- **Cultural encounters**
  The process which encourages the healthcare professional to directly engage in face-to-face cultural interactions and other types of encounters with clients from culturally diverse backgrounds in order to modify existing beliefs about a cultural group and prevent possible stereotyping.

- **Cultural desire**
  The motivation of the healthcare professional to *want to* (desire motivation) engage in the process of becoming culturally aware, culturally knowledgeable, culturally skillful, and seeking cultural encounters; not the *have to (compliance motivation)*. Cultural encounters is the pivotal construct of cultural competence that provides the energy source and foundation for one's journey towards cultural competence.

Source: Adapted from Campinha-Bacote (2002) with permission from SAGE Publications Ltd.

Cultural safety

The concept of cultural safety is drawn from the work of Maori nurses in New Zealand and is defined by Williams (1999) as:

> An environment that is safe for people: where there is no assault, challenge or denial of their identity, of who they are and what they need. It is about shared respect, shared meaning, shared knowledge, and experience of learning, living and working together with dignity and truly listening. (p. 213)

Cultural safety requires that people are cared for in full regard *for*, rather than regardless of, the aspects and elements of their life which make them unique. Providing full regard to all aspects and elements of the person's life, practitioners must reflectively engage the whole person, including the cultural, religious, socio-economic, and historical realities of the person they are engaged with. People feel unsafe if they believe that they need to hide aspects of themselves in order to be accepted, included, affirmed, and understood. The key to cultural safety, therefore, is the attitude change on behalf of the professional towards each person with which they engage (Jones, 2017).

For Aboriginal people, those who identify as LGBTQI+, and Aboriginal LGBTIQ+ people, a culturally safe environment is one where safety and security in identity, culture, community, and other existential elements pertinent to their unique identities, are both prioritised and centred. Health practitioners and healthcare organisations, together with the health systems in which they work, need to be engaged and committed to progressing towards cultural safety and critical consciousness. There must be preparedness to critique the 'taken for granted' power structures and to challenge their own culture and cultural systems rather than prioritise becoming 'competent' in the cultures of others (Curtis et al., 2019).

Cultural humility

Cultural humility is an approach and process that can help facilitate strong working alliances between therapists and diverse clients, leading to better outcomes (Mosher et al., 2017). It is a 'lifelong process of self-reflection and self-critique whereby the individual not only learns about another's culture, but one starts with an examination of her/his own beliefs and cultural identities' (Tervalon & Murray-Garcia, 1998; Yeager & Bauer-Wu, 2013).

Cultural competency is characterised as a *skill* that can be taught, trained, and achieved and is often described as a necessary and sufficient condition for working effectively with diverse patients, with the underlying assumption that the greater the knowledge one has about another culture, the greater the competence in professional practice realms. Cultural humility, by contrast, requires a more nuanced, reflective, and empathic engagement, which involves 'entering a relationship with another person with the intention of honouring their beliefs, customs, and values, and entails an ongoing process of self-exploration and self-critique combined with a willingness to learn from others' (Stubbe, 2020). Ultimately, it encourages an interpersonal stance that is curious and other-oriented. Campinha-Bacote (2019) states that in differentiating between cultural competency and cultural humility in professional practice, cultural humility:

- requires less emphasis on knowledge and competency;
- places a greater emphasis on a lifelong commitment;
- encourages nurturing of self-evaluation and critique;
- addresses power imbalances;
- promotes interpersonal sensitivity;
- requires an attitude of openness and egolessness;
- involves supportive interaction;
- entails maintaining an interpersonal stance that is other-oriented;
- necessitates learning from differences.

Three aspects of cultural humility (Waters & Asbill, 2013)

The first stage is specific to a lifelong commitment to self-evaluation and self-critique (Tervalon & Murray-Garcia, 1998). Pertinent to this stage is the knowledge that the learning is never complete. Professionals must have the courage and commitment to audit themselves critically and willingly undertake more learning.

The second stage of cultural humility is a desire to rectify or dismantle power imbalances. Recognising the inherent value of individual and that each person has something important to express or contribute. Acknowledging that the client is the expert on his or her own life, including all of the experiences they have had and how they have perceived them. The practitioner's power lies in their professional expertise, and the clients' power lies in the expertise of their own life – the relationship must, therefore, be one of equal collaboration.

The final stage of cultural humility includes aspiring to develop partnerships with people and groups who advocate for others. Positive change can be progressed by individual practitioners; however, the collective power of groups and communities can create more profound impacts on unbalanced structures and systems. By advocating for systemic macro change, the practitioner can take a more nuanced approach towards their commitment to self-reflection, self-evaluation, and in the rectifications of power imbalances.

Working with Aboriginal LGBTIQ+ people

When working with Aboriginal LGBTIQ+ people, there are a variety of factors and influences that must be considered in order to understand the complexity of the lived experiences of those individuals and communities with this particular range of intersecting identities.

Minority identity

Over many years, the term *minority* has been defined in a vast number of ways. Presenting one of the earliest definitions of the term minority, Wirth (1945, p. 347) states:

> We may define a minority as a group of people who, because of their physical or cultural characteristics, are singled out from the others in the society in which they live for differential and unequal treatment, and who therefore regard themselves as objects of collective discrimination. The existence of a minority in a society implies the existence of a corresponding dominant group enjoying higher social status and greater privileges.

Characteristics that have been linked to minority group identity include sex, gender, sexual orientation, disability, ethnicity, nationality, race (without debating the validity of that concept), language, culture, and religion (Viladrich & Loue, 2010). These characteristics act as levers to distinguish specific people from the dominant group due to differences in physiology, language and expression, customs, patterns of culture, or a combination of all these factors. Othered and perceived as inherently different from the dominant group, minorities are either implicitly or explicitly (consciously or unconsciously) excluded from full participation in life within the particular *dominant* culture.

It is important to remember that, whilst the common term of minority may indicate a numerical standpoint (the majority being larger in number than a minority), the term in the context of sociology is more accurately reflected from the standpoint of subordination in regards to power, status, and opportunity (Schermerhorn, 1970). It has been suggested by Yetman (1991) that a helpful way to think about minority and majority groups is to consider minority as a synonym for a *subordinate,* and majority as a synonym for *dominant.*

Being Blak

Aboriginal and Torres Strait Islander People have a complex and holistic worldview, in which all aspects of life are perceived as connected and interdependent. Culture consists of a body of collectively shared values, principles, practices and customs, and traditions, *where connection to culture* refers to Aboriginal and Torres Strait Islander peoples' capacity and opportunity to sustain and (re-)create a healthy, strong relationship to their Aboriginal or Torres Strait Islander heritage, which includes all of the associated systems of knowledge, law, and practices that comprise this heritage (Gee, Dudgeon, Schultz, Hart, & Kelly, 2014).

There is no single Aboriginal and Torres Strait Islander culture or group, but numerous groupings, languages, kinships, and tribes, as well as ways of living. Central to each is the connection to identity, knowledges, and culture. This includes aspects such as connection to kin (both current and ancestral), community and Country, language, ceremony and traditions, stories, philosophies, and spirituality. Ways of knowing, doing, and being are vast and unique and rooted in philosophies, structures, systems, and practices garnered from over 65,000 years of uninterrupted culture (Adams, Faulkhead, Standfield, & Atkinson, 2018).

For Aboriginal people, the historical and current impacts of colonisation have perpetuated, and continue to perpetuate, devastating impacts on individuals and communities at every level. Since the landing of the first British fleet, settler-colonisation has encompassed practices including war, displacement, forced labour, the removal of children, relocation, ecological destruction, massacres, genocide, slavery, unintentional and intentional spread of deadly diseases, regulation of marriage, assimilation, the banning of Indigenous languages, and the eradication of social, cultural, and spiritual practices (Doyle, 2011; Paradies, 2016).

> The legacy of traumatic experiences and oppression sustained through ongoing colonisation has ensured that the injury experienced has not been given an opportunity or space to heal. Grief and loss have been felt deeply and in ways, people were not able to effectively deal with; instead, they had to fight just to survive. The legacy of this unacknowledged trauma and unresolved grief has resulted in its internalisation and festering of wounds which have been labelled as dysfunctional behaviours of the individual and collective sufferers. (Sherwood, 2015, p. 1)

Aboriginal health considerations

> Aboriginal health does not mean the physical wellbeing of an individual, but refers to the social, emotional, and cultural wellbeing of the whole community. For Aboriginal people this is seen in terms of the whole-life view. Health care services should strive to achieve the state where every individual is able to achieve their full potential as human beings, and must bring about the total wellbeing of their communities. (Gee et al., 2014)

Indigenous peoples view health in a holistic context that encompasses mental health, physical, cultural and spiritual health, and wellbeing, not only in the individual but also for the whole community. Land and Country are central to wellbeing, and when the harmony of these interrelations is disrupted, Aboriginal and Torres Strait Islander ill health persists (Ganesharajah, 2009). In professional practice with Aboriginal and Torres Strait Islander People, these factors must be acknowledged, and universal prevention strategies, which promote strong, resilient communities and focus on restoring social and emotional wellbeing, should be implemented through the development of collaborative strategies in partnership with the community one is serving.

Box 2.3 Factors That Impact on Social and Emotional Wellbeing

* Connection to Body
* Connection to Mind and Emotions
* Connection to Family and Kinship
* Connection to Community
* Connection to Culture
* Connection to Country
* Connection to Spirit, Spirituality, and Ancestors

Source: Gee et al. (2014)

Throughout the literature, it is evidenced that Aboriginal Australians experience higher levels of psychological distress than any other group, and the historic and ongoing effects of colonisation through genocide, assimilation, family separation, the loss of traditional lands, social inequity, racism and marginalisation, the loss of culture and identity, and issues of transgenerational trauma on Aboriginal health and wellbeing are well recognised (Balaratnasingam et al., 2019; Krieg, 2009; Paradies, 2016; Yu-Tang et al., 2018). Grief, loss, and trauma are significant factors in psychological distress and deeply impactful concerning poor social and emotional wellbeing and, if unresolved by the survivor, can be directly transmitted from one generation to another in a process known as intergenerational (or transgenerational) trauma. The mechanism for this transmission is via a secondary traumatic exposure, that is, bearing witness to past traumatic events of family and community members, as a result of colonisation, forced removals, and other government policies.

To be Blak in Australia

Historically, both in Australia and around the world, particularly in white and/or settler-colonial dominated societies, the term Black has been used to imply something negative, demeaning, stereotyping, stigmatising, and dis-empowering for the people who have been the target of race-based violence. The term *Black* was used to denigrate and violate the cultural and racial origin of an individual or community (Watego, n.d.), to justify and normalise discourses, behaviours, and practices of white supremacy and domination.

For Aboriginal and Torres Strait Islander Peoples, *Blak* is a deeply political expression reclaimed and redeployed in defiance of those who for so long successfully weaponised their non-*whiteness* against them. It is used by Aboriginal people to reclaim historical, representational, symbolical, stereotypical, and romanticised notions of Black or Blackness (Watego, n.d.). It is a term that is intensely rooted in the seizing back of power, authority, agency, and self-determination, in the dismantling of settler-colonial socio-political ideals and practices that marginalise, harm, violate, and oppress Aboriginal people. To be Blak is to be engaging actively with the complex process of freedom from the impositions and expectations of coloniality. It is the perception, thinking, feeling, and knowing of the world from a Blak standpoint, one where *whiteness* is not only disarmed, but is not even considered. Blak is the mechanism of unshackling the mind and the heart from the vast prison that *whiteness* has attempted to place one in. It is unapologetic presence, power, and survival.

Strength not deficit

It is critical that any person working with Aboriginal people understands that processes and actions must always be as a *collaboration* with the community one seeks to serve. It is imperative that each professional working with mob has a contextual understanding of the historical and current factors that have created, and continue to create, such significant social, health, and economic disparities in Aboriginal and Torres Strait Islander populations. Communities must also not be framed from deficit discourse perspectives, which refers to 'disempowering patterns of thought, language and practice that represent people in terms of deficiencies and failures' (The Lowitja Institute, 2018). Deficit discourse places responsibility for issues and problems with the affected individuals or communities, overlooking the larger socio-economic structures in which they are embedded.

Aboriginal and Torres Strait Islander People are strong, adaptive, and powerful, with robust cultures and considerable histories. This is evidenced by their continued survival and thriving, successfully countering all attempts by the colonisers to complete the genocide of First Peoples on this continent. Strengths-based approaches when working with the mob must be elementary. This allows professionals to move away from the traditional problem-based paradigm and offer a different language and worldview for engagement.

Being LGBTIQ+

The acronym LGBTIQ+ refers collectively to people who are lesbian, gay, bisexual, trans, intersex, queer, or questioning (those who are exploring their orientation and identity). The '+' is used to include people with alternate sexual, orientation, or sex or gender identities who do not identify with the terms contained within the 'LGBTIQ' acronym. The term LGBTIQA+ may also be used, with the 'A' referring to people who identify as asexual (LGBTIQIA+ Resource Center, 2018, https://lgbtqia.ucdavis.edu/). Alternatively, the 'A' has also been utilised to refer to allies of LGBTIQ+ communities (Kelly, 2014); however, this usage is still considered controversial as it recentres people with dominant and socially privileged heterosexual identities as principally aligned to the minority and socially disadvantaged LGBTIQA+ community.

'Queer', a historically derogatory, abusive, and deeply harmful term, has recently been 'reclaimed' by some individuals as a political term as a means of challenging homophobia, and in the active resistance of heterosexist constructions and enforcement of sexuality and binary gender. Given its historical usage, many in the LGBTI community have varying relationships with the word, and some may find it offensive (Smith et al., 2014).

> Sexual diversity can include people who are lesbian, gay or bisexual, as well as a range of other expressions of sexuality. This may include people who identify as asexual (experiencing an absence of sexual attraction, distinct from celibate) or pansexual (experiencing sexual or romantic attraction that is not based on gender identity or sex). (Smith et al., 2014)

Trans or TGD (trans and gender diverse) are commonly used to describe a broad range of non-conforming gender identities or expressions, including transgender, agender (having no gender), bigender (identifying as both a woman and a man), or non-binary (neither woman nor man). The term transsexual may be used to refer to a person who has an internal sense of gender that differs from their birth sex. People may also describe themselves as MTF/M2F (male-to-female), FTM/F2M (female-to-male), AFAB (assigned female at birth), or AMAB (assigned male at birth). The terms genderqueer and gender fluid are also used to refer to shifting gender identity. Using preferred names and pronouns is important for TGD people. These may include, for example, 'he/him', 'she/her', 'they/them' or 'zi/zem'. Some Aboriginal and Torres Strait Islander peoples use the term Sistergirl to refer to male-assigned people who live partly or fully as women and Brother boy to refer to female-assigned people who live partly or fully as men (Smith et al., 2014).

People born with intersex variations encompass a diversity of experiences. Intersex traits are a naturally occurring biological phenomenon, with at least

40 different variations. People may use diagnostic or chromosomal labels for their variations, including XXY, Complete Androgen Insensitivity, XY Woman, Swyer Syndrome, or Turner Syndrome (Intersex Human Rights Australia, 2013).

Social exclusion and marginalisation

Social exclusion and marginalisation are the complex processes of relegating specific groups of people to the lower or outer edge of society by blocking them from (or denying full access to) various rights, opportunities, and resources that are normally available to members of a different group, and which are fundamental to social integration and observance of human rights within that particular group (United Nation, 2016). This includes factors such as housing, employment, healthcare, civic engagement, democratic participation, and due process. It pushes certain groups of people to the margin of society economically, politically, culturally, and socially and denies marginalised and excluded individuals and communities the realisation of their productive human potential and opportunities for their full capacity utilisation (Shah, 2017).

Membership of a highly stigmatised group greatly increases the risk of exclusion and marginalisation. Stigmatisation occurs when a personal attribute is recognised as different (from dominant or *norm*) and the person or group is devalued because of this attribute (Simons, Houkes, Koster, Groffen, & Bosma, 2018). Stigmatised groups are often spoken about in derogatory terms by others. Cruwys et al. (2013), in their research of marginalised Australians over ten years, state that 'individuals can also be subject to stigma due to following an unusual developmental pathway, such as having children when very young or very old, retiring very early or studying later in life. This "doing the right thing at the wrong time" was a significant marker of marginalisation in our study.' Being discriminated against and excluded from society due to being labelled the 'wrong type' of person, or doing things at the 'wrong time' in life is a key component in marginalisation.

Major and Eccleston (2004) state that exclusion is not just an incidental aspect of stigmatisation, but an essential one. For those that exclude, excluding the stigmatised serves several functions, including self-esteem enhancement, anxiety reduction, system justification, and reduction of the costs associated with group living. For those exposed to the stigma-based exclusion, however, it is a considerable stressor with direct impacts on wellbeing (Pachankis, 2007; Quinn & Earnshaw, 2013) as well as limiting access to the kind of resources that are needed to improve one's life circumstances.

The gender binary and heteronormativity

The term *gender binary* describes the socially constructed system which allocates its members into one of two sets of gender roles, gender identities, and attributes based on the type of genitalia – that is, female and male (Lorber & Moore, 2011). In Western civilisation, the gender binary has been seen as a concept that is valid and immutable and assumes heterosexuality and cisgender identity for all (Shearer, 2019).

The gender binary, which is still extensively enforced (and often violently), fails to consider the vast biological, psychological, and existential diversity that exists within human lives. This has included the covert, overt and often-violent erasure, pathologising, stigmatisation, marginalisation, and exclusion of people whose bodies and identities exist outside of the narrow classifications of the ideology (Reiker & Reid, 2017). Evidence is well established in the literature which reflects negative attitudes towards sexual minorities (Dermer, Smith, & Barto, 2010; Herek, 1988), and the behavioural manifestations emerging from such attitudes have been directly correlated to in social, medical, and legal discrimination, and harassment and threats to personal safety towards sexual minorities (Herek, 1990). This includes common features such as bullying, intimidation, hate crimes, rejection, and estrangement from family and friends, and occupational and housing discrimination. In the worst instances (which are distressingly still too commonplace), physical, psychological, and sexual violence are enacted, in many cases with devastating, and fatal, consequences.

Habarth (2015) suggests that 'even ambient heterosexism – not targeted directly at observers but shaping psychosocial and institutional environments – can cause significant stress for sexual minority individuals'. In the case of those with sexual variances and intersex identities, forced binary compliance through coercive surgery and pharmaceutical-based interference has been commonplace, often performed in childhood without their understanding, right to body integrity, autonomy, and agency, and without their informed consent (Fausto-Sterling, 2000a, 2000b).

The persistence of negative beliefs, attitudes, and behaviours towards sexual minorities, including how discrimination expresses itself, suggests an implicit social contract that centres and privileges heterosexuality as normal or natural and defines the boundaries of what *is*, and what *is not*, acceptable and normal heterosexuality. Heteronormativity defines the frameworks on what is socially acceptable relationships and identities, and limitations on what is not, enforcing compliance with culturally determined and gendered heterosexual roles (Habarth, 2015). Having defined 'normal' and acceptable, and together with the heavily policed social pressures to conform to socially acceptable gender roles and sexual behaviour, heteronormativity activates the genesis and proliferation of heterosexism and heterosexist prejudice.

Discrimination and racism

The Australian Human Rights Commission (n.d.) states that 'direct discrimination occurs when a person, or a group of people, is treated less favourably than another person or group because of their background or certain personal characteristics'. Indirect discrimination occurs 'when an unreasonable rule or policy applies to everyone but has the effect of disadvantaging some people because of a personal characteristic they share'.

'Racism can be understood as an organised system based on the categorisation and ranking of racial/ethnic groups into social hierarchies whereby ethnic groups are assigned differential value and have differential access to power, opportunities, and resources, resulting in disadvantage for some groups and advantage for others' (Stanley, Harris, Cormack, Waa, & Edwards, 2019). Longstanding power relationships reinforce systems of racism, which, specifically in the Australian context, relate to historic and ongoing colonial processes. Racism is a key determinant of the health and wellbeing of Indigenous Australians and a key underlying factor to the unremitting gap in health and socio-economic outcomes between Indigenous and non-Indigenous Australians (Markwick, Ansari, Clinch, & McNeil, 2019).

From an individual perspective, racism refers to 'the beliefs and attitudes that members of certain groups have of their superiority concerning other groups who are regarded as inferior, based on race, ethnicity or cultural background' (Sanson et al., 1998), where those who are assumed to be inferior are treated differently and unfavourably.

From an institutional perspective, racism refers to 'the ways in which racist beliefs or values have been built into the operations of social institutions in such a way as to discriminate against, control and oppress various minority groups'. This type of racism, also known as systemic racism, is covert or even unrecognised by the agents involved in it (Bolt, 2001). The term defines how ideas of white superiority are captured in everyday thinking at a systems level in unquestioned social structures systems, including laws, policy, and regulations, and provides differential access to goods, services and opportunities of society by race. In systemic racism, white superiority is assumed individually, ideologically, and institutionally – which may be conscious, or unconscious. Individuals may not perceive themselves as racist, however, they still benefit from structures and systems that privilege certain (most often white) faces and voices (O'Dowd, 2020).

For Aboriginal LGBTIQ+ people, the experience of multiple levels of discrimination based on Aboriginal identity, sexual orientation, gender identity, or intersex status may exacerbate the effects and impacts of racism and heterosexism. This can lead to increased isolation from Aboriginal, LGBTIQ+, and/or mainstream communities.

Aboriginal peoples place high regard and prioritise family and community connections, including the authority, wisdom, and leadership of Elders. For Aboriginal people who are LGBTIQ+, discrimination leading to family and community estrangement, the loss of a sense of belonging, particularly for those who relocate from rural and remote communities to regional and metropolitan settings, can have a significant negative effect on their health and wellbeing.

> One of the most persistent aspects of today's discourse regarding racism in Australia is the very denial of its existence. (Augoustinos & Every, 2007)

Intersectional considerations: Being Blak and LGBTIQ+

Aboriginal LGBTIQ+ people are an amalgamation of a range of identities, with each individual (and the community) impacted cumulatively by powerful systems of oppression and discrimination that have significant effects on their daily lives (BeyondBlue, 2020; Paradies, Harris, & Anderson, 2008).

Intersectionality acknowledges that discrimination and systemic oppression are experienced very differently depending on one's gender, race, ethnicity, class, ability, age, and sexual orientation, and for those that fit into more than one identity or marginalised group, the impacts and effects of the discrimination, violence, and oppression are multiplied and magnified (Bowleg, 2012). As a gender deeply impacted by structural oppression that is rooted in patriarchal systems and privilege, intersectionality is traditionally applied to women; however, a person of any gender may be affected by this phenomenon of overlapping minority status. Although born from the feminist movement, intersectionality also understands the complex issues of how men with particular identities are marginalised and oppressed also (Crenshaw, 1989).

Intersectionality acknowledges the combined impacts on an individual, or marginalised community, of racism, sexism, heterosexism, ableism, classism, and xenophobia (Pilling, 2013). If a person is Indigenous and also identifies as one or more of female, disabled, lesbian, gay, bisexual, intersex, Brotherboy, or Sistergirl, the impacts on that individual and their life outcomes are multiplied by however many of those identities lie at their core.

Intersectional explorations within Indigenous health research, practice, and discourse, particularly within an Australian context, have been lacking, with *Indigeneity* alone being chiefly prioritised and privileged. Indigenous health and wellbeing have (for far too long) predominantly been the sole domain of reductionist biomedical model explorations where paternalism, pathologising, and deficit discourse is allowed to thrive, as the Australian healthcare system privileges it. In this rigid biomedical environment, and the tenets it promotes and sustains, we lose sight of the interconnected and complex social issues that drive health and wellbeing disparities (Farre & Rapley, 2017).

Identity in all of its forms is vastly complex, nuanced, and very, *very* personal. There are many Indigenous people whose 'other' identities are just as critical to their self-expression and lived experiences as their Indigeneity, yet all too frequently these 'other' identities are almost entirely deprioritised, or at worst ignored and excluded, in the context of their cultural identity – particularly in health and wellbeing policy and practice.

Elevating intersectional identity narratives and practices means that we recognise, honour, and respond to the whole person, whatever combination of intersectional identity expression. Without holistically perceiving and deeply considering the whole person, we are maintaining and privileging the systems of white colonial oppression (inclusive of gender-binary and heteronormative assumptions and enforcement), systems that control the individual and communities through an unsophisticated singular lens, and allocate regulation and resourcing accordingly (Braveman, 2006). Intersectionality must be prioritised by all in order to fully embrace the very diverse experiences of Indigenous identity (Farrell, 2015; Maddison & Partridge, 2014) and make more informed and culturally safe decisions about how to strengthen and optimise existences and outcomes for *all*.

The elevation of awareness, discussions, respect, and safety around other inherent identities beyond Indigeneity alone, in no way devalues, degrades, or harms the fundamental importance of Indigenous identity. It merely seeks to appreciate, deeply consider, and honour the beautiful diversity of identity and experiences within First Nations people.

Resilience

Fall down seven times, get up eight. (Japanese Proverb)

Resilience is identified as the process of managing taxing circumstances, expending effort to solve personal and interpersonal problems, and seeking to master, minimise, reduce, or tolerate stress or conflict (Riopel, 2020). It is defined as the 'bouncing back' from difficult circumstances and stressors, such as those that challenge and disrupt established routines or challenge a person's physical, social, or psychological resources. Resilience literature generally affirms that the concept encompasses not merely *surviving*, but includes both thriving and having benefited from the stressor experience (Social Work Policy Institute, 2004).

> The term resilience is reserved for unpredicted or markedly successful adaptations to negative life events, trauma, stress, and other forms of risk. If we can understand what helps some people to function well in the context of high adversity, we may be able to incorporate this knowledge into new practice strategies. (Fraser, Richman, & Galinsky, 1999)

Research also shows that resilience is not a trait that people either do or do not possess. It involves behaviours, thoughts, and actions that can be learned, developed, and harnessed by anyone. Research (Werner & Smith, 1992, 2001) shows that the primary factor in resilience is having caring and supportive relationships within and outside the family – relationships that create love and trust, provide role models, and offer encouragement and reassurance help bolster a person's resilience.

Other factors include:

- The capacity to make realistic plans and take progressive steps to carry them out
- A positive view of oneself and confidence in strengths and abilities
- Skills in communication and problem solving
- The capacity to manage strong feelings and impulses
- Reframing adversity as an opportunity for growth

Box 2.4 Traits, Qualities and Characteristics of the Resilient Person

Conner and Davidson (2003) have ascertained, through their research, that resilient people have certain characteristics. These may include:
- Viewing change as a challenge or opportunity
- Commitment
- Recognition of limits to control
- Engaging the support of others
- Close, secure attachment to others
- Personal or collective goals
- Self-efficacy
- Strengthening effect of stress
- Past successes
- Realistic sense of control/having choices
- Sense of humour
- Action-oriented approach
- Patience
- Tolerance of negative affect
- Adaptability to change
- Optimism
- Faith

The concept of resilience (or resiliency) has deep roots in social work practice, although social work research related to it is relatively recent (Social Work Policy Institute, 2004). As social-model aligned professionals, such as those positioned in social work, mental health, and behavioural and social science practitioners, transitioned from a deficit (pathology) orientation to a strengths-based perspective, increased attention has been paid to the prioritising of personal attributes, qualities and social influence that promote health and wellbeing.

> Resilience thinking enables a focus on strengths and opportunities, reorienting the conversation within impoverished communities where the usual focus is on maladjustment and deficiency. (Walsh-Dilley & Wolford, 2015)

Resilience *as problematic*

Whilst a term used extensively to represent strength, agility and adaptability, particularly across the breadth of health and social science professions and vernacular, embedded within the term *resilience* are neoliberalist assumptions of equitable access and resourcing, level playing fields, and every individual and community having equal opportunities. It assumes that, regardless of structural determinants, intermediary determinants, and socio-economic position (Solar & Irwin, 2010), each individual (and community) can succeed in the face of adversity and thrive on an equal footing with the rest of society under the power of their own volition. Unspoken within these assumptions lies the insinuation that the failure to succeed becomes the culpability of the individual (or the community), not of incongruent, unjust, defective, or unworkable structures and systems. Those who are strong and competitive, work hard, succeed, and survive, do so on merit; the weak and lazy fail, are unworthy of success or survival, and have nobody else to blame but themselves.

> The Anglo-Saxon understanding of resilience, in particular, is best understood as a neoliberal form of governmentality that places emphasis on individual adaptability. (Joseph, 2013)

Resilience demands an acceptance of and compliance with social structures, systems, and institutions that prove not only difficult to access (if at all), but that were built, progressed, sustained, and enforced with only the already centred, resourced, and privileged in mind. The burden of resilience falls upon those in society who are most disadvantaged, whose lives and histories are littered with trauma and dispossession, whose rights have been eroded, oppressed, or denied, their identities and ways of existing stigmatised, marginalised, or erased. Evans and Reid (2013) state that 'The resilient subject is a subject which must permanently struggle to accommodate itself to the world, and not a subject which can conceive of changing the world, its structure and conditions of possibility'.

The huge burden of *resilience* must not lie on the shoulders of disadvantaged, marginalised, and oppressed individuals and communities. Those with power – the centred and privileged whose lives greatly benefit from retaining status quo structures, systems, and institutions – must be the ones to adapt, re-interpret, and re-orient themselves in the journey towards transformation. The accommodation, ultimately, must come from those that have far more to give, motivated not by insular self-service and perpetual resource acquisition, but by the altruistic motivation to dismantle obstacles and barriers that prevent equity and empowerment for all.

Transformative existences, not *resilience*

Within fields of professional practice that seek to facilitate, energise, and sustain the empowerment of individuals and communities, strengths-based personal, cultural, and existential prioritisation and centring must lie at the foundation of discourse and application. Strengths-based, person-centred practices such as self-reflection, self-awareness, perception transformation, capacity-building, and resourcing, together with socially transformative practices such as advocacy, institutional reform, and structures and systems re-orientation, provide an incredible foundation from where *power and control* can be re-positioned and harnessed by individuals and by communities.

Instead of focusing on resilience as the outcome of practice, consider the facilitation of a knowledge-centred suite of transformative practice, one that welcomes each individual to discover themselves and their existence both within and outside the culture and structures in which they find themselves, and create innovative practices that free them from discomfort and pain. When one knows and understands oneself deeply, has an awareness of the multitude of social constructs and systems that impact upon them and the ways in which they influence their lives, and is able to navigate difficult situations and systems through perceptive shifts and solutions-oriented behaviours, one feels a great sense of control over one's life. To be self-empowered, with a robust sense of self-authority and agency, provides the internal environment that organically grows and nurtures the inherent features of *resilience*; strength, self-efficacy, flexibility, adaptability, agility, and transformative capability.

Self-sovereignty and self-determination

Self-sovereignty is the concept of property in one's own person, expressed as the moral or natural right of a person to have bodily integrity and be the exclusive controller of one's own body and life. Self-determination, a right of 'peoples' rather than the individual, is an 'on going process of choice' to ensure that peoples (in specific relevance to this chapter, Indigenous peoples and communities) are able to meet their social, cultural, and economic needs (Australian Human Rights Commission, 2013).

Sovereignty of wellbeing

Sovereignty of wellbeing alludes to the pursuit of wellness, to the ability of people to live in a society where optimal wellbeing is attainable through informed daily choices, and where individuals and communities can make informed choices because they possess the information and the tools to make such decisions (Kuartei, 2015). This means that the health professionals that individuals and communities engage with inherently understand the health and social issues that impact them, and can provide both the knowledge and freedom for each person to make robust informed decisions about their health and wellbeing.

Sovereignty of wellbeing is the fundamental freedom to choose health, pursue wellness, and achieve wellbeing in the full expression of our individual and unique identity and inherent humanity. Authentic self-expression is possible if each of us feels incredible freedom and safety to be exactly who we are; to live in the world as the ultimate versions of ourselves.

Without self-determination it is not possible for Indigenous Australians to fully overcome the legacy of colonisation and dispossession; yet without full sovereignty we can't do that either. If people with diverse identities cannot see real representations of themselves in the world, cannot connect to others like them, and are bound by the colonial structures of oppression and violence that prevent them from living authentically within their identities, how are they ever to reach a point where they can ultimately just be themselves and live liberated and with unapologetic agency and authority?

Conclusion

If social workers are committed to contributing to the advancement of Aboriginal and Torres Strait Islander health and wellbeing in Australia, it is critical to begin exploring intersectionality within a First Nations context as it provides additional insight into how people and communities with intersectional identities can be additionally impacted from structural inequities, discrimination, stigma, and social exclusion. Elevating and prioritising intersectional narratives and practices is critical if professionals are to privilege and honour the inherent humanity, agency, and sovereignty of *all* people. Every person must feel free to express themselves within the uniqueness of their intrinsic identities, including those expressed alongside ethnic and/or cultural identity.

Social work leadership requires critical self-reflection of past and present practices, and must prioritise how shifts can be made in order to create better future outcomes. Across the Australian healthcare system, difficult conversations must be had, new paths explored, and innovations made. It is only through the centring of Aboriginal LGBTIQ+ people, together with new ways of thinking, speaking, and being, that social workers can aspire to contribute to the critical changes required for the optimal health and wellbeing outcomes for Indigenous people. It is critical to remember that self-determination of Aboriginal people, without compromise, must lay at the very foundation of *every* pathway forward.

This chapter seeks to reiterate that the current research and practice models that continuously and consistently focus on Indigenous people as a homogeneous group are obsolete at best, and harmful at worst. It was my intent on writing this chapter, to inspire social workers and researchers into the field of intersectionality, and awaken curiosity, knowledge-seeking, and capacity-building amongst policy-makers, health professionals, and community. It is imperative that each of us seeks to promote and progress health and social justice for Aboriginal people with intersectional identities by creating more innovative, holistic, and client-centred models of thinking and doing in Aboriginal LGBTIQ+ health and wellbeing.

References

Adams, K., Faulkhead, S., Standfield, R., & Atkinson, P. (2018). Challenging the colonisation of birth: Koori women's birthing knowledge and practice. *Women & Birth, 31*(2), 81–88. doi:https://doi.org/10.1016/j.wombi.2017.07.014.

Agency for Healthcare Research and Quality. (2014). *Improving cultural competence to reduce health disparities for priority populations.* Retrieved from https://effectivehealthcare.ahrq.gov/sites/default/files/pdf/cultural-competence_research-protocol.pdf

Augoustinos, M., & Every, D. (2007). The language of "race" and liberal-practical politics. *Journal of Language Social and Psychology, 26*(2), 123–141. Retrieved from https://search.ebscohost.com/login.aspx?direct=true&AuthType=sso&db=edsmai&AN=edsmai.48942&site=eds-live&scope=site

Australian Bureau of Statistics. (2018). *Estimates of Aboriginal and Torres Strait Islander Australians – June 2016.* (Catalogue No. 3238.0.55.001). Retrieved from https://www.abs.gov.au/ausstats/abs@.nsf/mf/3238.0.55.001

Australian Government. (2020). *Our people.* Retrieved from https://www.australia.gov.au/about-australia/our-country/our-people

Australian Human Rights Commission. (2011). Chapter 4: Cultural safety and security: Tools to address lateral violence – Social Justice Report 2011. Retrieved from https://www.humanrights.gov.au/our-work/chapter-4-cultural-safety-and-security-tools-address-lateral-violence-social-justice

Australian Human Rights Commission. (2013). *Right to self determination.* Retrieved from https://humanrights.gov.au/our-work/rights-and-freedoms/right-self-determination

Australian Human Rights Commission. (n.d.). *Discrimination.* Retrieved from https://www.humanrights.gov.au/quick-guide/12030

Australian Institute of Aboriginal and Torres Strait Islander Studies [AITSIS] (2018). Indigenous Australians: Aboriginal and Torres Strait Islander people. Retrieved from https://aiatsis.gov.au/explore/articles/indigenous-australians-aboriginal-and-torres-strait-islander-people

Balaratnasingam, S., Chapman, M., Chong, D., Hunter, E., Lee, J., Little, C., Mulholland, K., Parker, R., Watson, M., & Janca, A. (2019). Advancing social and emotional well-being in Aboriginal and Torres Strait Islander

Australians: Clinicians' reflections. *Australasian Psychiatry, 27*(4), 348–351. doi:https://doi.org/10.1177/1039856218789765.

Belyh, A. (2017). *Degrees of cultural awareness*. Retrieved from https://www.cleverism.com/lexicon/cultural-awareness/

BeyondBlue. (2014). *Working therapeutically with LGBTIQ clients: A practice wisdom resource*. Retrieved 24 March 2020, from https://www.beyondblue.org.au/docs/default-source/default-document-library/bw0256-practice-wisdom-guide-online.pdf

BeyondBlue. (2020). *The impact of discrimination*. Retrieved from https://www.beyondblue.org.au/who-does-it-affect/lesbian-gay-bi-trans-and-intersex-lgbti-people/the-impact-of-discrimination

Bolt, R. J. (2001). *It's just how you've been brought up! An Aboriginal perspective on the relationship between the law, racism and mental health [honours thesis]*. Sydney, NSW: University of Sydney.

Bowleg, L. (2012). The problem with the phrase women and minorities: Intersectionality – An important theoretical framework for public health. *American Journal of Public Health, 102*, 1267–1273. Retrieved from https://ajph.aphapublications.org/doi/10.2105/AJPH.2012.300750

Braveman, P. (2006). Health disparities and health equity: Concepts and measurement. *Annual Review of Public Health, 27*(1), 167–194. doi: https://doi.org/10.1146/annurev.publhealth.27.021405.102103.

Campinha-Bacote, J. (2002). The process of cultural competence in the delivery of healthcare services: A model of care. *Journal of Transcultural Nursing, 13*(3), 181–184. doi:https://doi.org/10.1177/10459602013003003.

Campinha-Bacote, J. (2019). Cultural competemility: A paradigm shift in the cultural competence versus cultural humility debate – Part I. *The Online Journal of Issues in Nursing, 24*(1). doi: https://doi.org/10.3912/OJIN.Vol24No01PPT20.

Conner, K. M., & Davidson J. R. T. (2003). Development of a new resilience scale: The Connor-Davidson Resilience Scale (CD-RISC). *Depression and Anxiety, 18*(2), 76–82. Retrieved from http://static1.squarespace.com/static/51abe64ee4b0a1344208e98a/t/51d3ce77e4b001d5c13a7e87/1372835447995/CD-RISC+%28Connor+%26+Davidson%2C+2003%29.pdf

Crameri, P., Barrett, C., Latham, J., & Whyte, C. (2015). It is more than sex and clothes: Culturally safe services for older lesbian, gay, bisexual, transgender and intersex people. *Australasian Journal on Ageing, 34*, 21–25. doi:https://doi.org/10.1111/ajag.12270. Retrieved from https://www.latrobe.edu.au/__data/assets/pdf_file/0008/814769/Culturally-safe-services-for-older-LGBTI-people.pdf

Crenshaw, K. (1989). Demarginalizing the intersection of race and sex: A black feminist critique of antidiscrimination doctrine, feminist theory and antiracist politics. *University of Chicago Legal Forum, 1989*(1), Article 8. Retrieved from: http://chicagounbound.uchicago.edu/uclf/vol1989/iss1/8

Crosby Kile, N. (2018). *What are the stages of cultural awareness?* Retrieved from https://www.continued.com/early-childhood-education/ask-the-experts/what-stages-cultural-awareness-23104

Cross, T. L., Bazron, B. J., Dennis, K. W., & Isaacs, M. R. (1989). *Towards a culturally competent system of care* (Vol. 1). Washington, DC: Georgetown University Child Development Centre.

Cruwys, T., Berry, H. L., Cassells, R., Duncan, A., O'Brien, L. V., Sage, B., & D'Souza, G. (2013). *Marginalised Australians: Characteristics and predictors of exit over ten years 2001–2010*. University of Canberra, Australia. Retrieved from https://melbourneinstitute.unimelb.edu.au/assets/documents/hilda-bibliography/other-publications/2013/Cruwys_etal_marginalised_Australians.pdf

Curtis, E., Jones, R., Tipene-Leach, D., Walker, C., Loring, B., Paine, S., & Reid, P. (2019). Why cultural safety rather than cultural competency is required to achieve health equity: A literature review and recommended definition. *International Journal for Equity in Health, 18*(1). doi: https://doi.org/10.1186/s12939-019-1082-3.

Dermer, S. B., Smith, S. D., & Barto, K. K. (2010). Identifying and correctly labeling sexual prejudice, discrimination, and oppression. *Journal of Counseling & Development, 88*(3), 325–331. doi:https://doi.org/10.1002/j.1556-6678.2010.tb00029.x.

Doyle, K. (2011). Modes of colonisation and patterns of contemporary mental health: Towards an understanding of Canadian Aboriginal, Australian Aboriginal and Maori Peoples [online]. *Aboriginal and Islander Health Worker Journal, 35*(1), 20–23.

Evans, B., & Reid, J. (2013). Dangerously exposed: The life and death of the resilient subject. *Resilience, 2*, 83. Retrieved from http://explore.bl.uk/primo_library/libweb/action/display.do?tabs=detailsTab&gathStatTab=true&ct=display&fn=search&doc=ETOCvdc_100033222639.0x000001&indx=1&recIds=ETOCvdc_100033222639.0x000001

Farre, A., & Rapley, T. (2017). The new old (and old new) medical model: Four decades navigating the biomedical and psychosocial understandings of health and illness. *Healthcare, 5*(4). doi:https://doi.org/10.3390/healthcare5040088.

Farrell, A. (2015). Can you see me? Queer margins in Aboriginal communities. *Journal of Global Indigeneity, 1*(1), 2015. Retrieved from http://ro.uow.edu.au/jgi/vol1/iss1/3

Fausto-Sterling, A. (2000a). *Sexing the body. Gender politics and the construction of sexuality*. New York, NY: Basic Books.

Fausto-Sterling, A. (2000b). The five sexes, revisited. *Sciences, 4*, 18.

Frankland, R., Bamblett, M., & Lewis, P. (2011, May/June). 'Forever business': A framework for maintaining and restoring cultural safety in Aboriginal Victoria [online]. *Indigenous Law Bulletin, 7*(24), 27–30. Retrieved from https://search.informit.com.au/documentSummary;dn=211255923549358;res=IELAPA. ISSN: 1328-5475.

Fraser, M. W., Richman, J. M., & Galinsky, M. J. (1999). Risk, protection, and resilience: Toward a conceptual framework for social work practice. *Social Work Research, 23*(3), 131–143.

Ganesharajah, C. (2009). *Indigenous health and wellbeing: The importance of country*. Acton, ACT: Native Title Research Unit, Australian Institute for Aboriginal and Torres Strait Islander Studies.

Gay and Lesbian Health Victoria. (2013). *GLBTI inclusive practice audit for health and human services*. Australian Research Centre in Sex, Health and Society, La Trobe University. Retrieved from https://quac.org.au/wp-content/uploads/2017/09/GLBTI-inclusive-practice-audit_2013.pdf

Gee, G., Dudgeon, P., Schultz, C., Hart, A., & Kelly, K. (2014). *Aboriginal and Torres Strait Islander social and emotional wellbeing*. In P. Dudgeon, H. Milroy, & R. Walker (Eds.), *Working together: Aboriginal and Torres Strait Islander mental health and wellbeing principles and practice* (2nd ed., pp. 55–68). Canberra, ACT: Department of the Prime Minister and Cabinet. http://www.mhcc.org.au/media/80434/working‐together‐aboriginal‐and‐wellbeing‐2014.pdf

Habarth, J. M. (2015). Development of the heteronormative attitudes and beliefs scale. *Psychology & Sexuality, 6*(2), 166–188. doi:https://doi.org/10.1080/19419899.2013.876444.

Herek, G. M. (1988). Heterosexuals' attitudes toward lesbians and gay men: Correlates and gender differences. *The Journal of Sex Research, 25*(4), 451–477. doi:https://doi.org/10.2307/3812894.

Herek, G. M. (1990). The context of anti-gay violence: Notes on cultural and psychological heterosexism. *Journal of Interpersonal Violence, 5*(3), 316–333. doi:https://doi.org/10.1177/088626090005003006.

Higa, D., Hoppe, M. J., Lindhorst, T., Mincer, S., Beadnell, B., Morrison, D. M., Wells, E. A., Todd, A., & Mountz, S. (2014). Negative and positive factors associated with the well-being of lesbian, gay, bisexual, transgender, queer, and questioning (LGBTQ) youth. *Youth & Society, 46*(5), 663–687. doi:https://doi.org/10.1177/0044118X12449630.

Hofstede, G. (1994) *Cultures and organizations: Software of the mind*. London: HarperCollinsBusiness.

Intersex Human Rights Australia. (2013). *What is intersex?* Retrieved from https://ihra.org.au/18106/what-is-intersex/

Jones, J. (2017). Going back to the source: Cultural safety in diverse societies. *Whitireia Nursing & Health Journal, 24*, 9–12.

Joseph, J. (2013). Resilience as embedded neoliberalism: A governmentality approach. *Resilience, 1*(1), 38–52. doi: https://doi.org/10.1080/21693293.2013.765741.

Kelly, M. (2014). Adding 'allies' to LGBT acronym sparks controversy. *Iowa State Daily*, 29 October. Available at: http://www.iowastatedaily.com/news/article_50e5e8f6-5edc-11e4-a17f-f77a797314c5.html. Accessed 23 March 2020.

Krieg, A. (2009). The experience of collective trauma in Australian Indigenous communities. *Australasian Psychiatry, 17*(1_suppl), 528–532. doi: https://doi.org/10.1080/10398560902948621.

Kroeber, A. L., & Kluckhohn, C. (1952). Culture: A critical review of concepts and definitions. *Papers. Peabody Museum of Archaeology & Ethnology, Harvard University, 47*(1), viii, 223.

Kuartei, S. (2015). *Sovereignty in health – Towards a new paradigm in the Pacific*. Paper presented at The 13th National Rural Health Conference, Darwin, Australia. Retrieved from http://www.ruralhealth.org.au/13nrhc/images/paper_KN_Kuartei%2C%20Stevenson.pdf

Lavizzo-Mourey, R., & Mackenzie, E. R. (1996). Cultural competence: Essential measurements of quality for managed care organizations. *Annals of Internal Medicine, 124*(10), 919–921.

Lorber, J., & Moore, L. J. (2011). *Gendered bodies: Feminist perspectives* (2nd ed.). New York, NY: Oxford University Press.

Maddison, S., & Partridge, E. (2014). Agonism and intersectionality: Indigenous women, violence and feminist collective identity. *Research in Social Movements, Conflicts & Change, 37,* 28.

Major, B., & Eccleston, C. (2004). Stigma and social exclusion. In D. Abrams, M. Hogg, & J. Marques (Ed.), *Social psychology of inclusion and exclusion.* New York, NY: Psychology Press. doi:https://doi.org/10.4324/9780203496176.

Markwick, A., Ansari, Z., Clinch, D., & McNeil, J. (2019). Experiences of racism among Aboriginal and Torres Strait Islander adults living in the Australian state of Victoria: A cross-sectional population-based study. *BMC Public Health, 19*(1), 1–14.

Mosher, D. K., Hook, J. N., Captari, L. E., Davis, D. E., DeBlaere, C., & Owen, J. (2017). Cultural humility: A therapeutic framework for engaging diverse clients. *Practice Innovations, 2*(4), 221–233. doi:https://doi.org/10.1037/pri0000055.

Murden, R., Norman, A., Ross, J., Sturdivant, E., Kedia, M., & Shah, S. (2008). Occupational therapy students' perceptions of their cultural awareness and competency. *Occupational Therapy International, 15*(3), 191–203. doi:https://doi.org/10.1002/oti.253.

National Prevention Information Network. (2020). *What is cultural competence?* Retrieved from https://npin.cdc.gov/pages/cultural-competence#what

Nursing Council of New Zealand. (2011). *Guidelines for cultural safety, the Treaty of Waitangi and Maori health in nursing education and practice.* Retrieved from http://pro.healthmentoronline.com/assets/Uploads/refract/pdf/Nursing_Council_cultural-safety11.pdf

O'Dowd, M. F. (2020). Explainer: What is systemic racism and institutional racism? *The Conversation.* Retrieved from https://theconversation.com/explainer-what-is-systemic-racism-and-institutional-racism-131152

Pachankis, J. E. (2007). The psychological implications of concealing a stigma: A cognitive-affective-behavioral model. *Psychological Bulletin, 133*(2), 328–345. doi:https://doi.org/10.1037/0033-2909.133.2.328.

Paradies, Y. (2016). Colonisation, racism and indigenous health. *Journal of Population Research, 33*(1), 83–96. doi: https://doi.org/10.1007/s12546-016-9159-y.

Paradies, Y., Harris, R., & Anderson, I. (2008). The impact of racism on Indigenous health in Australia and Aotearoa: Towards a research agenda, Discussion Paper No. 4, Cooperative Research Centre for Aboriginal Health, Darwin. Retrieved from https://www.lowitja.org.au/content/Document/Lowitja-Publishing/Racism-Report.pdf

Pilling, M. D. (2013). Invisible identity in the workplace: Intersectional madness and processes of disclosure at work. *Disability Studies Quarterly, 33*(1), 1.

Quinn, D. M., & Earnshaw, V. A. (2013). Concealable stigmatized identities and psychological well-being. *Social and Personality Psychology Compass, 7*, 40–51. doi:https://doi.org/10.1111/spc3.12005.

Reiker, P. P., & Reid, J. P. (2017). The health gender gap. In M. P. Sanchez-Lopez & R. M. Limina-Gras (Eds.), *The psychology of gender and health: Conceptual and applied global concerns*. San Diego, CA: Elsevier, Inc.

Riopel, L. (2020). *Resilience skills, factors and strategies of the resilient person*. Retrieved from https://positivepsychology.com/resilience-skills/

Samovar, L. A., & Porter, R. E. (1994). *Intercultural communication: A reader*. Belmont, CA: Wadsworth.

Sanson, A., Augoustinos, M., Gridley, H., Kyrios, M., Reser, J., & Turner, C. (1998). Racism and prejudice: An Australian psychological society position paper. *Australian Psychologist, 33*(3), 161–182.

Schermerhorn, R. A. (1970). *Comparative ethnic relations: A framework for theory and research*. New York, NY: Random House.

Shah, S. (2017). *Role of civil society (NGOs) in the empowerment of marginalised people in India*. Retrieved from https://www.sociologydiscussion.com/society/role-of-civil-society-ngos-in-the-empowerment-of-marginalised-people-india/861

Shearer, J. (2019). Enforcing the gender binary and its implications on nonbinary identities: An exploration of the linguistic and social erasure of nonbinary individuals in the United States. Alpenglow: Binghamton University. *Undergraduate Journal of Research and Creative Activity, 5*(1). Retrieved from https://orb.binghamton.edu/alpenglowjournal/vol5/iss1/7

Sherwood, J. (2015). Intergenerational trauma isn't just another determinant of Indigenous People's health. *Journal of Ethics in Mental Health*, 1–7.

Simons, A., Houkes, I., Koster, A., Groffen, D., & Bosma, H. (2018). The silent burden of stigmatisation: A qualitative study among Dutch people with a low socioeconomic position. *BMC Public Health, 18*(1). doi: https://doi.org/10.1186/s12889-018-5210-6.

Smith, E., Jones, T., Ward, R., Dixon, J., Mitchell, A., & Hillier, L. (2014). *From blues to rainbows: Mental health and wellbeing of gender diverse and transgender young people in Australia*. Melbourne, VIC: The Australian Research Centre in Sex, Health and Society. Retrieved from https://www.beyondblue.org.au/docs/default-source/research-project-files/bw0268-from-blues-to-rainbows-report-final-report.pdf?sfvrsn=6f2e60ea_2

Social Work Policy Institute. (2004). *Resiliency*. Retrieved from http://www.socialworkpolicy.org/research/resiliency.html

Solar, O., & Irwin, A. (2010). A conceptual framework for action on the social determinants of health. Social Determinants of Health Discussion Paper 2 (Policy and Practice). Retrieved from https://www.who.int/sdhconference/resources/ConceptualframeworkforactiononSDH_eng.pdf

Spencer-Oatey, H. (2012) *What is culture? A compilation of quotations. GlobalPAD Core Concepts. Available at GlobalPAD Open House*. Retrieved from http://www.warwick.ac.uk/globalpadintercultural

Stanley, J., Harris, R., Cormack, D., Waa, A., & Edwards, R. (2019). The impact of racism on the future health of adults: Protocol for a prospective cohort study. *BMC Public Health, 19*(1), 1–10. doi:https://doi.org/10.1186/s12889-019-6664-x.

Stubbe, D. (2020). Practicing cultural competence and cultural humility in the care of diverse patients. *FOCUS, 18*(1), 49–51. doi: https://doi.org/10.1176/appi.focus.20190041.

Tervalon, M., & Murray-Garcia, J. (1998). Cultural humility versus cultural competence: A critical distinction in defining physician training outcomes in multicultural education. *Journal of Health Care for the Poor and Underserved, 9*(2), 117–125. doi:https://doi.org/10.1353/hpu.2010.0233.

The Lowitja Institute. (2018). *Deficit discourse and Aboriginal and Torres Strait Islander health policy – Summary report.* Retrieved from https://ncis.anu.edu.au/_lib/doc/ddih/Deficit_Discourse_summary_report_WEB.pdf

United Nations. (2016). *Leaving no one behind: The imperative of inclusive development.* Retrieved from https://www.un.org/esa/socdev/rwss/2016/full-report.pdf

Viladrich, A., & Loue, S. (2010). *Minority identity development.* In S. Loue (Eds.), *Sexualities and identities of minority women.* New York, NY: Springer. doi:https://doi.org/10.1007/978-0-387-75657-8_1.

Walsh-Dilley, M., & Wolford, W. (2015). (Un)Defining resilience: Subjective understandings of "resilience" from the field. *Resilience, 3,* 173. Retrieved from doi:https://doi.org/10.1080/21693293.2013.765741.

Watego, L. (n.d.). *Why blak not black.* Retrieved from https://sites.google.com/site/australianblakhistorymonth/extra-credit

Waters, A., & Asbill, L. (2013). *Reflections on cultural humility.* Retrieved from https://www.apa.org/pi/families/resources/newsletter/2013/08/cultural-humility

Werner, E. E., & Smith, R. S. (1992). *Overcoming the odds: High risk children from birth to adulthood.* Ithaca, NY: Cornell University Press.

Werner, E. E., & Smith, R. S. (2001). *Journeys from childhood to midlife: Risk, resilience, and recovery.* Ithaca, NY: Cornell University Press.

Williams, R. (1999). Cultural safety – What does it mean for our work practice? *Australian and New Zealand Journal Of Public Health, 23*(2), 213–214. doi: https://doi.org/10.1111/j.1467-842x.1999.tb01240.x.

Wirth, L. (1945). The problem of minority groups. In R. Linton (Ed.), *The science of man in the world crisis* (pp. 347–372). New York, NY: Columbia University Press.

Yeager, K. A., & Bauer-Wu, S. (2013). Cultural humility: Essential foundation for clinical researchers. *Applied Nursing Research, 26*(4), 251–256.

Yetman, N. R. (1991) *Majority and minority: The dynamics of race and ethnicity in American life* (5th ed.). London. Pearson.

Yu-Tang, S., Radford, K., Daylight, G., Cumming, R., Broe, T. G. A., & Draper, B. (2018). Depression, suicidal behaviour, and mental disorders in older Aboriginal Australians. *International Journal of Environmental Research and Public Health, 15*(3), 447.

3 From The Margins of the Other's Other: Indigenous Queers and a Crisis of Recognition

Todd J. Fernando

Indigenous queers in Australia are going through a crisis of recognition.

Maddee Clark (2014)

This chapter uses Indigenous standpoint theory and queer theory to frame its approach to the topic of Indigeneity and queerness. Standpoint is theoretically summarised as the way in which social positioning, epistemology, axiology, and ontology guide the research process (Walter & Andersen, 2013). The theory of standpoint helps to acknowledge the world around us, our social positioning in it, and how this positioning relates to others and society. My standpoint as an Aboriginal queer person from the Wiradjuri nation has contributed to the way in which this chapter is conceptualised and written. Additionally, I am employed within a tertiary education institution and I am noted as a leading scholar on the study of queer Indigenous history, culture, and identity.

Introduction

In their 2019 article, 'Teaching cultural humility for social workers serving LGBTQI Aboriginal communities in Australia', Bindi Bennett and Trevor G. Gates sparked a conversation for educators in the Australian field of social work to consider the use of a cultural humility framework to be more inclusive of the social and cultural issues facing Lesbian, Gay, Bisexual, Transgender, Intersex, and Queer (LGBTIQ) Indigenous people. Bennet and Gates also challenged researchers to become aware and subsequently reflective of the historical underpinnings that have shaped those who are often marginalised by Australia's colonial project. Bennett and Gates identified that queer Indigenous experiences are significantly omitted from mainstream Indigenous narratives within the field of social work. As a result, they noted the paucity of social work research and knowledge on queer Indigenous people limits how to appropriately work with and to build frameworks for this population. In thinking about proactive educational approaches to mitigate the lack of cultural, social, and historical understandings of queer Indigenous Australians, Bennett and Gates suggest that 'social work education needs to be based on a participatory model that recognizes the importance of lived experiences' (Bennett & Gates, 2019, p. 610).

Bennett and Gates have identified a phenomenon that is currently happening in many fields across Australia. There is a significant learning deficit when it comes to the full breadth of understanding the diversity of Indigenous Australia societies, and this is also the case for knowledge pertaining to the experiences of queer Indigenous people. Part of this learning deficit is that limited research has been conducted on the lives of queer Indigenous Australians. While this is a significant part of the problem, there exist a growing number of scholars who are producing literature that speaks to the queer Indigenous experience. Many of these scholars have suggested that the redoing of Indigenous histories is required – an approach based on telling Indigenous histories from the queered perspective.

To continue the conversation started by Bennett and Gates, I have written this chapter with the following in mind: it is widely accepted that many Australians have limited knowledge when it comes to Indigenous history; to assume that these people also understand the queer Indigenous experience is an overreach. Additionally, this chapter will provide a narrative of just some of the histories of queer Indigenous people in Australia, and internationally. In doing so, I urge others to highlight and tell these stories too. It is clear from social work literature that it is critical for social work education to find leadership to fill an empty space and allow queer narratives to be brought into the classroom. This chapter, therefore, continues their initial conversation by showcasing some of the events that have shaped the lives of LGBTIQ Indigenous people, both in Australia and internationally.

Conceptual framework

The emerging field of queer Indigenous research and studies is, at times, situated in opposition to default narratives within Indigenous communities. As this chapter will show, the narratives of Indigenous queerness have prompted an ideological challenge to the heteronormative lens that exists within mainstream Indigenous research and knowledge. By displaying the personal and public Indigenous socio-cultural practices, this chapter operates as a modality to assert and understand forms of sexual expressions and realities within gendered identities and in response to Indigenous heteronormativity and non-Indigenous concepts of sexuality.

For many decades, the Indigenous rights movement and queer liberation have run side by side (Altman, 2001). These movements have seen important transitions for both communities, such as the push for constitutional recognition or marriage equality. For queer Indigenous people, a system of co-existence between queerness and Indigeneity is viewed as a core identity. Like white feminism for Indigenous women, gender also complicates and makes complex the narrative of identities of queer Indigenous people. There is a current tradition of writings on and about Indigenous peoples through a heteropatriarchal lens. In an article titled 'Queering Resurgence: Taking on Heteropatriarchy in Indigenous Nation Building', author Leanne Simpson (2012) writes that,

> It is not enough for us to say 'patriarchy was not part of our traditions' because the pervasive and insidious nature of heteropatriarchy means that for hundreds of years Indigenous children have been taught to uphold these systems. Thanks to imperialism and conquest, heteropatriarchy is a world-wide phenomenon. It is impossible for Indigenous communities to be completely immune from it. (Simpson, 2012)

Current research about the lifestyles of Indigenous Australians portrays them primarily as heterosexual figures (Farrell, 2015). Moreover, Indigenous scholarly literature subconsciously assumes heteropatriarchy in Indigenous Australian societies as not just the norm but a critical feature of cultural organisation, land tenure, social life, and customs. In colonial and queer literature, however, this is magnified and distorted to portray Indigenous bodies as leading dreary, savage, and brutal lives (Smith, 2015; Arvin, Tuck, & Morrill, 2013; Driskill, 2011), while other authors have interrogated heteropatriarchy in Indigenous and non-Indigenous communities on the construction of decolonising feminism (Arvin et al., 2013), queer settler colonialism (Morgensen, 2011; Giuliani, 2015; Tatonetti, 2014), and homonationalism (Sykes, 2016; Sharif, 2015).

Emerging queer Indigenous literature has highlighted the importance of recognising heteronormative biases and social schemas within Indigenous frameworks as a way to shift and strengthen Indigenous socio-cultural and community knowledge (both historically and contemporarily – queered and non-queered). Across the globe, particularly in Anglo-sphered countries, queer narratives are quickly becoming mainstream.

Despite this trepidation, Indigenous people often prioritise issues relating to education (Nakata, 2002; Battiste, 2002; Battiste, Bell, & Findlay, 2002), health (Vos et al., 2009), land (Barbour & Schlesinger, 2012), economics (Langton, Mazel, & Palmer, 2006), and a search for culture (Nakata, 2006), over the understandings of the characteristic diversity amongst Indigenous communities. These factors remain a priority – and for good reason – but mean nothing if there is a continuation of violence perpetrated by heteronormative and heteropatriarchy behaviours that continue to influence Indigenous ways of doing and knowing in modernity.

Finding appropriate language

One of the major critiques in sexuality studies assumes that the language to describe sexuality diversity within modern societies is, at times, problematic (Altman, 2017). Many scholars, from an array of fields, argue that the problematic nature of this language extends to the relationship modern sexuality has with whiteness and religion; this is most certain when thinking about sexuality within Anglo-sphered countries, though at times it transgresses non-white populations (Altman, 2017; Farrell, 2015; Clark, 2015). Many terms and definitions used to describe sex, sexuality, gender diversity, and so forth often occur outside heteronormative binary systems within Western, Anglo-sphered societies. As such, it is important to recognise that these terms – Lesbian, Gay, Bisexual, Transgender, Intersex, and Queer (LGBTIQ) – are inherent, though not exclusively, Western concepts. There is a possibility that perhaps these terms do not necessarily provide an adequate understanding of the range of gender and sexual diversity (including experiences) of non-white populations. This is particularly the case for Indigenous societies globally (Driskill, 2011).

Troy-Anthony Baylis, a queer Indigenous artist, argues that this diversity of language is recognised within Indigenous Australian societies, insofar as terms such as Brotherboy and Sistergirl are used to describe the experiences of Indigenous Australian transgender people (Baylis, 2014). These phenomena also extend internationally, for example, where Maori cultural history and language use the term Takatāpui to describe a population that identifies as both gay and Maori (Murray, 2003). From 1990, Native American populations (and, to an extent, Canadian First Nations) moved to the use of a more inclusive term, Two-Spirit, which opposed the use of the imposed anthropological term 'berdache' and has come to refer to contemporary native identities and roles, past and present, including individuals who are gay or lesbian or prescribe to gender non-conforming roles (Jacobs, Thomas, & Lang, 1997).

Beyond the use of Brotherboy and Sistergirl to describe Indigenous transgender populations, no Indigenous term exists or is widely accepted to represent queer Indigenous Australians homogeneously. This places limitations and certain complications to describe this population without inference to the Western concept of the LGBTIQ umbrella and its associated identities' values and ways of being. Queer Indigenous writer Andrew Farrell adopts the term queer as a non-complacent descriptor to refer to sexuality and gender differences within the Indigenous Australian population (Farrell, 2016). Despite the term's historical baggage of association to acts of violence and oppression, the term queer has been reclaimed to reflect on the sexual, social, and political liberation and pride of diverse gender populations, including the intersecting experiences of queer Indigenous people (Baylis, 2014). The term queer is slowly becoming a widely used term by queer Indigenous people themselves, and, as such, I have come to use the term queer in my writing and research to describe LGBTIQ Indigenous populations.

Framing the redoing of histories

There is a growing movement to understand the relationship between queer and non-queer Indigenous people, resulting in the queering of Indigenous histories being seen as an important task (Freccero, 2013; Hodge, 2015; Hutchings & Aspin, 2007). The scarcity in the literature that understands queer Indigenous epistemology reveals not much is known about how queer Indigenous people emerged or how Aboriginal communities understood them before 1788. Limited and undiscovered evidence makes it not entirely possible to understand the role queer Indigenous populations played in traditional forms of Aboriginal society. While there are glimmers throughout early settler encounters with what was considered 'perverted homosexual behaviour', one could never firmly attest how those communities understood the phenomena of queerness. It is clear from most available writings from early colonial anthropologists to contemporary Indigenous research, there are few observations of sexuality (and non-heteronormative gender), and other than some salacious pseudo-anthropological erotica, the non-heteronormative practices and customs of pre-colonial Australia are almost absent.

It is a critical endeavour of this chapter to acknowledge both Indigenous and non-Indigenous – queer and not queer – who have spent considerable time researching and presenting knowledge of and about Indigenous queerness. Because of their ability to do so, the (re)generation of literature regarding queer Indigenous realities is located betwixt and between the partitions of 'a mirror'. This mirror was described in the first critical yet edifying works about Indigenous queerness, 'Peopling the Empty Mirror: The prospects for lesbian and gay Aboriginal history' (Dunn-Holland et al., 1994). Anthropological by nature, the Gays and Lesbians Aboriginal Alliance conceives this mirror by way of a revelation by lesbian writer Adrienne Rich who writes,

> When someone with the authority of a teacher, say, describes the world and you are not in it, there is a moment of psychic disequilibrium, as if you looked into the mirror and saw nothing. (Dunn-Holland et al., 1994, p. 3)

As a result of recognising the fissure held by the 'authority-fraught looking-glass of written texts' (Dunn-Holland et al., 1994, p. 3), the Alliance started a new, innovative phase of building the 'first step towards the development of a field of lesbian and gay Aboriginal history' (Dunn-Holland et al., 1994, p. 3). This queerly Indigenous 'social process' mission challenged the subordinated subjectivity of Indigenous sexualities and formed a foundational bedrock of a type of canon on queer Indigenous experiences, knowledge, and ways of knowing.

Aileen Morton-Robinson perplexes the anthropological constructions of Aboriginal women in her 1998 article, 'When the object Speaks:

A Postcolonial Encounter: anthropological representations and Aboriginal women's self-presentations'. Moreton-Robinson concerns herself with criticising the anthropological weaponry that subjugates Aboriginal subjectivity to show that historical forms of the anthropological methodology are problematic towards constructing 'Aboriginal womanity' in relation to what she calls 'spheres of interdependent cultural domains' (Moreton-Robinson, 1998, p. 278). Morton-Robinson describes,

> The sites analysed reflect or symbolise those sites under interrogation in Western society by the women's movement, such as: marriage; kinship; women's economic activity; sexuality; reproduction; ritual; and socialisation. This is not to say that the Aboriginal women about whom they are writing are not concerned with these aspects of their lives. What is at issue is that it is not they who set the terms of reference for investigation, nor are they the intended audience of this literature...The literature is written about them, not by them, for them or with them. (Moreton-Robinson, 1998, p. 278)

What is revealed in her assertion is the need to redefine the position of object and subject when exploring or creating textual analysis concerning an Aboriginal inquiry. For Morton-Robinson, Aboriginal women were showcased as subjects of inferiority when written as objects, but later observed an essential change when Aboriginal women became the subjects of their imagining. It is only 'when the object speaks' we understand that the assumed default positions become challenged (Moreton-Robinson, 1998, p. 278).

In navigating queer Indigenous subjectivity, Troy-Anthony Baylis posits that 'the sexual and gender diversity of Aboriginal peoples remains mostly absent in the recordings and interpretations of Australian histories, and these absences reinforce a hetero-centric reading of Aboriginal cultures' (Hodge, 2015, p. 1). The absences Baylis describes closely resembles the psychic disequilibrium employed by The Gay Alliance, penned by Adrienne Rich. Baylis points to the 'academy as a colonised space' as one reason for the gap in knowledge about Aboriginal ontologies of sexualities (Baylis, 2014). While queer Indigenous literature concerns mostly heterogeneous life stories, not all of them sit outside the academy. The author and historian Dino Hodge asserts that held within the literature by queer Indigenous peoples is that,

> A complexity always exists surrounding who is telling a story or documenting a topic, in what manner, and from which perspective. Some contributors have chosen to share oral histories or to write life stories. Others have prepared essays addressing specific topics or events. And some have written utilising an academic framework. (Hodge, 2015, p. viii)

Hodge raises a distinction to the strength and possibilities of 'redoing' histories of sexualities, especially for the Indigenous experience. The complexity that Hodge refers to is about the curation and provocation of texts and knowledge that informs narratives of Indigenous queerness. What is informed by this is more than a series of anthologies. Instead, the ability of queer Indigenous studies extends beyond the navigations of contemporary portrayals and sometimes even beyond the limits defined in an academic arena. By doing so, queer Indigenous literature provides a framework to transform the oral traditions of Indigenous Australians and inscribes history in the here and now amid the past and the future. Similarly, historian James Davidson writes:

> Restoring local traditions has now become an urgent task, both for Orientalists provoked by 'queer theory' in other branches of the Humanities, and, more urgently, by local people themselves, concerned to rediscover a local same-sex-oriented sexual identity. Homosexuality, however, is a difficult field for historians. Its materials require a high level of expertise in language and gesture, politics, and irony. There are problems in knowing what is actually in a particular text when words are so often misread or omitted... even before one gets to problems of tone and interpretation. (Davidson, 2007, p. 725)

The privilege of 'restoring local traditions' lends itself to the capacity to build a specialist framework that recognises and makes meaning of 'language and gesture, politics and irony' in order to deconstruct then reconstruct the 'tone and interpretation' provided in seemingly problematic texts (Davidson, 2007, p. 725). In this way, as Davidson's notion somewhat suggests, the challenge for queer Indigenous studies and research lies in its ability to formulate new meanings of history that remain visible or hidden. This is an important distinction to understand, particularly for institutions or fields – such as social work – who wish to engage with more diverse and inclusive content. The following display of queer Indigenous narratives and experiences are but a glimmer of ontological inquiries about queer Indigenous peoples and history.

Queering Aboriginalities/Indigeneity

In 2010, at the age of 21, I took a trip back to Wiradjuri Country, to my hometown of Condobolin. Wiradjuri Country is one of beauty. While I acknowledge that most Aboriginal people stake the claim that their Country is the most beautiful, the Western plains of Wiradjuri Country can only be described as majestic. This trip back to Country was one that I have done more times than I can recall. This particular drive back to Country, however, was one of reflective significance. It was my first on Country as an out queer man.

When queer people come out for the first time, it can often be a remarkable personal experience. And, of course, some queer people come out to violent response. Nonetheless, coming out allows one to uncover once hidden or dormant traits and attributes. The drive across Country allowed me to think about this. It forced me to deeply ponder who I now am and who I now will become. I often thought about the idea of who I am as a Wiradjuri person or as an Aboriginal person. Aboriginal people are often asked these questions about them: the 'What does it mean to be Aboriginal?' one. At times, it is easy to respond to Aboriginality. There are clear rules and protocols. Clear boundaries and limitations. There exist historical, personal, public, self-determining responses. But this trip forced me to ask a different question: 'What does it mean to be a queer Wiradjuri person?'

Aboriginal schema is built and remade, as Marcia Langton suggests (Langton & Bowers, 1993). It is discussed in a dialog between ourselves as Indigenous and non-Indigenous. It is constructed and reconstructed in place. Around the kitchen table. In and outside of the classroom. Present in media, film, art, and throughout the matrix of social media. Aboriginality can often be described violently, restricting its narrative from evolving beyond the savage flesh that demarcates Indigenous bodies as primitive. The historical relevance of Aboriginality, as a homogenously salient ontology, has been defined by state agents 67 times (McCorquodale, 1986, p. 9). As Aboriginal people, however, we often create space to escape the colonial reality. We carve a place to sit, to put down the loaded baggage. These locations often progress assemblies of men and women to do business. In these spaces, however, restrictions occur. In many ways, these spaces silently ask queer Indigenous people to go back into the closet. The constructions of these conversations weave discourse in very heteronormative ways.

In 2015, during the Cultured Queer/Queering Culture symposium, Andrew Farrell highlighted the ways queer Indigenous people are invisibilised and marginalised within Indigenous communities when they asked, 'Can you see me?' (Farrell, 2015, p. 1). In response, Farrell asserted that queer Indigenous people 'act as a conduit across realms', that their bodies are mere 'sites of contention between worlds' (Farrell, 2015, p. 1). The underlying theme explored by Farrell concerns how queer Indigenous people and their relationships – to themselves, to their families, and to their lovers – become legitimised. The contention between worlds reveals a type of desire queer Indigenous people seek to find validation, often from an authority that is largely unknown, that their existence extends beyond colonialism, into a type of uncolonised static traditionalism. As a result, these modern forms of queer Indigenous identities seek affirmation through a series of personal and public interfaces. Similarly, the link between past and present exposes the fraught tension between queer and non-queer Indigenous relationships, subsequently probing an ideological challenge to understand how Indigenous heteronormativity became the default that rendered queer Indigenous a broken, alienated, unknowable body. To this extent, Farrell suggests that the emergent definition of Aboriginality 'has radically transformed and become tested by queerness' (Farrell, 2015, p. 1).

The nexus of Indigenous rights and advancements in policy, citizenship, and participation in politics is met with the awkward reality that queer Indigenous populations are further minoritised by this progress mainly because Indigenous heteronormativity contributes to their silence. It becomes increasingly clear that the other side of this relationship – the heteronormative in Indigenous knowledge holding – bears a discomforted unknowingness about the diversity that exists within Indigenous societies. A significant factor of Indigenous heteronormativity perhaps blames contact with religion and colonialism, privileging ignorance as a tactic over acceptance and tolerance to the actualities of Indigenous diversity. But it is not only queer Indigenous Australians who have faced queer erasure; in fact, queer Indigenous people globally have experienced some form of heteronormative assimilation.

In 2011, Qwo-Li Driskill and others reimagined queer Indigenous literature as a place to understand, provoke, and awaken queer Indigenous studies as a site of interrogation of theory, politics, and research. The seminal text, *Queer Indigenous Studies*, presents the 'emergence story about the current work of activists, artists, and scholars to address the theoretical specificities of Indigenous gay, lesbian, bisexual, transgender, queer, and Two-Spirit (GLBTQ2) lives and communities' (Driskill, 2011, p. 1). This collection of queer Indigenous narratives 'asks us to imagine what critical Indigenous GLBTQ2 theories look like, and what impact they have on our practices as scholars, activists, and artists' (Driskill, 2011, p. 1).

Centred around the decolonising work of Linda Tuhiwai Smith, Driskill et al. embarked on an intellectual project to decolonise queer knowledge and its underpinning methodologies. Driskill et al. suggest that queer Indigenous studies must take a 'methodological turn to Indigenous knowledges', in order to build, assess, and centre queer Indigenous narratives, and 'the multiplicity, complexity, contestation, and change among knowledge claims by Indigenous people' (Driskill, 2011, p. 3). As such, queer Indigenous studies and research moves toward a global Indigenous resurgence of queer knowledge – a pledge to understand the relationship queer Indigenous people have with themselves and their communities. Similarly, many queer Indigenous people globally took charge of ensuring that queer Indigenous knowledge is lifted out of the margins.

In Australia, Dino Hodge's intellectual work Did You Meet Any Malagas? (Hodge, 1993), Peopling the Empty Mirror (Dunn-Holland et al., 1994), and Colouring the Rainbow – Blak Queer and Trans Perspectives (Hodge, 2015) remain the canonical core of the cultural significance of the Indigenous Australian queer landscape. For example, Hodge's Did You Meet Any Malagas? (Hodge, 1993) offered one of the first published accounts of an Aboriginal understanding of homosexuality. The text is useful to dispel myths that, '"queer" Aboriginal people do not exist, and demonstrate that the sexualities of Aboriginal people are diverse and complex and may have been so before colonisation' (Baylis, 2014). Historian Robert Reynolds considers similar inferences about Hodge's text in an essay entitled 'Writing Queer Cultural Histories' (Reynolds, 1995). Reynolds asserts,

> Hodge does far more than reclaim a pure gay history of the Northern Territory. His questioning of gay white men reveals the way in which class and race intersect to create a commercial sub-culture dominated by relatively affluent white men... It is in Hodge's interviews with Aboriginal and Asian gays, and two white men in close contact with Aboriginal communities, that the contextual and relational nature of homosexuality becomes clear. His interviews with Aboriginal gays indicate an understanding of sexuality that cannot be reduced to a Western model of sexual identity. This is not to construct Aboriginal sexuality as monolithic and static, or as an exotic other to the West, but rather to further contextualise dominant understandings of homosexuality and sexual identity. It may well be through such cross-cultural analysis that Western concepts of sexuality will be most seriously challenged. (Reynolds, 1995, pp. 70–71)

Over time, more researchers, scholars, and thinkers have begun to look to understand queerness in more nuanced and intersecting ways. Another example is Hodge's Colouring the Rainbow (Hodge, 2015), a text which reimagines the vivacity of contemporary Indigenous Australia, one that sits well outside of the considered norm by shifting the way we think about the Indigenous experience. Hodge's collection of queer Indigenous narratives calls for the (re)centring of a modern queer Indigeneity. It is for that reason – the breaking down of homogeneities – that allows the queering of Indigenous histories, concepts, and ways of being to create a stronghold of statements that says the diversity of sexuality within Indigenous knowledge remains valid and legitimate; no ifs, and, or buts. Māori scholars too have produced seminal texts that expose the broadening depth of Māori queerness. Author, Clive Aspin asserts that

> In traditional Māori society, sex and sexuality were openly discussed and represented in art. This changed as Europeans introduced Victorian morals to New Zealand, and traditional songs and stories were censored. In the 21st century sexual diversity was again recognised as an important part of wellbeing. (Aspin, 2019)

Much work has been done in Aotearoa/New Zealand to centre queer Māori knowledge and literature. These examples include, 'I didn't have to go to finishing school to learn how to be gay': Māori gay men's understanding of cultural and sexual identity (Aspin, 2002), Maori Sexuality (Aspin & Hutchings, 2006), Reclaiming the past to inform the future: Contemporary expressions of Maori sexuality (Aspin & Hutchings, 2007), and Sexuality and the stories of Indigenous people (Hutchings & Aspin, 2007). Like Aspin and Hutchings, a recognition of the work of Ngahuia Te Awekotuku is required. A deep thinker who, for many decades, has worked to revitalise queer Indigenous knowledge, especially for Maori's Takatāpui populations (Nikora & Te Awekotuku, 2016; Awekotuku, 2001).

Evoked by the presence of queer Indigenous ancestry, these texts have moved, shaped, and produced a series of frameworks to queer Aboriginality and/or Indigeneity, globally. In essence, these works are (re)telling the stories, realities, and lived experiences of Indigenous people in ways Indigenous literature has refused to do so before. Across the world, particularly Australia, New Zealand, the United States, and Canada, queer and non-queer, Indigenous and non-Indigenous scholars have infiltrated the academy to ensure queer Indigenous studies has no bounds. Of all these queer Indigenous texts, one theme, in particular, runs deep and connects the redoing of histories for queer Indigenous people globally and that theme is religion. A topic in which many queer Indigenous scholars argue lay at the core of Indigenous homophobia (Ross, 2020; Clark, 2014).

Organised religious stronghold

Religion has played, and continues to play, a fundamental role that silences and erases queer identity from Indigenous Australian ontology (Baylis, 2014). The continuation of colonial mentalities in Indigenous Australia compounds the development of understanding queer Indigenous histories, cultures, and identities. While the government enforced marginalisation of Indigenous Australians, the era of missions and reserves saw, in many ways, a shift of Indigenous kinships and family systems. Controlled mainly by missionaries of various theologies, these missions and reserves acted in part to disrupt Indigenous forms of life, including that of gender and sexuality norms. Dunn-Holland et al. argues that assumed Indigenous sexual and gendered identities at times justified the fracturing of Indigenous families. In a discussion on Indigenous sexualities globally, Aspin and Hutchings (2007) describe similar colonisation techniques that affect Maori populations today:

> This continuation of the colonisation of sexuality took hold in the US in the mid-twentieth century and has had a profound effect on Indigenous forms of sexuality around the world (Altman, 2001). In this account of the global influences on sexuality, Altman provides numerous examples of how indigenous sexual cultures look to Western concepts of 'gay' and 'lesbian' to inform the way in which they view themselves and, as a result, their sexual identities. Indigenous peoples who have moved some way towards defining their sexuality according to their own traditional values and beliefs have an important role to play in ensuring that this influence does not overwhelm and subjugate the essential elements of indigenous sexuality. (2010, p. 1)

The similar disparities of informed cultural understandings faced by Maori have relevance to techniques used to underpin the colonial warfare faced by Indigenous Australians. Since the primary goal of the mission and reserve era was in part to assimilate Indigenous Australian to a Western ideal of society, it comes to no surprise that colonial tropes were aiding this era, including the need to 'civilise the savages' and to 'breed out the black'. These exact phrases offered a new lens for early settlers, organised religions, and state agents to view the assimilatory work as a way to save the 'savage beasts' from their dysfunctioning, primitive society.

Troy-Anthony Baylis argues that 'the lived realities of colonisation have constructed a silencing force that mutes Queer-Aboriginality' (Baylis, 2014). He also argues that Australia's religious and colonial 'history has constructed Aboriginality as being so pure and so savage, so purely savage, that if tainted by the complexity of sexuality and gender, mixed ethnographies, mixed geographies, and mixed appearances, the whole look would be ruined. Aboriginal people would be regarded as not pure, not savage' (Baylis, 2014). Here, Baylis provides an interesting viewpoint to reimagine that the outcome of defining savagery could have easily been different had early explorers understood the uniqueness of sexual diversity. However, since the laws of England were reproduced throughout its colonies, particularly the Buggery Act of 1533 which rendered homosexuality practices illegal by the death penalty, it becomes more apparent as to why a sexuality lens was not in use. Nevertheless, Baylis argues that during pre-colonial times, homosexual relationships were considered an average experience for Indigenous men and women (Hodge, 2015). He further claims that these relationships were controlled by kinship systems that were produced outside of Western gender binaries. This knowledge, however, becomes lost as it remains non-existent or undiscovered in the writings of early colonial Australian histories.

Other types of writings about pre-colonial queer Indigenous histories underscore the argument that homosexual practices occurred during this period. These validating accounts do much more than reimagining the diversity of sexuality in pre-colonial Indigenous societies, but begin to undo the heteronormative realities that were reported by early settlers and researchers, that unfortunately continues in the present. In part two of Peopling the Empty Mirror, A View of the Past: 'Beastly and Un-Christian', Jim Wafer introduces the notion that many researchers who supported the argument that homosexuality never existed were, in fact, mistaken positions. Wafer here, of course, is contending that arguments such as 'nor have we found any homosexuality among full-blood people in whom tribal lore is maintained' (Ivor Jones, see Dunn-Holland et al., 1994) and David Moore's 'I never heard of homosexuality among Aborigines' pave a false premise that assumed queerness is solely located within Anglo culture and that, as a result of invading, ideologies queerness infected Indigenous ontologies (See, Dunn-Holland et al., 1994). Peopling the Empty Mirror (Dunn-Holland et al., 1994) goes on to reveal pre-colonial homosexual practices – and the key themes are noted:

- early accounts;

- boy-wives;

- kinship and homosexual relationships;

- Variations in homosexual practices and attitudes towards them;

- homosexual practices among women;

- homosexuality in rituals;

- stories.

These subsections of part two moreover push the boundary for understanding the processes inherent in colonisation by highlighting the intersections of Indigeneity and sexuality, in addition to Christian values and taboos. Overall, these themes showcased the danger that recorded pieces of evidence of homosexual behaviour and practices have become so tainted that they were indeed denied, ignored, misinterpreted, and completely erased from accounts of Aboriginal life. As John Newfong asserts, these accounts 'reacted to what they [settlers and researchers] saw as beastly, un-Christian practices with shocked excitement' (see Dunn-Holland et al., 1994, p. 27). Nonetheless, 'Peopling the Empty Mirror' provides sufficient data to capture the notion that sexuality was indeed a part of pre-colonial Indigenous social life. The extent to the value of such participation, however, remains somewhat unknown.

To provide contrast, of the many accounts noted about homosexual Indigenous practices and behaviours few dared to record women in homosexual roles. Early literature may suggest that this mainly could be explained by the notion that the female ceremony was conducted away from the white, male research gaze or that women's sexuality was deemed of less interest (Dunn-Holland et al., 1994, p. 28). Nevertheless, there exist records of female homosexual relations being conducted in ritual, story, and dance ceremonies. For example, there are accounts of women performing a 'love magic song' where they would show their labia to each other (Blackwood, 1986, p. 12). Although there is some debate as to whether this is considered a homosexual practice (Baylis, 2014).

The discussions on pre-colonial histories provide a further understanding that early colonial records fail to account for sexuality and cultural differences. While this is not new concerning knowledge about how Indigenous peoples are recorded throughout histories, it instead allows the reimagining of queer Indigenous narratives retrospectively. The recording of pre-colonial histories cannot possibly understand queer Indigenous ontologies as 'homosexuality', or terms used throughout this early period because it is inherently Western that the two could not correlate. As noted by Dunn-Holland et al. (1994) it is essentially impossible to understand the extent to which Indigenous sexual practices correspond to this notion. An important point to make and to take into consideration is that the possible version of recorded history was intentionally masked by Indigenous peoples deliberately to provide misleading information to Europeans to conceal particular kinds of knowledge (Dunn-Holland et al., 1994, p. 28). This silence contributes to the present-day erasure of the queer Indigenous voice. Nevertheless, despite the many problems with early colonial records, these accounts do provide evidence consistent with the claims of Dunn-Holland et al. (1994), and others, that gender and sexual variation has always existed within Indigenous Australian culture. It remains clear, however, that the tensions produced in understanding oral and recorded histories of Indigenous Australian sexuality are as Maori scholars Aspin and Hutchings describe as a result of an 'imposition of colonialist institutions including the Christian religion' (Aspin & Hutchings, 2007, p. 418). This imposition has granted some Indigenous people with an assumed right to express homophobia.

Indigenous homophobia

The first episode of Season 2 of ABC's hit television series *Redfern Now* (ABC, 2012) opened with a character named Frank; 'an Aboriginal man in a gay relationship navigating parenting, grief, sex, family, and responsibility' (Clark, 2014). What followed was an online social media onslaught by Indigenous and non-Indigenous communities popularised by sportsman Anthony Mundine who viciously added:

Watching Redfern Now and they're promoting homosexuality! Like it's ok in our culture. That ain't in our culture and our ancestors would have their head for it! Like my dad told me GOD made ADAM & EVE not Adam and Steve.

This attack on queerness by Mundine polarised Indigenous communities across Australia. It further silenced queer Indigenous people who watched, as many shared, commented, and supported the notion offered by Mundine. Furthermore, it compelled many Indigenous people who might be afraid to 'come out of the closet' to revert and hide their sexuality, even more, affecting them negatively, particularly on mental and social-emotional wellbeing (Clark, 2014). Mundine's confrontation must also be juxtaposed against a largely heteronormative Indigenous system of health who offered little support towards ensuring the safety of queer Indigenous peoples. Similarly, his commentary also extends to a relationship of homophobia built and produced by and within a religious stronghold.

Homophobia is a nasty disease. It is heavily entrenched within Indigenous societies. In his article 'Against Authenticity', Bundjalung queer writer Maddee Clark analysed Mundine's thoughts:

> The controversial Redfern Now episode brilliantly captured the perils of being Indigenous and queer, particularly the complexities of dating, casual sex, parenting, and family. But what was represented on screen hardly garnered a mention during the culture war that followed Mundine's statement. Instead, as is so often the case, the conversation fell back on familiar narratives around authenticity. (Clark, 2014)

Clark's response highlights many vital topics within Indigenous society on the notions of authenticity. The continuation of the erasure of queer Indigenous narratives and experiences causes much concern. The impact homophobia plays in the role of suicide is disturbing, causing negativity that leads to lateral violence which tends to increase (Wilson, 2004; Quinn & Meiners, 2011). Clark further adds,

> But it is not only Mundine who is aligning pre-contact Aboriginal cultures with heterosexuality. Arguments for tolerance often centre on an assumption that tradition and the past are necessarily heterosexual and intolerant, hence the common refrain it's the twenty-first century – get over it. In the grand narrative of social progress, sexual diversity is associated only with certain 'civilised' societies, while homophobia is – with or without evidence – used as a marker of backwards traditional societies. The supposed reluctance of Aboriginal people to accept LGBTIQ people is inevitably connected with 'ancient' culture... (Clark, 2014)

Steven Ross, a Wiradjuri gay man and author, argues that Mundine further aggravates the continuation of heteronormative behaviour within Indigenous society:

> Some argue that our culture would have oppressed such behaviour. This raises some interesting questions, as well as some colonial mythologies. Which traditional Aboriginal culture is being referred to here? When white people colonised Australia, there were hundreds of Aboriginal cultures. To know the mores and values of every single Aboriginal culture would be a major feat of anthropological prowess – one of which I doubt Mundine and his ilk are capable. (Ross, 2019)

In 2015, some Indigenous people posing as Indigenous leaders and elders petitioned the Australian federal parliament to oppose same-sex marriage (Walker, 2016). The group contested the notion of non-heteronormative relationships entering into a marriage, stating on the basis that 'traditional unions' between a man and a woman have always been upheld by the oldest living culture on earth. Group leader, Peter Walker, further commented:

> As Aboriginal leaders, we applaud the High Court's unanimous decision to reject homosexual marriage in the ACT. I speak on behalf of these leaders from the premise of an Australian indigenous Christian leader and elder's perspective. Aboriginal people, the first nation people of Australia, have a strong culture of heterosexual marriage and have practiced marriage between male and female for thousands of years, long before white man came to this land. Homosexuality was never accepted in our culture, the change came with the introduction of western culture. Redefining marriage would change the whole meaning of marriage, from traditional Aboriginal marriage between a man and women, to two people of the same sex. This is not the true Australian way. This goes against the moral code of ethics that I have grown up with and respect. (Walker, 2016)

This claim, once again, affirms the notion that some Indigenous people and communities do not support queerness, and do this while hiding behind a religious standpoint (much like Mundine's). Indigenous peoples are, in many ways, a nation divided on issues of sexuality and gender. The effects of homophobic attitudes that permeate Indigenous communities requires further research. It is clear that there exists a gap to understand the implications Indigenous homophobia has on queer Indigenous people, particularly at a time where psychological impacts from homophobia for queer people in Australia are alarmingly high. Suicide plays a horrible role in all communities, The *Growing Up Queer* report released by Young and Yell CRC found that,

> In the national online survey, at least two out of five acknowl-edged thinking about self-harm (41%) and/or suicide (42%). In addition, 33% of queer young people who participated in our sur-vey have harmed themselves in the past, and 16% have attempted to take their own lives. (Robinson et al., 2014, p. 4)

Contrastingly, higher rates of suicide exist in Australian Indigenous com-munities (Hunter & Harvey, 2002; Nasir et al., 2017; Dudgeon, Calma, & Holland, 2017). However, the extent to understand the relationship between Indigenous suicide and sexual shame or homophobia is not yet entirely clear and requires rigorous research. Indigenous societies globally must begin the work to 'decolonise' the heavily entrenched heteropatriarchy. As author Lea Simpson asserts:

> The interrogation of heteropatriarchy needs to become part of our decolonizing project. We must decolonize our framing of Indigenous governance and politics so that we can recognize the nation-building work of women and the LGQB2 community, in all the forms it takes. We need to examine how the internalized het-eropatriarchy of colonialism serves to disconnect some of our most vital people from the land and our knowledge systems, and we need to continue to vision and build strong Indigenous nations based on a celebration of diversity, a fluidity around gender, indi-vidual self-determination and the Indigenous philosophies that allowed our Ancestors to do just that. (Simpson, 2012, p. 100)

Indeed, the literature on Indigenous queerness has revealed post-colonising impacts have made coming out as queer challenging for some Indigenous peoples; often this is explained with the 'otherness' of being queer com-pounded by the 'otherness' of being Indigenous. Nevertheless, there is a growing movement of queer Indigenous people pushing back against imposed homophobia and transphobia and are subsequently reclaiming queer Indigenous traditional mores. The emergence of queer Indigenous studies as a discipline has provided the opportunity to review and decon-struct the claim that queer culture was never a part of Indigenous culture, and to create a new account that transforms the past, present, and future (Baylis, 2014). The narratives and experiences of queer Indigeneity are now being produced and disseminated.

One of the major impacts of Australia's colonial project was a severing of knowledge between 'untouched' and current, modern-day Aboriginal socie-ties. To be clear, while tangible links remain to what it is pre-invasion

Indigenous people thought about their world in the sense of epistemologies and ontologies, the entirety of known, factual knowledge cannot be claimed. Part of this sever includes knowledge about sexuality – more specifically, what Indigenous people thought about sexuality; its nature and its origins. This is important to understand because it allows the knowledge of sexuality to be assessed against current concepts which are primarily understood by Western discourse.

Heteronormative assimilation

Assimilation is a vastly complicated process, and when woven into the thread of sexuality, the concept of assimilation becomes multilayered. As such, it becomes clear that the defining themes of sexuality – as enforced by Western ontological systems – depend profoundly on a homosexual/heterosexual paradigm to successfully compartmentalise an ideal order of Western society (Aspin & Hutchings, 2007). The assumed standard of the West's standpoint to sexuality is quickly undone when juxtaposed against difference. In this way, the complexities of sexuality as understood in non-Western domains would do more to fracture the strict and rigid version of sexual identities produced throughout Western history, perhaps leaving their ontological belief tattered and torn. The power of Western theological epistemology of sexuality provided a foundation to enforce such ideals to claim that any system of sexuality outside this sphere could be easily demarcated as an undesirable falsehood.

Indigenous communities in Australia, and indeed globally, faced a relentless stripping of culturally integral sexuality and gender identities once coming into contact with theologised doctrines that upheld assimilatory techniques. Aspin and Hutchings note:

> Integral to this colonising influence was the imposition of various manifestations of the Christian religion, which in turn had a profound impact on Maori sexuality. This ongoing tension between Indigenous culture and Western religion continues to be played out in modern-day New Zealand life. (Aspin & Hutchings, 2007, p. 416)

This process of colonisation of sexuality included aligning sexuality and gender constructions under a doctrine strongly tied to Christianity and other similar theologies. The project of colonialism and its assimilatory techniques provides a significant deficit in knowledge about sexuality and gender identities resulting in many Indigenous communities to adopt a view that actively promoted deep-seated homophobia and transphobia. These phobias play a significant role in the building of a heteronormativity in Indigenous Australia. This disruption of Indigenous epistemology to sexuality had profound effects on Indigenous communities globally. Arvin, Tuck, and Morrill argue that Indigenous heteropatriarchy has infiltrated Indigenous nation-building primarily because the 'social systems in which [Indigenous] heterosexuality and patriarchy are perceived as normal and natural' thus those outsides of this framework or those of 'other configurations are perceived as abnormal, aberrant, and abhorrent' (Arvin et al., 2013, p. 23).

The reality that we may never know how Indigenous Australians understood sexuality before the introduction of organised religion and the role it played during colonisation. It must become widely understood how much of a role religion played in formatting how Indigenous people prescribed meaning to distinct cultural elements such as sex, gender, and sexuality. It is important to understand these intersecting elements as mechanisms that changed Indigenous mind sets. In almost all Indigenous populations across the globe, cultural stories hold meaning and truths about genders and sexuality that exist beyond the boundary of meanings placed by Anglo-sphered countries like Australia, New Zealand, the United States, and Canada. Many queer Indigenous scholars from these countries emphasise the significant cultural linkage between these societies separated by seas. Indeed, these societies have mirroring impacts from religions, who held formal positions as savours to the savages.

Conclusion

For many queer Indigenous people, the erasure of Indigenous sexualities has caused a gap in their history (Cameron, 2005), an erasure of their cultural ties to an ancestral knowledge of queerness (Freccero, 2013), and the suppression of their legitimate roles in gender-specific social organisation, such as those social and ritual matters now deemed as either as men's or women's business (Smith & Kēhaulani Kauanui, 2008). As such, this erasure has contributed to adverse effects of personal normalisation and an increase in the phenomenon of personal shame. Queer theorist Chris Finley asserts that, in Indigenous communities, 'sexual shame has been passed down for generations' (Finley, 2011, p. 344). It is this 'sexual shame' that continues to permeate Indigenous communities as non-queer Indigenous people continue to silence gender and the diversity of sexuality from conversations or a seat at the table. Thus, it is increasingly evident that queer Indigenous people remain an absent minority forced to promote normalisation and individuation within their own families and communities.

It is increasingly clear that queer Indigenous people remain an absent minority forced to promote normalisation and individuation within their own families and communities. As illustrated in this chapter, queer Indigenous people historically have been positioned as an Indigenous subgroup who sit outside the 'cultural' norm as if to say: 'they are only queer because of colonisation'. This rhetoric causes much concern for the health and wellbeing of queer Indigenous people. What prevails is a failure to seek an understanding of who queer Indigenous people are concerning what queer Indigenous people are.

There is an urgency to recognise heteronormative biases and social schemas within Indigenous frameworks as a way to shift and strengthen Indigenous socio-cultural and community knowledge away from the heteronormative colonial gaze that has become normalised in the field of Indigenous studies. From this departure, I believe it is important that the conversation started by Bennett and Gates must now challenge the default narratives that exist in Indigenous knowledge and communities at all levels – including the biases that exist within social work and other similar agencies.

Despite the many problems identified with colonial records and the impacts of assimilation, evidence that Indigenous Australian Queer culture pre-dates colonisation is being reclaimed as an important and enduring aspect of Indigenous Australian culture within contemporary nationhood. Nowhere is this more evident than in the growing movement to document the oral histories of traditional queer culture within the emerging discipline of queer Indigenous studies, and in the many community-based activists and support groups and initiatives available for Australian Indigenous people who identify as queer. Ultimately, further research is needed to understand better the complexities surrounding queerness within both historical and contemporary Indigenous Australia.

Given that Australia is a large immigrant population, it is crucial to recognise that there are many Australians who, because of religious, cultural, or nationhood factors, consider homosexuality to absolutely unacceptable. Therefore, it must be acknowledged that these beliefs promote tension and conflict within queer and non-queer communities that give rise to homophobia and transphobia which undoubtedly cause many people to remain in the closet at certain times or periods throughout one's life. This has immeasurable effects on health and wellbeing and also one's overall quality of life (Robinson et al., 2014).

To conclude, it is clear that we can become easily complicit to biases produced throughout histories that govern Indigenous and non-Indigenous and queer and non-queer relationships. The heteronormative lens reproduced in Anglo-sphered psyches often describes queer Indigenous as a margin of the other's other. The complexity of colonialism and assimilation must now be fused to the idea that modern colonisation is not just about land; it is about the body, and in this case, queer Indigenous bodies.

References

ABC TV. (2012, October 30). *The making of Redfern now*. http://www.abc.net.au/tv/redfernnow/webextras/. Accessed 15 February 2015.

Altman, D. (2001). Global gaze/global gays. *Contributions to the Study of World Literature*, 101, 1–18.

Altman, D. (2010). 21 exporting moralities. In *Routledge handbook of sexuality, health and rights* (p. 193). London: Routledge.

Altman, D. (2017). Discontents: Identity, politics, institutions. *Griffith Review, 57*, 80.

Arvin, M., Tuck, E., & Morrill, A. (2013). Decolonizing feminism: Challenging connections between settler colonialism and heteropatriarchy. *Feminist Formations, 25*(1), 8–34.

Aspin, C. (2002). I didn't have to go to a finishing school to learn how to be gay. Maori gay men's understandings of cultural and sexual identity. In *The life of Brian. Masculinities, sexualities and health in New Zealand* (pp. 91–103). Dunedin: University of Otago Press.

Aspin, C. (2019) Hōkakatanga – Māori sexualities, Te Ara – The Encyclopedia of New Zealand. http://www.TeAra.govt.nz/en/hokakatanga-maori-sexualities/print. Accessed 20 February 2020.

Aspin, C., & Hutchings, J. (2006). Maori sexuality. In *State of the Maori nation: Twenty-first-century issues in Aotearoa* (pp. 227–235). Auckland: Reed Publishing.

Aspin, C., & Hutchings, J. (2007). Reclaiming the past to inform the future: Contemporary views of Maori sexuality. *Culture, Health & Sexuality, 9*(4), 415–427.

Awekotuku, N. T. (2001). Hinemoa: Retelling a famous romance. *Journal of Lesbian Studies, 5*(1–2), 1–11.

Barbour, W., & Schlesinger, C. (2012). Who's the boss? Post-colonialism, ecological research and conservation management on Australian Indigenous lands. *Ecological Management & Restoration, 13*(1), 36–41.

Battiste, M. (2002). *Indigenous knowledge and pedagogy in First Nations education: A literature review with recommendations*. Ottawa: National Working Group on Education.

Battiste, M., Bell, L., & Findlay, L. M. (2002). Decolonizing education in Canadian universities: An interdisciplinary, international, indigenous research project. *Canadian Journal of Native Education, 26*(2), 82.

Baylis, T. (2014) The art of seeing Aboriginal Australia's queer potential. *The Conversation*. Available at: http://theconversation.com/the-art-of-seeing-aboriginal-australias-queerpotential-25588. Accessed 1 March 2017.

Bennett, B., & Gates, T. G. (2019). Teaching cultural humility for social workers serving LGBTQI Aboriginal communities in Australia. *Social Work Education, 38*(5), 604–617.

Blackwood, E. (1986). Breaking the mirror: The construction of lesbianism and the anthropological discourse on homosexuality. *Journal of Homosexuality, 11*(3–4), 1–18.

Cameron, M. (2005). Two-spirited Aboriginal people: Continuing cultural appropriation by non-Aboriginal society. *Canadian Woman Studies, 24*(2), 123–127.

Clark, M. (2014). Against authenticity CAL-connections: Queer-Indigenous identities. *Overland, 215*, 30.

Clark, M. (2015). Indigenous subjectivity in Australia: Are we queer? *Journal of Global Indigeneity, 1*(1), 7.

Davidson, J. (2007). *The Greeks and Greek love: A radical reappraisal of homosexuality in ancient Greece.* London: Weidenfeld & Nicolson.

Driskill, Q.-L. (Ed.). (2011). *Queer Indigenous studies: Critical interventions in theory, politics, and literature.* Tucson, AZ: University of Arizona Press.

Dudgeon, P., Calma, T., & Holland, C. (2017). The context and causes of the suicide of indigenous people in Australia. *Journal of Indigenous Wellbeing, 2*(2), 5–15.

Dunn-Holland, W., et al. (1994). Peopling the empty mirror. The prospects of lesbian and gay Aboriginal history. In R. Aldrich (Ed.), *Gay perspectives II. More essays in Australian gay culture* (pp. 1–62). Sydney, NSW: University of Sydney.

Farrell, A. (2015). Can you see me? Queer margins in Aboriginal communities. *Journal of Global Indigeneity, 1*(1), 3.

Farrell, A. (2016). Lipstick clapsticks: A yarn and a Kiki with an Aboriginal drag queen. *AlterNative: An International Journal of Indigenous Peoples, 12*(5), 574–585.

Finley, C. (2011). Decolonizing the queer Native body (and recovering the native bull-dyke): Bringing 'sexy back' and out of Native studies' closet. In *Queer-Indigenous studies: Critical interventions in theory, politics, and literature* (pp. 31–42). Tucson, AZ: University of Arizona Press.

Freccero, C. (2013). Queer spectrality: Haunting the past. In *The spectralities reader. Ghosts and haunting in contemporary cultural theory* (pp. 335–359). New York/London: Bloomsbury.

Giuliani, G. (2015). Book review: Spaces between us: Queer settler colonialism and Indigenous decolonization. *Feminist Review, 109*(1), e17–e19.

Hodge, D. (1993). *Did you meet any Malagas?: A homosexual history of Australia's tropical capital.* Nightcliff, NT: Little Gem Publications.

Hodge, D. (Ed.). (2015). *Colouring the rainbow: Blak queer and trans perspectives: Life stories and essays by First Nations People of Australia.* Mile End: Wakefield Press.

Hunter, E., & Harvey, D. (2002). Indigenous suicide in Australia, New Zealand, Canada and the United States. *Emergency Medicine, 14*(1),14–23.

Hutchings, J., & Aspin, C. (Eds.). (2007). *Sexuality and the stories of indigenous people.* Wellington: Huia Publishers.

Jacobs, S.-E., Thomas, W., & Lang, S. (Eds.). (1997). *Two-spirit people: Native American gender identity, sexuality, and spirituality.* Urbana, IL: University of Illinois Press.

Langton, M., & Bowers, J. (1993). *Well, I heard it on the radio and I saw it on the television...: An essay for the Australian Film Commission on the politics and aesthetics of filmmaking by and about Aboriginal people and things.* Sydney, NSW: Australian Film Commission.

Langton, M., Mazel, O., & Palmer, L. (2006). The 'spirit' of the thing: The boundaries of Aboriginal economic relations at Australian common law. *The Australian Journal of Anthropology, 17*(3), 307–321.

McCorquodale, J. (1986). The legal classification of race in Australia. *Aboriginal History, 10*, 7–24.

Moreton-Robinson, A. (1998). When the object speaks, a postcolonial encounter: Anthropological representations and Aboriginal women's self-presentations. *Discourse: Studies in the Cultural Politics of Education, 19*(3), 275–289.

Morgensen, S. L. (2011). *Spaces between us: Queer settler colonialism and indigenous decolonization*. Minneapolis, MN: University of Minnesota Press.

Murray, D. A. B. (2003). Who is Takatāpui? Māori language, sexuality and identity in Aotearoa/New Zealand. *Anthropologica, 15*(2), 233–244.

Nakata, M. (2002). Indigenous knowledge and the cultural interface: Underlying issues at the intersection of knowledge and information systems. *IFLA Journal, 28*(5–6), 281–291.

Nakata, M. (2006). Australian Indigenous studies: A question of discipline. *The Australian Journal of Anthropology, 17*(3), 265–275.

Nasir, B., et al. (2017). An Australian Indigenous community-led suicide intervention skills training program: Community consultation findings. *BMC Psychiatry, 17*(1), 219.

Nikora, L. W., & Te Awekotuku, N. (2016). Moehewa: Death, lifestyle & sexuality in the Maori World. *Journal of Indigenous Wellbeing, 1*(2), 2–8.

Quinn, T., & Meiners, E. R. (2011). Teacher education, struggles for social justice, and the historical erasure of lesbian, gay, bisexual, transgender, and queer lives. Studying diversity in teacher education, 135–151.

Reynolds, H. (1995). *The other side of the frontier: Aboriginal resistance to the European invasion of Australia*. Melbourne, Australia. Penguin.

Robinson, K. H., et al. (2014). *Growing up queer: Issues facing young Australians who are gender variant and sexuality diverse*. Melbourne, VIC: Young and Well Cooperative Research Centre.

Ross, S. (2019). Homosexuality and Aboriginal culture: A lore unto themselves. *Archer Magazine*. http://archermagazine.com.au/2014/10/homosexuality-and-aboriginal-culture-a-lore-unto-themselves/. Accessed 1 March 2019.

Ross, S. L. (2020, October 31). Not in our culture? Open hearts helped me grow up Indigenous and gay. *The Guardian*. Retrieved from https://www.theguardian.com/commentisfree/2014/oct/31/not-in-our-culture-open-hearts-helped-me-grow-up-indigenous-and-gay

Sharif, R. (2015). White gaze saving brown queers: Homonationalism meets imperialist Islamophobia. *Limina, 21*(1), 1–19.

Simpson, L. (2012) Queering resurgence: Taking on heteropatriarchy in Indigenous Nation Building. *Leanne Betasamosake Simpson*, June 1. Blog, available via http://leannesimpson.ca/queering-resurgence-taking-on-heteropatriarchy-inindigenous-nation-building/. Accessed 12 February 2020.

Smith, A., & Kēhaulani Kauanui, J. (2008). Native feminisms engage American studies. *American Quarterly, 60*(2), 241–249.

Smith, L. T. (2015). Decolonizing knowledge: Toward a critical Indigenous research justice praxis. In *Research justice: Methodologies for social change* (pp. 205–210). Bristol: Policy Press.

Sykes, H. (2016). The sexual and gender politics of sport mega-events: Roving colonialism. In *The sexual and gender politics of sport mega-events* (pp. 13–31). London: Routledge.

Tatonetti, L. (2014). The erotics of sovereignty: Queer native writing in the era of self-determination by Mark Rifkin. *The American Indian Quarterly, 38*(1), 119–122.

Vos, T., et al. (2009). Burden of disease and injury in Aboriginal and Torres Strait Islander Peoples: The Indigenous health gap. *International Journal of Epidemiology, 38*(2), 470–477.

Walker, L. E. (2016). *The battered woman syndrome*. Springer.

Walter, M., & Andersen, C. (2013). *Indigenous statistics: A quantitative research methodology*. Walnut Creek, CA: Left Coast Press.

Wilson, J. (2004). Racism and internal hatred within the queer community. *Queer Vertigo, 7*.

4 A Culturally Supportive Ethics of Care: Working with Aboriginal Children and Young People

Jessica Russ-Smith and Amelia Wheeler

Introduction

Aboriginal children and young peoples (CYP) hold sovereignty, strength, and voice. However, too often social work and human service practice negates this, in effect harming the wellbeing of Aboriginal CYP. This chapter examines a range of contexts, systems, and discourses that affect Aboriginal CYP and proposes a culturally supportive ethics of care to transform current colonial social work practices. This framework situates ethical practice with Aboriginal CYP as practice that is decolonising, caring, just, and meaningfully inclusive. This framework emerges from our relationships with and legacies of the ancestors and mentors we have both been fortunate to know and honour.

As an Indigenous and a non-Indigenous/white social worker, we honour Indigenous sovereignty and acknowledge that we stand on the shoulders of the ancestors and leaders who have come before us and continue to guide us. From these leaders we continue to learn and to transform our social work practice in order to adopt, embed, and embody critical and decolonising approaches. Thus, this chapter critically explores historical and contemporary colonial, paternalistic, and white forces in social work practices and invites the readers to actively commit in solidarity to a process of critical and decolonising practice.

It is important to note that we refer to 'practice' in a broad sense. We see 'practice' as encompassing both 'direct' (micro-level casework, counselling or case management) and 'indirect' (macro-level, i.e. policy, education, research, and academia) social work. We make a conscious choice not to distinguish between 'indirect' and 'direct' practice. This can serve to create a false dichotomy in which the individual and structural concerns of social work never meet. This polarising approach echoes the very white colonial ideologies which we aim to critically deconstruct in this chapter. As explored below, this dichotomy is antithetical to the mission of critical social work and to an embodied, situated approach to social work ethics that is culturally supportive of Aboriginal CYP.

Context: Protectionism, whiteness, and practice

A critical exploration of current practice and contexts is essential for our profession to engage honestly and authentically in decolonisation. This chapter aims to provide a conceptual and ethical re-situation of Aboriginal CYP to decolonise current practice and propose ethical ways of working alongside Aboriginal CYP. We emphasise the point that this chapter is not a practical guide on how to be culturally competent when working with Aboriginal youth, as these approaches perpetuate the idea that Aboriginal culture can be learned and owned by others in a way that echoes colonial legacies. Rather, this chapter argues that we need to stop, listen, and reflect to encompass our ethics truly and continuously in our practice with Aboriginal people.

The interplay of child protection systems and whiteness in practice with Aboriginal people has a great impact on the wellbeing of Aboriginal CYP. It is imperative that social work critically explores and acknowledges the white and colonial foundations of practice with Aboriginal people, including CYP. The majority of discourse and practice derives from a child protection space, echoing white saviourism and a power hierarchy of white 'experts'. Social workers are present within child protection systems, and our ethics in practice directly resist or feed white protectionist and colonial agendas towards Aboriginal youth. The following sections will discuss contextual aspects of social work practice with Aboriginal CYP, highlighting the flaws of current protection and risk-driven systems.

Nationally, Aboriginal and Torres Strait Islander children are vastly over-represented in Out Of Home Care (OOHC) and are in foster care placements at 11 times the rate of non-Indigenous young people (Child Family Community Australia, 2020). This chapter attempts to continue a critical dialogue upon these statistics that resists the deficit narrative of Aboriginal families and youth by instead turning the lens onto issues with practice. Central to these arguments is a critique of the emphasis on 'best interests' for Aboriginal children and young peoples. Historical and contemporary practices of child protection with Aboriginal CYP emphasise 'safety' and 'best interests' based upon presenting risks, as opposed to centring self-determination and empowerment of Aboriginal children, young people, families, and communities.

It is important to note the history of cultural genocide of child protection practices in Australia, commonly referred to as the Stolen Generations (Bennett, 2019). Historically, white Australian policies and practices allowed for the forced removal of Aboriginal children from their families to 'save' the children and assimilate them into white society (Bennett, 2019). These colonial actions of the past directly impact the current state of child protection systems and the State's practice with Aboriginal CYP, relating to discourses of white safety and deficit narratives of Aboriginal people and parents:

> It was not just racism that drove governments to remove children, it was a way of dispossessing Aboriginal people of their land and controlling distinctive groups that were perceived as threatening. (Bennett, 2019, p. 14)

These actions of dispossession and forced intervention have continued to pervade the wellbeing of Aboriginal CYP today. Recent major reports, including 'Family is Culture' in NSW and 'Our Booris Our Way' in the ACT, highlight the emphasis on the alarming absence of Aboriginal CYPs' voices in child protection interventions. These systems place professionals in positions of power and influence to make decisions about Aboriginal CYP, which inevitably affects their wellbeing. Social work plays a key role in decolonising current white protectionist systems and practices. Now is the time for social work to listen, learn, and act through a culturally supportive ethics of care.

Recently, two major reviews of the experiences of Aboriginal CYP in OOHC have been published. In NSW 'Family is Culture' (2019) and in the ACT 'Our Booris Our Way' (2019) have shown that current practice with Aboriginal CYP and their families does not align with the Aboriginal and Torres Strait Islander Child Placement Principle (ATSICPP), especially in the area of self-determination and Community-Controlled Organisations. The reports provide evidence that current practice with Aboriginal CYP is not up to standard and fails to be culturally and ethically supportive (Davis, 2019; Our Booris Our Way Steering Committee, 2019). In relation to the 'Family is Culture' NSW Report, it is argued that the Department of Community Services has lost sight of achieving the central goal of the ATSICPP, which is to keep Aboriginal CYP 'connected to family, community, country, and culture' and the recognition of community as a strength (Davis, 2019, p. xiv). The 'Family is Culture' report brings to light the pervading risk-averse and compliance culture of government services that take priority over critical and ethical practice with Aboriginal CYP (Davis, 2019, p. xvii).

There were similar findings in the 'Our Booris Our Way' 2019 Report. This review aimed to evaluate and propose recommendations for the ACT Government to implement, so as to decrease alarming statistics which 'found that Aboriginal and Torres Strait Islander children in the ACT were twelve times more likely to be in OOHC than other groups of children', higher still than the national average (Our Booris Our Way Steering Committee, 2019, p. 23). The review assessed the implementation of the three aspects of the

Aboriginal and Torres Strait Islander Children Placement Principles (ATSICPP) in the ACT, which are:

1. Prioritising placement of Aboriginal and Torres Strait Islander children in order, with their Aboriginal and Torres Strait Islander family, community, or other Aboriginal and Torres Strait Islander families, where such placement is safe for the child.
2. Requiring consultation with Aboriginal and Torres Strait Islander families, communities and organisations about child protection intervention, and child placement and care.
3. Ensuring that Aboriginal and Torres Strait Islander children in out-of-home care are supported to maintain connection to their family, community and culture, especially children placed with non-Indigenous carers. (SNAICC, 2013)

The ATSICPP is divided into five domains of placement, prevention, partnership, participation, and connection (SNAICC, 2018). The review found that the application of all five domains was rarely seen in reviewed cases (Our Booris Our Way Steering Committee, 2019, p. 20). The report also found significant inconsistency in child protection practice with Aboriginal CYP, stating that 'it appears to be the luck of allocation that determines whether the child and family receive culturally sensitive practice, appropriate supports and are appropriately engaged throughout the process or will simply be administered to collect evidence for court proceedings' (Our Booris Our Way Steering Committee, 2019, p. 21). These inconsistencies and lack of culturally and ethically supportive practice have devastating and continuous impacts upon the wellbeing of Aboriginal CYP.

Within these inconsistent and unethical practices, the 'best interests' of Aboriginal CYP are used to support decisions to remove or prevent restoration of Aboriginal CYP from their families (Our Booris Our Way Steering Committee, 2019, p. 19). However, this practice neglects to consider and integrate foundational aspects of Aboriginal wellbeing: family and culture. As such, this approach to practice forces ongoing separation and dislocation from family and culture, which are in fact 'the very source of their safety and identity' (Our Booris Our Way Steering Committee, 2019, p. 12). Therefore, these practices echo protectionist ideologies as they are conducted under the justification of the 'best interests' and 'safety' of Aboriginal CYP from a perspective that does not consider how Aboriginal CYP identify their own best interests, safety, and wellbeing. Here the idea of colonial superiority and authority, especially regarding the care of Aboriginal children and young people, is present.

The 'Family is Culture' and 'Our Booris Our Way' reports highlight the need for systemic *and* micro-practice change concerning how professionals, including social workers, practice with Aboriginal CYP. This transformation must incorporate a culturally supportive ethics of care approach by organisations and professionals, to deconstruct dominating colonial ways of working with Aboriginal CYP. This process encompasses critical analysis and approaches to working with Aboriginal CYP with acknowledgment of intergenerational trauma (Our Booris Our Way Steering Committee, 2019, p. 103) and the white protectionist ideologies embedded within the system and practices. To improve wellbeing, this shift centres around the role of empowerment and right of self-determination for Aboriginal people, which is outlined in the Australian Association of Social Workers Code of Ethics (2010). The role of professionals in advocating and creating space for self-determination holds great power in enhancing the wellbeing of Aboriginal CYP now and in the future:

> The right to self-determination is not about the state working with our people, in partnership. It is about finding agreed ways that Aboriginal people and their communities can have control over their own lives and have a collective say in the future of wellbeing of their children and young people. As the Uluru Statement from the Heart implores: 'when we have power over our destiny our children will flourish. They will walk in two worlds and their culture will be a gift to their country.' (Davis, 2019, p. xviii)

The whiteness of social work

The above discussions regarding child protection systems and their practice with Aboriginal CYP highlight an important reality that is too often denied by social workers: that *Australian social work practice is white*. The whiteness of social work is often ignored because of white invisibility, white fragility, white superiority, and relationships with the race of 'others' under the name of 'inclusion' (Walters & Baltra-Ulloa, 2019, p. 72). Ironically, the aim of inclusion based on other people's race actively maintains the narrative that whiteness is not a race, thus upholding its invisibility and excluding white people from responsibility. The dominance of whiteness in Australian social work greatly impacts the wellbeing of Aboriginal CYP and highlights the urgent need to transform practice to a culturally supportive ethics of care.

Whiteness is political and personal as it is systemically embedded within all aspects of life and social work, awarding privilege and advantages to white people. These privileges are so deeply entrenched within everyday life and history that they have become the norm and thus invisible to white people and social work. White fragility has played a key role in maintaining the invisibility of whiteness. White fragility manifests into behaviours and responses of anger, affection of victimhood, argumentation, emotional incapacitation, and withdrawal (Walter & Baltra-Ulloa, 2019, p. 68; DiAngelo,

2011), which use white race power 'to stop discussion or shift focus and restore the racial status quo of the white person's racial comfort' (Walter & Baltra-Ulloa, 2019, p. 67). The continued status quo of white invisibility continues the danger that whiteness is not critically examined and transformed, and race oppressions against Indigenous people continue.

As social workers, we have an ethical commitment to 'raising awareness of structural and systemic inequities' (AASW, 2010, p. 8). Thus, social workers have an ethical responsibility to acknowledge whiteness and deconstruct the structural advantages and disadvantages it powerfully creates and sustains, especially relating to Aboriginal CYP:

> To understand whiteness in social work is to understand the profession as a product of Western culture. With this understanding, we can begin to imagine how it is that social work can disrupt epistemological and ontological roots to begin to have some relevance to Indigenous peoples. (Walter & Baltra-Ulloa, 2019, p. 71)

The invisibility of whiteness in social work is evident within our teaching and practice, as both rarely encompass critical reflection of what it means to be white and the implications of race relations embedded within Australian social work (Walter & Baltra-Ulloa, 2019). Social work education attempts to address cultural diversity through subjects or content based on raced 'others'; however, this too often lacks a critical examination of whiteness, in effect further fuelling the invisibility of whiteness in social work practice:

> No one thinks to ask a white person to stand in front of a class and describe their personal and family privilege. For all these paradigms, white culture remains the invisible vertical and black culture the alien oblique. (Walter & Baltra-Ulloa, 2019, p. 76)

A similar criticism lies in relation to the Code of Ethics (AASW, 2010) and Practice Standards (AASW, 2013):

> The code provides the foundations for the practice standards. It outlines the values and responsibilities that characterise social work; while the practice standards articulate what is expected of social workers in practice. Both these documents make explicit mention of the importance of cultural sensitivity in practice, and of the demonstration of respect for and knowledge of cultural diversity. However, they do so from an implicit position of superiority...Not at any point do these documents deal with social work as a product of Western knowledge and values, or how these are embedded in whiteness. This limits the extent to which social work can be a culturally sensitive practice. (Walter & Baltra-Ulloa, 2019, p. 72)

Thus, whiteness becomes the dominant position from which decisions and actions are made in social work practice. The invisibility of whiteness has sat hand in hand with power, superiority, and 'voice'. Having a voice is a 'given', although not necessarily for CYP. Whiteness generalises. Whiteness frames the CYP as 'universal' and homogeneous. Whiteness deliberately minimises race and can centre 'resilience' approaches as a tool of continuing deficit narratives of the raced 'other'. We need to be sceptical of resilience narratives. Indigenous people have strength and resilience. However, 'resilience' can be easily co-opted by the establishment to encourage adaptation to current systems, as opposed to the system examining and reconstructing itself. The invisibility of whiteness directly connects with white saviourism, paternalism, and hierarchical relationships between professionals and Aboriginal CYP. The invisibility of whiteness and lack of attention and accountability to whiteness serves to drastically increase the power differential between the non-Indigenous, particularly white, workers and Aboriginal CYP, without actually naming the power differential. The harm from this relationship is significant and has been enacted throughout Australian, and Australia social work's, histories.

Therefore, in this chapter, we aim to make whiteness visible and to enact a process of decolonisation of practice. Core to this process is the role of self and identity, critical reflection, and decolonisation of practice. Identity is an important aspect seen universally across social work theories and approaches to practice. Identity is central to wellbeing; however, the focus on wellbeing in practice too often focuses only on the identity of the client. Such an approach neglects critical consciousness of whiteness, which in turn translates to a focus on the raced 'other' when working with Aboriginal CYP. Working with Aboriginal CYP must encompass active and continuous reflection of the identity of the social worker as an individual and as a part of a white profession and history. Critical reflection of self and profession is key in transforming social work practice with Aboriginal peoples, and this reflection must consider race relationships within the context of colonisation (Green & Baldry, 2008; Walter & Baltra-Ulloa, 2019). The continuation of practice that actively resists this crucial transformative work is a continuation of colonial practice and therefore holds devastating effects upon the wellbeing of Aboriginal CYP. In order to authentically commit to and engage in this transformative process of culturally supportive ethics of care, the decolonisation of social work *must* take place.

Culturally supportive ethics of care: The framework

We propose a culturally supportive ethics of care framework for social work with Aboriginal CYP and their families (Figure 4.1). Our work builds upon Green's (2019) cultural support framework, with application to the field of

Figure 4.1 Culturally supportive ethics of care framework

practice with Aboriginal CYP. Our framework is informed by a critical, decolonising approach that honours Indigenous sovereignty, an ethics of care that encompasses professional decolonisation, social justice, and meaningful inclusion of Aboriginal CYP in social work practice. This framework was constructed in the process of writing this chapter but applies to various fields of practice. In the context of this chapter, we critically apply the framework in relation to working with Aboriginal CYP.

We actively resist the idea that social work ethics exists only 'out there', as a code to be memorised or a set of standards to be achieved (further explored below). We also actively resist the framework of 'cultural competency', which, as Green notes, carries with it the danger of appropriating Indigenous knowledges rather than focusing on 'what we are doing, how we are doing it, what are our assumptions, and how are they informed by race and whiteness' (Walter, 2013, p. 238; within Green, 2019, p. 179). We instead frame practice *as* ethics and social workers as active agents whose attendance to the ethical base of our profession compels us to counter white colonial practices within ourselves and our organisations. In the following sections, we unpack the culturally supportive framework, exploring the areas of decolonising social work, practice *as* ethics, and the critical reframing of justice, care, and meaningful inclusion in relation to Aboriginal CYP. The proposed culturally supportive framework is intended to provide social workers and social work students with some key concepts and a basis for reflection when working with Aboriginal CYP and their families, which we encourage you to apply in your unique context and informed by the Country which you work upon.

Decolonising *as* ethics: Decolonising social work

Colonial and white approaches to social work maintain relationships of power differentials based upon race. Indigenous ways of knowing and caring challenge this assumption, as they view a world based upon relationships of care and connection, rather than hierarchies of power (Green, 2018; Russ-Smith, 2019). We aim to weave these ways of knowing, being, and doing into this chapter and this supports our purposeful resistance to not distinguish between 'theory' and 'practice'. We are a part of knowledge, and knowledge is a part of us. We exist in relationship to, with, and through knowledge. Research, 'direct' social work, policy, academia: all are learning, all are ethics, all are social work 'practice'. The knowing is embedded within the doing. The doing is embedded in the knowing. And both are embedded in our way of being as a collective professional identity. Our ways of knowing, being, and doing in social work are dominantly shaped through whiteness. We must collectively challenge whiteness and commit to decolonising our practice to ensure culturally supportive ethics of care when working with Aboriginal CYP.

Decolonisation of social work calls for action beyond approaches of 'equity', 'equality', and 'cultural inclusion' to a social justice movement. Equity, equality, and cultural inclusion possess power to maintain deficit narratives of the raced 'other' in practice. For example, these three approaches are based upon what the non-white 'other' does not have or needs access to, as opposed to focusing upon the injustice of the system that creates these needs. Decolonisation as a social justice movement centres critical analyses of power (Russ-Smith, 2019), making whiteness and its power visible and open to reconstruction. As Gray argues, 'care must be connected to justice or it would become a random practice' (2010, p. 1805). Thus, decolonisation calls us to transform our practice through the relationship between care with social justice. Care *is* ethics. Social justice *is* ethics. And, importantly, the relationship between care and social justice *is* ethics.

The process of decolonising social work encompasses active and continuous learning of self. Part of this attention and focus is upon impact *over* intention. Responses of white fragility and tears are too often reactions to non-white people bravely sharing their experiences of racism, cultural unsafety, and oppression (Green, Russ-Smith, & Tynan, 2018; Hamad, 2019). Caring about Aboriginal people and CYP is not sufficient to practice ethically. Actions *must* reflect a culturally supportive ethics of care. Intention is not valued the same as impact. Just 'being nice' or 'caring' about Aboriginal CYP, human rights, or wellbeing does mean that your practice is culturally supportive or ethical. Equally, coming from a position of protecting Aboriginal CYP does not mean that your practice is culturally supportive or ethical. The impact of action is not just measured or felt within the direct micro space of interaction or working relationships, but links to wider social injustices that continue to oppress and silence Aboriginal people, CYP, communities, and sovereignty.

In addition, a caring or kind intention does not give an Aboriginal CYP rights. This attitude of intention over impact negates the best interests, rights, and voice of Aboriginal CYP as it reflects a white protectionist lens, prioritising the invisibility and assumed untouchability of whiteness over the wellbeing of Aboriginal peoples. This hierarchy illuminates how whiteness conceptualises Aboriginal peoples and CYP as having little agency, in need of saving and protecting. We need to decolonise practice to reframe this dominant discourse enforced by whiteness, especially when working with Aboriginal CYP because this assumed lack of agency is directly linked to the intergenerational trauma of colonialism.

Decolonisation calls for the active inclusion and guidance of Aboriginal CYP voices and agency. Whiteness tells us to not be inclusive of these voices; it tells us to do *for* Aboriginal CYP because they *need* help and that white people are their 'saviours'. This is an approach that centres the safety of the professional and preserves the status quo of white institutions, organisations, and people as superior and therefore the *only* powers that can make decisions regarding CYP safety. But this is not safety for Aboriginal CYP. This paternalistic white saviourism further damages wounds of colonialism, trauma, and oppression. White fragility justifies this harmful practice as it aims to maintain the superior and saviour complex, when in fact this very actioning of fragility harms Aboriginal CYP.

This existence of intention over impact in social work practice highlights the reality that we are not neutral; instead, we 'are political agents who hold power to influence change towards social justice or further colonisation' (Russ-Smith, 2019, p. 108). Critical consciousness of self, profession, and wider society is a core aspect of a culturally supportive ethics of care. Critical consciousness, like decolonisation, is not a metaphor, but an active responsibility, action, and way of being.

Decolonisation and critical consciousness call upon non-Indigenous, especially white, social workers to label, examine, and deconstruct their white power, privilege, and fragility (Russ-Smith, 2019; Green & Baldry, 2008; Briskman, 2008). It is here, in this transformation of white knowing, being, and doing, that the saviour complex and deficit narratives can be rewritten. This transformative process demands an ongoing commitment to being, knowing, and doing decolonising work. Decolonisation by white social workers must encompass admission to and of colonial practice:

> Colonialist practice is often not overtly visible and not challenged. Most practitioners would deny that we operate within colonial structures and implicitly we believe we are operating in a post-colonial era. (Briskman, 2008, p. 87)

Colonisation remains an active and pervasive force within society and Australian social work. We are not *post* colonialism; we are in an active space of colonialism (Russ-Smith, 2019). To deny this reality is to evade an ethics of care and enact the invisibility of whiteness. A culturally supportive ethics of care is founded upon critical consciousness and decolonisation that embeds continuous critical reflection of self throughout all aspects of knowing, being, and doing. This process calls for social workers to *wayamiilbuwawanha*, a Wiradyuri concept meaning deep self-reflection (Russ-Smith, 2019, p. 113; Grant & Rudder, 2010). Social workers must commit and be accountable to the acknowledgment, critical analysis, and transformation of whiteness through deep self-reflection:

> Further to this, there is a need to be prepared to dismantle the power relationship and imbalance. This also means being able to challenge and dismantle accepted ways of knowing and practising, and ensuring that practice models and our individual practice is culturally aware, sensitive, safe, responsive and supportive. To do this, we as individuals must also ensure that we are culturally aware of our own and others' culture. (Green, 2019, p. 182)

Wayamiilbuwawanha, critical consciousness, and decolonisation invite us into a journey of unlearning, listening deeply, being continuous learners, and 'learning to let go of the familiar and comfortable position of power' (Walter & Baltra-Ulloa, 2019, p. 77). So, we invite you, the readers, political agents of change and power, to resist the comfort of power and certainty. We invite you to actively resist a clear step-by-step process, an order, especially as seen in child protection practice, which has become highly regulated and routine-based. We invite you to actively resist these urges for power and certainty in order to open up critically reflective spaces of *us* as a profession and individual social workers. Only through this process can we embody a culturally supportive ethics of care approach when working with Aboriginal CYP because we are in relationships when we are working with others. Our practice should not be about the expert and vulnerable person: it must be about existing within relationship *with* self and others, not in a relationship of or to an 'other'. Let us collectively resist whiteness to reimagine and redefine what ethical practice looks like because much of our current practice, especially that with Aboriginal CYP, is not ethical.

Practice *as* ethics – Resisting disembodied, deficit approaches to practice

Our ethical approach is infused in our everyday being, knowing, and doing as social workers, whether we are consciously aware of this or not. Banks uses the term 'ethics work' to refer to the efforts professionals put into 'seeing ethically salient aspects of situations, developing themselves as good practitioners, working out the right course of action and justifying who they are and what they have done' (2016, p. 36). Banks insist that we should not limit our moral awareness to classic 'ethical dilemmas' or difficult decisions encountered in practice, but that we should attend to the ethical aspects of our everyday work and in particular the ethical elements of our professional caring practices (2011, pp. 16–17). When working with Aboriginal CYP practice as ethics *must* guide relationships as current, dominant approaches frame work with Aboriginal families as an attempt to solve an 'ethical dilemma'. Here the colonial deficit narrative continues: that Aboriginal parents are incapable of caring for their CYP and that Aboriginal CYP need to be 'saved'.

A culturally supportive approach adopts an ontological ethic; it concerns who we are, how we live, and how we engage in professional relationships and practices. This is in contrast with a technical or 'textbook' approach to ethics (Banks, 2016, p. 35), which involves the outline of generalised ethical principles, emphasises normative ethical frameworks, and presents ethical dilemmas as a path to achieving ethical competency. A textbook approach can lead to disembodied ethics, devoid of context, and relationship. The textbook approach to ethics is evident in contemporary child protection practice where bureaucratic and neo-liberal systems dictate work with Aboriginal CYP. Here, ethics is centred around assessing and reducing 'risk', as a safety plan to follow, and as the gathering and thorough recording of 'evidence' in order to defend the individual practitioner, the organisation, or both, in the event, there are legal implications or processes. This textbook approach to ethics disembodies the relationship between professional and Aboriginal CYP, in effect negating culturally supportive ethics of care.

In contrast, we feel a situated, 'embodied' approach to social work ethics is essential to good practice when working with Aboriginal CYP. The significance of 'situated' frameworks within social work practice lies within their contextualisation in particular practice spaces (see Held, 1990, 1995, 2006; Tronto, 1995, 1998; Hugman, 2005; Ash, 2016). Situated, ontological ethics enables us to attend to emotion and relational care in real time. Understanding the 'why', the conceptual and critical thinking behind *how* we practice, helps us act as embodied social workers in a specific time, place, and context: with our values, ethics, theories, and practice in continuous, congruent connection. An embodied approach to social work connects directly with Aboriginal ways of knowing, being, and doing in that both are based upon the interrelatedness of self and others (Russ-Smith, 2019). Embodied ethical approaches to practice with Aboriginal CYP thus emphasise an acknowledgment of and active attention to the relationship between the worker, who they are and what they present, and the Aboriginal CYP.

Therefore, a culturally supportive ethics of care framework emerges from the foundation of the relationship. It brings together multiple forms of knowledge in an attempt to connect theory, research, practice, and people in the situated context of social work with Aboriginal CYP. This interrelated and connected way of being, knowing, and doing is the enactment of ethics as practice.

Moreover, a culturally supportive ethics of care entails a critical approach to social work with Aboriginal CYP. This approach of practice *as* ethics involves active resistance of dominating white oppressive ideologies. The work of Morley et al. (2019) provides a framework for understanding a conservative approach to social work, which we see as also encompassing a white and colonial approach to practice. The authors use the term 'establishment' social work to describe:

> ...a conservative understanding of social work dominant in most welfare systems today, which uncritically accepts existing social inequalities and helps people to cope with the impact of injustices instead of challenging them. It is also strongly associated with objective scientific methods for managing the marginalised in the most cost-effective and least disruptive manner. (Morley et al., 2019, p. 2)

This is a social work which centres a deficit approach to work with Aboriginal CYP. A 'deficit discourse' refers to a way of writing and speaking about a group in terms of deficiency and race-based stereotypes and which 'narrowly situates responsibility for problems with the affected individuals or communities, overlooking the larger socio-economic structures in which they are embedded' (Fogarty, Bulloch, McDonnell, & Davis, 2018, p. vii). Deficit discourse in relation to Aboriginal and Torres Strait Islander people is both 'a product of, and reinforces, the marginalisation of (Indigenous peoples') voices, perspectives and worldviews', reflects colonial relationships and appears highly likely to impact on the wellbeing and health of Indigenous people (Fogarty et al., 2018, p. xi). The devastating impacts of deficit discourses and establishment approaches are evident within the Northern Territory Emergency Response, which frames Aboriginal men and boys as sexually abusive, dangerous, and deviant people:

> The National Coalition of Aboriginal and Torres Strait Islander Social Workers Association has received reports from around the country of Aboriginal children, especially the boys, telling their parents that they didn't want to be Aboriginal anymore, as they fear they will grow up to be an Aboriginal man and 'Aboriginal men do bad things to their children and beat up their wives' and they then turn to their father and ask, 'Dad, are you going to hurt us?' The pain and anguish of the grandfathers, fathers, brothers and uncles have gone to the very heart of Aboriginal men, attacking their very being. Social workers of Australia, how will you respond, and how are you responding to this human crisis? (Fejo-King & Briskman, 2009, pp. 114–115)

This deficit discourse reinforces an establishment approach to practice, which is to remove Aboriginal CYP from danger and to 'protect' them from unsafe family spaces, reinforcing colonial narratives of Aboriginal CYP and people. This is a social work that focuses on individual Aboriginal people and communities as responsible for both the cause and the solutions of their 'issues'. This negates a critical approach that analyses the power of whiteness in constructing deficit discourses, in effect maintaining superiority through the demonisation and criminalisation of Aboriginal people and CYP. There may be some rhetoric about a 'trauma-informed' approach, as well as recognition of the history of colonisation, the Stolen Generations, and intergenerational experiences of trauma. But establishment social work cannot translate into a culturally supportive approach. In contrast, 'critical' social work forms an alternative approach:

> Critical social work is about acknowledging the limitations of our current society and the systems that characterise it and exposing oppressive conditions that impede human freedom and social justice (Mullaly, 2010) in order to think about how things might be different. (Morley et al., 2019, p. 2)

A critical approach to social work with Aboriginal CYP thus critically examines colonial legacies of deficit and raced 'other' narratives of Aboriginal people and actively decolonises practice to deconstruct the continuing harm of whiteness. One important part of a culturally supportive ethics is to bring into conscious awareness the dominant colonialist discourses that remain present in the institutions and organisations that routinely engage with Aboriginal CYP. We argue that white protectionist/paternalist approaches can be so embedded within systems that it can take deep reflection and conscious learning to bring them to our awareness. This can prove difficult in an environment where whiteness is so pervasive that it has become synonymous with popular managerialist approaches to social service delivery. Like white and colonial discourses, managerialism places 'an over-emphasis on risk and an under-focus on needs and rights (in addition to) a quest for objectivity and certainty' (Morley & Macfarlane, 2014, p. 339). This creates a so-called 'auditing culture' where routinisation, worker compliance with organisational standards, and managerial surveillance can be the everyday reality (Morley & Macfarlane, 2014, p. 339), particularly in the highly regulated child protection space. Non-Indigenous, and especially white, social workers have a responsibility to critically analyse established practices and actively resist the deficit-saturated, risk-centric discourse that is so often applied to Aboriginal CYP.

Justice and care *as* ethics: Listening to Aboriginal ways of care

Justice and care *as* ethics and also as a practice (Sevenhuijsen, 2003, p. 194) is an approach that can meaningfully inform our work with Aboriginal CYP, and it underpins our culturally supportive approach. We see social work as 'not simply a profession, but rather a way of being that is based upon values of respect and care' (Russ-Smith, 2019, p. 113). The construction of care and justice directly impacts what and how we define ethical practice. Critical reflection is imperative in understanding how we individually as social workers and as a profession construct and therefore 'do' care. Within our culturally supportive ethics of care framework, Aboriginal ways of caring and feminist ethics of care theory guide our constructions of care and justice. Furthering upon Aboriginal ways of care that are based upon relationships, care, and justice are interrelated aspects of ethics. Notions of care are inseparable from justice. And notions of justice are inseparable from care.

Aboriginal ways of caring are based upon relationships with all things, human and non-human. Green (2018) and Russ-Smith (2019) explore Aboriginal systems of caring for others and the environment through a Wiradyuri perspective. This is a care that transcends attendance to humans to also encompass care for animals, plants and land, language, story, past, present, and future (Green, 2018, pp. 140–141, 144–145; Russ-Smith, 2019, pp. 110, 111, 112). Foundational to Wiradyuri ways of care is the concept of *yindyamarra*. For Wiradyuri people, *yindyamarra* is a way of life that encompasses being deeply respectful to self, others, and environment, now and in the future (Green, 2018; Russ-Smith, 2019). *Yindyamarra* embodies the concept of *wirimbirra ngurambanggu*, caring for Country. Wirimbirra ngurambanggu is also a way of life that centres our ways of respect and relationships through the notion of care (Green, 2018; Russ-Smith, 2019). In Aboriginal communities, care is held collectively:

> the role of caring [is] not just situated with one person and an individual [is] not seen as being someone who [is] specially cared for, but rather everyone [is] cared for and everyone [plays] a role in caring and nurturing the family and community. (Green, 2018, p. 141)

Collective ways of caring hold great insight for culturally supportive ethics of care, as they centre the role of relationships. This approach to care resists disembodied relationships with the raced 'other' as the value of systems and networks become the way of being, knowing, and doing that guide practice with Aboriginal CYP.

Similarly, feminist care ethics views care as the primary principle or value from which all other values flow (Hugman, 2005, pp. 84–85). This approach recognises that all of us require care throughout our lives, and in turn, we will care for others in various ways (Sevenhuijsen, 2003, pp. 183–184). Feminist care ethics sees that care itself can be highly supportive of self-determination, provided that the views and perceptions of care receivers are respected (Sevenhuijsen, 2003, p. 184). This relates to decolonising practice with Aboriginal CYP as it actively resists notions of hierarchical care and white paternalistic approaches that echo saviour-centred ways of caring. A culturally supportive approach recognises the power differential between the white, adult 'giver' of care and the Aboriginal CYP, traditionally framed as the passive 'receiver' of care. Aboriginal ways of care and feminist care ethics, therefore, are key in our culturally supportive ethics of care framework as they resist colonial understandings of care and in effect enact processes of decolonisation through a collective way of caring. Thus, care *is* ethics.

Social justice is a second key concept that we consider as vital to 'caring', ethical social work practice with Aboriginal CYP. We construct justice as a critical approach to social work that emphasises the importance of systemic and structural analysis. Justice relates to wider notions of relationships and power within society. For Aboriginal CYP, this includes Aboriginal sovereignty. Therefore, sovereignty *is* justice. Acknowledgment of and solidarity with Aboriginal sovereignty *is* justice and *is* practice *as* ethics. Justice, as informed by Aboriginal and feminist ethics of care, thus resists purely working with 'individuals'. Rather, this approach acknowledges not only the relationship between the social worker and Aboriginal CYP but the wider relationships the Aboriginal CYP holds with their families, community, Country, and ancestors. Moreover, justice *as* ethics also relates to the impacts of historical, social, and contemporary forces of oppression upon Aboriginal CYP.

We also consider that a commitment to justice should include 'resistance to neoliberal practices and policies, with a focus on the quality of caring relationships over and above economic efficiency' (Wheeler, 2019, p. 213). This can prove difficult to achieve within the increasingly residualised and resource-scarce social welfare system. Ethical considerations of justice also apply 'a political awareness to understanding the constraints individual workers face, as moral agents who are also involved in dependent relationships with organisations and power structures' (Wheeler, 2019, p. 213). Utilising our professional and personal power to pursue both justice and care in our everyday work *is* possible. Both the ability and willingness to approach our employing organisations and institutions critically is an important part of pursuing justice in our work with Aboriginal CYP. As social workers, we must be able to frame ourselves as interdependent moral and professional actors, not only as organisational agents.

We have both the power and the responsibility to enact culturally supportive ways of being, knowing, and doing wherever we find ourselves. The pursuit of justice cannot be delegated to those practicing at a macro level – and likewise, working at this level does not guarantee the practitioner embodies a culturally supportive ethic. Here, the decolonisation of practice highlights the issue of white fragility in constructions of justice.

Non-Indigenous, and particularly white, social workers must be highly alert to their tendency to stop or shift discussion of race, including where we may frame this as an expression of 'care' i.e. over-apologising, expressing guilt or shame to Indigenous people. Prioritising white racial comfort serves to 'restore the racial status quo' (Walter & Baltra-Ulloa, 2019, p. 67), furthering colonisation, as opposed to a shift towards social justice (Russ-Smith, 2019, p. 108). Care 'must be about more than "good intentions"' (Hugman, 2014, p. 178). Care is thus interrelated to justice as a transformation is needed to give up white power and privilege in constructing care and giving this power to Aboriginal CYP.

Care and justice are so closely intertwined as to represent two parts of a whole. Resistance to colonial discourses is an expression of both social justice and deep, abiding care. As social workers, we must recognise that 'care' for Aboriginal CYP and their wellbeing is not possible without respect for sovereignty. Nor is it possible without attending to justice and pervasive colonial narratives. Culturally supportive ethics of care must grow from the understanding that justice and care *are* ethics.

Meaningful inclusion *as* ethics: Practice *as* decolonised, caring and just

Meaningful inclusion *as* ethics acknowledges the sovereignty of Aboriginal CYP and the crucial role of their agency in culturally supportive ethics of care. There have been growing calls for the participation of CYP in social work and social care practices. This is most recently reflected in the National Principles for Child Safe Organisations (AHRC, 2018), developed out of the Royal Commission into Institutional Responses to Child Sexual Abuse. At the time of writing, the States and Territories are still determining how the National Principles will be enacted and enforced. This is an important time in our history where we have an opportunity to reflect upon the past and envision the future of ethical practice with Aboriginal CYP.

What do we mean by 'inclusion?' A 'child-focused' or 'child-centred' approach has long been popular in the Australian human services sector. This is an approach that frames the CYP as the 'client' of the service, in which a focus on the CYP's 'best interests' directs practice. A child-centred approach may or may not involve the CYP directly in defining their 'best interests' or in determining the services they receive. We challenge social workers to critically reflect upon how they construct the 'best interests' of Aboriginal CYP and the implications that flow from these constructions. What may be in a CYP's 'best interests' is contestable, subject to conflicting criteria, and is likely to be framed by Western concepts of attachment relationships (Keddell, 2017, p. 324), as well as colonial constructions of care and deficit narratives of Aboriginal people. As such, the *meaningful* inclusion of Aboriginal CYP in social work practice is in need of transformation. Child-centred approaches when working with Aboriginal CYP continue to echo colonial and paternalistic relationships of care. Here, the decolonisation of social work, care, and justice *as* ethics interplay in guiding how meaningful inclusion of Aboriginal CYP is understood and enacted in practice. What we consider here is the essential nature of the inclusion of Aboriginal CYP in social work, and the nature of this inclusion as *meaningful inclusion*, not just 'technical' participation (Wheeler, 2019). A culturally supportive ethics of care challenges policy makers, organisations, and practitioners to pursue inclusion that is experienced as decolonised, meaningful, caring, and just by Aboriginal CYP.

Concerns for the safety of Aboriginal CYP – whether physical, emotional, or psychological – especially when constructed from a white saviour complex, can hinder the ability to meaningfully include Aboriginal CYP. Social work can hold a dichotomy that frames 'care' of Aboriginal CYP as *either* protection, *or* as rights and inclusion (Eriksson & Nasman, 2008, p. 265). We must recognise Aboriginal CYP's rights to service provision, protection and participation are *not mutually exclusive*, and *must* be considered in relationship with one another (Wheeler, 2019; see also Eriksson & Nasman, 2008, p. 271). Here, decolonisation of social work, and seeing ethics as practice, justice, and care, asks us to critically assess constructions of care and come to the following reflection: Colonial care *is* protective action done *to* Aboriginal CYP; in contrast, a culturally supportive ethics of care *is* meaningful inclusion undertaken *with* Aboriginal CYP. White saviourism can and does compound with paternalistic approaches to Aboriginal CYP to claim expertise in 'care' for the young person and knowledge of how to ensure their wellbeing. This, too, is an issue of justice. When Aboriginal CYP are framed as non-agentic, 'lacking' or in deficit, sovereignty is denied. Where sovereignty is denied, the wellbeing of Aboriginal CYP is threatened.

Conclusion

Aboriginal people and Aboriginal CYP have survived and thrived through generations of attempts by colonial powers (including social workers) to deculture, enslave, and exterminate them (Green & Baldry, 2008, p. 398). Aboriginal people and CYP alone can determine what is in their 'best interests': this is not the domain of the non-Indigenous, particularly the white, social worker. This assertion may feel threatening to the reader, especially white practitioners; let us reconnect with the importance of decolonising social work practice and the reconstruction of privilege, power, care, justice, and inclusion. Working with Aboriginal CYP *must* come from a culturally supportive ethics of care as it encompasses an embodied, critical approach to social work practice. If the social work profession and practitioners endeavour to uphold the three core values of respect for persons, social justice, and professional integrity AASW, 2010, a culturally supportive ethics of care and the processes it encompasses must be enacted. Core to this ongoing process is the role of deep listening and self-reflection, foundational to Aboriginal ways of caring. The absence of this action fails the wellbeing and rights of Aboriginal CYP and continues colonial practices, not the ethics of care that our profession holds claim to. Let us join collectively as social workers to ensure our practice *is* decolonising, *is* justice, *is* care, *is* ethics.

 ## Discussion Questions

1. Define 'whiteness'. Where do you see whiteness in your practice and/or education?

2. List the four tenets of the culturally supportive ethics of care framework. How might you apply each of these key concepts in your work?

3. What is your definition of 'meaningful inclusion' of Aboriginal children and young people in relation to your practice context?

References

Ash, A. (2016). *Whistleblowing and ethics in health and social care.* London: Jessica Kingsley Publishers.

Australian Association of Social Workers. (2010). *Code of ethics.* Canberra, ACT: AASW.

Australian Association of Social Workers. (2013). *Practice standards.* Canberra, ACT: AASW.

Australian Human Rights Commission. (2018). *National principles for child safe organisations.* Sydney, NSW: Australian Human Rights Commission.

Banks, S. (2011). Ethics in an age of austerity: Social work and the evolving new public management. *Journal of Social Intervention: Theory and Practice, 20*(2), 5–23.

Banks, S. (2016). Everyday ethics in professional life: Social work as ethics work. *Ethics and Social Welfare, 10*(1), 35–52. doi: https://doi.org/10.1080/1 7496535.2015.1126623.

Bennett, B. (2019). The importance of Aboriginal history for practitioners. In B. Bennett & S. Green (Eds.), *Our voices: Aboriginal social work* (2nd ed., pp. 3–30). London: Red Globe Press.

Briskman, L. (2008). Decolonising social work in Australia: Prospect or illusion. In M. Gray, J. Coates, & M. Yellow Bird (Eds.), *Indigenous social work around the world: Toward culturally relevant education and practice* (pp. 83–93). Surrey: Ashgate.

Child Family Community Australia. (2020). *Child protection and Aboriginal and Torres Strait Islander Children.* CFCA Resource Sheet: January 2020. Available online: https://aifs.gov.au/cfca/publications/child-protection-and-aboriginal-and-torres-strait-islander-children. Accessed 17 April 2020.

Davis, M. (2019). *Family is culture final report. Independent review into Aboriginal out-of-home-care in New South Wales*. Sydney, NSW: Family Is Culture.

DiAngelo, R. (2011). White fragility. *International Journal of Critical Pedagogy, 3*(3), 54–70.

Eriksson, M., & Nasman, E. (2008). Participation in Family Law proceedings for children whose father is violent to their mother. *Childhood, 15*(2), 259–275.

Fejo-King, C., & Briskman, L. (2009). Reversing colonial practices with Indigenous peoples. In J. Allan, L. Briskman, & B. Pease (Eds.), *Critical social work* (pp. 105–116). Crows Nest, NSW: Allen & Unwin.

Fogarty, W., Bulloch, H., McDonnell, S., & Davis, M. (2018). *Deficit discourse and indigenous health: How narrative framings of Aboriginal and Torres Strait Islander people are reproduced in policy*. Melbourne, VIC: National Centre for Indigenous Studies: The Australian National University, The Lowitja Institute.

Grant Snr, S., & Rudder, J. (2010). *A new Wiradyuri dictionary*. Wagga Wagga, NSW: Restoration House.

Gray, M. (2010). Moral sources and emergent ethical theories in social work. *British Journal of Social Work, 40*(6), 1794–1811.

Green, S. (2018). Aboriginal people and caring within a colonised society. In B. Pease, A. Vreugdenhil, & S. Stanford (Eds.), *Critical ethics and care in social work: Transforming the politics and practices or caring* (pp. 139–147). New York, NY: Routledge.

Green, S. (2019). Social work and cultural support. In B. Bennett & S. Green (Eds.), *Our voices: Aboriginal social work* (2nd ed., pp. 175–189). London: Red Globe Press.

Green, S., & Baldry, E. (2008). Building indigenous Australian social work. *Australian Social Work, 61*(4), 389–402. doi: https://doi.org/10.1080/03124070802430718.

Green, S., Russ-Smith, J., & Tynan, L. (2018). Claiming the space, creating the future. *Australian Journal of Education (Special Issue), 0*(0), 1–10.

Hamad, R. (2019). *White tears, brown scars*. Melbourne, VIC: Melbourne University Publishing.

Held, V. (1990). Feminist transformations of moral theory. *Philosophy and Phenomenological Research, 50*(1), 321–344.

Held, V. (1995). The meshing of care and justice. *Hypatia, 10*(2), 128–132.

Held, V. (2006). *The ethics of care: Personal, political, and global*. New York, NY: Oxford University Press.

Hugman, R. (2005). *New approaches in the ethics of the caring professions: Taking account of change for caring professions*. London: Palgrave Macmillan.

Hugman, R. (2014). Professionalising care – A necessary irony: Some implications of the 'ethics of care' for the caring professions and informal caring. In A. Gonzalez & C. Iffland (Eds.), *Care professions and globalisation: Theoretical and practical perspectives* (pp. 73–193). London: Palgrave Macmillan.

Keddell, E. (2017). Interpreting children's best interests: Needs, attachment and decision-making. *Journal of Social Work, 17*(3), 324–342. doi: https://doi.org/10.1177/1468017316644694.

Morley, C., & Macfarlane, S. (2014). Critical social work as ethical social work: Using critical reflection to research students' resistance to neoliberalism.

Critical and Radical Social Work, 2(3), 337–355. doi: https://doi.org/10.1332/204986014X14096553281895.

Morley, C., Macfarlane, S., & Ablett, P. (2019). *Engaging with social work: A critical introduction*. Cambridge: Cambridge University Press.

Our Booris Our Way Steering Committee. (2019). *Our Booris our way final report: December 2019.* https://www.strongfamilies.act.gov.au/_data/assets/pdf_file/0011/1457813/Our-Booris-Report-FINAL-REPORT.pdf

Russ-Smith, J. (2019). Indigenous social work and a Wiradyuri Framework to practice. In B. Bennett & S. Green (Eds.), *Our voices: Aboriginal social work* (2nd ed., pp. 103–116). London: Red Globe Press.

Sevenhuijsen, S. (2003). The place of care: The relevance of the feminist ethic of care for social policy. *Feminist Theory, 4*(2), 179–197.

SNAICC. (2013). *Aboriginal and Torres Strait Islander child placement principle*. Available at: https://www.snaicc.org.au/aboriginal-and-torres-strait-islander-child-placement-principle/. Accessed 25 March 2020.

SNAICC. (2018). *Baseline analysis of best practice implementation of the Aboriginal and Torres Strait Islander placement principle*. ACT.

Tronto, J. (1995). Care as a basis for radical political judgements. *Hypatia, 10*(2), 141–149.

Tronto, J. (1998). An ethic of care. *Generations, 22*(3), 15–20.

Walters, M., & Baltra-Ulloa, J. (2019). Australian social work is white. In B. Bennett & S. Green (Eds.), *Our voices: Aboriginal social work* (2nd ed., pp. 65–85). London: Red Globe Press.

Wheeler, A. (2019). *A situated ethical analysis of child inclusive practices in five relationships Australia NSW family relationship centres*. Unpublished doctoral dissertation. Sydney, NSW: University of New South Wales.

5 Working with Aboriginal Older Persons

Maddison Williams

Cultural Standpoint

I am an Aboriginal woman from the Wiradjuri Nation, Central NSW. My ancestors are the Galari people who lived along the Lachlan River. I have been raised by my mother and maternal grandmother who are also proud Wiradjuri women. This upbringing has assisted my standpoint regarding Aboriginal ways of knowing, being, and doing. In addition to this, most of my life has been spent in Westernised educational systems and workplaces. I am therefore mindful that this exposure may have some influence over my standpoint.

Introduction

The aged care sector is commonly documented as less appealing to social work students and practitioners than other fields of practice (Hughes & Heycox, 2006). However, with Australia's ageing population, it is anticipated that the need for aged care social workers will be a rapidly growing area of employment (Duffy & Healy, 2011; Phillips, 2018).

Aboriginal people over the age of 65 are expected to grow 200% by 2031, holding implications for Australia's aged care system (Australian National Audit Office [ANAO], 2017a, 2017b; LoGiudice, 2016). Coombes et al. (2018) explain that, despite literature arguing that Australian Government-funded aged care systems are being effectively delivered to Aboriginal people, there remains a paucity of culturally appropriate care and a lack of Aboriginal voices and knowledge influencing the processes and outcomes. The Government of South Australia (2018) add that Australia's aged care service providers and systems continue to lack the understanding that urban, rural, and remote Aboriginal communities each have differing language groups, cultural practices, and beliefs. It is further concerning that Westernised ideals seem to prevail in Australia's aged care sector, consequently neglecting the belief systems appropriate to Aboriginal culture.

This chapter will address the large gap in the knowledge and skills of working with an older population. Due to the disparity of age, this is a new area that needs awareness raised and challenges discussed. This chapter will explore current and future issues, as well as raising awareness of the needs of Aboriginal older persons. This chapter aims to broaden the knowledge and skills of social work students and practitioners; whilst allowing readers to understand the importance of their holistic psychosocial assessments, inventions, and advocacy skills.

Identification of Aboriginal older persons

Under the Aged Care Act 1997, the identification of Aboriginal older persons is defined as aged 50 years and over, compared with age 65 for their non-Aboriginal counterparts (ANAO, 2017a, 2017b). This is due to the multiple health and social disadvantages Aboriginal people in Australia face, specifically their lower life expectancies and more complex health care needs. In 2016, only 5% of Aboriginal people were aged 65 years and over, compared with 16% of non-Aboriginal people (Australian Institute of Health and Welfare [AIHW], 2018a, 2018b).

Health and healthy ageing

Coombes et al. (2018) explain that prior to colonisation, Aboriginal people led healthy lifestyles with access to clear air, fresh food, fresh water, and regular physical activity through 'walking, corroborees, gathering and hunting'. Coombes et al. (2018) further this by explaining that colonisation prevented Aboriginal people from this healthy lifestyle by removing them from their environments and introducing foreign diseases that they were not immune to and had not previously encountered.

Aboriginal people over the age of 55 are at higher risk of diabetes, cardiovascular disease, and respiratory disease (AIHW, 2018a, 2018b). The causes of inadequate health between Aboriginal people and non-Aboriginal people can be related to social determinants of health such as 'social and economic exclusion, unemployment, low income, poor housing and sanitation, poor education, and lack of adequate nutrition' (National Aboriginal Community Controlled Health Organization [NACCHO], 2019). Furthermore, it can be linked to social and political changes, lack of trust within Australian government systems, and absence of adequate public policy for the health and wellbeing of Aboriginal communities (LoGiudice, 2016; NACCHO, 2019).

Several research articles that centre on Aboriginal health have focused on the increasing prevalence of dementia in Aboriginal older people. The AIHW (2018a, 2018b), Neuroscience Research Australia (2020), and LoGiudice (2016) agree that Aboriginal people over the age of 60 have higher rates of disability than their non-Aboriginal counterparts, and have been found to be three times more likely to develop dementia in both urban and rural settings. Importantly, practitioners need to understand that dementia is largely unknown in Aboriginal communities, with many Aboriginal people not classifying dementia as a medical condition and instead theorising it as a 'sick or lost spirit looking for help' (Dementia Training Australia, 2017; LoGiudice, 2016, p. 83; Radford et al., 2014). This cultural understanding is vital for practitioners to understand and should inform their psychosocial assessments, provision of care, and psychoeducation (LoGiudice, 2016). To assist investigating dementia in Aboriginal people, the culturally appropriate 'Kimberly Indigenous Cognitive Assessment (KICA)' screening tool has been developed and is being widely used in both rural and remote Australia (Wall, 2010).

The notion of 'healthy ageing' differs in a Westernised context compared with an Aboriginal context. LoGiudice (2016) explains that healthy ageing for non-Aboriginal people includes 'optimizing opportunities for good health, so that older people can take an active part in society and enjoy an independent quality of life'. For Aboriginal older persons, healthy ageing is centred on 'the physical and mental ability to pass on traditional values, cultural knowledge, and cultural spirituality' (Coombes et al., 2018). In the 'Sharing the Wisdom of Our Elders' report, which is the outcome of the Koori Growing Old Well Study, the primary themes identified for healthy ageing for Aboriginal persons include (Radford et al., 2019):

- Connection to Country and culture;

- Respecting yourself, the Elders and all the mob;

- Resilience;

- Getting together, yarning, passing on knowledge;

- Keeping healthy to live a long life;

- Saying no to smoking, alcohol, and drugs;

- Education.

It is recommended that all readers familiarise themselves with the Sharing the Wisdom of Our Elders report which is found in the Further Reading section.

Social and emotional wellbeing

The concept of 'mental health' is commonly rejected by Aboriginal communities due to the concept being developed in a Westernised context which emphasises an individualistic view. The concept of 'social and emotional wellbeing' (SEWB) is therefore preferred, due to the notion holding a holistic view which incorporates factors such as kinship, connection to Country, and the impact of historical policies (NSW Department of Health, 2010).

The Australian Government Department of Health (2006) explain that these cultural differences have created problems for Aboriginal communities due to 'mental health' being the concept which has informed most policies, programs, and service provisions.

The Australian Government Department of Health (2006) explain that ongoing mental health care for Aboriginal people requires acknowledgement and respect for the interconnectedness of 'kinship, culture, law, land and spirituality; as well as an understanding of the effects of invasion, colonization and ongoing cultural stress'. In the Older Person's Mental Health Project (2010, p. 36) it was stated that the most common factors contributing to SEWB were 'alcohol (88%), drugs (72%), Australian social history (75%), Australian political history (63%) racism (78%), general health (81%), Sorry Business, violence (72%), over representation in prison and incarceration (66%), culture identity (66%), empowerment (69%), connection to country (56%), forced removal of children from families (66%), education opportunities (63%), employment opportunities (75%) housing (72%) and access to services (72%)'. In addition to these statistics, the NSW Department of Health (2010) stress that Aboriginal older people may not only experience a SEWB issue, but also may face the effects of SEWB in their communities as Elders and leaders (NSW Department of Health, 2010).

To address SEWB in Aboriginal older persons, the NSW Department of Health (2010) explain that practitioners need to understand the importance of culture and ensure the holistic health needs of Aboriginal people are met. Furthermore, practitioners must understand the importance of family and community connections (The NSW Department of Health, 2010).

Cultural responsiveness and culturally safe care

Coombes et al. (2018) explains that a lack of cultural responsiveness and culturally safe care negatively impacts the desire for Aboriginal older persons to seek and access government services and systems. The Department of Health and Human Services (DOHHS, 2016) explains that cultural responsiveness for Aboriginal people is centred on listening to, understanding, and demonstrating empathy for their specific needs, whilst also knowing and respecting community Elders, their land, and their culture. For social workers, Bender et al. (cited in AASW, 2016) and the AASW (2016) explain that a culturally responsive practice requires social workers to understand their own values, cultures, and position in society, while, respecting Aboriginal ways of knowing, being, and doing.

The Agency of Clinical Innovation (2020, p. 1) has provided the following guidelines to demonstrate a culturally responsive practice:

- An awareness and understanding of different cultures, with the ability to accept differences without judgements;

- The ability to identify risk factors among specific groups without stereo-typing people;

- An awareness of your own culture and understanding your inherent biases towards your own cultural values and behaviours;

- The ability to work with people from different cultures in a way that is safe and supportive and is not discriminatory or harmful;

- An understanding of the structures and services that are necessary to deliver cultural support and bring about systemic change.

The DOHHS (2016) describes cultural safety as allowing Aboriginal people to feel connected to culture, community, and Country, rather than feeling unwelcomed. The National Aboriginal and Torres Strait Islander Health Workers Association (2013) extend this by explaining that cultural safety aims to enhance the delivery of services by identifying power imbalances and requiring professionals to undergo a process of critical self-reflection on the influence that their culture may have on their practice.

Dementia Training Australia (2017), the Australian Government Department of Health (2019, p. 1), Price-Robertson and McDonald (2011), and the National Aboriginal and Torres Strait Islander Health Workers Association (NATSIHWA, 2013) have each contributed to culturally safe aged care principles for professionals to implement when working with Aboriginal older persons:

- Ensure Aboriginal older persons have opportunities to continue partici-pating in cultural events and activities that they enjoy;

- Understand the concept of Elders in Aboriginal culture and respect the roles and responsibilities they hold in the community;

- Understand the importance of the role of informal care givers in Aboriginal communities and support Aboriginal older persons and their families to continue such arrangements as required;

- Recognise and celebrate historical events of significance and important annual events as a normal part of business;

- Have appropriate buildings to allow for cultural activities, family visits and ceremonies;

- Encourage Aboriginal older people to remain engaged with their com-munity and respect cultural traditions e.g. men's and women's business;

- Involve cultural artefacts in services and everyday activities (e.g. tradi-tional Indigenous tools, foods, and artwork);

- Consider how internal and external spaces are used to support the physi-cal, social and emotional wellbeing of an Aboriginal older person;

- Consult and involve family, extended kin networks, and community members in service delivery;
- Co-design facilities under the direction, views, and opinions of Aboriginal Elders.

Group Exercise

1. Discuss the differences between cultural responsiveness and culturally safe care.
2. Brainstorm how you or your service can provide a culturally safe service to Aboriginal older persons.

Services and challenges

The Government of South Australia (2018) and South Australia Health and Medical Research (2020) agree that there are many challenges in ensuring Aboriginal older people have access to culturally appropriate services and care, specifically those who live in remote or very remote communities, and those who face economic disadvantage. The ANAO (2017) and the Wall (2010) explain that rural and remote areas of Australia remain under-serviced; with even successful, Aboriginal-led, culturally appropriate services not securing recurrent funding.

The Older Person's Mental Health Project Wall (2010) explains 'Aboriginal people and communities are more likely to access services where other Aboriginal people have reported positive experiences'. Unfortunately, older Aboriginal people frequently report negative experiences regarding services, including 'poor communication, inappropriate processes of care, culturally inappropriate interventions, stereotyping, and racial discrimination' (Older Person's Mental Health Project, 2010). These negative experiences are supported by qualitative research studies where participants have communicated that there is minimal understanding of Aboriginal needs and a lack of cultural safety (Coombes et al., 2018; Older Person's Mental Health Project, 2010). Further challenges regarding services include transportation problems, failure of staff to provide care in use of language, fear of the medical system, and a continued 'one size fits all' belief by policy, programs, and service providers (Wall, 2010).

The Wall (2010) explains that, to address these challenges, it is essential that an Aboriginal aged care workforce is employed and that there is 'ongoing, genuine community control of services'. Furthermore, the ANAO (2017) argues that the Australian Government must ensure Aboriginal-focused service providers are supported and that ongoing impacts of aged care policies and programs are sufficiently evaluated. Coombes et al. (2018) supports this point by expressing the need for culturally appropriate services that centre on the knowledge, belief systems, and realities of Aboriginal people.

Despite these points, it is also important to mention that some Aboriginal people have reported positive experiences in Aboriginal-specific services, due to the services understanding cultural expectations and cultural obligations (Radford et al., 2019).

Australia's aged care system

Australia's aged care system can be broken up into four main categories. These categories include Commonwealth Home Support Programs (CHSP), Home Care Packages (HCP), and Respite Care and Residential Aged Care Facilities (RACF). Linking Aboriginal people in these services via My Aged Care is a primary role of aged care social workers. For this book chapter, however, only RACF and the National Aboriginal and Torres Strait Islander Flexible Aged Care Program (NATSIFACP) will be discussed.

RACF (commonly known as nursing homes) are for older people who can no longer live at home due to increased care needs. In 2016–2017, the AIHW (2018a, 2018b) found that less than 1% of residents in RACFs identified as an Aboriginal person. Furthermore, the AIHW (2018a, 2018b) found that 26% of Aboriginal people in RACF were 'under the age of 65 years' compared with 3% of their non-Aboriginal counterparts. The Agency of Clinical Innovation (2020) and LoGiudice (2016) explain that, when an Aboriginal person enters a RACF, the experience can be one of 're-institutionalisation' and is frequently seen as a place people are sent to die. Sivertsen et al. (2019) support LoGiudice (2016) in that RACF are not only far from Country, but also frequently produce 'a sense of disconnection from place, land, kinship, spirit and soul'. The AAG (2010) and LoGiudice (2016) agree that social workers must therefore implement a culturally responsive practice and understand that Aboriginal older persons often have a desire to be cared for in their communities, where they can die on land.

The Australian Government Department of Health (2019) explains that the NATSIFACP is an Australian Government-funded strategy created to improve the quality and access to culturally appropriate aged care services for Aboriginal people. The AIHW (2018a, 2018b) states that, in 2017, the NATSIFACP had 820 operational places, primarily located in rural and remote Australia. The ANAO (2017a, 2017b) explains that, despite the NATSIFACP being a cost-effective strategy for delivering aged care services in remote and very remote communities, the current funding approach prevents new service providers from becoming involved. The ANAO (2017a, 2017b) concludes that the Department of Health therefore needs to ensure that 'the existing service providers, their location, and number of places' remain the most effective for Aboriginal older people and communities.

Box 5.1 Case Study

You are a hospital social worker employed in the acute care sector and are referred to an Aboriginal person, aged 57, due to carer stress. This individual is from Bourke, has complex health care needs, and requires assistance with several activities of daily living. His wife appears exhausted and overwhelmed. Prior to meeting this family, you are approached by a nurse, who explains that she has mentioned the National Disability Insurance Scheme (NDIS) to this family, as this patient is not eligible for My Aged Care services because of his age. The nurse informs you that the wife appeared interested in accessing help.

Reflective Questions for Practice

1. Should you discuss with this family the NDIS or My Aged Care services?
2. What actions can you do to provide a more culturally responsive and culturally safe service to this family?
3. If your patient denies needing services against his wife's wishes, can you still complete a referral on his behalf?

Future planning for Aboriginal older persons

Future planning is an essential area of getting older; however, many older people may find this process confusing and believe that the only legal requirement is a will. The NSW Trustee and Guardian (2015) explains, that, if an Aboriginal person passes away without any future planning, this can create a potential dispute with the Aboriginal person's family and community at Sorry Time. To assist your understanding about future planning; wills, powers of attorney, guardianships, and advanced care directives will be briefly discussed.

Wills

A will is a legal document that explains who the individual wants their belongings to go to when they pass away (NSW Trustee and Guardian, 2015). It can state where the individual wants to be buried, their wishes for their funeral arrangements, and it can be a way for Aboriginal people to pass on cultural information and secret knowledge when they die (Vines, 2015).

A major area for consideration when writing wills is the specification of beneficiaries due to the common law and customary law having different ways of thinking about family (Vines, 2015). Vines (2015) explains that, when writing a will, it is important that the beneficiaries are clearly named, i.e. an Aboriginal older person may regard 'X, Y and Z as their children in customary law however, common law only regards X as their child'.

Power of attorney

A power of attorney is a legal document which appoints a person to look after an individual's money if they can no longer do this themselves (NSW Trustee and Guardian, 2015). The NSW Trustee and Guardian (2015) emphasises, the importance of making this attorney 'enduring', which means that, if the individual loses their capacity, their chosen person will remain in this role. If the individual is no longer able to manage their finances and has not allocated an enduring power of attorney, an application to the NSW Civil & Administrative Tribunal (NCAT) can be made (NSW Trustee and Guardian, 2019). If it is decided that the individual needs assistance with financial decisions, a financial manager will be appointed either privately or publicly (NSW Trustee and Guardian, 2019).

Box 5.2 Case Study

At the weekly multi-disciplinary team meeting, you are involved in a case discussion between the medical team, occupational therapist, physiotherapist, and Aboriginal Hospital Liaison Officer (ALHO) regarding Shirley. Shirley is a respected Elder who lives alone and was admitted following a fall. During her current two-week admission, Shirley has been bedbound, has been diagnosed with Alzheimer's disease, and has been deemed to have extremely high levels of care needs.

Earlier this week, you participated in a family conference where the recommendation of discharge into a RACF was presented and agreed upon by staff. During this family conference, Shirley and several of her loved ones rejected this recommendation and explained that she can be cared for in the community.

Over the past couple of days, Shirley has remained adamant that she will not be discharged into a RACF. With this information, Shirley's geriatrician deems her to not have the capacity to make an informed decision and concludes that this case is for guardianship. You ask the AHLO to assist you in presenting this news to the family, however the AHLO expresses feeling uncomfortable with the knowledge that guardianship ultimately means that Shirley's rights for lifestyle and health decisions will be taken from her.

Reflective Questions for Practice

1. What reasons might the AHLO have for feeling uncomfortable with the decision to go for guardianship?
2. What reasons might Shirley and her family have for disagreeing with the recommendation that she enter a RACF?
3. How can the social worker in this scenario advocate for Shirley using a culturally responsive and culturally safe approach?

Enduring guardian

An enduring guardian is someone appointed to make lifestyle, health, and medical decisions if the individual is no longer able to do this themselves (NSW Trustee and Guardian, 2019). Ideally, prior to the person losing their capacity, the individual would have chosen who they would like their enduring guardian to be. If the individual has lost their capacity and has not appointed an enduring guardian, an application will be made to NCAT where an Enduring Guardian will be appointed (NSW Trustee and Guardian, 2019). If there are no suitable private candidates for this role, i.e. family conflict or the nominated person has questionable intent, NCAT may appoint a public guardian (NSW Trustee and Guardian, 2019).

Advance care directives

An advance care directive is a legal document which explains a person's wishes and directions in advance, in case they lose their mental capacity in the future (Vines, 2015). It contains information such as the older person's views of medical treatments (Vines, 2015). Like the power of attorney and enduring guardianship documents, the older person must have the capacity to understand the consequences of competing and signing an advance care directive (Vines, 2015).

Elder abuse in Aboriginal communities

When speaking about Elder abuse, it is firstly important to note the difficulties and concerns of the appropriateness of the term due to its specific meaning in Aboriginal communities (Australia's Law Reform Commission, 2016). While some Aboriginal communities use age to define who is an elder, others associate the term with those who have contributed to their communities and hold certain knowledge within their language groups, communities, and families (Gooda, 2012; Office of the Public Advocate, 2005). For this chapter, the term 'Elder abuse' will relate to those aged over 50 years and over.

Elder abuse is a growing area of concern in the Australian population and may include forms of abuse such as neglect, physical, psychological, financial, and sexual abuse (ALRC, 2016). The National Research Council (2003) explain that elder abuse is an 'intentional action that causes harm or serious risk of harm by a person who stands in a relationship of trust or, by a person failing to prevent some form of injury, deprivation or dangerous condition'. Despite evidence that elder abuse occurs in all societies and cultures, some argue the importance of separating Elder abuse in an Aboriginal context due differences in 'cultures, relationships and responsibilities' (Gooda, 2012). Gooda (2012) explains his belief that Elder abuse in an Aboriginal context is linked to the breakdown of Aboriginal cultural norms due to colonisation, dispossession, and oppression, which has affected the respect Aboriginal people previously had for their Elders.

For Aboriginal Elders living in rural and remote communities, it is thought that the help-seeking process for Elder abuse may be more complex due to Aboriginal Elders not wanting their community to know their family business (Government of South Australia, 2012). Furthermore, Aboriginal people may be reluctant to access services due to 'not feeling safe within mainstream services, oral and written language barriers, poverty, lack of access to transport, family obligations (children/grandchildren), racism, and lack of respect from service providers' (Government of South Australia, 2012, p. 1).

By reviewing relevant literature and research, the most common form of abuse affecting Aboriginal older persons is financial abuse. This is linked to issues such as 'entrenched poverty, substance abuse, and a breakdown of strong family structures' (Government of South Australia, 2012, p. 1). Wundersitz (2010) explains that perpetrators of Elder abuse are frequently grandchildren who take advantage of kinship-based obligations. ALRC (2016) extends this point by conveying that kinship-based obligations, and the cultural expectations attached, may complicate how abuse is experienced and understood in Aboriginal communities.

Risk factors of Elder abuse in Aboriginal communities can been broken down into the key headings of 'Historical and cultural risk factors', 'Socio-economic risk factors', and 'Health and social and emotional wellbeing risk factors' (Government of South Australia, 2012, p. 1). To find more risk factors and further your understanding of Elder abuse in Aboriginal communities, please refer to the resources listed in the Further Reading section.

How to work respectfully with Aboriginal older persons

The AASW (2015, p. 4) defines social work in aged care as focusing on the 'preservation and improvement of psychological and social functioning'. The profession's core values of human rights and social justice allow them to advocate for older people against the isolation, discrimination, and Elder abuse they may face (AASW, 2015). Furthermore, social workers are the primary contact for community service providers, aged care facilities, family members, and carers (Duffy & Healy, 2011).

In a hospital setting, social workers assist with providing information and education, counselling, mediation, negotiation, arranging support services, and assisting the individual to make significant life decisions (AASW, 2015). One of their most vital duties is their role in the NCAT; with guardianship and financial management processes (Duffy & Healy, 2011).

As stated throughout this chapter, it is essential that social workers working with Aboriginal people employ a culturally responsive and culturally safe practice. To further assist, some practice techniques on how to work respectfully with Aboriginal people are outlined below.

Time: It is essential that practitioners dedicate a flexible amount of time when working with Aboriginal people as this is required to build a trusting relationship (Benevolent Society, 2013). Furthermore, practitioners must not rush the Aboriginal person and must attempt to forget any time limits they may have (Queensland Health, 2015).

Active Listening: Aboriginal people frequently speak in a narrative communication style and may have trouble communicating their thoughts (Queensland Health, 2015). Practitioners need to use active listening skills and paraphrase what the Aboriginal person has said to demonstrate their understanding (Queensland Health, 2015).

Rapport: Aboriginal people value a 'person before business' approach, which means that practitioners need to dedicate an appropriate amount of time into establishing rapport, such as sharing stories about themselves and finding common interests (Queensland Health, 2015).

Language: Many Aboriginal people and communities have different languages or speak in Aboriginal English. It is important that practitioners do not use complex words, that they check the meaning of what has been said, and that they do not mimic how an Aboriginal person may be speaking, or attempt to speak in Aboriginal English (Queensland Health, 2015).

Silence: Silence during conversations is common in Aboriginal cultures and demonstrates respect. It is important that practitioners do not interpret this silence as a lack of understanding. Practitioners should observe this silence and body language to uncover when it is appropriate to speak (Queensland Health, 2015).

Eye Contact: For some Aboriginal people, they may feel uncomfortable with direct eye contact and can view this as disrespectful. Practitioners must observe the Aboriginal person's eye contact and modify theirs accordingly (Queensland Health, 2015).

Titles: In Aboriginal cultures, the terms 'Aunty' or 'Uncle' are used to show respect for someone older. Practitioners must only address an Aboriginal person with these terms if approval has been given and a positive relationship has been developed (Queensland Health, 2015).

Questioning: For most Aboriginal people, indirect questioning is preferred. Practitioners must avoid compound questions and should use 'round about' approaches such as using statements. Furthermore, practitioners must use plain English (Queensland Health, 2015).

Trauma-Informed Care: It is essential that practitioners take a trauma-informed care approach by understanding the impacts of trauma on individuals and communities. Trauma – informed care is a strengths-based approach that emphasises safety and provides individuals opportunities to rebuild a sense of control and empowerment (Australian Institute of

Family Studies, 2016). The core principles for trauma informed care include safety, trust, compassion, collaboration, choice, and empowerment (Manitoba Trauma Informed Education & Resource Centre, 2020).

Conclusion

Although the concept of healthy aging for Aboriginal people differs, their beliefs are frequently neglected in the creation of aged care policy, programs, and services. Furthermore, the challenges faced by older Aboriginal people are not new issues; however, they remain largely unresolved. Interestingly, when researching for this chapter, there appeared to be a paucity of data on the topics discussed. Furthermore, many resources regarding Aboriginal older persons seem to have been developed in South Australia. This is inadequate given Australia's aging population and demonstrates that more work and attention is required. Throughout this chapter, it has been highlighted that Aboriginal people have had primarily poor experiences with the aged care sector and that this negatively impacts the desire for Aboriginal people to seek help. Likewise, it has been shown that there is a great need for practitioners and service providers to utilise cultural responsiveness and culturally safe practices. It is hoped that this chapter has raised awareness for the needs of Aboriginal older persons, and that readers have gained knowledge on how to work effectively with Aboriginal older persons.

 ## Discussion Questions

1. How do Aboriginal people view healthy aging?

2. What are some factors that affect an Aboriginal older person's SEWB?

3. What future planning must Aboriginal people consider prior to dying?

4. What is the most common form of Elder abuse that Aboriginal people face?

5. What are some practice techniques that you can implement when working with an Aboriginal older person?

 ## Further Reading

Australian Institute of Health and Welfare (AIHW). (2018). *Older Australia at a glance.* Viewed 11 December 2019. https://www.aihw. gov.au/reports/older-people/older-australia-at-a-glance/contents/ health-and-aged-care-service-use/aged-care

Duffy, F., & Healy, J. P. (2011). Social work with older people in a hospital setting. *Social Work in Health Care, 50*(2), 109–123. doi: https://doi.org/10.108 0/00981389.2010.527786.

Gooda, M. (2012). *Elder abuse and neglect.* Viewed 16 December 2019. https://www.humanrights.gov.au/about/news/speeches/indigenous-allied-health-australia-2012-national-health-conference

Government of South Australia. (2012). *Elder abuse and people from an Aboriginal background.* Viewed 11 December 2019. https://www.sahealth.sa.gov.au/wps/wcm/connect/99a36f004a1d6bf1b48bf490d529bdaa/Elder+abuse+-+People+from+an+Aboriginal+background.pdf?MOD=AJPERES

Hughes, M., & Heycox, K. (2006). Knowledge and interest in ageing: A study of final-year social work students. *Australasian Journal on Ageing, 25*(2), 94–96. doi: https://doi.org/10.1111/j.1741-6612.2006.00158.x.

NSW Trustee and Guardian. (2015). *Taking care of business, planning ahead for Aboriginal in New South Wales.* Viewed 15 December 2019. https://www.planningaheadtools.com.au/wp-content/uploads/2015/06/Taking-care-of-business.pdf

Radford, K., Mack, H. A., Robertson, H., Draper, B., Chalkley, S., Daylight, G., Cumming, R., Bennett, H., Jackson Pulver, L., & Broe, G. A. (2014). The Koori growing old well study: Investigating aging and dementia in urban Aboriginal Australians. *International Psychogeriatrics, 26*(6), 1033–1043. doi: https://doi.org/10.1017/S1041610213002561.

Radford, K., Allan, W., Donovan, T., Delbaere, K., Garvey, G., Broe, G. A., Daylight, G., Anderson, M., Timbery, A., Sullivan, K., Nichols, M., & Lavrencic, L. (2019). *Sharing the wisdom of our elders final report.* Viewed 15 March 2020. https://www.neura.edu.au/wp-content/uploads/2020/02/FINAL-REPORT-sharing-wisdom-of-our-elders-finl-lres.pdf

Vines, P. (2015). *Aboriginal wills handbook, a practical guide to making culturally appropriate wills for Aboriginal people.* Viewed 11 December 2019. https://www.tag.nsw.gov.au/verve/_resources/Aboriginal_Wills_Handbook.pdf

References

Agency of Clinical Innovation. (2020). *Consumer enablement guide.* Viewed 2 February 2020. https://www.aci.health.nsw.gov.au/resources/chronic-care/consumer-enablement/guide/how-to-support-enablement/culturally-responsive-practice

Australian Association of Social Workers. (2015). *Scope of social work practice, social work in aged care.* Viewed 11 December 2019. https://www.aasw.asn.au/document/item/8305

Australian Association of Social Workers. (2016). *Preparing for culturally responsive and inclusive social work practice in Australia: Working with Aboriginal and Torres Strait Islander peoples.* Viewed 10 February 2020. https://www.aasw.asn.au/document/item/7006

Australian Government Department of Health. (2006). *Pathways of recovery: Prevention further episodes of mental illness.* Viewed 3 February 2020. https://www1.health.gov.au/internet/publications/publishing.nsf/Content/

mental-pubs-p-mono-toc~mental-pubs-p-mono-pop~mental-pubs-p-mono-pop-atsi

Australian Government Department of Health. (2019). *National Aboriginal and Torres Strait Islander flexible aged care program*. Viewed 12 January 2020. https://www.health.gov.au/sites/default/files/documents/2019/12/national-aboriginal-and-torres-strait-islander-flexible-aged-care-program-manual.pdf

Australian Institute of Family Studies. (2016). *Trauma-informed care in child/family welfare services*. Viewed 10 February 2020. https://aifs.gov.au/cfca/publications/trauma-informed-care-child-family-welfare-services/applying-trauma-informed-care

Australian Institute of Health and Welfare. (2018a). *Indigenous Australians*. Viewed 12 January 2020. https://www.aihw.gov.au/reports-data/population-groups/indigenous-australians/overview

Australian Institute of Health and Welfare. (2018b). *Older Australia at a glance*. Viewed 11 December 2019. https://www.aihw.gov.au/reports/older-people/older-australia-at-a-glance/contents/health-and-aged-care-service-use/aged-care

Australian Law Reform Commission. (2016). *What is elder abuse?* Viewed 16 December 2019. https://www.alrc.gov.au/publication/elder-abuse-ip-47/issues-paper-4/what-is-elder-abuse/

Australian National Audit Office. (2017a). *Indigenous aged care*. Viewed 5 February 2020. https://www.anao.gov.au/work/performance-audit/indigenous-aged-care

Australian National Audit Office. (2017b). *Indigenous aged care*. Viewed 10 February 2020. https://www.anao.gov.au/sites/default/files/ANAO_Report_2016-2017_53a.pdf?acsf_files_redirect

Benevolent Society. (2013). *Working with older Aboriginal and Torres strait islander people*. Viewed 10 February 2020. https://www.google.com/url?sa=t&rct=j&q=&esrc=s&source=web&cd=1&cad=rja&uact=8&ved=2ahUKEwj1jNet6rvnAhVa7HMBHbdxBRIQFjAAegQIBhAB&url=https%3A%2F%2Fwww.benevolent.org.au%2FArticleDocuments%2F340%2FOlderaboriginal_torresstraitislander_people.pdf.aspx&usg=AOvVaw0DWD3t723QHoY6VxGlNHTX

Coombes, J., Lukaszyk, C., Sherrington, C., Keay, L., Tiedemann, A., Moore, R., & Ivers, R. (2018). 'First Nation Elders' perspectives on healthy ageing in NSW. *Australian and New Zealand Journal of Public Health, 42*(4), 361–364. doi: https://doi.org/10.1111/1753-6405.12796.

Dementia Training Australia. (2017). *Cultural assessment for Aboriginal and Torres Strait Islander people with dementia: Guide for health professionals*. Viewed 5 February 2020. https://www.dta.com.au/wp-content/uploads/2017/03/2370_DTA_WA_DT_manual_5web.pdf

Department of Health and Human Services. (2016). *Improving cultural responsiveness of Victorian hospitals*. Viewed 2 February 2020. https://www.google.com/url?sa=t&rct=j&q=&esrc=s&source=web&cd=14&cad=rja&uact=8&ved=2ahUKEwiNzvb54rbnAhUk7XMBHaS2DDoQFjANegQIBBAB&url=https%3A%2F%2Fwww2.health.vic.gov.au%2FApi%2Fdownloadmedia%2F%25

7BF4318754-CB2B-4F6E-A995-FF43F3ECCADF%257D&usg=AOvVaw2rKD
lSGL2v1Z8wPhD1jyHs

Duffy, F., & Healy, J. P. (2011). Social work with older people in a hospital set-ting. *Social Work in Health Care, 50*(2), 109–123. doi: https://doi.org/10.108 0/00981389.2010.527786.

Gooda, M. (2012). *Elder abuse and neglect.* Viewed 16 December 2019. https://www.humanrights.gov.au/about/news/speeches/indigenous-allied-health-australia-2012-national-health-conference

Government of South Australia. (2012). *Elder abuse and people from an Aboriginal background.* Viewed 11 December 2019. https://www.sahealth.sa.gov.au/wps/wcm/connect/99a36f004a1d6bf1b48bf490d 529bdaa/Elder+abuse+-+People+from+an+Aboriginal+background. pdf?MOD=AJPERES

Government of South Australia. (2018). *Aboriginal mental health clini-cal practice guideline and pathways.* Viewed 10 February 2020. https://www.sahealth.sa.gov.au/wps/wcm/connect/c9265300414f31cab-52cb7e8f09fe17d/Aboriginal+Mental+Health+Clinical+Practice+Guid eline+and+Pathways.pdf?MOD=AJPERES&CACHEID=ROOTWORKSP ACE-c9265300414f31cab52cb7e8f09fe17d-mNBKYG

Hughes, M., & Heycox, K. (2006). Knowledge and interest in ageing: A study of final-year social work students. *Australasian Journal on Ageing, 25*(2), 94–96. doi: https://doi.org/10.1111/j.1741-6612.2006.00158.x.

Logiudice, D. (2016). The health of older Aboriginal and Torres Strait Islander peoples. *Australasian Journal on Ageing, 35*(2), 82–85. doi: https://doi. org/10.1111/ajag.12332.

Manitoba Trauma Informed Education & Resource Centre. (2020). *Principals.* Viewed 16 February 2020. https://trauma-informed.ca/about-us/mtiec-trainings-and-webinars/trauma-informed-organizations-and-systems/ principles/

National Aboriginal and Torres Strait Islander Health Workers Association. (2013). *Cultural safety framework.* Viewed 10 February 2020. https://www. natsihwa.org.au/sites/default/files/publications/NATSIHWA-Cultural%20 Safety-Framework%20Summary.pdf

National Aboriginal Community Controlled Health Organisation. (2019). *Aboriginal health.* Viewed 12 January 2020. https://www.naccho.org.au/ about/aboriginal-health/

National Research Council. (2003). *Elder mistreatment: Abuse, neglect, and exploitation in an aging America.* Viewed 11 December 2019. https://www.nap.edu/catalog/10406/elder-mistreatment-abuse-neglect-and-exploitation-in-an-aging-america

Neuroscience Research Australia. (2020). *Koori growing well study.* Viewed 25 January 2020. https://www.neura.edu.au/project/koori-growing-old-well-study-longitudinal-follow-6-years/

NSW Department of Health. (2010). *Aboriginal older person's men-tal health project.* Viewed 3 February 2020. https://www.aihw.gov. au/getmedia/6d50a4d2-d4da-4c53-8aeb-9ec22b856dc5/ctgc-ip12-4nov2014.pdf.aspx?inline=true

NSW Trustee and Guardian. (2015). *Taking care of business, planning ahead for Aboriginal in New South Wales*. Viewed 15 December 2019. https://www.planningaheadtools.com.au/wp-content/uploads/2015/06/Taking-care-of-business.pdf

NSW Trustee and Guardian. (2019). *What is an enduring guardian*. Viewed 15 December 2019. https://www.tag.nsw.gov.au/what-is-an-enduring-guardian.html

Office of the Public Advocate. (2005). *Mistreatment of older people in Aboriginal Communities Project – An investigations into elder abuse in Aboriginal Communities*. Viewed 16 December 2019. https://www.publicadvocate.wa.gov.au/_files/Mistreatment_older_aboriginal.pdf

Phillips, R. (2018). Emancipatory social work with older people: Challenging students to overcome the limitations of ageism and institutional oppression. *Social Work and Policy Studies: Social Justice, Practice and Theory, 1*(1), 1–23. Viewed 11 December 2011. https://openjournals.library.sydney.edu.au/index.php/SWPS

Price-Robertson, R., & McDonald, M. (2011). *Working with Indigenous children, families, and communities: Lessons from practice*. Viewed 10 February 2020. https://aifs.gov.au/cfca/publications/working-indigenous-children-families-and-communities

Queensland Health. (2015). *Communicating effectively with Aboriginal and Torres Strait Islander people*. Viewed 16 February 2020. https://www.health.qld.gov.au/data/assets/pdf_file/0021/151923/communicating.pdf

Radford, K., Allan, W., Donovan, T., Delbaere, K., Garvey, G., Broe, G. A., Daylight, G., Anderson, M., Timbery, A., Sullivan, K., Nichols, M., & Lavrencic, L. (2019). *Sharing the wisdom of our elders final report*. Viewed 15 March 2020. https://www.neura.edu.au/wp-content/uploads/2020/02/FINAL-REPORT-sharing-wisdom-of-our-elders-finl-lres.pdf

Radford, K., Mack, H. A., Robertson, H., Draper, B., Chalkley, S., Daylight, G., Cumming, R., Bennett, H., Jackson Pulver, L., & Broe, G. A. (2014). The Koori Growing Old Well Study: Investigating aging and dementia in urban Aboriginal Australians. *International Psychogeriatrics, 26*(6), 1033–1043. doi: https://doi.org/10.1017/S1041610213002561.

Sivertsen, N., Harrington, A., & Hamiduzzaman, M. (2019). Exploring Aboriginal aged care residents' cultural and spiritual needs in South Australia. *BMC Health Services Research, 19*(1), 1–13. doi: https://doi.org/10.1186/s12913-019-4322-8.

South Australia Health and Medical Research Council. (2020). *Culturally safe workforce models for rural and remote indigenous organisations*. Viewed 10 February 2020. https://www.sahmriresearch.org/user_assets/2fbfa9fdb1e1ee7c4ea2d0636eb537db5c6f6356/cultural_safety_for_older_aboriginal_people_summary.pdf

Vines, P. (2015). *Aboriginal wills handbook, a practical guide to making culturally appropriate wills for Aboriginal people*. Viewed 11 December 2019. https://www.tag.nsw.gov.au/verve/_resources/Aboriginal_Wills_Handbook.pdf

Wall, S. (2010). *Aboriginal aging*. Viewed 2 February 2020. https://www.aag.asn.au/documents/item/1438

Wundersitz, J. (2010). *Indigenous perpetrators of violence: Prevalence and risk factors for offending*. Viewed 16 December 2019. https://www.aic.gov.au/publications/rpp/rpp105

SOCIAL WORK IN PRACTICE SETTINGS

6 How The Practical Perspectives of Health Impact on Aboriginal Males, Family and Communities

Mick Adams, James Smith, and Jesse John Fleay

We would like to mention that the terms Aboriginal, Aboriginal and Torres Strait Islander, Indigenous, and men and males are used interchangeably throughout this chapter. Male is the preferred term as it is inclusive of all males.

Introduction

European colonialism and migration have had a severe and devastating impact on Indigenous people around the world. The ramifications of global Indigenous dispossession are evident and continues in present-day society. The effects of colonial assimilation have contributed to many of the obstacles and challenges Aboriginal peoples are confronted with. The methodical devastation of Aboriginal societies, social and kinship structures, cultural practices, language, and spirituality is recognised as a key factor in the erosion of Aboriginal and Torres Strait Islander spiritual wellbeing. The ongoing escalation of violence in Aboriginal and Torres Strait Islander communities is a continuation of the violent dispossession of land in early settlement and subsequent destruction of Aboriginal social and relationship structures.

Australia's Northern Territory Intervention, otherwise known as the Northern Territory Emergency Response (NTER), is a prime example of the continuation of colonial systems that impose restrictions on the exercise of individual rights of the members of Aboriginal communities. In 2007, the then Howard Government introduced, without consultation with Aboriginal people, a 'national emergency intervention' towards the eradication of child sexual abuse and violence against women in Aboriginal communities and town camps within the Northern Territory. This racially discriminated against, and infringed on, the human rights of Aboriginal people in the Northern Territory (Anaya, 2010; Australian Indigenous Doctors Association and the Centre for Health Equity Training, Research and Education, 2010). The NTER was framed in racial terms as the measures were intended to, and in fact applied specifically to, Aboriginal individuals and communities in the Northern Territory and not to others (Anaya, 2010, p. 6).

Based on the report, *Ampe Akelyernemane Meke Mekarle – 'Little Children are Sacred'*, (which received little attention from the Australian Government in relation to its overarching recommendations) and increased national attention to the problems of child abuse, the Howard Government paid particular attention to Aboriginal women and children. It used the NTER as a rationale for wanting women and children to live their lives free of violence and to enjoy the same rights enjoyed by other Australians.

Aboriginal women expressed anguish over not just the immediate impacts of various aspects of the NTER, but also about a deepening sense of indignity and stigmatisation brought about by the entire scheme (Anaya, 2010, p. 8). During this process, some consultations engaged with Aboriginal people through their own community and regional leadership structures, where women often played prominent roles in respective meetings (Anaya, 2010, p. 8). Yet, there was often minimal direct involvement of Aboriginal males (Central Australian Aboriginal Congress, 2008). This had a detrimental effect on Aboriginal males, not only in the Territory but nationally. Indeed, there were no special measures to engage Aboriginal males, until an Aboriginal Male Health Summit was held at Inteyerrkwe (Ross River), Northern Territory in July 2008. This was an important summit involving more than 400 Aboriginal males from across Australia. Participants worked collectively to produce the following statement:

> We the Aboriginal males from Central Australia and our visitor brothers from around Australia gathered at Inteyerrkwe in July 2008 to develop strategies to ensure our future roles as husbands, grandfathers, fathers, uncles, nephews, brothers, grandsons, and sons in caring for our children in a safe family environment that will lead to a happier, longer life that reflects opportunities experienced by the wider community. We acknowledge and say sorry for the hurt, pain and suffering caused by Aboriginal males to our wives, to our children, to our mothers, to our grandmothers, to our granddaughters, to our aunties, to our nieces and to our sisters. We also acknowledge that we need the love and support of our Aboriginal women to help us move forward. (CAAC, 2008, p. 2)

This was an important historic moment for a few different reasons. It promulgated a new public discourse about Aboriginal males that challenged negative societal stereotypes that had frequently depicted them as offenders and the perpetrators of child abuse and violence against women, towards an alternative strengths-based narrative which reflected a heartfelt and emotional response focused on their nurturing and caring qualities. It also provided an opportunity for Aboriginal males to apologise for the harmful actions of a small minority of Aboriginal males and emphasise the important role that Aboriginal females play in their lives. In turn, this emphasised the importance of working together – both Aboriginal males and females – to maintain the health, safety, and wellbeing of their children, partners, families, and community.

Many changes imposed on Aboriginal people by non-Aboriginal people have made it hard for Aboriginal men to bring up their kids with good support (Collard, Adams, Palmer, & McMullan, 2016). Much of Australian history has been a one-sided affair that misrepresents the position of Aboriginal societies, cultures and land tenure. The media images, too, of Aboriginal males have tended to focus on 'deficit' issues such as child abuse or domestic violence. There is no denying that many forms of violence and abuse are taking place in Aboriginal and Torres Strait Islander communities, but from both health promotion and Aboriginal health perspectives, relaying positive identities and strengths-based messages is the most effective mechanism through which to create more culturally safe environments and to promote positive health behaviour change (Fogarty, Lovell, Langenberg, & Heron, 2018).

In Aboriginal cultural settings, Aboriginal males have always helped one another learn about fathering and how to be effective in the role. Emerging scholarship about Aboriginal fathers and fatherhood has also provided guidance and new directions for creating more supportive and health-promoting environments for these men (Reilly & Rees, 2018; Canuto, Harfield, Canuto, & Brown, 2019; Canuto et al., 2019; Canuto, Harfield, Wittert, & Brown, 2019; Canuto, 2019). Indeed, one of the key features of Aboriginal traditions is that family helps out, so that men are not alone when it comes to looking after kids. As we move beyond the stereotypes suggesting that fathers are of little significance, many Aboriginal men have taken a more positive approach to maintaining their role within their communities (Wenitong, 2006, p. 466; Adams, 2006). Our history is also full of Aboriginal males who have quietly maintained their status as leaders and traditional bosses and who have been inspirational as fathers, uncles, and pops (Collard et al., 2016, p. 2).

In the context of this book, it is worth noting that there is an increasing focus on promoting equity and social justice through social work research and practice (Bennett, 2015). This has included discussion about gender equity, particularly concerning, with no disrespect, sexist attitudes and practices in social work contexts that have been challenged. While it is well recognised that men hold more power and privilege in most industrialised contexts, it has also been acknowledged in recent men's health promotion scholarship that the dualistic framing of gender equity has been particularly problematic for acknowledging and addressing the complex health and social inequities faced by marginalised groups of men, particularly those relating to race, age, sexuality, socio-economic status, geography, and disability (Smith, Watkins, & Griffith, 2020). This includes Aboriginal and Torres Strait Islander males, and we reflect on these struggles throughout this chapter.

Unfortunately, social work literature has offered relatively little about ways to engage with, and respond to the needs of, Aboriginal males – with a few notable exceptions (Adams, Mataira, Walker, Hart, & Fleay, 2019; Prehn, 2019). When entering their profession, many social workers have little knowledge of the history surrounding Aboriginal peoples. They cannot understand how and why the history of colonisation has continued to impact Aboriginal people and this is reflected in a range of health and social issues (Bennett, 2015). Many social work educators and students are puzzled by the fact that historical events, such as the Stolen Generations, remain significant for the thinking and behaviour of Aboriginal people and their communities (Bennett, 2015; Bennett & Green, 2019, pp. 2, 4).

Social work in Australia assumes a cloak of cultural sensitivity and cultural valour by 'allowing' Indigenous people and knowledges a space to be considered within the profession. However, the profession retains the power and privilege of determining and controlling how much space will be given, and where this space is allowed within the profession (Bennett, 2015; Smith, Christie, et al., 2019, p. 71). Social workers need to critically examine their role in the ongoing colonisation of Aboriginal people and how it can become an active agent in decolonising not only the social structures that form Australian society, but also social work practice (Bennett & Green, 2019, p. xviii).

Valuing Aboriginal males

Unsurprisingly, Aboriginal and Torres Strait Islander males, which also includes males from other marginalised population groups, are not necessarily considered as high-priority clientele within a social workers' scope of practice. We also recognise that social work is a female-dominated profession, which has historically placed a greater influence on the welfare of women and children and placed male social workers in an uncomfortable professional position with respect to their gender identity (Christie, 2006). The intent here is not to apportion blame, rather to note that there has been a gendered dimension to the way social work theory and practice has evolved over time. This has seen a gradual shift from situating males as the problem (i.e. as negligent offenders or perpetrators) towards males being perceived part of the solution (i.e. as emotionally intelligent carers and nurturers). This has been particularly evident in work relating to fathers (Maxwell, Scourfield, Featherstone, Holland, & Tolman, 2012; Pfitzner, Humphreys, & Hegarty, 2017), domestic and family violence (Casey, 2010), and child welfare (Maxwell et al., 2012). Such narratives help to shift negative societal norms associated with harmful and toxic forms of masculinity – such as those reinforced by health professionals (including social workers), people of authority and the media – that have historically positioned males negatively. However, there is more work to be done. It is difficult to change these discourses when there is overt gender discrimination and inequities experienced by Aboriginal males on a regular basis (Fredericks, Adams, & Best, 2014; Fredericks et al., 2017). The disproportionate representation of Aboriginal males in the justice system is one such example (Blagg, 2016). Blagg (2016) observed that, in many crucial respects, the fundamental nature of the relationship between the criminal justice system and Indigenous people has remained unchanged since invasion when the system was employed as a tool of dispossession. It is disappointing that there is so little focus on the critical efforts of Aboriginal males who work tirelessly with their female counterparts to protect, nurture, and encourage the next generation and maintain positive roles in community and family contexts. This would offer a much more productive focus.

Throughout the chapter we will attempt to unravel the mist and misfortune that is regularly applied to Aboriginal and Torres Strait Islander males. We acknowledge that addressing the health status of Aboriginal and Torres Strait Islanders is an ongoing concern for primary healthcare providers. One avenue of addressing this concern is to closely examine the relationship between Aboriginal culture and health through relevant and culturally appropriate methodologies. One such example includes the recent Lowitja Institute special funding round for a research study to investigate the processes of valuing Aboriginal and Torres Strait Islander young men. The aim was to establish a strengths-based approach to the cultural wellbeing for young Aboriginal and Torres Strait Islander males, in the most critical stages of their transition into adult life. This research is timely as it is emerging at the same time as a global movement that is seeing a reinvigoration of culturally based work (Collard et al., 2016).

Most of the participants (young, elderly, female) in the nationally focused Lowitja-funded research study acknowledged the lack of attention and time invested in young people to value their views, insight, and heartfelt desire to transform their lives. They highlighted the importance of family and communities, believing that their connection to Country and culture bestowed the characteristic strengths within many aspects of their lives. Many had experienced and were accustom to the process of being disadvantaged; living in poverty; marginalised through racism, unemployment, and limited education. They strongly emphasised their desire to become and take on leadership roles to achieve a productive life and the intention of building a safe and cohesive community for their families. These themes were also noted in other Lowitja funded Aboriginal male health research (Smith et al., 2019).

The evidence generated from the valuing Aboriginal and Torres Strait Islander young men research stipulates ample empirical confirmation that there are negative impacts placed on young Aboriginal and Torres Strait Islander male's wellbeing. Current psychological literature suggests that the effects of colonisation on young Aboriginal and Torres Strait Islander males in settled colonies have been a topic of great concern (Adams et al., 2017). The literature, and subsequent Aboriginal health policy responses, also point out that colonisation led to the loss of traditional beliefs, separation from the land, breakdown of traditional structures of leadership and community, and poor achievement in education and employment (Department of Health, 2015; Fisher, Battams, McDermott, Baum, & Macdougall, 2019).

There has been increased interest in recent years in understanding and responding to the relationship between the social and cultural determinants of health (Department of Health, 2015; Fisher et al., 2019). Such commentary has emphasised that community-based and culturally driven solutions to health and wellbeing are required for Aboriginal males to succeed and flourish. Aboriginal males participating in the research expressed the need to explore their diverse identities, strengths, and values; being connected to Country, spirits and to the past being guided by the storylines and songlines. Seriously attaining a clear understanding of what the elders and ancestors have been telling them.

Adams, Collard, Palmer, Fleay, and Bulman (2019) and Shwalb, Shwalb, and Lamb (2013) observed that there is no single way of thinking about respectably working with Aboriginal young males. This is partly because: (1) cultural traditions across the country have long been varied; (2) many contemporary approaches have been strongly shaped by introduced or European approaches to youth work; (3) there are a variety of old and emerging Aboriginal systems that influence families today; and (4) there is a very long and disruptive history of policy impositions on Aboriginal males. Importantly, there is limited evidence to suggest that people working with young Aboriginal males have sufficient experience, training, and competence to engage with this population effectively.

Nor is it the case that work with Aboriginal young males occurs in one place or context. Indeed, the care and support of Aboriginal young males is often shared across the community; has strong involvement across the generations; is built into a range of different organisational contexts and situations; is now being incorporated into modern institutions such as sport, Aboriginal community-controlled organisations, and ranger teams; and through old conventions such as law and cultural ceremony (Adams, Collard, et al., 2019).

The Quop Maaman: Aboriginal Fathering Project (Collard et al., 2016) confirmed that many Aboriginal males were keen on rebuilding their roles as fathers, brothers, uncles, grandfathers, and supporting their sons, nephews, grandchildren, and women. The evidence also demonstrated that a growing group of young men were very actively involved in 'culture'. The ABS data from 2008 (ABS, 2011) demonstrate very high levels of involvement in cultural ceremony with 24% of people 15 years or older attending a ceremony in the 12 months prior, with (47%) having attended a funeral of an Aboriginal relative. Aboriginal males residing in remote area communities are three times more likely to attend a ceremony compared with those in non-remote areas. The evidence also displayed that in the 2008 Aboriginal and Torres Strait Islander Social Survey, 65% of children and young people claim to have been to one or more selected cultural events (fishing and hunting, ceremonies, and NAIDOC events) in the past year. Almost all young people

(98%) said that they would like to participate in cultural events and cultural activities. Of these, 22% did so at least once a month, 29% did so several times a year, and 16% did so once a year (ABS, 2011). This was confirmed by the young males participating in The Quop Maaman: Aboriginal Fathering Project (Collard et al., 2016). Contrary to popular belief, therefore, Aboriginal males have strong connection to their culture. This can form one site where health outreach is delivered in an engaging and culturally responsive manner.

The valuing Aboriginal and Torres Strait Islander young men research project gave us the opportunity to build a strengths-based approach that included Aboriginal and Torres Strait Islander men's (and women's) participation through the use of yarning and film. The filmmaking was important, particularly its 'participatory' style, as it allowed local senior custodians (both males and females) to take on a more traditional and technical research methodology that might otherwise not have occurred. It involved a clear and, in many ways spatial, narrative approach in which collective cultural and traditional stories were shared (Collard et al., 2016; Adams, Collard, et al., 2019). The raw and edited footage was utilised to produce two short documentaries that recorded interviews with Aboriginal males and women talking about culture and health. The documentaries were designed to authenticate examples of cultural solutions in addressing issues associated with men's health. The documentaries are available via the Australian Indigenous HealthInfoNet webpage for Aboriginal communities, Aboriginal Health Workers and other health practitioners aiming to build their understanding of young Aboriginal male health and wellbeing, and as training resources for those working in Aboriginal men's health.

The collection of raw and edited data is an effective way of reporting and disseminating information. The images of senior lawmen and local senior custodians (males and females) provide an evidence-based example of how young Aboriginal males participate in cultural learning. It also demonstrates senior lawmen and local senior custodians sustaining leadership by guiding the young males though cultural ceremonies in the likelihood that they too will become leaders. Importantly, the cultural practices equip young males to endorse, endure, and preserve their cultural positions and values. This is evident and promoted through the documentaries providing a storyline on why we conducted the research and includes Traditional Lawmen talking to young males about the importance and processes of law and culture.

In a separate, but closely linked, Lowitja Institute-funded research project relating to health literacy among young Aboriginal and Torres Strait Islander males in the Northern Territory, yarning sessions and a novel Facebook photovoice approach were used to elicit the voices of this population (Smith, Christie, et al., 2019). This research revealed that young Aboriginal males conceptualise and negotiate health from both Western and Aboriginal paradigms and are constantly resisting and embracing different constructions of masculinity – sometimes simultaneously (Smith, Christie, et al., 2019; Smith, Watkins, & Griffith, 2020). Outreach health promotion efforts that incorporate a deeper focus on relationships between friends, family, and the broader community were highly valued, as were opportunities for the intergenerational exchange of cultural knowledge (Smith, Christie, et al., 2019; Smith, Watkins, & Griffith, 2020). In addition, efforts to embrace emerging social media platforms as a means to engage and interact with this population about their health and wellbeing were deemed to be important (Smith, Watkins, & Griffith, 2020).

These community-focused and participatory research approaches have surfaced a range of innovative practices to help young Aboriginal and Torres Strait Islander males adopt healthier lifestyles and to better understand and manage their chronic health conditions. It is crucially important that future health promotion initiatives tailored to this population concentrate on community-based and culturally relevant interventions. The range of innovative practices that can be adopted must demonstrate a commitment to addressing different dimensions of social and cultural determinants of health and wellbeing that embrace traditional Aboriginal and Torres Strait Islander cultural identity, values, and practices alongside those of Western society.

Understanding Aboriginal and Torres Strait Islander male health

It is well documented that Aboriginal and Torres Strait Islander people, both males and females, have much poorer health outcomes on nearly all measures of health and wellbeing when compared with non-Indigenous Australians (Australian Health Minister's Advisory Council, 2017; Smith, Drummond, Adams, Bonson, & Christie, 2019). In particular, Aboriginal males have a substantially lower life expectancy, higher rates of potentially preventable hospital admissions, and higher rates of suicide than non-Indigenous men (AIHW, 2017; Smith, Adams, & Bonson, 2018; Smith, Drummond, et al., 2019). This represents one of the most significant health inequities in Australia and is considered a global health concern in a broader international men's health promotion context (Smith, Drummond, et al., 2019; Smith, Watkins, & Griffith, 2020). Yet there have been minimal targeted investments to remedy this situation (Fredericks et al., 2017; Smith, Drummond, et al., 2019). Indeed, certain policy interventions – such as the NTER mentioned earlier in this chapter – have further stigmatised Aboriginal and Torres Strait Islander males and have done little to improve the social, environmental, and economic outcomes that impact on their health and wellbeing (Australian Indigenous Doctors' Association and Centre for Health Equity Training, Research and Evaluation, 2010). While there has been a long history of public health advocacy in relation to Aboriginal and Torres Strait Islander male health in Australia (Wenitong, 2002, 2006), the quantum of funding committed to this cause has been grossly insufficient to address the scale of the public health crisis these men face (Smith et al., 2018; Richardson et al., 2019).

It has long been argued that Indigenous male health is strongly affected by the social determinants of health, including economic opportunity, physical infrastructure, and social conditions (Wenitong, 2002; Working Party of Aboriginal and Torres Strait Islander Male Health and Wellbeing Reference Committee, 2004; Fredericks et al., 2017; Smith et al., 2018).

Indeed, a recent review of gendered Indigenous health and wellbeing in Australia identified that:

> Determinants such as housing, education, employment, access to services, social networks, connection with the land, racism, and rates of imprisonment continue to have an enormous impact on male health. Addressing Indigenous male health needs to take a social determinants approach and involve Indigenous males as important participants in defining their social roles, within their own communities and within the broader Australian context. (Fredericks et al., 2017, p. 53)

This unique social determinant of health orientation requires a deep understanding of the nexus between research, policy, and practice contexts as they relate to addressing Aboriginal and Torres Strait Islander male health. It also requires insight into the complex interplay between culture, race, age, and gender, in the way Aboriginal and Torres Strait Islander male identities are formed, shaped, negotiated, and enacted across their life course (Smith, Watkins, & Griffith, 2020). This is important because recent research examining intersections between gender, culture, and health has shown that there are positive cultural and gender attributes that shape the identities of Aboriginal and Torres Strait Islander males (Smith, Christie, et al., 2019). We start this exploration by briefly summarising the research, policy, and practice contributions that have contributed to shaping the Aboriginal and Torres Strait Islander male health discourse in Australia over the past two decades.

Research aimed at better understanding Aboriginal and Torres Strait Islander male health

As mentioned earlier in the chapter, the Lowitja Institute (and its previous iterations) – as Australia's primary national institute for Aboriginal and Torres Strait Islander health research – has played an important role in building the evidence base about ways to strengthen the health of Aboriginal and Torres Strait Islander males, including those intersecting with social determinants of health. It has funded various research projects in areas relating to art and health (McCoy, 2011); men's spaces/sheds (Bulman & Hayes, 2011);

parenting (Robinson, Tyler, Jones, Silburn, & Zubrick, 2012); and families (McEwan et al., 2008). Noteworthy is its relatively recent investment into a nationally competitive grant round that was dedicated to valuing the voices of young Aboriginal and Torres Strait Islander males – as already mentioned above. This resulted in five additional research projects explicitly focused on fathering (Canuto, Harfield, Canuto, & Brown, 2019; Canuto, Towers, Riessen, et al., 2019; Roe, 2020); health and wellbeing (Adams, Collard, et al., 2019; Adams, Mataira, et al., 2019); health literacy (Smith, Christie, et al., 2019; Smith, Drummond, et al., 2019); and rites of passage and Indigenous masculinities (Mukandi et al., 2019). Findings from these projects are only just starting to emerge. Additional research related to Aboriginal male sexual health; Aboriginal males' use of primary health care services (Adams, 2014; Adams, Collins, de Kretser, Dunne, & Holden, 2013; Adams, De Kretser, & Holden, 2003; Canuto, Brown, Wittert, & Harfield, 2018; Canuto, Harfield, Wittert, & Brown, 2019); and Aboriginal male incarceration and alcohol and other drug use (Doyle, Shakeshaft, Guthrie, Snijder, & Butler, 2019) have also emerged in recent years. These provide particularly useful insights into ways the health and prison systems can better accommodate the needs of Aboriginal and Torres Strait Islander males, in contrast to recommendations that place all the onus on individual men. While these studies are all unique in their own right, many of them emphasise the central role that culture, kinship, families, and community play as key determinants that shape Aboriginal and Torres Strait Islander male health. These should be fundamental considerations in subsequent health policy and practice responses.

Policy investments aimed at improving Aboriginal and Torres Strait Islander male health

The first ever *National Male Health Policy* was developed in Australia in 2010 (DHA, 2010a). This policy identified Aboriginal and Torres Strait Islander males as a priority population and directed people towards the *National Aboriginal and Torres Strait Islander Male Health Framework – Guiding Principles* (Department of Health and Ageing, 2010b). However, policy action in the area of Aboriginal and Torres Strait Islander male health preceded the release of this policy. Earlier policy advocacy efforts specific to Aboriginal and Torres Strait Islander male health culminated in key documents and frameworks to help guide program investments, particularly those focused on enhanced Aboriginal community control (Wenitong, 2002; Working Party of Aboriginal and Torres Strait Islander Male Health and Wellbeing Reference Committee, 2004). These early contributions provided a solid foundation from which to advocate for greater investment in Aboriginal and Torres Strait Islander male health at local, state, and national levels. Of course, these efforts have occurred in parallel to other community engagement and professional development opportunities aimed at raising awareness and understanding of Aboriginal and Torres Strait Islander male health. For example, we are about to enter the 10th National Aboriginal and Torres Strait Islander Male Health Convention that is held biannually along- side the National Men's Health Conference facilitated by the Australian Men's Health Forum. In addition, the National Aboriginal Community Controlled Health Organisation (NACCHO) has held multiple Ochre Days across various locations in Australia that have been led by Aboriginal males working in the health sector to identify and discuss emerging health and social issues relevant to the lives of Aboriginal and Torres Strait males and to share stories and insights about how these are best addressed. Noteworthy is the NACCHO *Aboriginal Male Health Futures Blueprint 2013–2030* that was developed during an Ochre Day event (NACCHO, 2013). This reflects a community-driven action plan that extends over a 17-year period with specific reference to social and cultural determinants of health (NACCHO, 2013). This clearly shifts the focus from policy intent to program invest- ment – akin to the mantra of less talk, more action.

Program and service investments aimed at improving Aboriginal and Torres Strait Islander male health

Health-related program and service investments have fluctuated significantly over the past two decades. In response, many Aboriginal Community Controlled Health Organisations have developed their own unique place- based men's health services or programs (Canuto et al., 2018; Canuto, Harfield, Wittert, & Brown, 2019). These include male-specific programs or services embedded with primary health care services, such as outreach programs and men's camps (Department of Health and Ageing, 2010a). However, we have also seen the establishment of dedicated Aboriginal corporations such as the Darwin Indigenous Men's Service and the Men's Outreach Service in Broome. This has placed a much sharper focus on the unique cultural and spiritual needs of Aboriginal and Torres Strait Islander males and provides a much broader conceptualisation of wellbeing than most mainstream health services currently offer. In addition, a number of organisations have also turned atten- tion to establishing healing spaces for Aboriginal men, such as Mibbinbah Spirit Healing and the Healing Foundation (Bulman & Hayes, 2011; Healing Foundation, 2015). This has been paralleled by a substantial growth in Indigenous men's sheds and groups (Southcombe, Cavanagh, & Bartram, 2014; Cavanagh, Shaw, & Bertram, 2016). These settings-based approaches are a welcome addition to the Aboriginal and Torres Strait Islander male health landscape and provide new and innovative ways of engagement that redirect attention towards making health programs and services more accessible and responsive to their needs. In addition, there have been multiple practitioner guides and resources developed to help health professionals better engage

Aboriginal and Torres Strait Islander males in discussion about their health (Healthy Male, 2018), again shifting the balance of responsibility from individual patients to health services and systems.

Health literacy abilities are generally conceptualised as skills essential to successfully navigating health – and are linked to increased wellbeing and improved health outcomes. Significantly, it is important for social workers to be understand that emerging scholarship locates culture, gender, and age as influential determinants of health literacy. This often overlaps with other factors that shape a person's identity, including their sexuality.

Gender politics, sexuality, and colonial practices in the context of young Aboriginal males

This section aims to highlight the intersections between gender politics, sexuality, and colonial practices as a useful example to guide social work practice relating to Aboriginal males. Historically, LGBTI people have faced exclusion and marginalisation. This has been exacerbated for Aboriginal people that identify as LGBTI that have unique ways of describing their distinct histories, experiences, needs, and understandings of their health and wellbeing. Aboriginal gay men have often felt left out of the conversation around masculinities. For decades, some nods toward the LGBTI space in an Aboriginal and Torres Strait Islander context has been increasingly Western-oriented and fairly tokenistic. Significant evidence is found through work undertaken in primary healthcare (Rosenstreich, Comfort, & Martin, 2011; Zeeman, 2019). Aboriginal gay men have significant leadership roles in their communities, and in families, because the role of male leadership for *all* Aboriginal men goes well and truly beyond the raising of one's own children. Aboriginal men are leaders, mentors, role models, and champions in a range of careers, social work, and in the home. Negative Western ideas about sex and masculinities have degraded the role of all men, but they have affected homosexual men double-fold, and Aboriginal homosexual men triple-fold. These cumulative impacts are important to unpack.

Culturally and emotionally, sex and sexuality are key in navigating a sense of self, and security, and is interwoven with forging relationships, invoking creativity, and paired crucially with a sense of purpose and being. The anonymity element of male apps such as Grindr, can negatively impact what should be a positive, safe experience (Jaspal, 2017). The ability to use these apps with complete anonymity leads to a culture of sex and other behaviour without consequence. Even anonymous sex needs to be carried out with the regard of the safety of others, which can be one with a better sense of community, services, and safe sexual health practices, and healthy males take responsibility and care in these areas of their lives, which challenges a notion of toxic masculinity (Callander, Holt, & Newman, 2015; Wiele & Tong, 2014).

Homosexuality among Aboriginal men is less about historical assumptions that have been made, but more of a contemporary human rights issue. Aboriginal gay men face a range of intersectional discriminatory obstacles in their social and economic lives, as well as their cultural and spiritual practices (Australian Human Rights Commission, 2018). They are at risk of being alienated by a range of people, institutions, and approaches that already devalue males. Generally speaking, they do not conform to traditional models of patriarchy, and actively resist white hegemony.

The ban on homosexual activity has been a largely British colonial practice, worldwide. The persecution and harsh treatment of the Irish under the British control manifest itself notably and historically in the 1895 trials of Oscar Fingal O'Flahertie Wilde, a world-famous Irish poet and playwright, who was a notable figure in the aesthetic movement before being criminally convicted of gross indecency for his sexual activity with young adult males. His imprisonment in Reading Gaol under a British regime led to his early death just three years after release, during his exile in France. The trials of *Wilde* v. *Queensberry* over libel and, subsequently, *Regina* v. *Wilde* brought homosexuality itself on trial:

> 'The love that dare not speak its name' in this century is such a great affection of an elder for a younger man as there was between David and Jonathan, such as Plato made the very basis of his philosophy, and such as you find in the sonnets of Michelangelo and Shakespeare. It is that deep spiritual affection that is as pure as it is perfect. It dictates and pervades great works of art, like those of Shakespeare and Michelangelo, and those two letters of mine, such as they are. It is in this century misunderstood, so much misunderstood that it may be described as 'the love that dare not speak its name', and on that account of it I am placed where I am now. It is beautiful, it is fine, it is the noblest form of affection. There is nothing unnatural about it. It is intellectual, and it repeatedly exists between an older and a younger man, when the older man has intellect, and the younger man has all the joy, hope and glamour of life before him. That it should be so, the world does not understand. The world mocks at it, and sometimes puts one in the pillory for it. (Wilde, 1895)

These laws – and British thoughts about sexuality – have had as much an influence in Australia as they have on Ireland through practices of colonisation. Sodomy laws, which targeted gay men, not lesbian women or heterosexual people, prohibited them from engaging in practices classed as sodomy under such laws. Homosexual men faced the death penalty, which was barely minimised to life in prison where people would die in unsanitary conditions or from hard labour, regularly (Aldrich, 2002).

Historical researchers such as Bill Stanner, Norman Tindale, A.P. Elkin, and Ralph Piddington have claimed that Aboriginal people had not been homosexual before colonisation (Australian Law Reform Commission, 2010). However, their research is more a product of their time and the social influences on their work, rather than any solid, objective evidence for such a claim. Stanner was a product of early Federation era thinking, Tindale took great liberties as a white cataloguer of Indigenous knowledges and Aboriginal practices, especially from a salvationist Christian position. Elkin was an Anglican clergyman, and Piddington was also an early Federation-era Australian. The backgrounds, and mindsets of these white – presumably heterosexual – men are of an undeniably anti-homosexual disposition, inconsistent with the ancient people they attempted to classify and categorise, as much as they are today with a contemporary zeitgeist of multicultural, humanistic, and diverse society.

It is extremely important to remember that, when serving these communities, the biggest struggle for those who identify as part of the LGBTI community is that they are currently not being treated with respect or in a socially just way that promotes health and social equity (Stecker, 2020). The LGBTI community have been struggling for decades for the same rights as their heterosexual counterparts. Though the struggles have given many rewards, there is still a stigma surrounding the health and needs of the LGBTI community.

A study in the United States showed a significant relationship between organisational LGBTI competence and individual LGBTI competence within schools of social work and that programs with greater LGBT competence also had students who felt more competent to work with sexual minorities. These findings suggest schools of social work can take substantive action at an organisational level to improve the professional LGBTI competence of future social workers (McCarty, 2018). While openness about sex and sexualities is still rather cloistered in Australia – and the primary target of a culture war – significant new work has been undertaken in social work, enhancing conversations about the everyday sexual lives lived by Australians, challenging assumptions made about diversity, homophobic behaviours and representations, as well as sexual orientation (Rowntree, 2013). This is timely, as social workers have an obligation to be culturally competent and sensitive to the unique needs of the communities they serve. When working with individuals in the LGBTI community, we must acknowledge the ways in which societal and social practices influence, oppress, and discriminate against them.

Fathering

In this section, we turn our attention to Aboriginal fathers. Globally, Indigenous fathers are arguably one of the most socially disenfranchised populations with monumental systemic barriers to wellbeing and little social advocacy (Ball, Roberge, Joe, & George, 2007; Canuto, Harfield, Canuto, & Brown, 2019; Canuto, Towers, Riessen, et al., 2019; Canuto, Harfield, Wittert, & Brown, 2019; Canuto, 2019). In recent studies and reviews the lasting negative impacts of colonial government interventions on Aboriginal fathers have been noted, with the dispersion and diminution of Indigenous families, clans, communities, and cultures; and the ongoing removal of Indigenous children from their families (Ball et al., 2007; Canuto, Harfield, Canuto, & Brown, 2019; Canuto, Towers, Riessen, et al., 2019; Canuto, Harfield, Wittert, & Brown, 2019; Canuto, 2019). Many Aboriginal fathers have identified historical and intergenerational trauma as a monolithic set of causal factors that have shaped their experiences. Many also felt that programs, policies, and society as a whole were biased towards favouring women and children (Ball, 2010, p. 14). For example, fathers raising their children as lone parents expressed the sense of being left without help to raise their child – noting that after separation or divorce there is a perception of bias in favour of awarding custody to mothers (Ball, 2010, p. 14). While this may be true in some circumstances, we recognise this field of research is complex and that parental alienation in the Australian family court system is a highly contested space (Rathus, 2020) for both Aboriginal and non-Indigenous males alike.

There appears to be little research that explores the positive aspects of Aboriginal fatherhood.

Research on fatherhood in Indigenous cultures, including Australian Indigenous communities, is underexplored when compared with research conducted with men from white, married, well-educated, and middle-to-high socio-economic backgrounds (Reilly & Rees, 2018, p. 423; Canuto, Harfield, Canuto, & Brown, 2019; Canuto, Towers, Riessen, et al., 2019; Canuto, Harfield, Wittert, Brown, 2019). The available literature tends to highlight responses virtually exclusively to the health and wellbeing of women and relating to the negative consequences of male behaviour. Furthermore, even where attention has been paid to a broader concept of male health, programs and action have remained predominantly small scale, underfunded, and unsustainable (Brown, 2004, p. 1). Anecdotal evidence and local knowledge, however, strongly suggests that the parenting role is positively associated with men's psychological well-being (Reilly & Rees, 2018, p. 423, Adams, 2006; Laliberté, Haswell, & Tsey, 2012; McCalman et al., 2006; Tsey, Patterson, Whiteside, Baird, & Baird, 2002; Tsey et al., 2004).

Antiquity demonstrates males have quietly maintained their status as leaders and who have been inspirational as fathers, uncles and grandfathers. Indigenous fathers' experiences unfold in a socio-historical context fraught with difficulties (Ball, 2010, p. 1). The erosion of Aboriginal and Torres Strait Islander (and Indigenous males globally) men's roles have profoundly affected their capacity to function as positive role models (Adams, 2006; Hammill, 2001). Aboriginal and Torres Strait Islander males have strong goals and aspirations as fathers, but have to overcome barriers that delayed their ability to achieve them. It is also important to note that cultural strengths and sources of resilience are often unseen in research and community programs driven by Western perspectives (Ball, 2010, p. 1).

Indigenous males and men of colour remain on the margins of mainstream society and have no visible representation (Smith, Watkins, Griffith et al., 2020). Their culturally traditional male roles and entitlements in family and community structures have been forcibly stripped from them by government policies (Ball, 2010, p. 3). In many Indigenous cultures' fatherhood is an important position within the family structure, but in many instances male parenting skills are vastly overlooked. In today's society, Indigenous males as fathers rarely rate a mention unless framed in the negative, or as the cause of dysfunctional family life (Reilly & Rees, 2018). Consequently, the roles and responsibilities of Aboriginal and Torres Strait Islander men within parenting have largely been neglected or ignored (Canuto, Harfield, Canuto, & Brown, 2019).

The history of post-colonial Australia has in part been negative by its attempts to destroy Aboriginal family systems and importantly removing and restricting Aboriginal men from their roles and involvement in fathering. Despite this, Aboriginal males have been able to continue to maintain a range of positive roles in the lives of their communities, central in traditional knowledge transmission, work, leadership, and the raising of children. Today, Aboriginal fathering practices have been greatly impacted on by a range of forces, including institutional child removal, access to traditional lands and economies, the imposition of market economies, the introduction of foreign technologies, forced language loss, the introduction of various forms of Christianity, Western epistemology, and modern expressions of culture. At the same time, many Aboriginal men continue to be shaped by a renaissance of culture, language, and expressions of identity. There is also good evidence that a range of Aboriginal men are participating in a movement to reacquaint others with strong fathering through their involvement in law and culture, projects to support family health and wellbeing, education, language regeneration, sport, and the arts (Collard et al., 2016).

Sequential accounts from Europeans settlers also acknowledge that traditional Indigenous fathers were kind and involved parents, and violence was an infrequent exception to the rule (Elkington, 2017, p. 3; Taonui, 2010, p. 195). Taonui (2010, p. 195) informs that 'the current high levels of violence towards women and children has genesis in the post-contact period'. International literature conveys similar effects of colonial practices amongst other Indigenous cultures that have jeopardised the family structure, hindering positive family outcomes and isolating families from support through colonisation, historical trauma, and urbanisation (Elkington, 2017; Taonui, 2010).

In recent years we have observed a significant increase in recognition of the prevalence and impacts of domestic and family violence in Aboriginal and Torres Strait Islander communities. However, it has only been recently that mainstream literature has offered limited insights into the pathways, trajectories, and context for violence within the Australian Indigenous context. Consequently, strategies to reduce disproportionate levels of violence in Indigenous communities have predominately relied on the supposed culturalisation of Western violence prevention programs, which assumes that the factors associated with violence are fundamentally the same. Aboriginal males emphasised the need to understand disproportionate levels of family violence in Aboriginal and Torres Strait Islander communities in the context of historical and continued colonial and systemic violence as a crucial step to negotiating support for a genuine Aboriginal and Torres Strait Islander framework for violence prevention. The failure to do this has led to many inappropriate and ill targeted strategies that have had limited impact on reducing violence to date (Healing Foundation, 2015, p. 5).

Over the years, the media, Government Ministers and other commentators have promoted negative portrayals in connection of family violence and child abuse in Aboriginal and Torres Strait Islander communities, often erroneously conflating this with culture. As stated earlier in the chapter, there is no denying that many forms of violence and abuse is taking place in Aboriginal and Torres Strait Islander communities and this is not to say that other Australians do not suffer from these maladies. However, such statistics are more commonly used to define Indigenous Australian men, families, and communities compared with other groups of men.

When identifying aspects of family violence and child abuse in Aboriginal communities, there is also a need to acknowledge the underlying factors that may be the causes associated with these anti-social behaviours, rather than the drawing on assumptions. For example, the media often associate violence in the wider community as being related to alcohol, drugs, and other substances, and sometime associate it with culture (e.g. The Northern Territory Intervention or NTER). As mentioned above, though, much research and personal accounts have revealed that the deep-seated causes of these issues often relate to historical trauma and the ongoing impacts of colonisation. Without programs actively targeting these underlying issues, our responses will not be effective.

Historically, a father's connection to his children has often been measured by their economic contribution to the family. Engaging men as fathers both in working towards providing safety for children and service provision can be difficult, particularly for those men who contend with issues of identity and social and economic inclusion. The increasing involvement of women in paid employment has forced a broadening of parenting roles and conceptualisations of fatherhood (Davis, Luchters, & Holmes, 2012, p. 3).

The significant social and cultural changes that continue to occur have resulted in greater social expectations of men's family roles and greater expectations of fathers themselves. Women's increased involvement in the paid labour market and the changing expectations and aspirations of men in their role as fathers has necessitated significant changes in both family composition and structure. There has been a broadening of fathering roles and men who identify or are identified as fathers. One of the significant challenges for men is to adapt to these changes in ways that provide positive meaning to their fathering role and identity, strengthen their relationships with their children and partner and focus on fathering behaviours that are nurturant, supportive, and protective (Davis et al., 2012, p. 11). Providing Aboriginal and Torres Strait Islander males with the resources and support to navigate these transitions is essential in producing happy and harmonious communities.

Collective fathering is beginning to be seen as essential in strengthening the bonds between men in their role as fathers and endorsing the importance of fatherhood to male identities. The growth of Aboriginal men's groups throughout Australia continues to facilitate the 'healing' of Aboriginal men and encourage dialogue around the importance of Aboriginal fathers to families and communities. The support of men's groups is central in providing a medium for Aboriginal men to voice their needs and aspirations (Reilly & Rees, 2018, p. 421). Anecdotal evidence and local knowledge, however, strongly suggests that the parenting role is positively associated with men's psychological wellbeing (Reilly & Rees, 2018, p. 421; Adams, 2006; Laliberté et al., 2012; McCalman et al., 2006; Tsey et al., 2002, 2004).

Indigenous society accepts that there is men's business and women's business and that this understanding is not based around inequality (Bessarab, 2006; Fredericks, 2010; Fredericks et al., 2014). Unlike Western societies, where gender has been a marker of empowerment (male) and subordination (female), gender in Aboriginal societies defines different fields of influence and empowerment (Brock, 2001). This gender-specific authority is protected by maintaining a separation between 'male and female spheres'. These 'male and female spheres' are known as men's business and women's business (Brock, 2001, p. 9). The activities and knowledges relating to each gender's business are not shared between the genders (Brock, 2001, p. 9; Fredericks et al., 2014). Even today, Indigenous people uphold the separation of men's and women's business, particularly in relation to health interventions (Fredericks et al., 2014). This does not mean that Aboriginal males and females are unable to work collaboratively from a gender-relations approach with respect to addressing a broad range of public health issues. Indeed, there are multiple examples of family- and community-oriented health promotion programs that successfully adopt a gender lens in a collaborative way. However, it is an acknowledgement there are some health spheres where gender-specificity is a cultural requirement and should not be ignored.

Future research is needed that involves Aboriginal and Torres Strait Islander women and men to build strong evidence of what works in improving gendered Indigenous health outcomes (Fredericks et al., 2017, p. 4). What we really need is research that builds on best practice, informed by intervention and measurement studies, so that we can build a better system for working with Aboriginal and Torres Strait Islander people (Fredericks et al., 2017, p. 56).

Conclusion

Generally, Aboriginal and Torres Strait Islander males had meaningful, active roles with authority and status. The kinship system ensured that everyone had clearly defined responsibilities and obligations. They are responsible for the management and maintenance of traditional obligations, sacred objects, spiritual matters, and the performance of rituals. They provided leadership, educated the young, and are custodians of the law. Young males had a clear passage to manhood; a test of worthiness and courage, designed to instil discipline, self-reliance, obedience, connectedness, and co-operation (Adams & McCoy, 2010).

Yet Indigenous men globally remain on the margins of mainstream society and have no visible representation. Their cultural roles and privileges in family and community structures and contexts have been effectively taken away from them (Ball, 2010, p. 3). Many Aboriginal and Torres Strait Islander males in Australia are floundering; feeling lost in the confusion of competing and conflicting pressures; cut loose from their cultural and historical bearings. However, most are constructing a variety of new identities in these personal journey: while keeping themselves deeply rooted in their ancient sources of Indigenous identity: in Country, Indigenous law, relationships, language, history, and culture (Lowe & Spry, 2002, p. 28). These Indigenous identities are also shaped by other factors that relate to gender, age, sexuality, geography, and disability. However, further research and strategy development is required to respond to these complex intersections more comprehensively.

Strategies that have often excluded the 'taboo' of homosexuality have put a significant cohort of gay and bisexual Aboriginal men at risk. The shame around sex, and the increasingly anonymous nature of same-sex behaviours on apps such as Grindr, present some of the most challenging psychological and physical risks to Aboriginal men in this decade. Assault and substance use are interwoven with homophobia, racism, and negative views on bodies and identities.

As mentioned, Australia's Northern Territory Intervention and *Little Children Are Sacred* report have had continuing colonial effects on Aboriginal and Torres Strait Islander males. There has been support from the Aboriginal community-controlled health sector and community groups to develop unique place-based men's health services or programs. This has focussed on the cultural and spiritual needs of Aboriginal and Torres Strait Islander males. It also provides a much broader conceptualisation of wellbeing than most mainstream health services currently offer.

Both Aboriginal males and females understand that this process of recovery requires support and partnership with each other. A powerful example of this partnership and support between Indigenous males and females occurred during the 3rd National Men's Health Conference in Alice Springs (1999). Indigenous women and children joined their men to present their issues and claims to the conference (Lowe & Spry, 2002, p. 46). This was followed by the Summit, initiated by the Central Australian Aboriginal Congress, which allowed nearly 400 men to discuss different strategies to assist Aboriginal men to resume their role as protectors of the family and the broader community. This was the first Aboriginal Male Health Summit titled 'Taking Care of our Children, Taking the Next Steps', where Aboriginal males reflected on the important connection between men's health, community wellbeing, and social relationships, and the participating men presented an apology (the *Inteyerrkwe* Statement) to Aboriginal women and children (Indigenous Law Bulletin, 2008), as already outlined earlier in this chapter.

We mentioned the NACCHO ten-point plan that focuses on innovation, leadership, and accountability, which reinforces the need to invest in capacity building, supporting, and expanding Aboriginal community-controlled health services to ensure more Aboriginal people can access more services in more places around the country, including urban, regional, and remote.

A recent Indigenous Male Research Strategy Think Tank held in the Northern Territory has made some significant inroads in the men's health promotion landscape in Australia (Smith, Drummond, et al., 2019). It identified multiple priority areas, observing that suicide has become one of the significant contributors to premature mortality among Aboriginal males – it estimated that suicide rates among Aboriginal people are at least 40% higher than the national average (Smith et al., 2018). The Think Tank added to the literature about understanding men's health inequities and possible investment in men's health in Australia (Smith et al., 2018; Smith, Drummond, et al., 2019).

The vision of male Indigenous leaders and men's groups has been to take greater responsibility themselves to improve the status of men's health and play their rightful role as leaders, fathers, uncles, husbands, and grandfathers. The empowerment of Indigenous males is achieved through holistic strategies that allow cultural healing and address the multiple determinants of men's health, such as discrimination, employment, education, high incarceration rates, and poor self-esteem (Adams & McCoy, 2010; Wenitong, 2002, 2006).

In order to understand the health and wellbeing of Aboriginal males, social workers need to accept and understand that the historical, cultural, physiological, psychosocial, economic, environmental, and political contexts faced by males are different from those faced by women (Brown, 2004, p. 1; Adams & McCoy, 2010). The occurrence, determinants, experience, prognosis, treatment, and prevention of ill health among males are different to that of women, and this needs to be better accommodated with social work practice. Furthermore, the process of accessing, interacting with, and utilising health systems for health gains are different because of intersections between gender and culture (Brown, 2004, p. 1; Adams et al., 2003, p. 3; Adams & McCoy, 2010). Social workers need to recognise that, despite the differences in the contexts in which Aboriginal and Torres Strait Islander males reside, whether it be urban, rural, or remote, traditional or non-traditional, the problems they face and the needs to be addressed are remarkably similar (Adams & McCoy, 2010). The social work profession has an important role to play in embracing these alternative ways of working to benefit the health and wellbeing of Indigenous males globally.

 ## Discussion Questions

1. How could I change the colonial processes within social work practice?

2. Has this chapter improved my knowledge about Aboriginal males, and do I have the confidence to address their issues?

3. As a non-Aboriginal person, how would I approach Aboriginal or Torres Strait Islander social workers to seek their advice on how to address Aboriginal needs rather telling Aboriginal people 'to get over it and move on'?

4. As an Aboriginal/Torres Strait Islander social worker, what course of action would I take to overcome the mistrust of Aboriginal and Torres Strait Islander people towards social workers?

5. What are the messages is the chapter telling me, and as a social worker, how would I address these issues?

 ## Further Reading

Adams, M., Mataira, P., Walker, S., Hart, M., & Fleay, J. J. (2019). Colonialism and the atrophy of Indigenous male identities. In B. Bennett & S. Green (Eds.), *Our voices*. Palgrave Macmillan Publications.

Smith, J., Drummond, M., Adams, M., Bonson, J., & Christie, B. (2019a). Chapter 31: Understanding men's health inequities in Australia. In D. Griffiths, M. Bruce, & R. Thorpe (Eds.), *Handbook on men's health disparities* (pp. 498–509). New York, NY: Routledge.

Blagg, H. (2016). *Crime, aboriginality and the decolonisation of justice* (2nd ed.). The Federation Press.

Collard, L., Adams, M., Palmer, D., & McMullan, J. (2016). *Quop Maaman: Aboriginal fathering project*. Perth, WA: Moodjar Consultancy.

Fredericks, B., Adams, M., & Best, O. (2014). Indigenous gendered health perspectives. In O. Best & B. Fredericks (Eds.), *Yatdjuligin: Aboriginal and Torres Strait Islander Nursing and Midwifery Care*. Melbourne, VIC: Cambridge University Press.

Fredericks, B., Daniels, C., Judd, J., Bainbridge, R., Clapham, K., Longbottom, M., Adams, M., Bessarab, D., Collard, L., Andersen, C., Duthie, D., & Ball, R. (2017). *Gendered Indigenous health and wellbeing within the Australian health system: A review of the literature*. Rockhampton, QLD: CQUniversity.

References

Adams, M. (2006). *Working towards changing the negative image of Aboriginal and Torres Strait Islander males*. In Proceedings from Victims of Crime conference, Darwin Airport Resort.

Adams, M. (2014). *Men's business: A study into Aboriginal and Torres Strait Islander men's sexual and reproductive health*. Canberra, ACT: Magpie Goose Publishing.

Adams, M., Collard, L., Palmer, D., Fleay, J. J., & Bulman, J. (2019). *Valuing Aboriginal and Torres Strait Islander young males: A systematic review*. Australian Indigenous Health*InfoNet*. Edith Cowan University (Unpublished).

Adams, M., Collins, V., de Kretser, D., Dunne, M., & Holden, C. (2013). Male reproductive health disorders among Aboriginal and Torres Strait Islander men: A hidden problem? *Medical Journal of Australia, 198*(1), 33–38.

Adams, M., De Kretser, D., & Holden, C. (2003). Male sexual and reproductive health among the Aboriginal and Torres Strait Islander population. *Rural and Remote Health, 3*, 153. Available: www.rrh.org.au/journal/article/153

Adams, M., Mataira, P., Walker, S., Hart, M., & Fleay, J. J. (2019). Colonialism and the atrophy of Indigenous male identities. In B. Bennett & S. Green (Eds.). *Our voices*. South Yarra, VIC: Palgrave Macmillan Publications.

Adams, M., Mataira, P. J., Walker, S., Hart, M., Drew, N., & Fleay, J. J. (2017). Cultural identity and practices associated with the health and well-being of Indigenous males. *Ab-Original Journal of Indigenous Studies and First Nations and First Peoples' Cultures, 1*(1), 42–62.

Adams, M., & McCoy, B. (2010). Lives of Indigenous Australian men. In R. Thackrah & K. Scott, (Eds.) *Indigenous Australian health and cultures. An introduction for health professionals* (pp. 127–151). Frenchs Forest, NSW: Pearson Australia.

Aldrich, R. (2002). *Colonialism and homosexuality*. New York, NY: Routledge.

Anaya, J. (2010). *Observations on the Northern Territory Emergency Response in Australia*. United Nations Special Rapporteur on the situation of human rights and fundamental freedoms of indigenous people.

Australian Bureau of Statistics. (2011). Culture, heritage and leisure: Connections with cultural groups and the land. In *Aboriginal and Torres Strait Islander wellbeing: A focus on children and youth*, 4725.0.

Australian Health Ministers' Advisory Council (AHMAC). (2017). *Aboriginal and Torres Strait Islander health performance framework: 2017 report*. Canberra, ACT: AHMAC.

Australian Human Rights Commission. (2018). *Brotherboys, sistergirls and LGBT Aboriginal and Torres Strait Islander peoples*. Canberra, ACT: Australian Human Rights Commission.

Australian Indigenous Doctors' Association and Centre for Health Equity Training, Research and Evaluation, UNSW. (2010). *Health impact assessment of the Northern Territory Emergency Response*. Canberra, ACT: Australian Indigenous Doctors' Association.

Australian Institute of Health Welfare. (2017). *The health of Australia's males*. Canberra, ACT: Australian Institute of Health and Welfare, Australian Government.

Australian Law Reform Commission. (2010). *Marriages in Aboriginal societies today*. Canberra, ACT: Australian Government. Retrieved from: www.alrc. gov.au

Ball, J. (2010). Indigenous fathers reconstituting circles of care. *American Journal of Community Psychology: Special Issue on Men, Masculinity, Wellness, Health and Social Justice – Community-based Approaches, 45*, 124–138. doi: https://doi.org/10.1007/s10464-009-9293-1.

Ball, J., Roberge, C., Joe, L., & George, R. (2007). *Fatherhood: Indigenous men's journeys*. Early Childhood Development, Intercultural Partnerships. The Social Sciences and Humanities Research Council of Canada.

Bennett, B. (2015). "Stop deploying your white privilege on me!": Aboriginal and Torres Strait Islander engagement with the Australian Association of Social Workers. *Australian Social Work, 68*(1), 19–31.

Bennett, B., & Green, S. (2019). *Our voices: Aboriginal social work* (2nd ed.). South Yarra, VIC: Palgrave Macmillan Publications.

Bessarab, D. (2006). *A study into the meanings of gender by Aboriginal people living in urban (Perth) and regional (Broome) settings*. Unpublished PhD thesis. Perth, WA: Curtin University.

Blagg, H. (2016). *Crime, Aboriginality and the decolonisation of justice* (2nd ed.). Annandale, NSW: The Federation Press.

Brock, P. (2001). Aboriginal women, politics and land. In P. Brock (Ed.), *Words and silences: Aboriginal women, politics and land*. Sydney, NSW: Allen & Unwin.

Brown, A. (2004). *Building on the strengths: A Review of male health in the Anangu Pitjantjatjara lands*. Nganampa Health Council. Menzies School of Health Research.

Bulman, J., & Hayes, R. (2011). Mibbinbah and spirit healing: Fostering safe, friendly spaces for Indigenous males in Australia. *International Journal of Men's Health, 10*(1), 6–25.

Callander, D., Holt, M., & Newman, C. E. (2015). 'Not everyone's gonna like me': Accounting for race and racism in sex and dating web services for gay and bisexual men. *Ethnicities, 16*(1), 3–21. doi: https://doi. org/10.1177/1468796815581428.

Canuto, K. (2019). Time to stop flogging a dead horse? *Medical Journal of Australia, 211*(1), 12–13.

Canuto, K., Brown, A., Wittert, G., & Harfield, S. (2018). Understanding the utilization of primary health care services by Indigenous men: A systematic review. *BMC Public Health, 18*(1), 1198. doi: https://doi.org/10.1186/s12889-018-6093-2.

Canuto, K., Harfield, S., Wittert, G., & Brown, A. (2019). Listen, understand, collaborate developing innovative strategies to improve health service utilisation by Aboriginal and Torres Strait Islander men. *Australian and New Zealand Journal of Public Health, 43*(4), 307–309. doi: https://doi.org/10.1111/1753-6405.12922.

Canuto, K., Harfield, S. G., Canuto, K. J., & Brown, A. (2019). Aboriginal and Torres Strait Islander men and parenting: A scoping review. *Australian Journal of Primary Health, 26*, 1–9. doi: https://doi.org/10.1071/PY19106.

Canuto, K., Towers, K., Riessen, J., Perry, J., Bond, S., Chee, D. A., & Brown, A. (2019). "Anybody can make kids; it takes a real man to look after your kids": Aboriginal men's discourse on parenting. *PLoS One, 14*(11), e0225395.

Canuto, K., Wittert, G., Harfield, S., & Brown, A. (2018). 'I feel more comfortable speaking to a male': Aboriginal and Torres Strait Islander men's discourse on utilizing primary health care services. *International Journal for Equity in Health, 17*, 185.

Casey, E. (2010). Strategies for engaging men as anti-violence allies: Implications for ally movements. *Advances in Social Work, 11*(2), 267–282.

Cavanagh, J., Shaw, A., & Bertram, T. (2016). An investigation of Aboriginal and Torres Strait Islander men's learning in Men's Sheds in Australia. *Australian Aboriginal Studies, 1*, 55–67.

Christie, A. (2006). Negotiating the uncomfortable intersections between gender and professional identities in social work. *Critical Social Policy, 26*(2), 390–411.

Collard, L., Adams, M., Palmer, D., & McMullan, J. (2016). *Quop Maaman: Aboriginal fathering project*. Perth, WA: Moodjar Consultancy.

Davis, J., Luchters, S., & Holmes, W. (2012). *Men and maternal and newborn health: Benefits, harms, challenges and potential strategies for engaging men*. Melbourne, VIC: Compass: Women's and Children's Health Knowledge Hub.

Department of Health. (2015). *Implementation plan for the National Aboriginal and Torres Strait Islander Health Plan 2013–2023*. Canberra, ACT: Australian Government.

Department of Health and Ageing (DHA). (2010a). *National male health policy*. Canberra, ACT: Australian Government.

Department of Health and Ageing (DHA). (2010b). *National male health policy supporting document: National Aboriginal and Torres Strait Islander male health framework – Guiding principles*. Canberra, ACT: Australian Government.

Doyle, M., Shakeshaft, A., Guthrie, J., Snijder, M., & Butler, T. (2019). A systematic review of evaluations of prison-based alcohol and other drug use behavioural treatment for men. *Australian and New Zealand Journal of Public Health, 43*(2), 120–130. doi: https://doi.org/10.1111/17536405.12884.

Elkington, A. (2017). The everyday lives of young Māori fathers: An explorative study. *Journal of Indigenous Wellbeing, 2*(3), Article 1. Published by Te Rau Matatini.

Fisher, M., Battams, S., McDermott, D., Baum, F., & Macdougall, C. (2019). How the social determinants of Indigenous health became policy reality for Australia's National Aboriginal and Torres Strait Islander Health Plan. *Journal of Social Policy, 48*(1), 169–89.

Fogarty, W., Lovell, M., Langenberg, J., & Heron, M. J. (2018). *Deficit discourse and strengths-based approaches: Changing the narrative of Aboriginal and*

Torres Strait Islander health and wellbeing. Melbourne, VIC: The Lowitja Institute.

Fredericks, B. (2010). Re-empowering ourselves: Australian Aboriginal women. *SIGNS: Journal of Women in Culture and Society, 35*(3), 546–550.

Fredericks, B., Adams, M., & Best, O. (2014). Indigenous gendered health perspectives. In O. Best & B. Fredericks (Eds.), *Yatdjuligin: Aboriginal and Torres Strait Islander nursing and midwifery care*. Melbourne, VIC: Cambridge University Press.

Fredericks, B., Daniels, C., Judd, J., Bainbridge, R., Clapham, K., Longbottom, M., Adams, M., Bessarab, D., Collard, L., Andersen, C., Duthie, D., & Ball, R. (2017). *Gendered Indigenous health and wellbeing within the Australian Health System: A review of the literature*. Rockhampton, QLD: CQUniversity.

Hammill, J. (2001). *The culture of masculinity in an Australian Indigenous community*. The Society for International Development. SAGE Publications.

Healing Foundation. (2015). *Our men our healing: Creating hope, respect, and reconnection. Evaluation report*. Canberra, ACT: Healing Foundation.

Healthy Male (Andrology Australia). (2018). *Clinical summary guide: Engaging Aboriginal and Torres Strait Islander men in primary care settings*. Melbourne, VIC: Healthy Male.

Indigenous Law Bulletin. (2008). Aboriginal Male Health Summit – "Inteyerrkwe Statement". *IndigLawB, 26*(2), 7.

Jaspal, R. (2017). Gay men's construction and management of identity on Grindr. *Sexuality & Culture, 21*, 187–204. doi: https://doi.org/10.1007/s12119-016-9389-3.

Laliberté, A., Haswell, M., & Tsey, K. (2012). Promoting the health of Aboriginal Australians through empowerment: Eliciting the components of the Family Well-being Empowerment and Leadership Programme. *Global Health Promotion, 19*, 29–40.

Lowe, H. J., & Spry, F. (2002) *Living male: Journeys of Aboriginal and Torres Strait Islander males towards better health and well-being* (Indigenous Male Health Discussion Paper). Male Health Policy Unit. Published by the Northern Territory Male Health Reference Committee.

Maxwell, N., Scourfield, J., Featherstone, B., Holland, S., & Tolman, R. (2012). Engaging fathers in child welfare services: A narrative review of recent research evidence. *Child & Family Social Work, 17*(2), 160–169.

McCalman, J., Tsey, K., Wenitong, M., Whiteside, M., Haswell, M., James, Y. C., & Wilson, A. (2006). *Indigenous men's groups – What the literature says*. Cairns, QLD: James Cook University.

McCarty, D. (2018). LGBT-competence in social work education: The relationship of school contexts to student sexual minority competence. *Journal of Homosexuality, 65*(1), 19–41.

McCoy, B. F. (2011). *Art into health: Puntu Palyarrikuwanpa* (Aboriginal Men Becoming Well). Melbourne, VIC: The Lowitja Institute.

McEwan, A., Tsey, K., & The Empowerment Research Team. (2008). *The role of spirituality in social and emotional wellbeing initiatives: The family wellbeing program at Yarrabah* (Discussion Paper No. 7). Darwin, NT: Cooperative Research Centre for Aboriginal Health.

Mukandi, B., Singh, D., Brady, K., Willis, J., Sinha, T., Askew, D., & Bond, C. (2019). "So we tell them": Articulating strong black masculinities in an urban Indigenous community. *AlterNative: An International Journal of Indigenous Peoples, 15*(3), 253–260.

National Aboriginal Community Controlled Health Organisation (NACCHO). (2013). *Aboriginal male health futures: Blueprint 2013–2030*. Canberra, ACT: NACCHO.

Pfitzner, N., Humphreys, C., & Hegarty, K. (2017). Research review: Engaging men – A multi-level model to support father engagement. *Child & Family Social Work, 22*(1), 537–547.

Prehn, J. (2019). How social work can improve the health and wellbeing of Aboriginal men. In B. Bennett & S. Green (Eds.), *Our voices: Aboriginal social work* (pp. 157–174). South Yarra, VIC: Macmillan International Higher Education.

Rathus, Z. (2020). A history of the use of the concept of parental alienation in the Australian family law system: Contradictions, collisions and their consequences. *Journal of Social Welfare and Family Law, 42*(1), 5–17.

Reilly, L., & Rees, S. (2018). Fatherhood in Australian Aboriginal and Torres Strait Islander communities: An examination of barriers and opportunities to strengthen the male parenting role. *American Journal of Men's Health, 12,* 420–430. doi: https://doi.org/10.1177/1557988317735928.

Robinson, G., Tyler, W., Jones, Y., Silburn, S., & Zubrick, S. (2012). Context, diversity, and engagement: Early intervention with Australian Aboriginal families in urban and remote contexts. *Children and Society, 26,* 343–355.

Roe, Y. (2020). *Tell my story: Hearing from the Dads in the Indigenous Birthing in an Urban Setting (IBUS) Study*. The University of Queensland.

Rosenstreich, G., Comfort, J., & Martin, P. (2011). Primary health care and equity: The case of lesbian, gay, bisexual, trans and intersex Australians. *Australian Journal of Primary Health, 17*(4), 302–308.

Rowntree, M. R. (2013). *Making sexuality visible in Australian social work education. Social Work Education: The International Journal,* 33(3), 353–364. doi: https://doi.org/10.1080/02615479.2013.834885.

Shwalb, D. W., Shwalb, B. J., & Lamb, M. E. (2013). *Fathering in cultural context*. New York, NY: Routledge.

Smith, J., Adams, M., & Bonson, J. (2018). Investment in men's health in Australia. *Medical Journal of Australia, 208*(1), 6–7.

Smith, J., Christie, B., Bonson, J., Adams, M., Osborne, R., Judd, B., Drummond, M., Aanundsen, D., & Fleay, J. (2019). *Health literacy among young Aboriginal and Torres Strait Islander males in the Northern Territory*. Report prepared for the Lowitja Institute. Darwin, NT: Menzies School of Health Research. ISBN:978-1-922104-60-1.

Smith, J., Drummond, M., Adams, M., Bonson, J., & Christie, B. (2019). Chapter 31: Understanding men's health inequities in Australia. In D. Griffiths, M. Bruce, & R. Thorpe (Eds.), *Handbook on men's health disparities* (pp. 498–509). New York, NY: Routledge.

Smith, J., Watkins, DC and Griffith, DM (2020) Equity, gender and health: New directions for global men's health promotion. Health Promotion Journal of Australia, Volum 31 Issue 2 p 161-165. https://doi.org/10.1002/hpja.337.

Southcombe, A., Cavanagh, J., & Bartram, A. (2014). Capacity building in Indigenous men's sheds and groups across Australia. *Health Promotion International, 30*(3), 606–615.

Stecker, S. (2020). Social workers and the LGBT community. Vocal.

Taonui, R. (2010). Mana Tamariki: Cultural alienation. *AlterNative: An International Journal of Indigenous Peoples, 6*(3), 187–202.

Tsey, K., Patterson, D., Whiteside, M., Baird, L., & Baird, B. (2002). Indigenous men taking their rightful place in society? A preliminary analysis of a participatory action research process with Yarrabah Men's Health Group. *Australian Journal of Rural Health, 10*, 278–284.

Tsey, K., Patterson, D., Whiteside, M., Baird, L., Baird, B., & Tsey, K. (2004). A microanalysis of a participatory action research process with a rural Aboriginal men's health group. *Australian Journal of Primary Health, 10*, 64–71.

Wenitong, M. (2002). *Indigenous male health: A report for Indigenous males, their families, and communities, and those committed to improving Indigenous male health.* Canberra, ACT: Commonwealth of Australia.

Wenitong, M. (2006). Aboriginal and Torres Strait Islander male health, wellbeing and leadership. *Medical Journal of Australia, 185*(8), 466–467.

Wiele, C. V. D., & Tong, S. T. (2014). Breaking boundaries: The uses & gratifications of Grindr. In *UbiComp '14: Proceedings of the 2014 ACM international joint conference on pervasive and ubiquitous computing.* doi: https://doi.org/10.1145/2632048.2636070.

Wilde, O. (1895). *The love that dare not speak its name.* Kansas, MO: University of Missouri-Kansas City Law School. Retrieved from: www.law.umkc.edu.

Working Party of Aboriginal and Torres Strait Islander Male Health and Wellbeing Reference Committee. (2004). *A national framework for improving the health and wellbeing of Aboriginal and Torres Strait Islander males.* Canberra, ACT: Commonwealth of Australia.

Zeeman, L. (2019). A review of lesbian, gay, bisexual, trans and intersex (LGBTI) health and healthcare inequalities. *European Journal of Public Health, 29*(5), 974–980. doi: https://doi.org/10.1093/eurpub/cky226.

7 Mental Health as Spiritual Health: Toward New Understandings of a Healing Approach

Joe Williams and Phill Pallas

Cultural standpoints

Joe is a proud Wiradjuri/Wolgalu, First Nations Aboriginal man born in Cowra, raised in Wagga Wagga in New South Wales. In 2018 Joe was awarded Suicide Prevention Australia's highest honour, a LiFE Award for his excellence in communities within the suicide prevention sector. In 2019 he was named a dual winner of the Australian Mental Health Prize. He continues to work with communities across Australia through his organisation The Enemy Within.

Phill's heritage is Greek, English, Irish, Scottish and Danish. He is privileged to work with Pitjantjatjara and Yankunytjatjara people in Central Australia and honours Anangu who have taken time to lead him into sacred learning spaces through culture, language and ceremony. He is a social worker and lecturer at the University of Newcastle.

Going public with my silent battle

Joe: The year is 2014, and from the outside looking in, I had it all together. Having played in the National Rugby League, I was a known sportsperson even before making the switch to professional boxing. In the week leading up to my defence of the World Boxing Foundation World Junior Welterweight title, the course of my life changed. My story of living with bipolar disorder and severe depression, which led to a suicide attempt in 2012, was made public in my hometown of Wagga Wagga. Because of my sporting career, people had seen me in the public eye for many years. At the time, I was living some of the peaks of that career as a fighter, but what people didn't realise is that I was battling my own unseen struggle for a very long time. In silence and behind closed doors, I was in the biggest fight of my life. When my silent struggles were made public via a short film in the Wagga film festival, my story went to the core of many people who were also battling in silence. In that moment, *The Enemy Within* was born.

My focus shifted from pursuing a career in sport to working in schools and communities to break down the stigma of talking about mental health. I was determined to raise awareness about wellbeing and promote the prevention of suicide. I had a passion to talk about the impacts of mental health and suicide in communities and help people understand how we can all be involved in the work of making things better.

In the weeks following the film festival, countless people came to me to share their story; stories of pain that people had often been sitting with, alone, for a very long time. In each and every person I connected with, I could feel a sense of relief. As I spoke with people, the weight that many had been carrying began to lift. The more people I talked to, the more I found that people were receiving something through our connection to begin their own journey towards healing. I quickly realised that I needed to be doing as much as I could to help people that were struggling in silence.

It's true that I have I had some opposition from people; 'You're not a professional; you're not a psychologist or a social worker. You're not equipped to give professional advice.' Some of these words played around in my own mind early on, until a person I was connecting with said to me, 'No, you aren't a professional, but you normalise the conversation. Your story is relatable to ours. You connect to our pain when we are struggling in silence.'

Over the past seven years, *The Enemy Within* has grown. With that growth, I have had the opportunity to connect with many people across our continent of Australia and many thousands of people across the USA.

The more I work 'on the ground' in community, particularly in rural and remote communities in Australia that are predominantly populated by First Nations people, I see that the way we view mental health is more than a little skewed. I want to emphasise that I am not a professional and what I offer in this chapter is not attack on anyone in the field who is trained to deliver their best work. What I am leaning into, however, is my experience of working in some 200+ communities – from highly populated metropolitan areas to the smallest of remote communities and islands accessible only by small aircraft. I am also drawing on my experience as a person who has accessed professional mental health services. Although the depth of what I have experienced for many years was kept hidden away, I still engaged with professional services whilst I was playing rugby league in the NRL and after a suicide attempt in 2012 which saw two separate stays in psychiatric facilities. The ideas I present to social workers in this chapter draw on this broad range of experiences with the hope of informing a better approach to working with First Nations people in the area of mental health.

The lens through which we see

Phill: 'Everything you think you know about yourselves and the way the world operates will be challenged.' She was right. It was day one of my social work degree, and I sat eagerly with a pen in my hand and cliché motivations of wanting to 'make a difference' in my heart. The lecturer's statement hinted at the rollercoaster of reflection and self-discovery that I was about to jump into. As a first-year social work student, I was eager to start my journey of formation towards professional practice. What I didn't realise is that my formation as a social worker began long before I walked onto campus that day.

This book explores the various fields of practice where social workers engage with Aboriginal people in Australia. For social workers, this requires us to consider the intersections between a particular field of practice (in this instance, mental health) and the gamut of cultural and other factors that inform the lived experience of Aboriginal people. In approaching our work in this space, we have to resist our often strong desires to homogenise or essentialise the experience of Aboriginal people to avoid formulaic approaches to our work. One of the dangers we are required to negotiate in our considerations is the temptation to fix our gaze solely on 'the client' and their situation, without reflecting critically upon the lens through which we make sense of another person's experience. Joe's story offers us important perspectives that can inform our work with Aboriginal people in the area of mental health. Many of us can either relate to or know someone who can relate to his experience. Joe's story offers even more than this, though. His story invites us to consider our own story. His story invites us into the same space of critical reflection that I was ushered into the first day of my social work degree.

As practitioners, we can never graduate from critically reflecting on our position. The way that we approach our work in the area of mental health with Aboriginal people is shaped by particular historical realities and narratives, as well as our early life experiences, that we carry with us. The dominant narrative that forms the historical backdrop against which our engagement with Indigenous peoples plays out is the imposing force of colonisation and its ongoing negative impact within Indigenous lives. Colonisation has had a detrimental effect on the lives of Indigenous people in almost every corner of the globe (see Smith, 1999, 2012; Gray, Coates, & Yellow Bird, 2008). Colonisation is about invading space to establish power and control. It is perpetuated by notions that certain 'others' are classifiable as 'underdeveloped economically and mentally' (Mignolo, 2009, 161). The historic justification for colonial advancement is found in the idea that not only are some inferior but the ideology that Indigenous people are less than human. Maori scholar Linda Tuhiwai Smith, in her book *Decolonizing Methodologies: Research and Indigenous Peoples* (1999), explains,

> One of the supposed characteristics of primitive peoples was that we could not use our minds or intellects. We could not invent things, we could not create institutions or history, we could not imagine, we could not produce anything of value, we did not know how to use land and other resources form the natural world, we did not practice the 'arts' of civilization. By lacking such values we disqualified ourselves, not just from civilization but from humanity itself. In other words, we were not 'fully human'; some of us

were not even considered partially human. *Ideas about what counted as human in association with the power to define people as human or not human were already encoded in imperial and colonial discourses...* (1999, p. 25, emphasis added)

Adopting a view of Indigenous people as primitive or without intellect is now often more subtle. Within our practice, it can be more hidden, more nuanced. However, it is not absent. This is part of what Joe encounters when someone questions his qualification to speak on issues related to mental health. This questioning is a challenge to the knowledge base from which Joe is operating. Paternalistic policy regimes and the foundational assumption that Aboriginal people need our help continue to abound and influence our work.

Social work practice literature appropriately highlights the arrival of the British and consequent government policies with the poor social and health status of Indigenous Australians today (Bennett, Green, Gilbert, & Bessarab, 2012; Briskman, 2007, 2014). However, we need to hold these realities in tension with a fuller narrative that captures Indigenous peoples' resistance, resilience, and strength. Wherever practitioners place a question mark over the legitimacy of Indigenous knowledges and experience, colonisation is present. If we are serious about seeing new ways of working in mental health with Aboriginal people, wherever we practice and whatever our cultural heritage, we must commit to interrogating the lens through which we view the world and allow new forms of knowledge to be foregrounded.

Mental health is spiritual health

Joe: My view of mental health gained a very different perspective when I was talking to a senior cultural elder that I hold close. I was on Country with Ngemba man Uncle Paul Gordon when my perspective on how I viewed not only my own mental health challenges, but those I had encountered within the many First Nations communities across the country, changed. I remember the conversation so vividly; sitting around the fire on a brisk winter night in western NSW. The conversation was centred around the work I was doing across many communities throughout Australia. Talking about my personal journey, Uncle Paul, a very humble and observant man, said to me, 'You don't have a mental illness, it's your spirit that is sick. You need to heal your spirit, but you also need to heal our ways, on Country. When you heal your spirit, you will get well.' His words really hit me as only moments earlier I had been talking to Uncle Paul about how mentally and emotionally stable I felt every time I was on Country, especially when I was in deep cultural practice.

When I left Uncle Paul that weekend, I concentrated on doing things that were good for my spirit. Unsurprisingly, I noticed this was having a positive impact on my personal wellbeing. As I noticed the positive change I was experiencing, I also I began to implement these learnings in the content I was delivering during my wellness and wellbeing sessions. It felt like everything was falling into place when I gained another perspective that backed up Uncle Paul's advice. It was at a cultural gathering where I found myself in deep conversation with another respected elder of the same first name. This time it was Uncle Paul Callaghan (Uncle PC). There were many lessons taught during that conversation; lessons from his struggles, and also mine. I remember the words he said to me when talking about being on Country, engaging in cultural practice, and healing. Uncle PC said, 'You stick close to culture, the practice and the lessons you learn out here (on Country) and your mental health challenges will all but go away.' Again I was greeted with another message about placing priority on healing the spirit.

No more than a few weeks after that conversation with Uncle PC, I was in the remote community of Yirrkala in North East Arnhem land when I was questioned about my delivery on the topic of mental health. In this region, the process of colonisation didn't occur until the mid-1940s. 'We don't have that mental health thing you talk about here', one community member said to me. In that simple statement I realised that I had to change my language to enable the local community to understand what it was that I was trying to deliver; a seminar on mental health and the effects on the individual. I quickly remembered my conversation with Uncle Paul about my spirit being sick.

There too, in Arnhem Land, I started talking about healing our spirit.

We know as First Nations people that when our spirit isn't well, or when our spirit is sick, there are elements of our total wellbeing that aren't well. When our spirit is sick, we show behaviours that could quite easily reflect those of someone in mental or emotional distress. When our spirit is sick, we look for other areas in our life to fill the void. It is often in times of distress that we turn to behaviours that may cause us further harm or damage; for example, alcohol misuse and violence.

Becoming well

Phill: It was more than dehydration. I had been out bush for a few days travelling Country, hunting, and learning with my brothers. It was hot, but I was drinking a lot of water. I sat leaning against a desert oak, quietly by myself. I had been with people all day, every day and I just wanted a moment to rest. I felt sick in my stomach and I had a headache. I had felt like this before, I wasn't worried at all, but I knew that I just needed some time by myself to rest and feel better. One of my brothers noticed me sitting by myself and walked over to check on me. I told him how I was feeling. A worried look came across his face as he turned and yelled out to about six of our brothers off in the distance, 'Wai, ngalya pitja.' They came to where we were sitting and in Pitjantjatjara, he continued, 'Our brother is feeling sick, come sit with him and tell him stories.' So, then I had company, sitting with me, telling me stories and laughing.

The concept of 'illness behaviour' (Mechanic, 1995) describes how we monitor our bodies, interpret what we are experiencing and take action to become well. It also captures how we engage with formal health care systems. A vital premise of the study of illness behaviour is that the way we experience being unwell, and becoming well, is shaped by sociocultural and other social-psychological factors regardless of biological basis. Western illness behaviour in Australia involves going to a doctor, a person often unknown to you, who undertakes several assessments on your body in a closed office setting. Usually, you and the doctor are the only people in the room. After conducting their assessment, the doctor commonly prescribes medication in the form of drugs and provides a written 'prescription' for this medication. Upon leaving the doctor you go to a chemist to buy the medication that has been prescribed, then you go home. When you get home, you isolate; you stay in your room, you avoid interaction with others, and you don't go to work. It is common to consume drugs that work on a biological level to make you well again. This approach to health is familiar to me as I have been socialised into this system from a very young age and have engaged in this type of illness behaviour throughout my life. It stands in stark contrast to the process of 'becoming well' that I experienced as I leaned against a desert oak that day, surrounded by stories and laughter.

The concept of illness behaviour, and how it manifests within mainstream Western contexts, is an important perspective to consider when seeking to change the way we view and approach mental health care with First Nations people. At no time did my brothers out bush that day suggest I head over to the clinic. They didn't rush to sit me in a room by myself. Their response was, in many ways, the opposite to the Western illness behaviours I have outlined above. In conversation with one of my brothers, I realised that many Western illness behaviours are about disconnection, but many First Nations illness behaviours are about increasing connection. 'How can we get well if we are by ourselves? We need other people around us, talking stories, that connection heals our bodies and makes us feel better.'

Without knowledge and appreciation of culturally and socially bound illness behaviours, we may unknowingly interpret and 'treat' behaviour from a perspective that reinforces disconnection and causes more harm, rather than promoting connection towards healing. More integrated ways of understanding wellbeing and becoming well require us to move from our reliance on models of mental health that draw heavily on Western knowledge and an interrogation of the very knowledge base of social work. A case can be made that the same ethnocentric foundations that informed and drove colonisation is at the core of historical developments of social work as well as the continued global expansion of our profession. The globalisation agenda, to take social work 'to the world', has involved the export of Western approaches to non-Western contexts. This has primarily occurred through education and academic discourse. Social work theories and methods from the United States, Britain, and other European nations have been adopted by the new schools of social work that appeared after the Second World War in what was then known as the 'Third World' (Midgley, 2008). Social workers and academics in Western nations facilitated this knowledge exchange (Midgley, 2008). Largely, the expansion to non-Western contexts was grounded in the belief that social work was based on universal values and practice methods that applied to all societies (Midgley, 2008).

The globalisation agenda and claims to 'universal' social work are not without their critics. Gray, Coates, and Yellow Bird (2008), in their significant contribution to the discourse in this area *Indigenous Social Work around the World*, note:

> We believe that an uncritical acceptance of the globalization agenda is paradoxical in a profession which values cultural responsiveness and that concerns with cultural relevance force us to rethink the universals in social work and be wary of homogenizing processes like the search for international definitions of social work and global standards of social work education. (xxv)

As we work with First Nations communities in the field of mental health, we need to acknowledge our shared histories and our dependence on Western knowledges and the contemporary challenges that we face. A culturally responsive approach that operates from a position where more integrated understandings of wellbeing guide our practice will lead us into greater capacities to learn from one another as we walk together towards healing.

Looking beyond behaviour

Over the years, I have seen many dedicated youth workers, social workers, and mental health workers approaching their work with great passion but struggling to achieve change. Too many times I have seen services operating within communities unaware of the historical, cultural, and political landscape. I have seen many professionals with good intentions head in to 'fix' issues in the community. Although many of these workers are extremely dedicated and have great intentions, I have found that many do not understand the full complexity of issues, including the generational impacts of trauma.

The effects of generational and transgenerational trauma have been widely researched and documented (see Atkinson, 2002). New understandings have emerged that show trauma is passed down through the generations on a cellular level. This means that babies are being born who are immediately impacted by the trauma of their parents, grandparents, and other ancestors. I describe transgenerational trauma to people by highlighting that many within the First Nations community may or will have preconceived ideas about non-Indigenous people. Sometimes these ideas are applied to non-Indigenous people generally, whilst First Nations peoples' ideas about non-Indigenous social workers, caseworkers, and other professionals are specifically impacted by the generational imprint that has been caused by the negative and ongoing impacts of colonisation.

When people have been bashed, beaten, and slaughtered for a couple of hundred years, the trauma, as you can imagine, is multi-layered. Physical trauma on top of physical trauma. Emotional trauma on top of emotional trauma. Mental trauma on top of mental trauma. When we approach the multilayered nature of trauma of generations across more than 230 years, we can begin to understand the depth of pain and why many First Nations people have a distrust of non-Indigenous professionals. The stealing of children throughout the stolen generations continues to mean that professionals are often met with barriers and disengagement.

When we begin to look at mental health through a lens that is trauma-informed, one that understands the impacts of trauma as outlined, we can see a different story. We can also see a collective of people who lived 'at one' with the land for many thousands of years. A collective of people who are struggling to walk between an ancient thriving world of rich empowerment, and a (relatively) new world that has been introduced. This new world has been forced onto culture and people who are struggling to adapt to it. A trauma-informed culturally responsive approach to mental health work with First Nations people requires us to acknowledge community capacities and adopt a view of behaviour as language.

Imagine professionals arrived to work in a community and instead of only noticing negative behaviours, they understood the many layers of trauma that have been forcibly impacted on communities due to the ongoing generational process of colonisation. Imagine we also looked at communities and acknowledged their generational resilience rather than judging the negative behaviours that we encounter. Sure, there are negative behaviours that have a big impact on how a community functions, but rather than focusing on the negative and repeated narrative, how would our view and our work change if we looked at the strengths that have kept these communities functional for thousands of years? How would our approach differ if we noticed the ongoing resilience of a community trying to rebuild from the destruction that colonisation has caused? Again, I recognise that this wouldn't eliminate certain negative behaviours immediately, but it would provide workers an appreciation of the strengths that exist within many families and the community as a whole. Adopting this viewpoint gives us a target to get back to. It gives us a positive narrative to encourage and empower individuals within the community to become the best possible version of themselves.

I have always gone into a community and operated from a strengths-based approach. One strategy that has assisted me greatly in this is viewing behaviour as language. If the behaviour is a result of trauma or a reaction to trauma, wouldn't we be better served in healing what is causing the behaviour? When we see destructive and negative behaviours in community, we need to first ask ourselves, 'Why is this behaviour occurring?', 'Where is the pain coming from?', or 'What is triggering the trauma that is causing this pain?' One thing we do know, and a view I like to encourage people to see before they make a prior judgement, is that 'hurt people, hurt (other) people'. In finding positive from a negative, whilst having the view that hurt people, hurt people, there is also a case to argue that 'healed people, heal people'. Simply, I believe the more healing that we see and is modelled in the community, the more positive actions and behaviours we will see in the community.

When we view behaviour as language, we are forced to focus our viewpoint on what is causing such behaviours, rather than the behaviour itself. If and when we begin to look at the behaviours as a product of something else, we can then begin to look at healing the root cause associated with those behaviours. That sounds like a pretty straightforward thing to do right? Except what we see in many communities around the country is services employed and millions of dollars spent on programs that effectively act as a band-aid; working to address individual behaviours, rather than what is causing the behaviours.

Bringing real change to practice

Phill: To appropriately approach our work with Aboriginal people in the area of mental health, practitioners need to learn ways to listen to Indigenous and decolonial academics in ways that bring real change to their practice. This involves making space to hear powerful counternarratives that challenge deficit narratives of Aboriginal communities and examination of the Western knowledge base of the profession. Decentring Western knowledges and acknowledging the validity of Indigenous knowledges is challenging because it involves 'losing privilege, power, and identity' (Walter & Baltra-Ulloa, 2019, p. 77). There is a strong call from Indigenous social work scholars for non-Indigenous social workers to consider their racial privilege and cultural assumptions should they desire to work with Aboriginal communities (Walter, Taylor, & Habibis, 2011; Young, 2005, 2008; Young & Zubrzycki, 2005). Beyond the discipline of social work, critical theorists and Indigenous scholars 'urge researchers and educators to consider the nature of their position by way of gender, class, culture, religion, and race and the associated institutional assumptions represented in research and education exchanges' (Osborne, 2016).

Practitioner-focused social work literature examines social workers' preparedness, cultural competence, and experience working with Indigenous communities. Bennett, Zubrzycki, and Bacon's (2011) article, 'What do we know? The experiences of social workers working alongside Aboriginal people', represents a standout contribution as they shift the focus from the Aboriginal client or population towards the practitioner and their experience. Whilst much of the literature in this space focuses on the complexities of working with communities that are experiencing significant disadvantage, the focus of their work is how practitioners' approach and facilitate relationships with Aboriginal people.

Despite the critique, the term 'cultural competence' is still often used in social work literature. At an organisational level, there are calls for mainstream service providers to become more culturally competent in their work with Indigenous populations by addressing racism and integrating understandings of trauma in their practice (Herring, Spangaro, Lauw, & McNamara, 2013). Intergenerational trauma is widely recognised as an ongoing impact of colonisation (Atkinson, 2002). Addressing systemic racism in mainstream organisations is imperative to addressing disadvantages that Aboriginal people face (Paradies, Harris, & Anderson, 2008). Other practice tools, such as cultural mapping tools that acknowledge the complexity of family and kinship structures, have also been promoted as pathways to culturally competent practice (Stewart & Allan, 2013), whilst Herring et al. (2013) advocate that an essential step in becoming more culturally competent in understanding the benefits of 'white privilege'.

Literature has also emerged that considers the intersections between social work and whiteness theory and calls for further integration of whiteness theory in social work education and practice. Moreton-Robinson (2004) defines whiteness as 'the invisible norm against which other races are judged in the construction of identity, representation subjectivity, nationalism, and the law' (viii). The invisibility of whiteness masks its privilege. Young (2008, p. 103) asserts that whiteness theory presents 'a description of how privilege is raced and invisible: a method of unsettling this privilege; and it offers guidance for more inclusive and respectful human relationships.'

Understanding how one's personal and cultural identity has been shaped by colonisation is fundamental (Bennett, Zubrzycki, & Bacon, 2011) to establishing appropriate connected relationships with Aboriginal and Torres Strait Islander people. Walter, Taylor, and Habibis critique whiteness within the social work profession, whilst Bennett (2015) presents research regarding barriers Aboriginal and Torres Strait Islander people experience in participating in the AASW. On the basis of interviews with 16 Indigenous social workers from across Australia, she argues that social work is 'socially, economically, culturally, geographically separated from Indigenous people and that the consequences for how social workers engage with their Indigenous clients have yet to be fully explored' (Bennett, 2015, p. 6). Thus, Bennett calls for the AASW to 'walk alongside us' by leaving 'their western comfort zone' (Bennett, 2015, p. 29) to become visibly involved with Indigenous communities.

In the area of mental health with Aboriginal people, we must become more forward-thinking, more nuanced, and more courageous than simply taking mainstream strategies, adding some dot painting around the borders, and declaring them fit for Aboriginal people everywhere.

Walking in two worlds, walking towards healing

Joe: In the travel I have done across many communities around Australia, I see the impacts of colonisation in our metropolitan and highly populated areas, and the contrasting impacts in many remote communities. What I have noticed is the evident struggle in the balance of two worlds. We have First Nation communities who are strong in the traditional ways of life; culture, story, song, and ceremony. We also see the opposite. I see the many brothers and sisters who walk strongly in the modern Western-introduced world of new foods, new substances, entirely new ways of living that involves finances, tax, utility bills, and the costs of general day-to-day living. There is a huge contrast between the two; one has a strong sense of identity, culture, and spirit that is struggling in a new world, and the other is strong in the new Western-introduced world with little understanding of the ancient ways of ceremony, story, spirit, and cultural responsibilities. What we don't see a great deal of is a strong balance where people walk between both. We see many First Nations people across the country struggling to do this. There is the ancient world of knowledges handed down through story, and the modern world, that was introduced just 232 years ago. That is where our spirit gets lost.

When looking at two people from those two worlds, we see one who is strong in one world and not the other; and another who is strong in the opposing world but without skills to navigate the other. We see a fight in balance and our spirit gets lost between the two worlds. Individuals and communities can become lost between a world dominated by a modernised colonial context and one that practices the same or similar customs that have been present for many thousands of years. Being lost in this way also plays out in behaviours that can be viewed as destructive and interpreted as mental health concerns. These behaviours are largely due to the impacts of colonisation and displacement, which have had massive repercussions on the spirit of people. It is these behaviours that we see interpreted as a reflection of an individual's mental state. Unfortunately, many services treat the symptoms of this mental health without recognition that these issues stem from trauma.

Would our approach be different if we began to view individual issues within the community from a trauma-informed lens, acknowledging the importance of healing the spirit, rather than focusing on behaviour? When our spirit feels lost, we experience disconnection, and a constant yearning to feel connected; connected to self, community, and a larger purpose. When an individual experiences loss of connection, identity, and purpose, it is impossible to find fulfilment. The path towards healing from this space can be complex for people to understand, and in accordance with First Nation belief systems, rests at a much deeper, ancient spiritual level.

One of the greatest pieces of advice I have ever been told in my journey, again, from Uncle Paul Gordon, 'We must walk with a foot in each camp, learn to walk between two worlds'. This idea is what informs my approach to working with mental health in many First Nations communities today. It is this very idea that social workers need to consider as they work with communities to address mental health concerns. Work with us, slow down to understand our ways and make room for us to navigate two worlds on our path towards healing.

 ## Discussion Questions

1. What is your cultural background, and how does this influence the way in which you approach your practice?

2. How do you make sense of the spiritual dimensions of wellbeing and integrate these understandings in your practice?

3. What is your current understanding of the trauma and intergenerational impacts on the mental health of Aboriginal people?

References

Atkinson, J. (2002). *Trauma trails: Recreating song lines*. Melbourne, VIC: Spinifex Press.

Bennett, B. (2015). "Stop deploying your white privilege on me!" Aboriginal and Torres Strait Islander engagement with the Australian Association of Social Workers. *Australian Social Work, 68*(1), 19–31. doi: https://doi.org/10.1080/0312407X.2013.840325.

Bennett, B., Green, S., Gilbert, S., & Bessarab, B. (2012). *Our voices: Aboriginal and Torres Strait Islander social work*. South Yarra, VIC: Palgrave Macmillan.

Bennett, B., Zubrzycki, J., & Bacon, V. (2011). What do we know? The experiences of social workers working alongside Aboriginal people. *Australian Social Work, 64*(1), 20–37.

Briskman, L. (2007). *Social work with Indigenous communities*. Sydney, NSW: Federation Press.

Briskman, L. (2014). *Social work with Indigenous communities: A human rights approach* (2nd ed.). Annandale, NSW: Federation Press.

Gray, M., Coates, J., & Yellow Bird, M. (2008). *Indigenous social work around the world: Towards culturally relevant education and practice*. Aldershot: Ashgate.

Herring, S., Spangaro, J., Lauw, M., & McNamara, L. (2013). The intersection of trauma, racism, and cultural competence in effective work with Aboriginal people: Waiting for trust. *Australian Social Work, 66*(1), 104–117. doi: https://doi.org/10.1080/0312407X.2012.697566.

Mechanic, D. (1995). Sociological dimensions of illness behavior. *Social Science and Medicine, 41*(9), 1207–1216.

Midgley J. (2008). Perspectives on globalization and culture: Implications for international social work practice. *Journal of Global Social Work Practice, 1*(1), 1–11.

Mignolo, W. (2009). Epistemic disobedience, independent thought and de-colonial freedom. *Theory Culture & Society, 26*(7–8), 1–23.

Moreton-Robinson, A. (2004). *Whitening race: Essays in social and cultural criticism*. Canberra, ACT: Aboriginal Studies Press.

Osborne, S. (2016). *Staging standpoint dialogue in tristate education: Privileging Anangu voices*. Doctoral thesis, Retrieved from http://vuir.vu.edu.au/32634/1/OSBORNE%20Samuel%20-%20Thesis.pdf

Paradies, Y., Harris, R., & Anderson, I. (2008). *The impact of racism on indigenous health in Australia and Aotearoa: Towards a research agenda*. Retrieved from https://www.lowitja.org.au/lowitja-publishing/C004

Smith, L. T. (1999). *Decolonizing methodologies: Research and Indigenous peoples*. London: Zed Publishing.

Smith, L. T. (2012). *Decolonizing methodologies: Research and indigenous peoples*. London: Zed Books.

Stewart, B., & Allan, J. (2013). Building relationships with Aboriginal people: A cultural mapping toolbox. *Australian Social Work, 66*(1), 118–129. doi: https://doi.org/10.1080/0312407X.2012.708937.

Walter, M., & Baltra-Ulloa, J. (2019). Australian social work is White. In B. Bennett & S. Green (Eds.), *Our voices: Aboriginal and Torres Strait Islander social work* (pp. 65–85). London: Red Globe Press.

Walter, M., Taylor, S., & Habibis, D. (2011). How White is social work in Australia? *Australian Social Work, 64*(1), 6–19. doi: https://doi.org/10.1080/0312407X.2010.510892.

Young, S. (2005). Social work theory and practice: The invisibility of whiteness. In A. Moreton-Robinson (Ed.), *Whitening race: Essays in social and cultural criticism* (pp. 104–118). Canberra, ACT: Aboriginal Studies Press.

Young, S. (2008). Indigenous child protection policy in Australia: Using Whiteness theory for social work. *Sites: A Journal of Social Anthropology and Cultural Studies, 5*, 102–123.

Young, S., & Zubrzycki, J. (2005). *Analysing policy and practice: Developing the ground for educating about whiteness*. Paper presented at the Whiteness and the Horizons of Race Conference. University of Queensland, Brisbane.

8 Child Protection Practice with Aboriginal and Torres Strait Islander Children, Families and Communities

Kaylene Malthouse and Fiona Oates

Introduction

To begin this chapter, we would like to locate ourselves within it.

My name is Kaylene Malthouse. Nalpajuwi is my Murri name. I am an Upper Malanbarra Yidinji woman. My name is derived from the Dancing Revitalisation Spirit. My mother, Grace Mary Ambrum, was a Yidinji Nadjan woman from the Atherton Tablelands in Far North Queensland. I have fond memories of my mother sitting with her mother and her sisters and aunties under the stars and each with their children wrapped in handmade quilts made by themselves from cloth, backed with open bags. My Great Grandfather's estate commences at Toohey's Creek waterways on the Atherton Tablelands which runs through the Gadgarra Forest into the Mulgrave River in the Goldsborough Valley, taking in the Gillies range southwest of Cairns in Far North Queensland.

From the age of seven, I worked in the potato farms in Atherton Tablelands supporting the senior women who worked there. This was my introduction into a traditional process of becoming a respectful, responsible, and resilient woman. This background assisted me to develop a career of advocacy for my people. When I was 13, my father, Nungabuna (George Davis), established the Biddi Biddi Housing Co-op in Atherton at a time when housing for Aboriginal and Torres Strait Islander people was scarce. This name comes from the metamorphosis of the Jumbun (witchetty grub) to a Biddi Biddi (White beetle). The Jumbun lives in the Candle Nut Tree and is gently cut out for food or bait for fishing.

I spent valuable time with my father being immersed in cultural practice while working with the linguist Professor Bob Dixon to document and revitalise his language. He taught me the importance of dedication, and I became a staunch advocate for my people in all things that effect their/our lives. I moved through the education system as a teacher's assistant and then into homework centres looking after the kids from remote communities in Cape York Peninsula, the Torres Strait Islands, and Mornington Island. I then moved into the child protection field. I have worked in the child protection field for approximately 14 years where I have advocated for the return of our children in care back home to their Kin. I am a strong advocate for the integration of Aboriginal history, knowledge, and ways of working into contemporary child protection systems, including the recruitment and retention of Indigenous practitioners.

In addition to my work with children and families, I Chaired the North Queensland Land Council for four years and was a Director on the Council for another 10 years. As part of my role as Chair with the North Queensland Land Council, I worked with my constituents to ensure their views were represented in the Uluru Statement from the Heart process – their views being truth, treaty, and a voice to parliament. I also Chair my local Traditional Owner Alliance and continue to advocate for our peoples in my parents' homelands.

Throughout the chapter, there are times when I would like to speak with you, the reader, directly. These times will be indicated in *italics*. Some of those times will be in an interview/yarn type format with Fiona.

My name is Fiona Oates. I am a non-Indigenous female with strong family and professional links to Far North Queensland. This is where I was born and where I reside today. Since completing my undergraduate degree in social work in 2003, I have worked in the area of child protection, in statutory and non-statutory settings as a practitioner, supervisor, and consultant. More recently, I have worked as an educator and researcher with the desire to contribute towards the education of the next wave of social work professionals.

I am of the firm view that the role non-Indigenous practitioners have in the disproportionate representation of Indigenous children in the child protection system needs thorough and ongoing examination. Having worked as an educator, I can say that the majority of non-Indigenous students have a deep desire to be 'culturally competent' and to ensure that they don't further harm Indigenous children or families. In my experience, I would say that is also true of the majority of non-Indigenous practitioners working in the child protection field. Unfortunately, the desires of non-Indigenous practitioners to work in a culturally responsive way has not decreased the number of Indigenous children removed from their families. There is a disconnect between the desire of non-Indigenous practitioners to deliver culturally competent services, the needs of Indigenous children and families, and the disproportionate numbers of Indigenous child removals. Something is missing. The continued disproportionate representation of Indigenous children in the child protection system is evidence that the current way of doing things is not working for Indigenous children and families.

Similar to Kaylene, there will be times when I would like to speak with you, the reader, directly. You will recognise these times as the paragraphs will begin with or contain the phrase 'as non-Indigenous practitioners'.

In addition to locating ourselves within this chapter, we wish to acknowledge that Aboriginal people are the Traditional Custodians of mainland Australia. We further acknowledge that Torres Strait Islander people are the Traditional Custodians of the Torres Strait Islands. We would like to acknowledge the tens of thousands of years that Aboriginal and Torres Strait

Islander people raised strong healthy children in culture on Country. We would also like to acknowledge the hard work and dedication of all the Aboriginal and Torres Strait Islander peoples who have fought, and continue to fight, for the restoration of sovereignty, including the right to raise strong healthy children in culture on Country, stolen as a result of colonisation.

When approached to write this chapter, we were asked to consider what skills and knowledge we thought were critical for non-Indigenous social workers to know and keep in the fore of their mind when working with Indigenous children and families in a child protection context. We were also asked to outline our thoughts on how practitioners might more effectively work with Indigenous children and families. With this in mind, there are three key sections in this chapter; namely, what has been in relation to child protection work with Indigenous children and families, how it is now, and some future practice considerations for practitioners.

Before proceeding with the chapter, we would like to acknowledge that child protection work is an extremely complex and difficult area of social work and human services practice. We have both worked in frontline child protection in statutory and non-statutory contexts for lengthy periods of time. We understand the complexities, the pressures, and the systems issues. Child protection work is essential work that is done in a chronically under-resourced environment that is often hostile externally and, at times, internally. The intention of the chapter is not to blindly criticise the statutory child protection system or non-Indigenous statutory child protection practitioners. The purpose of this chapter is to provide knowledge and opportunities for insight as well as to present alternative ways of working with Aboriginal and Torres Strait Islander children and families that still adhere to legislative requirements. We encouraged readers to engage with the material in this chapter within this context.

Also, a note on language. We recognise that Aboriginal and Torres Strait Islander peoples belong to two separate and unique cultural backgrounds, with distinct languages, customs, and belief systems. The terms 'Indigenous' and 'Aboriginal and Torres Strait Islander' have been used interchangeably for the ease of the reader, not as an indication that the two are homogeneous.

What has been

To have a strong understanding of the complexity that exists when undertaking child protection work with Indigenous children and families in Australia, one must first understand the history of the State's intervention into the lives of Indigenous people and communities in relation to the raising of children. When the British arrived in Australia in 1788, they determined that there was no evidence of civilisation because the land did not appear to be owned or cultivated in any way (Bennett, 2013; Prentis, 2009). As a result, the British declared the land now known as Australia to be 'Terra Nullius' – that is, the land was regarded as being owned by no one (Atkinson, 2002; Krieken, 1999). The British assessed the land to be empty of anything except flora and fauna, and subsequently free for ownership to be assumed (Bolt, 2009).

According to Tyson (2011), the declaration of Terra Nullius was underpinned by the colonisers' belief that they were superior to other cultures because they were 'civilised' and the other people (namely, the Aboriginal people) were not. Discourses at the time – including social evolutionary theory, Darwinism, and anthropological scholarship – deemed Aboriginal people to be primitive, inferior, and requiring a superior race to assume responsibility for them (Bennett, 2013; Muecke, 1992; Reynolds, 1987). Anthropologists used questionable research practices to determine that Aboriginal people were unable to evolve and assimilate into European society, and that they would subsequently eventually die out (Tatz, 1999).

The expectation of natural expiration of Aboriginal people heralded a period of protectionism beginning in the late 1800s. The protectionist period was designed by government officials to move Aboriginal people from their traditional lands and onto missions or settlements, so they could be segregated from the European community while they died out (Bennett, 2013). Any autonomy over oneself was extinguished by the authorities who controlled every aspect of an Aboriginal person's life, including freedom of movement; employment and wages; education; marriage; and access to resources, such as food, water, and other supplies (Sherwood, 2013; Tatz, 1999). Traditional cultural practices were forbidden, including the use of tribal names and language and participation in Ceremony (Reynolds, 1987). Tilbury (2009) wrote that 'State paternalism saturated every piece of legislation… the effect was to slowly extract any power that people had over their lives' (p. 58).

Despite the efforts of the colonisers, the Aboriginal population did not die out, and instead increased as a result of relationships, often non-consensual, between Aboriginal women and settler men (Bennett, 2013). As government authorities became increasingly concerned about the 'half-caste problem', they began strategising a solution. Paten and Robinson (2008) wrote that 'many settlers and government authorities believed that the most effective way to deal with the Indigenous population was to separate Aboriginal children from Aboriginal adults' (p. 502). 'Half-caste' children were viewed to have the capacity to be civilised, unlike their Aboriginal parents, they possessed British blood, if only in part.

To ensure that 'mixed-blood' or 'half-caste' children were 'protected' from their Aboriginality, the British colonies of Australia implemented legislation that would see the state assume the legal guardianship of all Aboriginal children, without parental consent or the right of appeal (Bennett, 2013). Aboriginal children were removed from their families and communities and were adopted by non-Indigenous families, sent to orphanages or group homes, or sent to work as farmhands and/or housemaids (Atkinson, 2002).

The removal of children as a tool of social control over marginalised 'problem populations' had been used throughout Europe prior to the colonisation of Australia. Krieken (1999) wrote that:

> the concept of 'rescuing the rising generation' had been central to European church and state agencies' policies in relation to the children of the poor and working class since the 16th century, and was a central element of the modern state's conception of the intersection of family life and liberal citizenship. (p. 302)

The strategy of forcefully removing children from their parents and communities to control the Aboriginal population was not a new idea – the colonisers brought it with them. This is, of course, in contradiction to the dominant political discourse at the time which was that forced child removal was philanthropic, promoted the health and welfare of children, and was altruistic on behalf of policy-makers (Atkinson, 2002; Bessant, 2013).

Role of social work in the forced removal of Indigenous children

It is important to remember that the social work profession played a central role in the enactment of policies that resulted in the removal of Indigenous children – the practice that was referred to by Indigenous Australian social work academic Bennett (2013) as an 'instrument of social control' (p. 19). Bennett (2013) further argued that social workers at the time were 'participants in the process of dispossession and oppression' (p. 20) of Aboriginal people and communities. The role of social workers in the forced removal of children created a deep sense of suspicion and distrust of the profession among Aboriginal and Torres Strait Islander people and communities in Australia (Gilbert, 1993; Harms et al., 2011). Indigenous Australian social work academics Menzies and Gilbert (2013) wrote that the sense of fear and suspicion towards social workers stems from social work being undertaken 'to' Aboriginal people, 'not with them', and from the perception that the profession can 'value a social system that privileged non-Aboriginal perspectives and values, or ways of life over that of Aborigines and Torres Strait Islanders' (p. 52).

Past trauma presents in a contemporary context

There is a strong evidence-based connection between colonisation practices, including the historical forced removal of children, and the social issues impacting Indigenous communities in a contemporary context (Atkinson, 2002; Bessarab & Crawford, 2013; Sherwood, 2013). Many researchers and academics state that the disproportionate representation of Indigenous children and families requiring the intervention of statutory child protective authorities is a demonstration of this nexus (Atkinson, 2002; Bennett, 2013; Menzies & Gilbert, 2013). Communities with a history of forced child removals experience deep trauma that manifests in behaviour that will likely cause children to receive the attention of current child protection services (Herring, Spangaro, Lauw, & McNamara, 2013; King, Smith, & Gracey, 2009). Cunneen and Libesman (2000) wrote that contemporary child removals by state child protective authorities have foundations linked to historical removals – namely, that the intergenerational effects of past separations, coupled with systemic racism and poor socioeconomic conditions, 'combine to produce the conditions which underlie contemporary removals' (p. 103).

It is essential that non-Indigenous practitioners understand the history of the State's intervention into the lives of Indigenous people in Australia and centrally, how children were to be raised, and by whom. This is critical to keep in the forefront of your mind when working with Indigenous families especially where engagement is difficult. Indigenous people have been excluded for generations by authorities in any discussion about how best to meet the care and protection needs of their children. It is not an unreasonable assumption that mainstream child protection systems are not particularly good at engaging Indigenous families and communities or that Indigenous families and communities know how best to have their voices heard by child protection authorities.

> Q: Kaylene, how could/should Cultural Knowledge be included into child protection work?
> *It is not Cultural Knowledge that needs to be included in child protection work, it is historical knowledge. Cultural Knowledge is about Our identity. Historical knowledge is about what has happened to us. Once you understand how colonisation and following government policy traumatised Us, once that framework of understanding is acknowledged, you will then see the behaviour of Indigenous parents more clearly, through a trauma-informed lens.*
>
> *Under the protection days when a lot of Our people were put into missions, those gates were not locked, but most didn't leave. They didn't leave because the oppression was normalised. Not having a voice or a role in decision making about anything was normalised. Being told what to do and how to be was normalised. People were fearful of what was outside those gates – fearful of things that might happen inside the gate too, constant fear. Then to now – you have parents who are evasive, don't show up to appointments, aggressive, hard to engage – they are trying to dodge you yes, but you need to ask why are they dodging? Don't just shake your head, think of what might be happening inside of them – they are fearful of what will*

*happen next – this is what trauma looks like for Us. A thorough under-
standing of historical truth is important because it is linked to present
day behaviours seen with Our parents.*

*You must first understand historical knowledge before Cultural
Knowledge will be revealed to you. Cultural Knowledge is about Our
identity. This information will flow naturally once historical truths are
acknowledged and safety is established. Cultural Knowledge will not
be shared with you when effort is not taken to establish rapport and
relationships. Relationships are key.*

It is critical for non-Indigenous practitioners to understand is how the
trauma caused by the forced removal of children generations before, presents
in the lives of Indigenous children and families today. What does the manifestation of intergenerational trauma look like on the front line when you are
assessing risk to an Indigenous child in a child protection context? What
elements are critical to consider? What parental behaviour would you be
likely to see and how would this impact your assessment? How is it, or is it,
different from how you would assess a child from a non-Indigenous
background?

What is now?

Contemporary child protection practice with Indigenous children and families

Several authors are critical of how child protection authorities work with
Aboriginal and Torres Strait Islander children and families within Australia
(Bennett, 2013; Briskman, 2014; Lewis & Burton, 2014). A lack of understanding of the ways in which historical trauma presents within Aboriginal
and Torres Strait Islander communities in a contemporary context is frequently cited (Atkinson, 2002; Bessarab & Crawford, 2013; Harms et al.,
2011; Menzies & Gilbert, 2013). My doctoral research explored the experiences of Indigenous child protection practitioners (Oates, 2018). The participants in the study were all experienced practitioners, in both statutory
and non-statutory child protection practice contexts within Australia.
Practitioners were invited to talk about child protection practice with
Indigenous children and families from their perspective. The voices of these
practitioners have been included in this chapter as they are the experts in
working with Indigenous children and families in a culturally safe child protection context. Collectively, they hold critical knowledge that should underpin our practice frameworks as non-Indigenous practitioners. Please note
that the names included in the direct quotes from participants are pseudo-
nyms they chose for themselves. A strong theme from practitioners in the
study was concern that non-Indigenous statutory child protection workers

did not have a thorough understanding of how historical trauma presents for Indigenous people and communities contemporarily:

> They don't understand the anger and the hurt behind it. I mean, some families still come in and say, 'Oh, you're just like the Stolen Generation, you're going to steal our children again, which is the Stolen Generation all over again'... I don't think we go back to the origins of that family and speak to their fear and history of the family. (Rosalyn)
>
> You have to have some empathy for people who have gone through – who are going through stuff. I think the department needs to be more empathetic when they do talk to our people about the history. They keep saying, 'it happened, whatever'. But it didn't happen a long time ago. It happened not long ago... it needs to be in the forefront of every department worker's mind. (Missy)

Of great concern to participants was that behaviour exhibited by clients during investigations is interpreted by non-Indigenous child protection workers to be a demonstration of parents' denial or minimisation of child protection concerns. Parental aggression, threats, attempts to intimidate or refusal to engage were interpreted by the participants to be a trauma response because of the presence of child protective authorities, rather than a minimisation of child protection concerns:

> Our interventions... need to be trauma informed because we're talking about people coming in who have got complex trauma, but we might say they're more oppositional, defiant or got mental illnesses. But they're just coming to us with complex trauma, so our more difficult clients who are angry and want things to happen straight away, and they can't think properly... they can't remember things. (Elvina)
>
> There was a Black mother with four children and [she] was notified on ... she went into fight or flight mode. Her automatic response is, 'Okay, now it's my turn to have my kids taken away from me'. Not able to love properly because of how they were raised... so they don't know how to love and engage... It's almost like being removed because of the symptom of transgenerational trauma, but, in fact, we're exacerbating and continuing that cycle and that trauma. There's no healing. (Mary)
>
> The thoughts and ideas of the old ways of being are still there. I think that, you know, legislation has to be different. They have to be different in the way they actually look at things and then the way that they actually work out whether the child is in need of

protection or not, you know. I think what needs to happen is they need to evaluate families better. If they evaluated the families better in a different way, they'll know whether those kids are safe. (Lisa)

Menzies and Gilbert (2013) argued that 'making the link between separation and assimilation and trauma may assist social workers to accurately identify the origins of behaviour and avoid inaccurate assessments and negative assumptions of Aboriginal clients' (p. 62). Participants held the view that the misinterpretation by non-Indigenous workers of these behaviours was a demonstration of them not 'making the link', which could potentially lead to premature removal because of a lack of proper assessment of their protective needs, rather than an actual risk of harm. Participant Sarah details an example of this below:

I've also found, because the Indigenous parents tend to not engage as well because of that transgenerational trauma, they just go, 'They've taken them. We're done now'. Or they get really aggressive. So they get listed as being aggressive and because they didn't engage well, that reunification is less likely to happen. (Sarah)

As an example of how Indigenous people experience intergenerational trauma, some participants spoke about the fear responses they experienced when engaging with child protection authorities as professionals:

There is still a bit of a – there's still fear of, like, white man and child safety ... Even myself, I guess... I still have that fear of even going to child safety meetings ... I do get really anxious. (Grace)

As demonstrated by participant Grace, the fear experienced by Indigenous people who come under investigation by child protection authorities cannot be underestimated.

An additional source of frustration for some participants was an observed lack of willingness by some non-Indigenous workers to learn and gain knowledge about the trauma related to previous child protection practices, including the period when State-sanctioned forced child removal policies were in place. One participant, Rosalyn, was herself taken and placed for adoption without her mother's consent. She shared that some workers did not believe that atrocities committed against Aboriginal people, such as the Stolen Generation, were of contemporary relevance:

The other part of it is that not everybody wanted to listen to that story, my story, because it happened so long ago, it's past

> history... the newer generation of staff coming through the door could not understand what that would feel like... it just doesn't happen. (Rosalyn)

Critical social work theorist Fook (2012) argued that the legitimacy of knowledge and its value is determined by the dominant group. Similarly, it is the privilege of mainstream structures to decide when knowledge has been used to its full capacity and is subsequently no longer viewed as significant. The experiences of the participants, particularly highlighted by Roslyn's quotation, appear to be consistent with Fook's work because the dominant non-Indigenous group does not place the same significance on intergenerational trauma and its contemporary presentation as does the Indigenous, more marginalised group.

From the narratives of the Indigenous child protection practitioners above, we would like to draw out some critical elements that non-Indigenous practitioners can implement in their practice with Indigenous families. Participant Elvina spoke about the need for trauma-informed practice when working with Indigenous children and families. She went on to say that the manifestation of intergenerational trauma within parents presents as parents not being able to think clearly or rationally when presented with concerns about their children. They are often quick to anger or behave aggressively. She also referred to parents not being able to remember things as a result of a trauma response being triggered by the presence of child protection authorities. With these behavioural presentations in mind, non-Indigenous practitioners can make some simple changes to the way they engage with Indigenous families that will allow them to form a better assessment of what is happening for children within their families. For example, asking parents to nominate a trusted friend or family member to be present so that they can repeat the information at a time when emotions are less heightened, involving a community-controlled partner organisation, or making a time to come back to talk about the concerns after you have outlined them may be strategies that address these behavioural presentations of complex trauma. Reflect on what other strategies you may be able to implement within your practice framework. What strategies could address the trauma-based behavioural presentation described by Elvina, that is, not being able to think clearly or not being able to remember things? This reflection activity will assist in working more effectively with all clients who have a complex trauma background, not just Indigenous children and families.

Over-reliance on cultural competency training

Another consistent criticism of child protection practice with Indigenous children and families is the lack of culturally competent practice possessed by statutory child protective workers (Bessarab & Crawford, 2013; Funston & Herring, 2016; Oates, 2019). Statutory child protection agencies rely heavily on cultural competency training as a strategy to upskill the non-Indigenous workforce to work appropriately with Aboriginal and Torres Strait Islander children and families. These workshops are typically one or two days as a one-off when a practitioner commences employment and, in some jurisdictions, yearly 'refresher' sessions offered either face to face or online.

The concept of 'cultural competency' and variations thereof is strongly criticised in the practice and research literature. An element of criticism relates to processes that frame cultural competence as a task for completion, rather than an ongoing process (Cross, 1989; Farrelly & Lumby, 2009; Sakamoto, 2007; Wells, Merritt, & Briggs, 2009). Other scholars have described cultural competency as a system that frames culture in neutral terms, affording no space for the critique of power or the oppression and marginalisation often faced by non-white groups (Pon, 2009; Sakamoto, 2007). It is our view that the oppression and marginalisation experienced by Indigenous people in Australia cannot be separated from contemporary child protection practice. *Our parents come into contact with the child protection system with a complete package of historical feelings and events that have been lived down through the ages and has accumulated into this moment, this moment where child protection gets involved – Aboriginal and Torres Strait Islander Australians are still trying to assimilate into a system that is neither fair or friendly to Our families.*

As stated previously in this chapter, the evidence base is clear that how Indigenous people were colonised has a direct impact on the current issues experienced by Indigenous families and communities, that is, the conditions that form the basis of contemporary removals. It must be acknowledged that statutory child protection agencies have progressed quite a way from historical draconian practices outlined in the beginning of this chapter. However, the way in which Indigenous children and families often experience the child protection system has not. This is as a result of families being caught in a continuous loop of trauma. The experience of trauma is often compounded by statutory authority practices that are not culturally safe for Indigenous children and families.

If not cultural competency training, then what?

Despite the criticism of cultural competency training in the literature, it is unclear what should replace it or be added on to make it more effective. However, the Indigenous child protection practitioners who were interviewed as part of my doctoral study offered some practical strategies to increase the culturally responsive practice of non-Indigenous practitioners. They too voiced concerns about the quality and effectiveness of cultural competency training. Outlined next are three of those strategies.

Indigenous practitioner-led and developed staff training packages and professional development

Practitioner Isabella presented an alternative way of thinking about the upskilling of non-Indigenous child protection workers that were not solely reliant on a formalised training package:

> What is the role that we can actually play outside of a formal cultural awareness training? Because I don't know if that has really the impact that we're looking for. I'm wondering about what is it that we can do if we're feeling strong enough to do that and capable enough doing that, where we can create safe places and safe spaces for our non-Indigenous colleagues to actually come to us. We create these places in organisations, in the workplace where non-Indigenous workers can actually come and ask the questions they're afraid to ask. Because how will the non-Indigenous ever learn? (Isabella)

Cultural supervision within agencies for non-Indigenous practitioners

Some practitioners in the study had been involved in receiving and delivering what they described as 'cultural supervision'. It was their view that non-Indigenous staff should receive cultural supervision from an experienced Indigenous child protection practitioner regularly as a way to strengthen their cultural competence and effectiveness when working with Indigenous families. This position is supported in the literature by Bessarab (2012), who argued that both Aboriginal and non-Aboriginal practitioners 'often require appropriate Aboriginal cultural supervision that can assist them to address and understand the cultural and political issues emerging in their work' (p. 75).

Creation of specialist Indigenous practitioner-led practice units within statutory child protection agencies

Many practitioners in this study raised their concern that the accuracy of assessments relating to the care and protection needs of Indigenous children was questionable and, at times, informed by ignorance and/or prejudice. Practitioner Missy raised during her interview that she would like to see specialist statutory child protection units that solely respond to Indigenous families at risk.

> Even if there was a specific unit that only worked with Aboriginal and Torres Strait Islander people that specialised in – rather than

just these random CSOs [Child Safety Officer] doing a mainstream job and then, oh, we've got an Indigenous job. Like there are actual specialised child safety officers who are completely over and understand and work with Aboriginal and Torres Strait Islander families only. I don't know why we don't have that. (Missy)

The model Missy suggested would be staffed by both Indigenous and non-Indigenous practitioners who would have access to specialist training, resources, and supervision.

A strong theme that emerged from the narratives of practitioners was how critical the involvement of experienced Indigenous practitioners in the upskilling of non-Indigenous practitioners is. Many of the practitioners discussed the issue that, even if non-Indigenous child protection practitioners receive quality cultural competency training, their ability to implement what they had learnt in the field was lacking.

> Q: Kaylene, how critical it is for non-Indigenous workers to include the expertise of Indigenous practitioners in a child protection context?
> *The inclusion of Indigenous practitioners when working with Indigenous children and families is critical. The way We communicate is different. The way We use and construct language is unique to Us – when non-Indigenous workers write down verbatim what Indigenous people say, they can misunderstand the meaning. The use of tone, context and non-verbal communication is at the core of how We communicate with each other, it is what defines Our communication with each other and is a central part of Our identity as Aboriginal people. Indigenous practitioners are attuned to listening and reading our Mobs.*
>
> *As a non-Indigenous person you will not be as familiar with Our communication style and therefore you will miss things, especially as things are already heightened – you will miss things, or misinterpret things – ineffective communication with Indigenous families about your processes often triggers aggressive responses from Our parents – this is not a sign they don't want to engage with you about your concerns, this is a sign they are frustrated by your communication style. Keep an Indigenous practitioner close to you until you can build rapport and trust, until you can understand the communication style of that family better. Also you need to understand that agreement is not understanding. An Indigenous practitioner will be able to give you an idea of whether or not you have been understood by the family and whether or not they agree with you or whether they are nodding to make you go away.*
> Q: Kaylene, what are your thoughts on cultural supervision and/or other Indigenous practitioner-led training for non-Indigenous workers?

I am supportive of cultural supervision for non-Indigenous workers. This will build the cultural capability of the non-Indigenous workforce. They need a place to unpack things like the behaviour of parents, things they might see but don't understand. It will help people understand that you might see a mother of children where there are concerns and you see her through that lens – the mother not looking after her children lens. Cultural supervision would help non-Indigenous workers understand that same mother, that Indigenous mother, is saturated in grief – grief of losing her children, grief related to the experience of abuse and violence, having loved ones around her die in large numbers one after one with no break – this is the reality for Our people.

Historically we were not allowed to grieve. We were not allowed to acknowledge Our family members. We were not allowed to grieve/ mourn their loss the way We needed to, Our way. Denying Us this was a strategy used by the colonisers to control and oppress Us. When there has been no truth telling, no healing, some of Us find it hard to process grief. Process trauma. That is what you see in that same mother when you have the historical knowledge of what happened to Us and what it looks like now.

Not being able to participate in decision making about Our lives was another way colonisers controlled and oppressed Us. No control over where We lived, who We married, where We went, how We look after Our children. Some of Our children were born of settler men raping Our women – We had no control over Our bodies. How that looks now is that Our people will desperately hold onto what little control they have, or they think they have. In child protection work, this might look like parents not attending appointments, not engaging in case planning decisions in the way or in the timeframe outlined by child protection. These behaviours are not necessarily signs that parents don't want to work with you. One on one cultural supervision sessions would give non-Indigenous workers a place to explore these links.

Future considerations

The rates of Indigenous child removal in Australia cannot continue. Fresh and innovative thinking that is more than just 'adding on' to a system that is already problematic for Indigenous children and families is desperately needed. A values and knowledge shift needs to occur. The non-Indigenous mainstream worldview of how an Indigenous child fits into an Indigenous family needs to be critically examined. The following case study highlights how the non-Indigenous worldview of the family is applied to an Indigenous child in the child protection system.

Q: Kaylene, what are your thoughts on working with Indigenous children and families where a long-term order has been made, like in the case study of Jane? What would be helpful for non-Indigenous practitioners to know?

Box 8.1 Case Study – Jane

This is Jane's story. Jane came to the attention of child protective services (CPS) as her mother, Anne, had been arrested by police for public intoxication. Anne had 6-month-old Jane with her at the time. Anne identified as Aboriginal and told police that she was from another state. Anne told police that she had no family in the area and that she didn't know anyone who could care for Jane. Police removed Jane from the care of Anne and she was placed into the care of CPS. CPS subsequently applied for a custody order on the grounds that Anne had a long history of homelessness, violent relationships, and problematic drug and alcohol use. Anne also had two older children in foster care in her home state. Anne would not disclose to CPS who Jane's father was. A one-year child protection order was made in relation to Jane and she was placed with non-Indigenous foster carers as there were no Indigenous foster carers available. Throughout this process, CPS did not make contact with Anne's family interstate as they intended to work with Anne so that Jane could safely return to her care.

One year passed and in that time Anne was not able to address the outstanding child protection concerns relating to Jane. CPS met with Anne to tell her that it was their intention to apply for a long term guardianship order in relation to Jane until she was 18 years of age. CPS told Anne that they didn't think she would be able to make the long-term lifestyle changes necessary to regain the care of her daughter even if they extended the short term custody order. CPS told Anne that they wanted stability for Jane and asked her if she could identify any appropriate family members who may be able to care for Jane as per their practice procedures. It was at this time that Anne identified who Jane's father was and stated that perhaps someone in his family could be a long-term carer.

Jane's father Peter was located by CPS. Peter was not in a position to care for Jane as he too had a long history of homelessness and problematic drug and alcohol use, as well as periods of incarceration due to violence. Peter stated that he had a very large family and nominated three people who may be able to care for his daughter. Peter stated he had had no contact with the three nominated people for many years due to his transient lifestyle. CPS contacted Peter's family members who stated that they were unaware that Peter had a child or that she had been in foster care for the past year. Two of the three family members stated they had capacity to care for Jane and wanted her placed with them as soon as possible.

Peter's family had the view that Jane was a missing piece of their family and kinship structure and that she should be returned to them. They also wished for the child protection order to be revoked as Jane would be with family and, in their view, no longer in need of protection. Both family members were assessed and formally approved as foster carers. CPS did not place Jane in the care of her extended family, however did arrange contact visits. Jane's mother was contesting the long term guardianship application while Jane's father was consenting on the condition that Jane live with members of his family. The position of CPS was that where Jane resided was irrelevant and that the court case should only focus on Jane's parents being unable to safely care for her.

CPS chose to continue with their application for long-term guardianship, despite the paternal family requesting Jane be placed in their care and the application for a child protection order be revoked. CPS cited that Jane had no relationship with her paternal family and had a very strong attachment to her current non-Indigenous foster carers where she had resided since being removed from her mother. The non-Indigenous foster carers viewed Jane as an important part of their family and indicated they would like to care for her on a long-term basis. CPS assessed that it would be in Jane's best interests long term to be cared for by her foster family until she was 18 years of age. CPS offered to facilitate contact between the paternal family and the foster family as part of Jane's cultural support plan. Neither of Jane's parents were present in court at the final hearing and as such a long-term order granting guardianship of Jane to CPS until she was 18 years of age was made in their absence.

Our position within Our families is seen by Us as a birthright. It doesn't matter whether a child is in care until they are 18, or whether the family lays eyes on them – that child has a place within their family and kinship structure. You might hear some of Our parents say, 'well take them now but they'll come back when they are 18' – that is not a sign that they do not want that child in their kinship structure, that is often them feeling helpless to change what is happening, what the government is doing. But you need to remember that Our bonds are stronger than your system.

Our people do not always understand that child protection processes are legal processes. They most times won't go and engage a solicitor as soon as their children are taken, which means Our people don't have proper legal representation to explain the process to them from the start. When CPS tells them they will be taking an order on their children for three days, they hear and believe those children will be returned in three days. When they are not, the anger, confusion and mistrust builds. Good communication is the key to this, communication that Our people will understand, not communication that is government talk. Our parents get stuck in the fight, trying to advocate for themselves in a system they don't understand. They get stuck there. They find it overwhelming to shift to the phase where they need to acknowledge the concerns CPS has and work with them to make changes. Our parents being stuck in the fight, this should not be taken as a sign they don't acknowledge or minimise the concerns or that they are not willing to engage – this is a sign that they are experiencing trauma, trauma you will recognise once you have an understanding of Our historical knowledge and truth.

All these things, the lack of communication that Our people understand, lack of legal representation from the beginning, barriers to being able to participate in decision making, trauma-based behaviours like evasion and/or aggression, sets Our children on a different path in the child protection system from non-Indigenous children. You should know your Act, your legislation but you should also know Our history if you want to work with Us properly.

Reflective Questions for Practice

Take a moment to reflect on the information presented in this chapter thus far and how you might have worked with Jane and her family.

1. What practice values are present in Jane's story? From the non-Indigenous social worker's view? From the worldview of the father and his family? From the non-Indigenous foster carer's view?

2. What are your thoughts on the child protection agency view that remaining with non-Indigenous foster carers is in 'Jane's best interest long term'?

3. What could the non-Indigenous social worker do to engage the family (with the Indigenous worldview of the family in mind)?

4. Do you think intergenerational trauma is a factor in this scenario? If so, how?

In Australia, Indigenous practitioners, advocates, academics, and researchers have told us that there are better ways to work with Indigenous children and families in a child protection context. Jane's story is an example of how Eurocentric and Indigenous worldviews of family and what is in a child's best interests significantly differ. From Jane's story, it is clear that both of her parents were not in a position to safely care for her. There were several factors the child protection agency took into consideration when determining what would be in Jane's best long-term interests. One example is the lack of 'relationship' between Jane and her extended family. Relationship, as defined by the CPS, included in-person contact over a period of time – which Jane had not had. This definition was also extended to Jane's father as he had had very little contact with his family over time due to his lifestyle. In contrast, Jane's family's worldview was that Jane already had a pre-determined relationship with them, regardless of physical contact, as she was the child of a family member and therefore a valuable part of their kinship network. The practice complexity demonstrated in Jane's story is that both options available to the CPS – that is, to place Jane with her non-Indigenous foster carers until she was 18 years of age or returning Jane to the care of her extended family – were within legislative requirements and adhered to the CPS's practice policies and procedures. The determining factor in relation to deciding what was in Jane's best interest was not the legislation, policies, or procedures of CPS, but the non-Indigenous worldview of family. The legislation, policies or procedures of CPS are often not the issue, the application of them is.

Indigenous children do not enter the child protection system as a singular entity even though statutory child protection practices and procedures are designed to view them that way. Indigenous children need to be acknowledged by non-Indigenous practitioners as a valuable piece in a larger sophisticated kinship network. Within Indigenous family and kinship networks exist processes and ways of managing the safety and protection of children when difficulties arise. However, these cultural methods are almost always disregarded or not considered in the first instance with the preference being to proceed with the colonist mainstream application of child protection approaches. Respectful collaboration with Indigenous families, communities, and colleagues by child protection practitioners could yield alternative ways of ensuring the care and protection needs of children are met in a culturally safe and respectful way. There are ways of achieving both outcomes – that is, the meeting of a child's care and protection needs as defined by mainstream child protection authorities that are culturally respectful and safe for Indigenous children and families.

> Q: Kaylene, what do non-Indigenous practitioners get wrong when working with Indigenous children and families? What are the key things they should know?
>
> *I feel that sometimes non-Indigenous workers lack the emotional intelligence to acknowledge they have a deficit in their knowledge. They might have done Indigenous studies at university but what does that mean? Can they make the links on the ground? Over the years I've had many non-Indigenous workers debate the point with me – I just want to say 'well are you Black then?' They won't accept that there is a gap in their practice, won't acknowledge a gap in their cultural capabilities.*

Why is that? Is it their own vulnerabilities? Standing back, allowing space, talking through and acknowledging the sensitive and difficult sections, shows understanding of Our Mob's journey and that you are not here to continue colonising.

Another key thing non-Indigenous people working with Our people need to understand is that we are human beings. Aboriginal people are always segregated, look on government forms, We are thought of, and seen as, different to non-Indigenous people – the government sanctions that – they see Aboriginality as a 'risk factor'. Risk factor for poor health, going to jail, not looking after kids. We are human beings. See Us. We are not just names on case lists or contents in affidavits. Don't let your case management tasks, end of month reports or legislative requirements dehumanise Us. We have the same right as everyone else. We are people who live, love and cry.

Concluding thoughts

Administering statutory child protection services that are Eurocentric to Indigenous children with a few 'add-ons' or 'cultural considerations', while well intended, have proven not to work over time. Practice frameworks that are underpinned by colonialist worldviews of how a child fits into a family structure have not been successful when working with Indigenous children and families. Maintenance of practices with a child protection system that is already problematic for Indigenous children and families will not address the disproportionate representation of Indigenous children in the system. Our key message to you is to take a minute to think about how you apply your agency's legislative requirements as well as their policies and procedures when working with Indigenous children and families. There are ways to ensure a child's care and protection needs are met as defined legislatively that are also culturally respectful and culturally safe. Be vulnerable, set to one side your professional fear and/or anxiety about being viewed as inadequate, and engage with Indigenous practitioner colleagues both inside and outside your agency with an open mind.

Discussion Questions

1. How can child protection systems more effectively include Indigenous worldviews of family and community into their work?

2. When making decisions about a child's 'best interests', what mechanisms would you include in your practice to ensure your dominant non-Indigenous worldview doesn't exclude Indigenous worldviews?

3. Given the knowledge in the chapter, how would you more effectively engage with Aboriginal and Torres Strait Islander practitioner colleagues?

4. What strategies would you use to ensure the impacts of intergenerational trauma are at the fore of your mind when working in child protection?

References

Atkinson, J. (2002). *Trauma tails recreating song lines: The transgenerational effects of trauma in Indigenous Australia*. Melbourne, VIC: Spinifex Press.

Bennett, B. (2013). The importance of Aboriginal and Torres Strait Islander history for social work students and graduates. In B. Bennett, S. Green, S. Gilbert, & D. Bessarab (Eds.), *Our voices: Aboriginal and Torres Strait Islander social work* (pp. 1–25). Claremont, VIC: Palgrave Macmillan.

Bessant, J. (2013). History and Australian Indigenous child welfare policies. *Policy Studies, 34*(3), 310–325. doi: https://doi.org/10.1080/01442872.201 3.803531.

Bessarab, D. (2012). The supervisory yarn: Embedding Indigenous epistemology in supervision. In B. Bennett, S. Green, S. Gilbert, & D. Bessarab (Eds.), *Our voices. Aboriginal and Torres Strait Islander social work* (pp. 73–92). South Yarra, VIC: Palgrave Macmillan.

Bessarab, D., & Crawford, F. (2013). Trauma, grief and loss: The vulnerability of Aboriginal families in the child protection system. In B. Bennett, S. Green, S. Gilbert, & D. Bessarab (Eds.), *Our voices: Aboriginal and Torres Strait Islander social work* (pp. 93–109). Claremont, VIC: Palgrave Macmillan.

Bolt, R. (2009). *Urban Aboriginal identity construction in Australia: An Aboriginal perspective utilising multi-method qualitative analysis*. Sydney, NSW: University of Sydney.

Briskman, L. (2014). *Social work with Indigenous communities: A human rights approach* (2nd ed.). Annandale, NSW: The Federation Press.

Cross, T. (1989). *Towards a culturally competent system of care: A monograph on effective services for minority children who are severely emotionally disturbed*. Washington, DC: CASSP Technical Assistance Center, Georgetown University Child Development Center.

Cunneen, C., & Libesman, T. (2000). Postcolonial trauma: The contemporary removal of Indigenous children and young people from their families in Australia. *Australian Journal of Social Issues, 35*(2), 99–115.

Farrelly, T., & Lumby, B. (2009). A best practice approach to cultural competence training. *Aboriginal and Islander Health Worker Journal, 33*(5), 14–22.

Fook, J. (2012). *Social work: A critical approach to practice* (2nd ed.). London: Sage Publications.

Funston, L., & Herring, S. (2016). When will the stolen generations end? A qualitative critical exploration of contemporary 'child protection' practices in Aboriginal and Torres Strait Islander communities. *Sexual Abuse in Australia and New Zealand, 7*(1), 51.

Gilbert, S. (1993). The effects of colonisation on Aboriginal families: Issues and strategies for child welfare policies. In J. Mason (Ed.), *Child welfare policy: Critical Australian perspectives*. Sydney, NSW: Hale and Iremonger.

Harms, L., Middleton, J., Whyte, J., Anderson, I., Clarke, A., Sloan, J., ..., Smith, M. (2011). Social work with Aboriginal clients: Perspectives on educational preparation and practice. *Australian Social Work, 64*(2), 156–168. doi: https://doi.org/10.1080/0312407X.2011.577184.

Herring, S., Spangaro, J., Lauw, M., & McNamara, L. (2013). The intersection of trauma, racism, and cultural competence in effective work with Aboriginal people: Waiting for trust. *Australian Social Work, 66*(1), 104–117. doi: https://doi.org/10.1080/0312407X.2012.697566.

King, M., Smith, A., & Gracey, M. (2009). Indigenous health Part 2: The underlying causes of the health gap. *The Lancet, 374*(9683), 76–85. doi: https://doi.org/10.1016/S0140-6736(09)60827-8.

Krieken, R. V. (1999). The 'Stolen Generations' and cultural genocide: The forced removal of Australian Indigenous children from their families and its implications for the sociology of childhood. *Childhood, 6*(3), 297–311. doi: https://doi.org/10.1177/0907568299006003002.

Lewis, N., & Burton, J. (2014). Keeping kids safe at home is key to preventing institutional abuse. *Indigenous Law Bulletin, 8*(13), 11–14.

Menzies, K., & Gilbert, S. (2013). Engaging communities. In B. Bennett, S. Green, S. Gilbert, & D. Bessarab (Eds.), *Our voices: Aboriginal and Torres Strait Islander social work* (pp. 50–69). Claremont, VIC: Palgrave Macmillan.

Muecke, S. (1992). Lonely representations: Aboriginality and cultural studies. *Journal of Australian Studies, 16*(35), 32–44. doi: https://doi.org/10.1080/14443059209387116.

Oates, F. (2018). *Working for the welfare: Exploring the experiences of Indigenous child protection workers*. PhD thesis, James Cook University, Cairns, Australia. Retrieved from https://researchonline.jcu.edu.au/56112/. doi: https://doi.org/10.25903/5bea03dc810f3.

Oates, F. (2019). Racism as trauma: Experiences of Aboriginal and Torres Strait Islander Australian child protection practitioners. *Child Abuse & Neglect*. Advance online publication. doi: https://doi.org/10.1016/j.chiabu.2019.104262.

Paten, J., & Robinson, S. (2008). The question of genocide and Indigenous child removal: The colonial Australian context. *Journal of Genocide Research, 10*(4), 501–518. doi: https://doi.org/10.1080/14623520802447818.

Pon, G. (2009). Cultural competency as new racism: An ontology of forgetting. *Journal of Progressive Human Services, 20*(1), 59–71. doi: https://doi.org/10.1080/10428230902871173.

Prentis, M. (2009). *A study in black and white: The Aborigines in Australian history* (3rd ed.). Dural, NSW: Rosenberg.

Reynolds, H. (1987). *Frontier: Aborigines, settlers and land*. Sydney, NSW: Allen & Unwin.

Sakamoto, I. (2007). An anti-oppressive approach to cultural competence. *Canadian Social Work Review/Revue Canadienne De Service Social, 24*(1), 105–114.

Sherwood, J. (2013). Colonisation – It's bad for your health: The context of Aboriginal health. *Contemporary Nurse, 46*(1), 28–40. doi: https://doi.org/10.5172/conu.2013.46.1.28.

Tatz, C. (1999). Genocide in Australia. *Journal of Genocide Research, 1*(3), 315–352.

Tilbury, C. (2009). The over-representation of Indigenous children in the Australian child welfare system. *International Journal of Social Welfare, 18*(1), 57–64. doi: https://doi.org/10.1111/j.1468-2397.2008.00577.x.

Tyson, L. (2011). *Using critical theory: How to read and write about literature* (2nd ed.). New York, NY: Routledge.

Wells, S., Merritt, L., & Briggs, H. (2009). Bias, racism and evidence-based practice: The case for more focused development of the child welfare evidence base. *Children and Youth Services Review, 31*(11), 1160–1171. doi: https://doi.org/10.1016/j.childyouth.2009.09.002.

9 Conversations on Practice in Criminal Justice

Steve Morgan, Clint Hanley, James Fa'Aoso, Claire Walker, Susan Rayment-McHugh, and Dimity Adams

Australia has an appalling record in criminal justice system responses to Aboriginal and Torres Strait Islander peoples. Chronic and increasing over-representation and over-incarceration is well documented, with Australian Indigenous peoples acknowledged as the most incarcerated on earth (where data are available; Anthony, 2017). Aboriginal and Torres Strait Islander peoples make up a significant 28% of current prisoners in Australia, but only about 3% of the national population (ABS, 2019). Whilst precise rates of imprisonment vary from state to state and year to year, it is reported that Aboriginal and Torres Strait Islander men are imprisoned at about 12.5 times the rate of non-Indigenous Australians (ALRC, 2017). This over-representation is even more pronounced for Aboriginal and Torres Strait Islander women, who are 21 times more likely to be imprisoned than non-Indigenous women (ALRC, 2017), and for youth, who are an alarming 28 times more likely to be detained (SCATSIA, 2011). This national crisis is attributed to a complex interplay of causal factors, including the destruction of Aboriginal society through colonisation, dispossession, and assimilation; intergenerational trauma; systemic racism; and entrenched disadvantage (PWC, 2017; Cunneen et al., 2016; Weatherburn, 2014).

These statistics are shocking and fundamentally unfair. The tragedy behind these figures becomes even most apparent, however, when the human impact is considered. People in the criminal justice system generally experience poorer physical health and higher rates of mental illness (AIHW, 2018). Imprisonment negatively impacts future employment, income, housing, and social inclusion (PWC, 2017). High imprisonment rates also have collateral impacts on children, families, and communities. For example, Aboriginal and Torres Strait Islander prisoners report difficulties maintaining relationships with their children, with distance and financial disadvantage restricting contact (Dennison, Smallbone, Stewart, Freiberg, & Teague, 2014). This in turn limits opportunities for these parents to be role models (Payer, Taylor, & Barnes, 2015), and may cause children distress and stigmatisation (Hagan & Dinovitzer, 1999). Further, research in the Northern Territory suggests that at any point in time between 4 and 14% of men aged 20–39 years may be absent from remote communities due to incarceration, ultimately chang-ing remote community composition and growth (Payer et al., 2015).

Re-offending and re-incarceration also contribute to Indigenous over-representation. Research consistently shows higher recidivism outcomes for Aboriginal and Torres Strait Islander clients in the correctional system (e.g. Rojas & Gretton, 2007; Smallbone & Rallings, 2013; Allan, Allan, Marshall, & Kraszlan, 2003; Broadhurst & Maller, 1992). Indeed, most (78%) Aboriginal and Torres Strait Islander prisoners have previously been incarcer-ated (ABS, 2019), whilst 43% of Aboriginal and Torres Strait Islander pris-oners have been in prison on at least five previous occasions (AIHW, 2018). Ineffective and irrelevant therapeutic programming and a lack of cultural responsiveness are recognised as key factors contributing to these poor results (e.g. Day, 2014; Hovane, Dalton, & Smith, 2014; Farrelly & Carlson, 2011). An examination of the criminal justice workforce sheds some light on these issues. Whilst 28% of prisoners identify as Aboriginal or Torres Strait Islander (ABS, 2019), the current criminal justice workforce employs only a small proportion of Aboriginal and Torres Strait Islander staff. Indeed, across Australia's many correctional departments, Indigenous employees typically make up 2–5% of the overall workforce (although the Northern Territory reports that 10.5% of the public service workforce identify as Aboriginal), most of whom are employed in the lower salary ranges (New South Wales Government, 2019; Northern Territory Government, 2015; Government of Western Australia, 2019; Victorian State Government, 2019; The State of Queensland, 2018). This snapshot exposes a jarring juxtaposition since, across the correctional system, Aboriginal and Torres Strait Islander peoples are more likely to be incarcerated than employed. In practice, this means that non-Aboriginal and Torres Strait Islander correctional staff are likely to be providing most of the supervision, rehabilitation, and transition services to Aboriginal and Torres Strait Islander clients. Given poor cultural responsive-ness is a key factor contributing to worse rehabilitation outcomes, the onus falls to these non-Indigenous criminal justice practitioners to contribute to improved outcomes.

Beyond the critical 'big picture' reforms recommended by multiple gov-ernment inquiries and reviews (e.g. a greater focus on prevention and early intervention, addressing disadvantage, law and justice reform, and improved rehabilitation and reintegration programming; ALRC, 2017; PWC, 2017), there is much that can be done at the level of the individual practitioner. Indeed, it is the individual practitioner who engages directly with Aboriginal and Torres Strait Islander clients, their families, and communities. The actions of these individual practitioners may impact client engagement, motivation, and success. For this reason, individual practitioners are respon-sible for ensuring they are culturally aware and responsive.

Too little has been written about culturally responsive practice within the criminal justice system. This chapter will advance this discussion, using reflections from some of the authors on their own experiences and observations. Reflections will centre on three key issues: (i) addressing power imbalances inherent within the criminal justice system; (ii) experiences of cultural supervision; and (iii) practice reflections. Collectively, these shared insights will showcase key considerations for individual practitioners in the criminal justice system to enhance culturally responsive practice and improve outcomes for Aboriginal and Torres Strait Islander peoples. Brief profiles are provided of the four authors who share their thoughts and experiences to contextualise their reflections.

Steve: Steve is a Kunindiri man who is passionate about 'building people from the inside out'. He is a family man, and a lifelong learner, and has over 20 years' experience working within the criminal justice system. He is committed to 'Closing the Chasm' and being a practitioner of cultural courage. His interests are in youth and personal leadership.

Clint: Clint is a Luritja man from Papunya, a community in the Western Desert of Central Australia in the Northern Territory. Over a 20-year career, he has been committed to supporting Aboriginal and Torres Strait Islander men to make positive choices in life through their participation in correctional programs. Clint's strong drive to assist men in introducing positive change to their story has been instilled in him by the many strong women in his life, such as his mother, his grandmother, his aunties, his sisters, and importantly, his wife of 25 years.

James: James descends from the Samu Augud, Koedal Augud (cassowary and crocodile clan) of the Torres Strait. He has spent over two decades working amongst First Nation communities, clan groups, and Elders around Australia. He is respected as a lead authority in leadership development with First Nation peoples in Australia and is a student of traditional knowledge practices and ancient wisdom of First Nation people.

Claire: Claire is a Wiradjuri woman who has over 20 years' experience working within the criminal justice system. She has a long-term commitment to enhancing outcomes for Aboriginal and Torres Strait Islander clients, including increasing the Aboriginal and Torres Strait Islander criminal justice workforce and decreasing the number of Aboriginal and Torres Strait Islander people who are imprisoned.

Author reflections

Power imbalances

Devastating practices triggered by European colonisation have led to inherent power imbalances for Aboriginal and Torres Strait Islander peoples in Australia and fostered a deep mistrust of government agencies. Involvement in the criminal justice system exacerbates these power imbalances, through punishment and the loss of freedom, choice, and decision-making, from the point of the first contact with police, through to periods of incarceration.

Without efforts to address this power imbalance, Aboriginal and Torres Strait Islander clients are less likely to engage with the criminal justice system, and outcomes will be compromised. It is crucial that steps are taken by practitioners to address this imbalance.

What are the practical steps for tackling power imbalances when you are working directly with a client in the criminal justice system?

James:

> When practitioners work with a client in the criminal justice system, they must understand the story of that individual, their family, and their cultural group. It is about knowing the background of First Nations clients. These individuals breathe the oxygen of over 200 years of disadvantage. An empathic understanding of this history is a crucial first step to being able to address power imbalances.

Steve:

> Addressing power imbalance begins with leveling the room. Bringing in Aboriginal and Torres Strait Islander staff as soon as you can into the professional relationship, if possible, from the first time you meet the client, whether that's at court or after sentencing. This can assist to break down cultural barriers. Consider how you physically set up an interview room and aim to balance the number of Indigenous and non-Indigenous people in the room. It is important to make sure that Aboriginal and Torres Strait Islander voices, the voice of the client and their family, carry equal weight. This is all part of building cultural safety for criminal justice system clients.

Clint:

> Aboriginal and Torres Strait Islander clients commonly share dispossession of identity. Although this can be the case for many people in custody, it is far more prevalent for Aboriginal and Torres Strait Islander peoples. For many, choices are something that have been hard to come by since invasion, and this is perpetuated in the criminal justice system. So, I try to provide my clients with opportunities to make choices, highlighting the fact that they can make positive choices in life. For example, my clients can decide if they engage in an interview with me or a fellow colleague. They can start making 'better choices' by deciding when and where an interview is conducted, acknowledging that in some correctional settings there are limitations to the options that are available.
>
> Establishing a culturally safe environment within the correctional setting is also important for addressing power imbalances. This could begin by simply getting clients to identify where they are from, who their family is, and where they have a cultural connection too. I will always provide the same information when requested to do so by the client as this will complete the process of circular communication.

Claire:

The first thing practitioners must do is take the time to build an environment of trust with the client. Practitioners must understand that past paternalistic policies and experiences, like the stolen generation, have significantly impacted Aboriginal and Torres Strait Islander people and continue to do so. These policies have resulted, for some, in generational losses, like loss of language, marriage lines, dance, ceremony, art, songlines. This results in trauma and a loss of belonging, which contribute to power imbalances, and must be understood.

There is also a need for practitioners to understand and respect the heterogeneity of Aboriginal and Torres Strait Islander cultures because belief systems and cultures can differ. Lumping people together into one culture is not helpful. The client is the cultural expert, and practitioners should adopt a culturally appropriate strengths-based model that respects the client's expertise. Practitioners should also think through issues like where to meet with the client, what will be safest for the client; this something to negotiate together. To further address power imbalances use language that is free of technical jargon and acronyms, have an awareness of gratuitous concurrence, and communicate *with* the client not *at* them.

Cultural supervision

Cultural supervision has been recommended as a key strategy for enhancing individual practice within the criminal justice system. Many Aboriginal and Torres Strait Islander professionals will have been asked to provide cultural supervision for newer Indigenous staff or non-Indigenous colleagues. Some will also have experienced cultural supervision themselves at some point in their career.

What is your experience with cultural supervision?
Clint:

I was previously employed as a cultural supervisor within the criminal justice system, where it was mandatory to have cultural supervision when facilitating an Aboriginal and Torres Strait Islander program or when facilitators required cultural support during specific sessions. Cultural supervision provided a predominately young non-Aboriginal workforce with the support and confidence they needed to establish culturally responsive programs for Aboriginal and Torres Strait Islander clients. The realities of cultural supervision are that those participating in it should be allowed to feel like they can ask any question they want and that there is no right or wrong, no racism, and no ignorance for the hour or two that they spend with you. They should be made to feel like they can ask you anything so that they become better cultural practitioners. If the practitioners providing a service to our people are offered appropriate cultural support, then Aboriginal and Torres Strait Islander clients in the criminal justice system benefit from this.

Steve:

> By providing cultural supervision, if I help non-Indigenous professionals do better, then I am helping my people. I see the provision of cultural supervision as a journey that I take with each practitioner. It's a process that fosters growth, where questions can be asked, and cross-cultural practice can be explored and debriefed. But it's important that practitioners really want this supervision, and that they are not just doing this because it is a workplace expectation.
>
> Whilst I haven't experienced formal cultural supervision myself as such, I have had the experience of intentional, targeted, sought-out relationship building with someone whose work I admire, in order to learn and enhance my practice. What is vital for me is to draw on local knowledge systems to build my skills; with the intent to be the best practitioner I can be.

Claire:

> Historically, there has been limited emphasis placed on cultural supervision within the criminal justice system, which has been detrimental to both clients and practitioners. When it occurs it is often sporadic and can be viewed as tokenistic, just ticking a box. This reduces the capacity to really learn from this experience. The value of cultural supervision is often dependent on management valuing the input of Aboriginal and Torres Strait Islander professionals and passing this onto the staff.

James:

> Cultural supervision is a place for practitioners to ask questions about their work with Aboriginal and Torres Strait Islander clients. It should be a safe place to have this dialogue and to help practitioners to prevent making mistakes with their clients.

Practice reflections

Reflecting on current practice within the criminal justice system is also crucial to enhancing practice. Whilst largely unintentional, mistakes are made in practice, which impact outcomes for Aboriginal and Torres Strait Islander clients in the criminal justice system. Reflecting on these mistakes provides an important source of learning and guidance for future practice. Exploring examples of good practice is equally important, highlighting key factors for future implementation.

What are the common mistakes you see professionals make in their practice with Aboriginal and Torres Strait Islander Peoples within the criminal justice system?
Steve:

> Not building authentic, purposeful relationships. Relationships are everything. Without a connection, you can't work effectively. Culturally respectful relationships are key to good practice. This is the only way that meaningful work can occur. When our relationships are strong, we all lift, we all rise.

When our relationships are poor, we all lower or sink. I call this the 'tides of relationships' and this should guide practice with Aboriginal and Torres Strait Islander clients. It is a practitioner's responsibility to establish, build, and grow respectful relationships, with their clients and the community.

When considering building and maintaining authentic relationships, think about them as a bank balance – if you have made no deposits, then you are unable to make any withdrawals. You want your 'relationship account' to be in abundance, so you have what is needed to be effective and can do so with confidence. The last thing you want is to be scraping the bottom of your 'relationship account', which causes you to be ineffectual and not able to obtain the best results for your client.

Claire:

I commonly observe mistakes around communication. Issues like speaking on behalf of Aboriginal and Torres Strait Islander peoples; a practitioner thinking they know what is best for us without consultation; not listening, and not understanding that English may not be the first language. Also, not taking the time to create culturally safe environments for clients; not taking the time to build the engagement that is needed for the best outcomes. Practitioners should look for connections with their clients, with sharing an important part of this process.

Disregarding gender issues is another mistake. Many program delivery officers are young, non-Indigenous females, but are regularly working with men on men's business. This can be insensitive to our mob. Cultural supervision is important in this situation.

Clint:

Many professionals are unaware of the diversity of Aboriginal and Torres Strait Islander people and the cultural, lore, language, and kinship differences we have between country or region. The professionals that I have worked with have had little understanding of the number of languages spoken in Australia before the invasion and the languages still spoken in this country even today.

Another common mistake that professionals make is that they are too scared to ask questions about Aboriginal and Torres Strait Islander people. There is usually an element of fear or hesitation that professionals present with when they ask questions about Aboriginal and Torres Strait Islander culture. The question professionals ask is typically primed by the professional stating 'I don't want to sound racist' or 'I don't want to be ignorant'. My usual response would be to encourage practitioners by stating that 'there is no such thing as a racist, ignorant or silly question if you genuinely don't know'.

James:

Mistakes occur when a few basic principles are not followed. These principles include respect, communication, silence, and patience. Respect is paramount. There needs to be a level of respect in how we communicate and do business within the criminal justice system. Practitioners also need to understand that if they want to share something, you don't talk directly, you must go around and around like a spiral until you get to the point. You need to give conversations time. You might only get a little information in the first few meetings, then more over time.

Practitioners also need to understand silence, when speaking with Aboriginal and Torres Strait Islander clients. It is important for practitioners to understand that they don't need to fill the space. The silence is people gathering their thoughts and their words, considering the implications of their response for themselves, their families and communities, and internalising and translating this in order to communicate and share in a way that practitioners will understand. So, when there is silence, practitioners need to understand this space. Practitioners also need to have patience. They need to understand that things happen in the client's timeframe, even though this can conflict with timing expectations or deadlines within the criminal justice system. This means adding space and buffer time, including extra time for appointments.

It is also important to understand that First Nations professionals can experience difficulties when non-Indigenous practitioners make mistakes. If they are associated with a non-Indigenous practitioner, they may bear the brunt of any mistakes or poor practice. This could impact their own credibility in the community.

What is the most damaging practice you have seen from a non-Indigenous justice professional in the criminal justice system?
James:
It is disrespectful and can be damaging when practitioners visiting remote communities don't follow protocols for engaging with the community. When they make promises they can't deliver on, or when there are inconsistencies between what they say and do, ultimately proving themselves unreliable, and validating historic mistrust of authorities. This can damage client engagement in the criminal justice system. And of course, racism. It's prevalent, it's still there.

Clint:
Most professionals who work in corrections don't go about their day intentionally trying to upset Aboriginal and Torres Strait Islander clients. They are mostly well intended and have a genuine desire to assist and support all people adjusting to a custodial setting. Many would give you the shirt off their back. But I have witnessed practitioners who struggle to integrate cultural responses into their clinical work. The practitioner will often turn to what they know best and have spent a large part of their education learning about – clinical or western therapy. You can't really blame practitioners for this. But the sticking point is this, once you take the time and effort to support that professional with cultural training and then provide them with ongoing support and consultation, and they still

intentionally don't make any cultural considerations or even dismiss culture altogether when providing future clients with support, then that clinician has just done their profession an injustice and they risk damaging practice. In the cases where a professional chooses the path of clinical over cultural, Aboriginal, and Torres Strait Islander clients rarely receive adequate support or intervention. As a professional, it is vital to understand that Aboriginal and Torres Strait Islander peoples within the criminal justice system need both clinical and cultural aspects of their interventions.

Steve:

A 'white is right' mentality is damaging. This is about practitioners thinking that the client, their family, and the community know nothing. This attitude closes practitioners off to learning about the client, their history and culture, and thus serves as a barrier to practitioners integrating Indigenous perspectives into their interventions. Ultimately, this reflects a lack of respect which is crucial to engagement.

It is also vital that non-Indigenous practitioners 'walk the talk' of culturally informed practice. This is more than just receiving cultural awareness training; this cannot just be about ticking a box. It is the practitioner's responsibility to 'walk the talk' once they know it, to consider what this looks like in their day to day practice.

Claire:

This comes back to a lack of understanding of basic cultural norms and protocols. I've seen people try to launch into therapeutic work with a client without first creating a culturally safe environment. Talking from a very clinical perspective can be frightening, and clients won't feel confident to yarn if they don't feel safe. Practitioners must take the time to build that safety and relationship. Another concern is re-traumatising clients by repeatedly asking them to re-live their trauma, which can happen every time there is a new caseworker. Sharing trauma histories in a group setting may also trigger traumatic responses in other clients, highlighting the importance of a trauma-informed approach.

What counselling and support skills have you seen non-Indigenous justice professionals use effectively in cross-cultural practice within Aboriginal and Torres Strait Islander clients in the criminal justice system?

Claire:

When practitioners apply both a cultural and a clinical lens in their work and are able to understand behaviour from a cultural perspective, not only from a clinical point of view. When they are open-minded and non-judgemental, and work holistically with the client – with the whole person. When practitioners focus on the client's story and their journey and give the client time and space to answer questions and consider their response. This is when the best engagement occurs; when clients are given time to share their stories. Practitioners should appreciate our culture is an oral culture and give people time to tell their story.

James:

Examples of effective practice include the integration of art therapies, somatic therapies, and cultural activities such as weaving into correctional programs. Effective counselling for First Nations people is not about two people sitting in a room talking, this is quite foreign. Instead, if it's a sit-down, it should involve a cup of tea and biscuits. But preferably effective practice involves practical activities through which you can yarn and discuss important issues. It also involves family.

First Nations peoples talk about healing the spirit. From a First Nations perspective, good practice acknowledges the need to strengthen the spirit to protect against trauma, and to connect with ancestors, and to change the narrative. When these spiritual connections are integrated into correctional interventions, they will produce change. Effective practice also acknowledges intergenerational trauma.

Clint:

Effective counselling supports the use of traditional healers when assisting Aboriginal and Torres Strait Islander clients and utilises Elders and family networks as cultural supports when appropriate to improve cultural safety for clients.

Steve:

Good practice involves utilising Aboriginal and Torres Strait Islander workers, who can answer questions, and provide mentorship. In the Aboriginal culture we talk about men's and women's business, so having male and female Aboriginal and Torres Strait Islander workers is important. Good practice also involves being flexible with venues for meetings with community-based clients, choosing settings that might enhance client safety. The use of artwork and cultural imagery can also be effective. Trauma-informed practice is also important.

A former colleague of mine routinely talked to clients about what he would learn from them, not just what he could teach them. This commitment to a two-way process of learning reflects authentic respect and engagement. This authenticity, openness, and interest exemplifies good practice.

Discussion

The ongoing reality in Australia is that Aboriginal and Torres Strait Islander peoples are over-represented within the criminal justice system. Sweeping system-wide reforms have been recommended to address this over-representation. Such reforms, whilst crucial, are likely to occur slowly, consisting of incremental change made over years if not decades of dedicated, persistent, revolutionary work. In contrast, significant changes and improvements to the way Aboriginal and Torres Strait Islander People are engaged in correctional interventions and rehabilitative work can be made immediately by on-the-ground criminal justice practitioners. These are not large-scale systemic changes, but rather individual changes and adjustments to the way intervention and rehabilitation with correctional clients are being undertaken (e.g. Day, 2014; Jones, Masters, Griffiths, & Moulday, 2002; Willis & Moore, 2008). It is hoped that such changes (as small as they may seem) may go some way to improving the experience of Aboriginal and Torres Strait Islander people involved in the justice system and may contribute to meaningful changes to the experience and outcomes of incarceration, rehabilitation, and recidivism.

Given the overwhelming majority of criminal justice, practitioners do not identify as Aboriginal and Torres Strait Islander peoples, it is unsurprising that reflections shared by some of the authors of this chapter highlighted the importance of effective cross-cultural practice in the criminal justice field. Moving beyond the popular jargon of 'competence' or simply 'acquiring knowledge of Aboriginal and Torres Strait Islander histories', the need for a much deeper understanding and integration of cultural knowledge is asserted. This includes a meaningful understanding of how issues like power imbalances, personal and collective histories, and colonial experiences are expressed and perpetuated within the criminal justice system in everyday interactions with prisoners. Practitioners must acknowledge, however uncomfortable it may be, that each time they enter the therapeutic space with an Aboriginal or Torres Strait Islander client in the criminal justice system, they may represent the 'majority', the 'system' and at times the 'oppressor'. Translating this knowledge into new ways to approach and engage clients in the intervention process becomes the individual responsibility of every practitioner. By changing the manner in which we 'do' the work of rehabilitation (process) we can enhance the effectiveness of programming and provide correctional clients with an authentic, trusting, therapeutic relationship through which real and lasting change can occur.

Genuine, long-lasting, collaboration between Aboriginal and Torres Strait Islander workers and their non-Indigenous counterparts working in the criminal justice system is another strong message. We implore practitioners to begin the development of long-lasting, respectful, and reciprocal relationships with their Aboriginal and Torres Strait Islander colleagues. Open and reflective non-Indigenous practitioners are likely to learn much about the process of therapy with Aboriginal and Torres Strait Islander peoples, community engagement, cultural norms, and practice from their Aboriginal and Torres Strait Islander colleagues. In the spirit of reciprocity, we encourage these practitioners to respect, prioritise, and action these learnings, building them into their day-to-day practice. When an Aboriginal or Torres Strait Islander criminal justice professional provides non-Indigenous colleagues with cultural supervision, however informal this may be, it must be acknowledged that the supervisee's practice is likely to reflect on the supervisor and may impact their standing with other colleagues and within their community. Engaging in a cultural supervisory relationship is therefore a risky proposition for Aboriginal and Torres Strait Islander professionals, and in response, non-Indigenous professionals should explicitly acknowledge both the risk the supervisor is absorbing and the trust their supervisors are placing in them by engaging in such a relationship.

The building, retaining, and supporting of a strong Aboriginal and Torres Strait Islander workforce is part of the solution to effect positive change within the criminal justice system. The correctional system must explicitly value the vital contributions of these staff and support them as they navigate the challenging waters of criminal justice system rules and expectations, whilst balancing the expectations and needs of their cultural connections and obligations (Day, Giles, Marshall, & Sanderson, 2004). For many Aboriginal and Torres Strait Islander correctional professionals, their motivation for working within this system stems from a desire to help their community, and the correctional system should support them to effectively do so (Day et al., 2004).

 Discussion Questions

1. What key messages are you taking away from this chapter?

2. What have you done in your practice to address power imbalances?

3. Have you engaged in cultural supervision? How has this impacted your practice?

4. Critically examine your recent practice. What mistakes have you made? Have you engaged in any of the damaging practices outlined by the authors? How well is your practice aligned with the recommendations made in the chapter?

5. What will you change in your practice, in response to key messages in this chapter?

Constraints with the criminal justice system are inescapable. The justice system has its own set of timeframes, expectations for what and how information is shared, and the need for a custodial environment that restricts freedom and movement. Even within these confines, however, individual criminal justice practitioners can make significant and lasting changes to client's lives and experiences of incarceration and rehabilitation. Whilst efforts towards radical systemic change must continue, practitioners can play their part by changing how they approach intervention and therapeutic work with Aboriginal and Torres Strait Islander peoples who come into contact with the justice system. Whilst we continue advocating for an Aboriginal and Torres Strait Islander workforce, which is large in number to reflect the population of the justice system, responsibility also lies with non-Indigenous practitioners to improve their cross-cultural practice to enhance individual outcomes for correctional clients.

References

ABS (Australian Bureau of Statistics). (2019). *4517.0 – Prisoners in Australia, 2019*. https://www.abs.gov.au/ausstats/abs@.nsf/PrimaryMainFeatures/4517.0?OpenDocument

AIHW (Australian Institute of Health and Welfare). (2018). *The health of Australia's prisoners* (Cat. No. PHE 246). Canberra, ACT: AIHW. https://www.aihw.gov.au/getmedia/2e92f007-453d-48a1-9c6b-4c9531cf0371/aihw-phe-246.pdf.aspx?inline=true

Allan, A., Allan, M., Marshall, P., & Kraszlan, K. (2003). Recidivism among male juvenile sexual offenders in Western Australia. *Psychiatry, Psychology and Law, 10*(2), 359–378.

ALRC (Australian Law Reform Commission). (2017). *Pathways to justice: An inquiry into the incarceration rate of Aboriginal and Torres Strait Islander Peoples* (Final Report No. 133). https://www.alrc.gov.au/wp-content/uploads/2019/08/final_report_133_amended1.pdf

Anthony, T. (2017). FactCheck Q&A: Are Indigenous Australians the most incarcerated people on Earth? *The Conversation*, June 6.

Broadhurst, R. G., & Maller, R. A. (1992). The recidivism of sex offenders in the Western Australian prison population. *British Journal of Criminology, 32*, 54–80.

Cunneen, C., Baldry, E., Brown, D., Borwn, M., Schwartz, M., & Steel, A. (2016). Penal culture and hyperincarceration: The revival of the prison. In *New advances in crime and social harm*. Farnham: Routledge.

Day, A. (2014). Culturally responsive CBT in forensic settings. In R. C. Tafrate & D. Mitchell (Eds)., *Forensic CBT: A handbook for clinical practice*. Chichester: John Wiley & Sons.

Day, A., Giles, G., Marshall, B., & Sanderson, V. (2004). The recruitment and retention of indigenous criminal justice agency staff in Australian state. *International Journal of Offender Therapy and Comparative Criminology, 48*(3), 347–359. doi: https://doi.org/10.1177/0306624X03261268.

Dennison, S., Smallbone, H., Stewart, A., Freiberg, K., & Teague, R. (2014). 'My life is separated': An examination of the challenges and barriers to parenting for Indigenous father sin prison. *The British Journal of Criminology, 54*(6), 1089–1108.

Farrelly, T., & Carlson, B. (2011). Towards cultural competence in the justice sector. *Indigenous Justice Clearinghouse, 3*(June), 1–8.

Government of Western Australia. (2019). *Department of Justice: Annual Report 2018/19*. https://department.justice.wa.gov.au/_files/annual-reports/DoJ-Annual-Report-2018-2019.pdf

Hagan, J., & Dinovitzer, R. (1999). Collateral consequences of imprisonment for children, communities and prisoners. *Crime and Justice, 26*, 121–162.

Hovane, V., Dalton, T., & Smith, P. (2014). Aboriginal offender rehabilitation programs. In P. Dudgeon, H. Milroy, & R. Walker (Eds)., *Working together: Aboriginal and Torres Strait Islander mental health and wellbeing principles and practice*. West Perth, WA: Kulunga Research Network.

Jones, R., Masters, M., Griffiths, A., & Moulday, N. (2002). Culturally relevant assessment for Indigenous offenders: A literature review. *Australian Psychologist, 37*, 187–197.

New South Wales Government. (2019). *Department of Justice: Aboriginal employment strategy 2019–2022.* https://www.justice.nsw.gov.au/Documents/aboriginal-employment-strategy.pdf

Northern Territory Government. (2015). *Aboriginal employment and career development strategy refresh.* https://ocpe.nt.gov.au/__data/assets/pdf_file/0018/711252/AECDS-Refresh_2015-2020_WEB.pdf

Payer, H., Taylor, A., & Barnes, T. (2015). *Who's missing? Social and demographic impacts from the incarceration of Indigenous people in the Northern Territory* (Research Brief, Issues 5). Northern Institute, Charles Darwin University.

PWC (Pricewaterhouse Coopers). (2017). *Indigenous incarceration: Unlocking the facts.* Pricewaterhouse Coopers Australia. https://www.pwc.com.au/indigenous-consulting/assets/indigenous-incarceration-may17.pdf

Rojas, E. Y., & Gretton, H. M. (2007). Background, offence characteristics, and criminal outcomes of Aboriginal youth who sexually offend: A closer look at aboriginal youth intervention needs. *Sexual Abuse, 19*, 257–283. doi: https://doi.org/10.1177/107906320701900306.

SCATSIA (Standing Committee on Aboriginal and Torres Strait Islander Affairs). (2011). *Doing time – Time for doing: Indigenous youth in the criminal justice system.* Canberra, ACT: Commonwealth of Australia. https://www.aph.gov.au/binaries/house/committee/atsia/sentencing/report/fullreport.pdf

Smallbone, S., & Rallings, M. (2013). Short-term predictive validity of the Static-99 and Static-99-R for Indigenous and Nonindigenous Australian Sexual Offenders. *Sexual Abuse, 25*, 302–316. doi: https://doi.org/10.1177/1079063212472937.

The State of Queensland. (2018). *Queensland corrective services annual report 2017–2018.* https://corrections.qld.gov.au/documents/publications/

Victoria State Government. (2019). *Department of Justice and Community Safety: Annual report 2018–2019.* http://www.justice.vic.gov.au

Weatherburn, D. (2014). *Arresting incarceration: Pathways out of indigenous imprisonment.* Canberra, ACT: Aboriginal Studies Press.

Willis, M., & Moore, J. (2008). *Reintegration of Indigenous prisoners.* Canberra, ACT: Australian Institute of Criminology.

NICHE FIELDS AND EMERGING TRENDS

10 Rural and Remote Social Work with Aboriginal People

Stuart McMinn, Clayton Cruse, Racheal Howard, Nathan Murgha and Phil Pallas

Stuart McMinn: Stuart is a cultural man from the Dharug and Gubbi Gubbi nations. He is the Practice Specialist for Aboriginal Services at Interrelate and Owner of Durrungan Cultural Immersions. Stuart's passion is cultural education and facilitation.

Clayton Cruse: I identify as having Adnyamathanha, Yankunytjatjara and Kamilaroi heritage. I have worked in the education sector since the late 1990's, on and off, and am currently working as a teacher in country South Australia. This role has increasing student wellbeing responsibilities, so I will be working with the school, families and wider department with regard to student welfare and achievement.

Rachael Howard: I am a Burra Burra woman of Gundungurra country. I am a social worker currently working for an Aboriginal Community controlled primary health service in remote communities outside Alice Springs. I honour the old ones who have walked before me and guide my path in this field.

Nathan Murgha: Nathan is a Gunggandji man from Yarrabah. He works for the Clontarf Foundation where he brings a wealth of experience and cultural knowledge to educational engagement and retention for young people. He is passionate about empowering people through love, comfort, support and encouragement through his organisation Club Fight Back.

Phill Pallas: Of Greek, English, Irish, Scottish and Danish heritage, I am privileged to have cultural connections and work with Pitjantjatjara and Yankunytjatjara people in Central Australia. I honour Anangu who have taken time to lead me into sacred learning spaces through culture, language and ceremony. I am a social worker and lecturer at the University of Newcastle.

Introduction

When we were approached to contribute to this chapter, we were collectively motivated by the hope that something we would write could change the way social workers engage with Aboriginal people living in rural and remote communities. As we came together, many of us meeting one another for the first time, conversation flowed easily. We have shared connections, relationships with Country, and lived experiences that made *coming together* easy. We began to talk through what we would like social workers to know (and see and understand and feel) so that they could work in ways that make sense for Aboriginal people living in the communities in which they find themselves working. We asked ourselves, 'What can we offer in this chapter that is unique? What could we write that is not written in other places? Could we write something that changes the conversation about how social workers engage in this space?'

We are acutely aware of the historical and contemporary injustices that face Aboriginal people. We have all experienced poor government policy and poor engagement by social workers and other human service workers in our own families and/or the communities that we are privileged to work with. In all honesty, we could easily fill the pages of this chapter with horror stories of workers' engagement in rural and remote places; workers whose actions we feel have done more harm than good. But we have chosen a different approach in this chapter. We offer our perspectives and our lived experience of living and working in rural and remote contexts across Australia to light a path towards a better way for social workers to engage and practice in those places.

In this chapter, we invite you to join our conversation. We ask you to move slowly through our words in the hope that you will see a new way forward together.

Social work with Aboriginal people in rural and remote contexts

Social services play an ever-increasing presence in the social and political lives of Aboriginal people in rural and remote communities in Australia. The engagement of a variety of service provision models exist whereby some social service organisations *place* a worker in a community over an extended period of time, whilst others engage in periodic visits by drive-in, drive-out, or fly-in-fly-out arrangements from regional centres. The second model is particularly common in remote and very remote communities. Often social workers arrive in rural and remote communities from places that are geographically, culturally, and linguistically different from the communities in which they have grown up and been educated. This reality invites a level of complexity that the social worker is required to negotiate, particularly in terms of challenging their cultural lens and the western frameworks they have been trained to employ in their work. Additionally, social workers need to challenge their constructions of Aboriginality that have often been formed in an education system that does not present a whole or inclusive view of history and presents Aboriginal people in deficit terms.

As a result of colonisation and a consistent comparison to health and other disparities between Aboriginal and non-Aboriginal Australians, narratives of Aboriginal people are often framed in deficit terms. This is often emphasised in remote contexts where the difference between Western and local priorities can be more pronounced. This is overlain with constructions of remoteness being *in the middle of nowhere* that reinforce descriptions of Aboriginal people in deficit terms. Characterisations of Aboriginal people as needing to be *saved, protected,* and *civilised* have reinforced the position of Aboriginal people as inadequate (see Smith, 1999). Such constructions are grounded social Darwinism, the framing of contact history, and ensuing policy eras. There are significant works, however, that challenge these constructions by asserting the active participation of Aboriginal people in history (see Pascoe, 2014; Gammage, 2011).

Deficit narratives of Aboriginal people are further reinforced in contemporary settings by popular film media, where constructions are not simply matters of artistic representation, but political acts that reinforce power and oppression (Hickling-Hudson, 1990; Rekhari, 2008). The construction of Indigenous people as 'the other' and innately inadequate is not new (see Hickling-Hudson, 1990) and social workers are not immune to the influencing force of films and popular media that depict Aboriginal people as 'passive or background players in a story whose main actors are white' (Hickling-Hudson, 1990, p. 264; see Langton, 1994). Within contemporary practice in remote communities, these roles can be replicated, thereby reinforcing the dominant white worker as centre stage and the hero of the narrative. There is need, therefore, for social workers to question their constructions of Aboriginality and come to terms with the reality that their profession has been complicit in the trauma, control, dislocation, acculturation, and colonisation of Indigenous peoples (Gilbert, 2001, 2009; Green & Baldry, 2008). Practitioner readiness to engage in social work with Aboriginal people living in rural and remote communities also requires considerable thought.

There is an emerging body of literature within social work that relates to practitioner readiness to work effectively with Aboriginal people. Within this space, 'cultural competence' is often set as an aim for practitioners wanting to engage with Aboriginal clients. Cultural competence emerged as a framework for practice as a response to working with culturally and linguistically diverse communities in the 1990s (Betancourt, Green, Carillo, & Ananeh-Firempong, 2016). By positioning the need to be 'culturally competent' with the culturally different 'other', the concept of cultural competence has come under criticism in that it minimises the cultural location of the practitioner. Hollinsworth (2013) critiques cultural competence as a process of gathering expert knowledge about the other, turning complex and relational ways of seeing, thinking, being, and acting into rigid and static cultural differences that are determining of people's behaviours. Interestingly, he notes that 'we' (those positioned as dominant racially or culturally) 'often do not experience our own cultural backgrounds as so powerful in determining our own decisions and thoughts' (p. 1051). For Hollinsworth, the key to building effective therapeutic relationships with Aboriginal people lies in the practitioner's ability to critically listen to a client in order to identify the aspects of their lives that are significant to them, rather than homogenised understandings that assume what is of importance to a group of cultural 'others'. Similarly, Furlong and Wight (2011) argue that, academic institutions, rather than teaching cultural competence (which is often positioned as an add on to professional education), foster an allegiance to 'critical awareness' to promote reflecting on one's own cultural location, as well as a continual critiquing of received professional knowledges. They highlight the concept of 'not knowing', originating from the field of family therapy as a helpful construct for developing culturally relevant practice. They call on social workers to become aware of possible shared lived experiences, without assuming that those things are universally experienced.

Despite the critique, the term 'cultural competence' is still often used within social work literature. At an organisational level, there are calls for mainstream service providers to become more culturally competent in their work with Aboriginal populations by addressing racism and integrating understandings of trauma in their practice (Herring, Spangara, Lauw, & McNamara, 2013). Intergenerational trauma is widely recognised as an ongoing impact of colonisation (Atkinson, 2002). Addressing systemic racism in mainstream organisations is imperative to addressing the disadvantages that Aboriginal people face (Paradies, Harris, & Anderson, 2008). Other practice tools, such as cultural mapping tools that acknowledge the complexity of family and kinship structures, have also been promoted as pathways to culturally competent practice (Stewart & Allan, 2013), whilst Herring et al. (2013) advocate that an essential step in becoming more culturally competent is understanding the benefits of 'white privilege'.

More recently, literature has emerged that considers the intersections between social work and whiteness theory and calls for further integration of whiteness theory in social work education and practice. Moreton-Robinson (2004) defines whiteness as 'the invisible norm against which other races are judged in the construction of identity, representation subjectivity, nationalism, and the law' (p. viii). Young (2004, p. 103) asserts that whiteness theory presents 'a description of how privilege is raced and invisible: a method of unsettling this privilege; and it offers guidance for more inclusive and respectful human relationships'. Young asserts that social work 'has yet to fully engage with an understanding of itself as racialised and to explore what this might mean for practice' (2004, p. 104). They conclude similarly with Dumbrill and Green (2008) that 'social work education continues to be taught from a Eurocentric perspective in a manner that perpetuates the colonization of Indigenous peoples' (p. 489).

As a response to these realities, we seek to present powerful counternarratives that incorporate Aboriginal epistemologies in this chapter. We seek to contribute to this developing dialogue that seeks to embed Aboriginal ways of knowing, being, and doing in practice and advocate for culturally responsive practice that works with Aboriginal people in rural and remote contexts in ways that are collaborative and relational.

Practice principles

We offer the following practice principles for working with Aboriginal people in rural and remote contexts. These principles have been formed from our practice experience. We hope these principles invite you into deep reflection as you seek to engage locally, wherever you are.

1. Examine your cultural lens.

Our cultural lens dictates our values, moral standards, and how we see the world. It is primarily influenced by the society in which we grew up. As many Australians, and most Australian social workers, have grown up in a Western society, they have developed a Westernised lens through which they view the world. Practising social work through this lens can mean that it may be difficult to understand behaviours and values from non-Western cultures. When working across points of language and culture there is much room for confusion and misinterpretation between the social worker and the community in which they find themselves. This can result in social workers making judgements about the behaviour of community members that are misinformed and ill-considered. Such judgements can be devastating when they manifest in professional interactions, especially when it comes to making decisions about the safety of community members from Westernised frameworks.

Assessing the potential risk of harm to children is a common task for social workers, whether the practitioner is directly employed within a child protection role or a more generalist role. Consider this scenario: whilst working in a remote community, a social worker notes that two young brothers are consistently spending time with grandparents and aunties and uncles, but not with their parents. The children seem to be constantly fed by these relatives, but no care seems to be provided by the parents. One day the worker hears that the parents have 'taken off to Port Augusta' and the worker begins to develop grave concerns for the welfare of the two boys. From the outside looking in, and without acknowledging the influence of Westernised views on social work framing and risk assessment processes, it is easy to make the assumption that the two boys are being neglected by their natural parents. This assumption is informed through a Western lens without consideration of Aboriginal communities' complex kinship systems. These systems may dictate that the grandparents or certain uncles and aunties have an obligation to feed, teach, and take care of the two brothers. In turn, the parents of the children may have a similar relationships and obligations with other young people (and may be in Port Augusta fulfilling those very obligations).

It is important that we challenge our cultural lens when working with Aboriginal people in rural and remote contexts. It is imperative that we interrogate the factors that influence our decisions before digging deeper and developing an in-depth understanding of why a particular practice or behaviour is evident within the community. The type of attitude and behaviour that ignores the ways in which a Westernised cultural lens influences our decisions led to the forcible removal of many First Nations children from their parents, known as the Stolen Generations (Human Rights and Equal Opportunity Commission, 1997). People thought that First Nations children would be better off being raised away from their families and forced to assimilate. The evidence to pause and interrogate the lens through which we interpret, understand and act is compelling, and the impacts significant.

2. Get rid of checklists and wrestle with nuance.

Social and political life within rural and remote contexts is often complex and not easily understood by those who have grown up outside the community. This is especially true for people who have limited experience working with First Nations people and for those who have not interrogated the lens through which they make sense of the world. Commonly, we see workers arrive in a community with an academic understanding of how the community operates, the challenges the community faces, and preconceived ideas about the best 'solutions' for 'their problems'. This is what we refer to as a 'read' understanding of the community. By 'read' understanding we mean those understandings that are formed by reading information produced by academic institutions and researchers. This type of understanding is limited at best, and at worst perpetuates a complete misunderstanding of community dynamics and priorities.

We also see workers arrive in communities with a checklist of hard and fast rules for engagement that reinforce homogenised ideas regarding Aboriginal communities and cultures. For example, we see workers desperate to avoid any eye contact in conversations with older people, so that they do not cause offence. This approach is problematic as it negates the social worker having to wrestle with the nuances of complex relational exchanges to consider where such rules may and may not apply, or when this practice may or may not be helpful. What if there are times when it is disrespectful to *not* make eye contact? This mode of operating leads to non-genuine and often paternalistic interactions that generally result in community members not respecting or trusting the worker. What is revealed in such interactions is the worker's lack of knowledge and respect for the lived experiences of people within extremely developed social systems. Social workers need to develop the ability to wrestle with nuance and complexity as they negotiate complex relationships informed by the local context.

3. Approach community engagement with patience, humility, and respect.

When first entering a community, it is important to display patience, humility, and respect. The attitude with which you approach people and carry yourself is the first step to building rapport. An everyday scene in a very remote community in central Australia is seeing a white Toyota arrive with one or two workers strapped into the front seats. They stop their vehicle, park nearby the clinic, hop out, and walk in to see the community nurse. They emerge a short time later and walk across to the community store to buy some water. What they often don't realise is that their work of 'engaging with the community' has already begun. Their every move is being observed; the way they carry themselves, the pace of their steps, the expression on their face, the way they spoke to the shopkeeper. Before a single word is exchanged, many people have already decided how safe they feel around the worker and what their level of engagement with that person will be.

Approaching our work with patience, humility, and respect requires us to move slowly. The pace of our work needs to provide space for culturally informed decision-making processes that may require people to seek the input of familial and kin relations. Moving slowly also creates space for social workers to adopt the stance of a learner. Holding loosely 'read' understandings of the context and prioritising patience can allow new understandings informed by local ways of knowing, being, doing to emerge in your consciousness. Moving slowly allows you to be seen and known before you receive the standing to speak and collaborate. Having the ability to be still and settled internally reflects a grounded spirit to the community. Aboriginal communities see great value in someone that can be strong within themselves whilst sitting still. Many members in the community, particularly senior people, will look into you and really see you. Elders and other senior community members often have the ability to know a person's motivations that will inform how they will interact with you. This doesn't mean that you only have one chance to make an impression, but it does mean that you need to be conscious of your interactions, remembering that presenting a true and genuine self contributes to an overall view of your intentions and engagement style.

The red dust became my classroom
Phill Pallas

What I didn't learn in my formal education has been imparted to me through more than a decade of relationship with Pitjantjatjara and Yankunytjatjara people in Central Australia.

Whilst dysfunction and grief are common features of the landscape in many remote Aboriginal communities, paradoxically in that space, I have found a great sense of community and healing.

By sitting in the red dust and listening, I have learned of the great loss that Indigenous people have experienced: the loss of culture, the loss of language, the loss of land, and the loss of human rights. As the new settlement from the other side of the globe advanced, whole communities of Aboriginal people were displaced, disease-ravaged entire tribes, and whole communities were violently massacred. As time progressed, many children were stolen or forcibly removed from their parents simply because of the colour of their skin. Fast-forward to 2007 and the Howard Government initiated the Northern Territory Intervention, suspending our nation's Racial Discrimination Act in order to pass the inherently discriminatory legislation. So great was the disruption of that day the tall ships arrived on this land now called Australia and the days that followed, that almost 230 years on my Aboriginal friends are still fighting for basic human rights and a better future.

But this is more than a story of dislocation and destruction – this is also a story of strength and survival. Aboriginal people right across this country have adapted, resisted, survived, and thrived despite the continued onslaught of colonial regimes, programs, and policies.

Since being welcomed in as a stranger more than a decade ago, there are now many Aboriginal people living in the desert and around Australia that I call family. Brothers, Sisters, Mothers, Fathers, Ngalungkus... that I care for deeply and who care for me. And these families of mine have humbled me as they have shared the story of our nation through their eyes.

For me, all of these stories and more are true and sit with me deeply. As I have sat and listened, I have learned that Aboriginal people know a lot more about the way forward than I do. As old men have graciously sat with me and shared Tjukurpa, the stories and laws and principles that have been present for thousands of years and continue to provide answers for Aboriginal people today, it is in these moments that I have become more integrated – with myself, my creator, humanity and creation.

I have learned that the past lives in the present. And with that learning, comes responsibility. And that responsibility is to continue to listen deeply.

4. Withhold advice and solutions by becoming an inquisitive learner.

Do not be quick to offer solutions. Instead, look, listen, and learn from the people you are working with. This is a real challenge when you have organisational directives, funding outcomes, and timeframes that may be at odds with community priorities and ways of working. Taking the time to find out what the community needs from their perspective requires us to adopt the stance of an inquisitive learner rather than the expert. When time is taken to listen and learn you will find there is much wisdom within the community.

You will also start to see gaps that can be filled by service provision differently. Once you begin developing rapport, small opportunities to build trust with members of the community will start to present themselves. These opportunities will come in many forms. It is imperative that these opportunities are taken up and that you deliver an outcome. From these interactions comes trust that will be built over a period of time. It is important to remember that you are a guest in another community and that you need to treat people as such. If you were to go to someone's house for the first time you would ensure that you were respectful, polite, and courteous. First and ongoing interactions with community members should be no different. When meeting community members, especially Elders, it is vital that you come with an empty cup. A cup that can be filled with direction and guidance gained in cross-cultural interactions. People will appreciate your humility and be more receptive to including you. As you progress further towards deeper community relationships, it is important to maintain this empty cup approach and allow yourself to be guided and driven by community needs. There will be opportunities to apply your knowledge and utilise your skills, but it is so important you do this with humility and respect.

Cross-cultural interaction can be confusing and somewhat spiritually, emotionally, and physically draining. As you need to work hard at understanding what the community is trying to say or convey. Every community has a certain protocol and behaviours that are considered appropriate to understand in order to engage effectively. Whilst we warn of the wholesale adoption of checklists and encourage wrestling with nuance, we can state with confidence that it is important to not speak when Elders are speaking. To speak when an Elder is talking is considered rude and impolite and shows a lack of understanding of the cultural protocol. You have two ears, two eyes, and one mouth, so you should look and listen twice as much as you talk. Aboriginal communities all have their own social culture and nuances that operate. Just like any community there are do's and don'ts and, of course, this will vary from any Aboriginal community you work in. Therefore, remember to consider this and develop an understanding that what may have been considered appropriate behaviour for one community may not be appropriate for another. It is imperative that you look and listen to what is going on in a community so you can learn to read the non-verbal cues and subtle ways of communicating. This is why it is highly important to sit listen and learn before you start to address the community in any formal organisational engagement.

In summary, community interactions and first impressions are extremely important, but what is equally important is carrying yourself with humility and respect. Aboriginal communities have many non-verbal and subtle cues that need to be watched and learned from. There are times to be quiet and listen and times to be more proactive, but understanding when to enact either of these strategies can only come from a practice of looking listening and learning.

You've got to come with your cup empty

Nathan Murgha

I started Club Fight Back in my community of Yarrabah for two reasons. Firstly, there was a need. Secondly, I have always wanted to play a big part in my community, particularly with making positive change for young people. Club Fight back works with young people in our local community through a cultural framework and is self-funded. The experience that I have gained from birth informs how I interact with young people on my community. I have been dragged through the mud at particular times in my life. I have been to the lowest point of life – to know that, experience that, acknowledge that and accept that, it has been a big part of my journey and why I want to reach out to others and invite them to live a different way.

We don't often see programs that operate from the ground up. This program is different. It's different because I am from Yarrabah. If you have troubles and you live in my community, I am going to ride with you, and I am going to be there with you. The work that I do comes from my heart and at the end of the day, I don't leave the community and go back to Cairns or get on a plane. I am here amongst it and I walk with my people. This isn't an 8 a.m. to 4 p.m. job for me. I want to invite people into a different way to live, that they can take back into their families. The way I engage in cultural practices such as hunting restores joy and begins to mold people.

When new workers ask me how to best work with my community, I tell them simply, 'You've got to come with your cup empty.' If you are not willing to empty your cup, then it is not going to work. We are observant people. We do not like sitting down asking millions of questions, we are watching. We are always watching. If you want to work with my community but are not willing to empty your cup it's going to be a long difficult road only to come to the point of realising that what you are doing is not working. One of the things I have become familiar with is the idea of Professional Development (PD). I want to tell you that if you want to engage in real PD, sit down around the fire and listen to the old people. That is the starting point.

5. Rethink 'I'm here to help'.

It is important to define what you want to achieve and your motivation for working in rural and remote Aboriginal communities. If you think you are 'here to help' you need to dig deeper than that. Aboriginal people are resilient, strong, resourceful, and capable people, and the idea that Aboriginal people living in rural and remote contexts need external people to 'help' is an assumption that Western society holds. Many Aboriginal people living in rural and remote contexts are navigating complexities that are difficult to see and understand for those who have not grown up in the community. This involves living in 'two worlds'; one world that has existed since time immemorial, with culturally ground priorities that are enacted through ceremony and everyday interactions, and another world that has been introduced and requires participation in local and global economies to survive and thrive. Consider approaching your work with the goal of empowering people to navigate a system that has not been built to empower them, so that they can continue to navigate through these two worlds to the best of their ability.

Help is often misunderstood as doing everything for someone else. This can be because the worker does not believe the individual or community has the capacity to do a particular task themselves. In some cases, this may be true. For example, when it comes to complicated issues such as dealing with courts and complex medical challenges, the impacts of colonisation and language barriers can make it difficult for Aboriginal people in rural and remote locations to navigate on their own. However, any 'help' needs to be grounded in a respectful relationship and collaboration. Modes of 'helping' that take the form of a worker assuming the role of a parent and treating the individual or community like a child result in further disempowerment.

At times, community may request the input of your knowledge and skills. In these moments, it is important to seek empowerment by scaffolding individual and collective skill development. Similar to building a scaffold during physical construction, you need to start at the bottom and build upon each layer. If you find that community is unable to undertake a task due to a gap in skills it is important to ask the community if they would like to learn how to undertake training or learning in order to learn how to do the skill. This can be done informally or formally, but it is important to consider and consult the community. Capacity building can take many forms and the decision on the best course of action needs to rest with the community. Letting go of the preconceived belief that the professional is the only expert can seem as counter-intuitive to what is taught in the university system; however, embracing the idea that the community has a deep understanding as to what they need is a path that will see you in great respect. Treading softly and listening carefully builds good relationships and allows mutual relationships to thrive.

6. Consider the language you speak.

Language is a powerful platform for the exchange of ideas and a site of complex negotiations that social workers need to reflect on to consider the nuances of cross-cultural communication and opportunities for connection. In very remote communities, particularly in the Northern Territory, Western Australia, and the far northwest of South Australia, Indigenous languages are commonly the first spoken language. It is not usual for three, four, or even more languages to be spoken in a single discrete community, with English only being used to interact with 'outsiders'.

Senior Pitjantjatjara woman, Rene Kulitja, in her presentation with Tjulapi Carrol and Nyunmiti Burton from the Anangu Pitjantjatjara Yankunytjatjara lands at the Lowitja Institute's 2019 International Indigenous

Health and Wellbeing Conference (Kulitja, Carrol, & Burton, 2019), speaks about the critical importance of Indigenous language for wellbeing from an Anangu standpoint. Kulitja sat cross-legged on the floor of the stage and pulled a large blanket over her body and head until the audience could barely see her eyes. 'This is English,' she said through interpreter Beth Sometimes from underneath the blanket, 'this is representing English, which is coming and pressing down on me and I can only see out through a tiny hole. Why is it like this? I'm not an English person. I'm a Pitjantjatjara person.' The presentation powerfully captures the importance of culture and language and the impact of colonisation on Indigenous peoples. It highlights the vital considerations that social workers must wrestle within their work with Aboriginal people, particularly in very remote communities.

The English language has been used as a weapon of colonisation at many sites of interaction between non-Indigenous and Aboriginal people in Australia. In education, the English language has been used as a means to undermine Aboriginal peoples' socio-economic position in Australia. The overwhelmingly poor standard of living for many Aboriginal people, particularly in rural and remote contexts, has been an outcome of consistent state and national education and other government policies. Here, one of our authors, Clayton Cruse, reflects on these policies from the context of education and provides critical considerations for social workers seeing to understand and interact in rural and remote contexts.

Aboriginal education has been like a bad science experiment for our people

Clayton Cruse

When I think about Aboriginal disadvantage in Australia as it is today, as a teacher I tend to think about Aboriginal peoples' interaction historically with consecutive state and national education departments.

There are historical examples of missionaries learning local languages to teach Indigenous children a western education, with good results recorded in some cases, but the fact is that Aboriginal children were expected to learn a western curriculum without being able to understand the language being used in schools. There is no doubting that culturally unresponsive education has placed Aboriginal and Torres Strait Islander students at an overwhelming disadvantage historically when compared to other Australians, and it is this educational disadvantage that continues to keep Aboriginal and Torres Strait Islander children, families and communities among the lowest socio-economic demographic in the country.

These results don't exist in a vacuum, in that poor educational outcomes sit alongside overall poor key life indicators like health, social mobility, and life expectancy for Aboriginal and Torres Strait Islander Australians.

While most Aboriginal people speak English and Aboriginal English as their first language, the majority of Aboriginal people who have identified as speaking an Aboriginal language in the 2011 census, lived in remote areas. In these instances, English can often be a third or fourth language. It is no surprise then that outcomes for Aboriginal students in these areas are poor, given they are educated at mostly English-only schools. Generally speaking, Aboriginal students in any community in Australia have not been schooled in their heritage language long term, and their cultures and experiences have not been valued within the curriculum to support holistic student development.

Bilingual education is concerned with teaching a student to read and write in their heritage language, giving the student the foundational skills of learning. Once reading and writing skills have been acquired, students then learn developmentally, working their way through being able to comprehend the same information that would be presented in a western educational setting.

The bilingual education movement which began in the early 1970s was developed using best practice for the education of people for whom the target language was not the home language. Bilingual education is not a new concept and has been used for centuries. The model here in Australia was achieving results for Aboriginal students, but not after issues with the program were 'ironed out'. The chart of Aboriginal student achievement saw that while progress initially for students was slow, once they had learnt the foundational skills of reading and writing, their progress increased rapidly, to the point where some Aboriginal students from remote areas were outperforming their non-Aboriginal peers in the larger coastal cities.

There is no denying that the social disadvantage of Aboriginal Australians is in part due to the denial of culturally reflective curriculum and pedagogy. This has created an environment for the hyper-interaction we see today between Aboriginal people and social work practice.

Educational disadvantage not only impacts Indigenous peoples in Australia. Generations of non-Aboriginal Australians have been denied a truly representative and inclusive version of Australia's history, which has had devastating impacts on race relations in this country. This is then clearly a concern for social work graduates in Australia working effectively with Aboriginal and Torres Strait Islander Australians.

We must consider how social work graduates can work effectively with Indigenous Australians when their own educational institutions do not present or support a truly representative and inclusive account of Australian history. It is vital that we consider the following critical questions:

What are social work students learning through 20 or so years of formal education that will enhance their ability to effectively work with Aboriginal Australians? Do the majority of social workers in Australia share the same heritage as those who sought to marginalise Indigenous peoples in this country? How do we reconcile these pasts in order to work together in the future?

Go forward with cultural humility

In review, our discussions in this chapter and the practice principles we offer are undergirded by a practitioner's ability to adopt a stance of cultural humility. Cultural humility is about maintaining integrity in practice and a deep ability to let go of one's pride; to be guided rather than be the guide. Development of true cultural humility is a game-changer. It means that people no longer are grouped into boxes; rather, they are met as individuals that are on an individual and collective journey. That journey may be a medical journey, social and emotional wellbeing journey, educational journey, or casework journey. Adopting a humble stance allows workers to come from a place of genuine and respectful curiosity instead of having to be an expert. When the worker and community members are on this journey together, the development of a relational interface that leads to greater facilitated outcomes is afforded. This relational model provides an opportunity for both people to develop a deep understanding of individual needs and how to meet these needs in healthy, culturally informed ways. This model allows for individual and collective empowerment that bucks the trend of ongoing systemic dependency. The model also facilitates genuine relational interaction that develops rapport and respect between the professional and the client.

We would like every social worker to ask themselves the question, 'How do I assist the community I am working with to move to a place of true self-determination?' Through a process of skill development and capacity building, every social worker should be working towards their role being performed by someone local to that community. We would ask social workers to recall their commitment to social work values and critically reflect on their motivations in every aspect of their work. The work that social workers do with Aboriginal people in rural and remote communities cannot be about making the professional look good and feel needed. This type of attitude only leads to further disempowerment of the individuals and the community. First Nations people of Australia have lived through countless ice ages and through over 100,000 years of global adversity. The innate ability to overcome and thrive through this adversity demonstrates significant strength and adaptability. We implore social workers not to be quick to dismiss the ability of community members to learn new skills or utilise knowledge from the past in order to grow as and manage their own communities, with assistance being given when needed and asked.

First Nations culture is a relational culture. It revolves around social interaction, social inclusion, and social obligation. The irony of teaching this information through a textbook is not lost on us. This form of education does not offer to follow up discussion nor discourse around how the person reading it will interpret the information. Therefore, it is a critical approach engagement in rural and remote communities as a whole person, not only as a worker. If the community only sees the worker there is no genuine interaction. Allowing people to 'see' you will allow you to find a place and provide space for people to interact with you. This means dropping the façade of expert and be willing to learn. Where appropriate, show vulnerability, and a willingness to learn and be guided. Action speaks louder than words so you will find it extremely valuable to ensure that you under promise and over-deliver. This means that you should ensure that if you say you will provide a service or support that you fulfill this commitment and where possible deliver more than what was promised.

To meet people with true cultural humility as a social worker is a wonderful gift. It represents dropping the guard of professionalism and allowing people to be people without prior judgement. This gift is one that Aboriginal communities have rarely been given. In the spirit of real cultural humility, we encourage you to take this learning and use it like a dilly bag of information to be drawn on when the right situation arises. Utilise knowledge from a wide range of sources, but don't let it own you or be your only guide. Use your intuition in the varied and wonderful interactions you have. Walk slowly, sit still, read the situation, then reach into your dilly bag and pull the right wisdom for that moment. Plant the seed and water it when the time is right. Aboriginal communities can bring to you much learning and enrichment from the world's oldest living culture. Look, listen, learn, and grow.

 ## Discussion Questions

1. What stories were you told about Aboriginal people at different stages in your education, and how have they informed your ideas about your work with Aboriginal people?

2. What is your motivation for wanting to work in a rural and remote context? If your answer includes 'to help', try to see if you go deeper and find what is at the core of that motivation.

3. How do you access and make sense of Indigenous knowledges pertinent to the context in which you are working?

References

Atkinson, J. (2002). *Trauma trails: Recreating song lines.* Melbourne, VIC: Spinifex Press.

Betancourt, J. R., Green, A. R., Carrillo, J. E., & Owusu Ananeh-Firempong, I. I. (2016). Defining cultural competence: A practical framework for addressing racial/ethnic disparities in health and health care. *Public Health Reports.*

Dumbrill, G. C., & Green, J. (2008). Indigenous knowledge in the social work academy. *Social Work Education, 27*(5), 489–503. doi: https://doi.org/10.1080/02615470701379891.

Furlong, M., & Wight, J. (2011). Promoting "critical awareness" and critiquing "cultural competence": Towards disrupting professional knowledges. *Australian Social Work, 64*(1), 38–54.

Gammage, B. (2011). *The biggest estate on earth: How Aborigines made Australia.* Crows Nest, NSW: Allen & Unwin.

Gilbert, S. (2001). Social work with Indigenous Australians. In M. Alston & J. McKinnon (Eds.), *Social work – Fields of practice* (pp. 46–57). South Melbourne, VIC: Oxford University Press.

Gilbert, S. (2009). Aboriginal issues in context. In M. Connelly & L. Harms (Eds.), *Social work context and practice* (2nd ed., pp. 94–106). Melbourne, VIC: Oxford University Press.

Green, S., & Baldry, E. (2008). Building indigenous Australian social work. *Australian Social Work, 61*(4), 389–402.

Herring, S., Spangaro, J., Lauw, M., & McNamara, L. (2013). The intersection of trauma, racism, and cultural competence in effective work with Aboriginal people: Waiting for trust. *Australian Social Work, 66*(1), 104–117. doi: https://doi.org/10.1080/0312407X.2012.697566.

Hickling-Hudson, A. (1990). White construction of black identity in Australian films about Aborigines. *Literature/Film Quarterly, 18*(4), 263–271.

Hollinsworth, D. (2013). Forget cultural competence; ask for an autobiography. *Social Work Education, 32*(8), 1048–1060. doi: https://doi.org/10.1080/02615479.2012.730513.

Human Rights and Equal Opportunity Commission (HREOC). (1997). *Bringing them home: Report of the National Inquiry into the Separation of Aboriginal and Torres Strait Islander Children from their Families.* Sydney, NSW: Human Rights and Equal Opportunity Commission.

Kulitja, R., Carrol, T., & Burton, N. (2019). *I want to light a fire in you with the knowledge of my ancestors.* Presentation at Lowitja Institute International Indigenous Health and Wellbeing Conference [interpreted by Beth Sometimes]. Retrieved from https://www.youtube.com/watch?time_continue=6&v=wG49UQux_cQ&feature=emb_logo

Langton, M. (1994). Aboriginal art and film: The politics of representation. *Race & Class, 35*(4), 89–106. doi: https://doi.org/10.1177/030639689403500410.

Moreton-Robinson, A. (2004). *Whitening race: Essays in social and cultural criticism.* Canberra, ACT: Aboriginal Studies Press.

Paradies, Y., Harris, R., & Anderson, I. (2008). *The impact of racism on Indigenous health in Australia and Aotearoa: Towards a research agenda.* Retrieved from https://www.lowitja.org.au/content/Document/Lowitja-Publishing/Racism-Report.pdf

Pascoe, B. (2014). *Dark emu: Black seeds: Agriculture or accident?* Broome, WA: Magabala Books.

Rekhari, S. (2008). The "Other" in film: Exclusions of Aboriginal identity from Australian cinema. *Visual Anthropology, 21*(2), 125–135. doi: https://doi.org/10.1080/08949460701857586.

Smith, L. T. (1999). *Decolonizing methodologies: Research and Indigenous peoples*. London: Zed Publishing.

Stewart, B. J., & Allan, J. (2013). Building relationships with Aboriginal people: A cultural mapping toolbox. *Australian Social Work, 66*(1), 118–129. doi: https://doi.org/10.1080/0312407X.2012.708937.

Young, S. M. (2004). Social work theory and practice: The invisibility of Whiteness. In A. Moreton-Robinson (Ed.), *Whitening race* (pp. 104–118). Canberra, ACT: Aboriginal Studies Press.

11 First Nation Leaders' Lessons on Sustainability and the Environment for Social Work

Michael Woodley and Dyann Ross

Introduction

We begin the chapter with an acknowledgement of First Nation activists who provide leadership in environmental sustainability and stewardship at this time in Australia. As the authors, our standpoint is forged from an earlier writing relationship based on common interests that span our different backgrounds and identities. Michael is a Yindjibarndi leader in the Pilbara, and Dyann is a white social work academic from Queensland. We present the environmental justice work of Mr. Ghillar Michael Anderson, Dr. Anne Poelina, Ms Michael Woodley (co-author), Mr. Adrian Burragubba, Ms. Murrawah Johnson, and the Youth Verdict organisation. The path-breaking work and activism of these leaders and their communities are highlighted with case studies. Case study 1 outlines Poelina's work, which relates to her role as a guardian of the Fitzroy River catchment area in northwest Kimberley region. The chapter describes her regional Earth-Centred Governance model which seeks directly to enable the sustainability of the environment. Case study 2 shows the ideas and activism of Anderson who is an Euahlayi Elder from northwestern New South Wales. Anderson has provided leadership in the struggle for sovereignty for many decades and, more recently, against coal seam gas mining. Case study 3 focuses on the concerns of Woodley and the Yindjibarndi People in the Roebourne area of Western Australia. It outlines the importance of having their story heard and Australians understanding the Yindjibarndi Peoples' struggle to protect their homelands. The issue relates to community division and impact by Fortesque Metals Group (FMG), which is one of Australia's largest iron ore mining companies. Case study 4 outlines the ideas and work of Burragubba and

Johnson who are First Nation Elders of the Wangan and Jajalingou Family Council from central Queensland. The Queensland government has extinguished native title to their land to make way for Adani, a major coal mine. Finally, the fifth case study is about the young Aboriginal and non-Aboriginal Australians who have formed Youth Verdict and currently have a legal challenge active against the Waratah coal mine on human rights grounds. As emerging leaders in the environmental sustainability space, this group of young people show an inter-racial partnership way forward that others can follow.

The chapter is written predominantly for social workers and calls on the profession to stand with First Nation People at this time. The task is one of partnering with First Nation activists to support their stewardship of the country (Green, 2018). The aim is to ensure environmental sustainability and integral to this, to care for nature upon whom all life is dependent. The first step towards partnerships with First Nation People is learning about their ideas and work. Further, for non-Indigenous Australians, the forming of partnerships in a racist society (Bennett, 2019; Bennett & Green, 2019) will need to involve a commitment to de-colonising our personal beliefs and actions (Yellow Bird, Coates, & Gray, 2013; Poelina, 2020a). The terms First Nation People and First Nation Peoples are given preference in the chapter to keep the focus on the unresolved issue of sovereignty and nationhood claims. Additionally, the intention is to emphasise the diversity of nations who comprise the traditional owners of Australia.

The issue of environmental unsustainability

Social work has a mission to contribute to social justice and peoples' wellbeing (International Federation of Social Workers, 2018) which can encompass a diverse range of fields of practice. An extension of social justice is to be inclusive of environmental justice (White, 2009). Winter explains that 'all issues of justice are already issues of environmental justice' (2017, n.p.). This is about sustainability, which refers to intergenerational, human, and trans-species equality and wellbeing where natural resources are protected against exploitation to ensure the flourishing of all life (Ross, 2015). Social work's attention and response are needed in a more ecological and holistic way (Boetto, 2019) alongside other professions, First Nation People, justice groups, and global citizens. This requires the re-framing of social work's famous dictum 'the person in the environment' to be inclusive of the natural environment as well as the milieu of the social work client (Jones, 2013). Without substantial justice, in areas of exploitation and harm to the environment (Gaard, 2011), the sustainability of life on the planet is impossible.

The issues of environmental unsustainability, interlinked with the denial of First Nation Peoples' sovereignty, profoundly impact humans' relationship with each other and with the natural environment and other species (O'Faircheallaigh & Saleem, 2017). First Nation People have provided stewardship of Australia's environment for tens of thousands of years and continue to do so at this time. There are many instances where First Nations are leading the struggle on behalf of all Australians to protect wild and sacred land, waterways and ecosystems (Woodley, 2020; Poelina, 2020a; Anderson, 2020; Wangan & Jagalingou Family Council, 2020a, 2020b, 2020c). As a profession, social work is not visible as a supporter of this struggle, but social workers often witness the transgenerational loss and trauma of colonisation and dispossession of First Nations People (Bennett, 2019) which in turn affects the planet.

First nation leaders' activism for their homelands and environmental sustainability

Pilger explains that 'political power in Australia often rests in the control of resource-rich land. Most of the uranium, iron ore, gold, oil, and natural gas is in Western Australia and the Northern Territory on Aboriginal land' (2011, n.p.). The vested interests of the power elites of society are thus increasingly in direct conflict with First Nation Peoples' stewardship responsibilities for their lands. It is in the area of ecological conflict that the linked issues of the denial of First Nation Peoples' sovereignty and environmental unsustainability are most evident (O'Faircheallaigh & Saleem, 2017).

Permission was sought by the authors to include the material from their publications and websites in the following case studies, which we acknowledge as significant goodwill towards us. In some instances, one or both of us did not have a relationship with the people approached. We have endeavoured to represent their ideas and work in carefully paraphrased summaries to maintain accuracy and their voices, with the key references identified at the beginning of each case study and in the reference list.

Box 11.1 Case Study 1

Ghillar Michael Anderson, Convenor Sovereign Union, Elder of Euahlayi Peoples' Republic, New South Wales.
(Anderson, 2012, 2014, 2015, 2020; Geia, 2013; Hooper, 2012).

Anderson was one of four land rights activists who set up the Aboriginal Tent Embassy in Canberra in the early 1970s and is a leader in the current call for sovereignty through the Sovereign Union movement. The sovereignty struggle has many dimensions and has been long-standing whereby First Nation People assert their pre-existing and continuing legal claims to the land and natural resources of Australia. Anderson understands it as a liberation struggle that has the parallel tasks of educating white Australians, building First Nations' capacity for independence, and seeking redress for harm done. History has shown that the dominant interests in Australian society will resist these calls and often will deny lawful claims, undermine community cohesion, and fight to maintain the status quo. The lack of constitutional recognition and equality and the persistence of racism in Australia compounds the Euahlayi Peoples' efforts to protect their homelands.

A breakthrough in the recognition of the rights of First Nation People occurred with the *Native Title Act 1993*, which established that the country of Australia was occupied prior to the white settlers. As such, First Nation People are recognised as having legal rights to their homelands. However, the vested interests of mining companies to these lands has resulted in complex contestations and very few First Nation People being awarded exclusive land rights. Nevertheless, Anderson's activism continues to challenge mining companies who are using loopholes in the Native Title legislation to gain mining rights against local First Nations' stewardship responsibilities.

For example, Anderson (2012, 2020) has been at the forefront of activism against coal seam gas mining on his country. The extractive industry is recognised internationally as having deleterious impacts on the environment (Cleary, 2012, 2017; Ransan-Cooper, Ercan, & Duus, 2018). However, the Goomeri region is rich in gas and other natural resources and as such is regarded as central to New South Wales' wealth into the future. In 2012, twenty-one Aboriginal Nations, including the Euahlayi Peoples' Republic, united on the basis of their non-ceded sovereignty to protect their most sacred water spirits (Hooper, 2012). They called on the government to protect the region's waterways and underground water systems, including from the harm caused by coal seam gas mining. The situation remains unresolved but continues to favour the dominant interests of mining companies.

Box 11.2 Case Study 2

Anne Poelina, Nikini Traditional Custodian, Managing Director of Madjulla Inc., Chair Martuwarra Fitzroy River Council, Pilbara, Western Australia. (Poelina, 2020a, 2020b),

Poelina (2020a) describes herself as a woman who belongs to the Mardoowarra [the Fitzroy River]. She describes the impact of colonisation on the river catchment in the remote Kimberley region of Western Australia as an invasion that was violent and brutal. It resulted in First Nation People in the Kimberley area experiencing subjugation and slavery. It also resulted in wealth creation by private and foreign interests at the expense of First Nation's lands and waters.

Poelina lives her life by upholding her customary responsibilities as required by Warloogarriy First Law. This involves a recognition that she is owned by, and responsible for, the Mardoowara river. She understands that the law is in the land and not in the people. The layers of significance of Poelina's ideas are profound; they not only challenge colonialist and capitalist ideologies but also provide the beating heart to moral claims for loving and sustaining nature. A key implication is the obligation to live in peaceful coexistence with nature and not to control or exploit it.

She writes that 'traditional ecological knowledge is Indigenous science' (2020a, p. ix) and Poelina believes First Nation Peoples' understandings are central to the needed re-imaging towards sustainable development. Thus, the reference to Country, called 'Booroo', is about both place and the spirituality of belonging, family, identity, and culture. Significantly, this involves mutual respect between human and non-human beings, a recognition of their interconnection, and an appreciation of shared livingness.

In line with these ideas, Poelina has worked to develop the Earth-Centred Regional Governance approach, which seeks sustainability of nature and sets limits to development. It is an approach based on dialogue between all stakeholders to enable the responsible management of the river and the surrounding natural resources. Further, the aim is to work towards the transition away from unsustainable and invasive development towards sustainable, clean, and green industries and thriving communities and cultures.

The Fitzroy River Management Plan of 2019 which is being used as a basis for multi-stakeholder research, dialogue, and decision-making is an example of this work. The signatories' preferred position is for a moratorium on the issuing of water licences until a consensus that works with the limits of nature and the cultural interests of First Nation People has been achieved.

Box 11.3 Case Study 3

Michael Woodley, Yindjibarndi First Nation, Chief Executive Officer Yindjibarndi Aboriginal Corporation, Pilbara, Western Australia.
(Woodley, 2020; Cleary, 2017).

Woodley is a leader of the Yindjibarndi People, who were forced off the high Country of the Pilbara tablelands in the early 1900s and placed into the Kujura Reserve. He explains the stark contrast between their living conditions and lack of free movement and the increasing influx of white people into the Pilbara as the mining boom ramped up in the 1960s. The Yindjibarndi people were displaced from their homelands because the Pilbara is rich in natural resources and poor in recognition of First Nation People. This pattern of domination continues to the present day and has had the effect of stopping them from their sovereignty and denied the wealth that was their birthright.

The whole Pilbara area was increasingly subject to mining development with the pegging of mining leases. Nevertheless, in 2007, as a result of sustained activism, the Yindjibarndi were granted native title and limited access to 30% to their ancestral Country. A decade later, they won exclusive rights over their land with a Federal High Court ruling. However, FMG, the mining company at the centre of this struggle, mounted an appeal against the decision. Estimates suggest that FMG stands to gain A$200 billion from mining on Yindjibarndi lands. The traditional owners will receive as little as 0.5% royalty. If the FMG appeal is successful, the Yindjibarndi People will have no option but to get the best compensation payment possible.

Woodley adds that a key threat to Yindjibarndi has been the 'divide and conquer' tactics undertaken by FMG who have gained support from some of the community to proceed with initial explorations for suitable sites without the relevant agreements with the Yindjibarndi people. The community was split when FMG paid one group to support them against the legally authorised Yindjibarndi Ngurra Aboriginal Corporation. Woodley explains that his people typically conduct their business in such a way that either everybody agrees or there is no agreement. This collective decision-making was undermined by FMG's actions. He sees the buying out of some of his people as corruption at the expense of collectiveness and power and money versus uncertainty and the history of deprived people.

This conflict was very harmful to the Yindjibarndi Peoples' cohesion as a community of approximately 800 people. In the context of dispossession and external divisive influences, Woodley and his partner, Lorraine, have worked to protect and support their peoples' culture and heritage with the development of the Juluwarlu Group Aboriginal Corporation. This is a place where the Yindjibarndi People can re-connect, value their history, language, and culture, and resist the threats to their community. Woodley holds a vision of justice where all the dispossessed land is reclaimed and First Nation People have control over property purchases. He concludes that the notion of free and informed consent would be upheld and First Nations could then rule Country through an economic means that recognises just terms compensation.

Box 11.4 Case Study 4

Adrian Burragubba and Murrawah Johnson, Elders, The Wangan and Jagalingou Family Council, Carmichael and Belyando Rivers area, Queensland. (Wangan Jagalingou, 2019a, 2019b, 2020a, 2020b).

The Wangan and Jagalingou First Nation People are on the frontline of trying to resist one of the world's largest proposed coal mines by Adani in the Galilee Basin area which covers 1385 hectares of their Country, including the ancient and sacred Doongmabulla Springs. In 2019, Burragubba, a W&J Elder, claimed they had been made trespassers on their own Country and now needed Adani's prior consent to enter the disputed area. He believes the government partnered with Adani and caused dispossession, suffering to his people, and harm to their ancestors.

Earlier, the Federal Court had rejected the W&J challenge against Adani, and this was followed by the anticipated state government's decision to extinguish native title. When this came to pass it was understood to be part of a mining corporation's legally sanctioned land grab. Some of the complexity occurred where a majority of native claimants supported the Adani mine and only one dissenting vote remained after Adani directly negotiated to get consent from the other claimants. Johnson, an Elder of the W&J First Nation People, was the singular dissenting voice and protested to the government about the mining company's tactics, undermining how his people made decisions as a collective. The Western legal system has supported a major multinational mining company to systematically buy the support of claimants through a similar divide and conquer process identified by Woodley. Burragubba faces imprisonment if he tries to enter the Adani-controlled area for sacred ceremonies on Country. His people became trespassers when the government changed the land title to freehold and gave it to Adani. The Wangan and Jagalingou First Nation People believe the loss is profound, going beyond the destruction of their homeland and extending to the stories and songlines in their land which teaches them how to live. They believe that without this connection to Country they cease to exist and will not be able to pass their culture onto future generations.

The broader public became aware of some level of the environmental issue when the black-throated finch was threatened with Adani's intrusion into their habitat (Slezak, 2016). Additionally, there has been an ongoing national-level campaign based on the pollution caused by coal and the environmental harm the mining and use of coal will cause (Stop Adani, 2020). The loss, if the Adani mine begins production, however, sits differently and goes deep into the hearts of the First Nation People. The W&J Family Council believe they are not just on the frontline of this major ecological struggle, but that they *are* the frontline. At the time of writing, they are holding a blockade at a key entrance road to the Adani mine site 'saying they have "re-established control" of land' (Smee, 2020).

Box 11.5 Case Study 5

Youth Verdict.
(Youth Verdict, 2020; Bell-James, 2020; Environmental Defender's Office, 2020a, 2020b; Wangan Jagalingou, 2020c).

The activist group is comprised of young people from a range of backgrounds and places who wish to stand with First Nation People in their struggle for cultural and land rights. Youth Verdict believes their own life experience of major floods, bushfires, and drought highlights the link between the adverse impacts of climate change, extractive industries, and harm to the environment. We sought out information about Youth Verdict upon hearing a news report of the concerns related to the continuation of government approvals for major coal mines. Their organisation is being enabled by the Queensland Environmental Defenders Office to undertake legal action against one of a number of major coal mining proposals in the Galilee Basin in Central Queensland. The mine in question, the Waratah Coal mega-mine, will be an estimated four times larger than the nationally contentious Adani coal mine. It has been given the green light at the federal government level and a draft environmental approval by the state government.

Youth Verdict is the first activist group to be utilising Queensland's *Human Rights Act* (Queensland Government, 2019) to claim their human rights will be compromised by the impact of such a massive coal mine. Youth Verdict, which includes First Nations and non-Indigenous young people, explains their concern that the Waratah mine is yet another 'carbon bomb' that the country cannot afford. Thus, the climate change impacts from the mining and use of fossil fuels are compromising their human rights to safe, secure life and employment which is environmentally sustainable.

The W&J Family Council is one First Nation that is actively supporting Youth Verdict's case. They argue that there is a chance for the courts to step up where the governments have tended to fail. The legal action brings together concerns about human rights, the impact of climate change, and Aboriginal culture and law. Johnson explains that 'when our moieties, our totems, our reference points in Country are destroyed, we can no longer be who we are as the people from that land' (Wangan Jagalingou, 2020c, n.p.).

Lessons for social work

What is happening in Australia is cause for moral, spiritual, emotional, and intellectual outrage and the case studies presented in this chapter lead us to call on social work to use this outrage to stand in solidarity:

- Listen to and learn from what the stewards of the land are saying;
- Educate self and others about the scientific and evidence-based reports of unsustainability and harm;
- Protest about the range of impact and the size of the mega-mines and polluting industries;
- Seek accountability for what the mining companies are doing and taking and,
- Question and challenge how the governments have a narrow economic view of what is in the public's interest.

First Nation People, in Australia and internationally, are providing a master class in what humans need to do to survive, sustain, and flourish. For example, the Redstone Statement is an internationally recognised document that expresses Indigenous environmental philosophy which claims that:

> We must assure the well-being of both humanity and nature. This requires a unification of diverse people who are open to ideas; people who are wise, clear, and profoundly human; and people who can transcend the self-imposed limits of their minds, reaching deep into their conscience and spirit for solutions. (2010, p. 2)

The lessons for social work are presented in the next section under two main themes and related implications with examples of possible action-oriented strategies related to First Nation Peoples' activism.

Theme: Stewardship of the environment for sustainability is a shared responsibility.

Environmental social work implication: Actively support First Nation Peoples' stewardship and, in particular, join ecological activism efforts against mining and other exploitative and polluting industries.

In relation to the First Nation Peoples' current activism, possible action-oriented strategies could include:

- Acting to stop the undermining of Native Title Land Rights – as per the example of the Yindjibarndi Peoples' struggles to protect its homelands against one of Australia's largest iron ore mining companies, FMG (Woodley, 2020);
- Protesting to show that the extinguishing of native title rights is a nationally significant ecological conflict – as per the example of activism against

Adani by the Wangan and Jagalingou People (Wangan Jajalingou, 2019b, 2020a, 2020b, 2020c; Smee, 2020);

- Acting to stop unsustainable industries before they start as per the example of Youth Verdict (2020) young people's activism against the Waratah coal mine proposal in the Galilee Basin;
- Making personal contact with First Nation Peoples' organisations as per the Sovereign Union (Anderson, 2020) website to lend support to their efforts as might be needed to protect the waterways and underground water systems of the Murray–Darling basin, and to resist coal seam gas proposals being approved on sacred land;
- Supporting the care and cultural work in First Nations as per the Yindijbarndi Peoples' cultural centre, Juluwarlu Group Aboriginal Corporation (2016);
- Lobbying key government officials and departments to endorse and adopt the co-operative regional Earth-centred Governance Model (Poelina, 2020b) as best practice for water management and other environmental disputes; and
- Making a connection with the W&J Family Council to give moral and other types of support to them at this time when they are facing prosecution by Adani if they enter their ancestral lands (Wangan Jagalingou, 2020b; Smee, 2020).

Theme: Showing love by listening deeply to First Nation People and emerging leaders.

Environmental social work implication: Acknowledge First Nation sovereignty as a key justice goal that will help heal the country and its people.

The leadership by First Nation People, and the young emerging leaders, are showing the ways forward that can create sustainability, justice, and healing of the people, animals, and the land. An ethic of love (hooks, 2000) suggests that nothing will change even if we take heed of the master class and notice matters of ethical concern and even if we have some guidance on action-oriented strategies. Justice will not be valued and sought without love of people, animals, and nature (Ross, 2020; Godden, 2017). Love is needed to sustain the activism and efforts that can take years, even decades, to achieve justice.

In relation to the influence of the First Nation People and young emerging leaders, love can be shown by listening deeply to what they are saying, then standing in solidarity, using a range of strategies with them to address issues such as:

- The politicisation of the Native Title Act of 1993 with powerful vested interests in the mining industry and government reducing the intent of the Act;
- The Yindjibarndi Peoples' experience of being divided and brought off by FMG which undermined their traditional, collaboration decision-making processes and solidarity;

- The challenges involved in First Nation Peoples' bringing test cases that set legal precedents for recognising that their spiritual rights are inseparable from the land;
- The politics behind some First Nation Elders conducting a walkout from the Uluru meeting as a protest calling for the strengthening of claims of the Uluru statement to include a specific requirement of First Nation Peoples' sovereignty;
- The lack of recognition of the significance of the belief that the law is in the land not in the people, that humans are in and of nature; and,
- Youth Verdict's concerns and ideas relating to mega mines and the threats to the environment and their human rights and our collective future.

Conclusion: Towards an environmental social work field of practice

Australia is a settler society that continues to perpetuate a colonialist governance structure which is actively resisting First Nation Peoples' calls for sovereignty (Pilger, 2011; Anderson, 2020). In turn, Australia's neoliberalist capitalist economic system is based on the exploitation of the environment and some species of animals (Brueckner & Ross, 2020). The governance structure and economic system create intersectionalities of oppression based on a mutually reinforcing ethic of domination (Poelina, 2020b). Social work is a profession located at the nexus of this ethic of domination in all its embodied and material forms of discrimination, inequality, and harm. The lessons from First Nation Peoples' ideas and activism can guide social workers in how to extend social justice to include environmental justice. The need for this expansion of social work's mission and ethical concern is evident in situations of ecological conflict.

The activism of leaders from several First Nations and emerging leaders have been acknowledged to convey the pressing moral imperative for social workers to develop an ecological commitment by undertaking broad-ranging justice work strategies. The Uluru Statement of the Heart, developed by a gathering of First Nation People at the 2017 National Constitutional Convention, notes:

> In 1967 we were counted, in 2017 we seek to be heard. We leave base camp and start our trek across this vast country. We invite you to walk with us in a movement of the Australian people for a better future. (Referendum Council, 2017, p. 2)

The invitation has been given. To date, justice has not occurred. At the same time, and not unrelatedly, mining continues at a pace and on a scale not witnessed in the history of Australia, for the wealth of a few white people.

The chapter concludes with a set of questions to guide the personal and professional ethical premises of an environmental social work field of practice:

– Are you willing to regard all sentient beings and nature as of equal moral worth?
– Are you willing to contribute to the stewardship of the environment?
– Are you willing to stand with First Nation People and their struggle for sovereignty?

We recommend that social workers critically reflect on the questions, seek answers, and develop a plan on how to respond in their professional supervision. Further, in relation to each of these questions, be proactive in answering this last question in your practice:

– If so, what is a step you can take to demonstrate this socio-environmental justice commitment?

Social work needs to cultivate a critical mass of practitioners who take up this commitment to an environmental social work field of practice to gain traction in the profession. Wherever social workers live and work, as is the case for all people, we are always in and of nature. As such, there are ever-present opportunities to respond to the person and the environment simultaneously. The sustainability of the planet and all life forms alongside the sovereignty of all peoples of the world can be considered to include the full moral implication of social work's social justice mission.

Discussion Questions

We ask you to reflect upon the chapter and discuss the following with your family, friends, neighbours, and colleagues:

1. Why does the Australian public overwhelmingly support reconciliation between Aboriginal and Torres Strait Islander People, and yet allow the noted travesties of justice?

2. Do you think there should be limits placed on the way mining companies engage with and seek to influence different First Nation groups in an area where the companies have a mining lease?

3. Relatedly, do you think governments should be able to extinguish native title for economic reasons when this threatens the human and other rights of First Nation People?

4. Do you think the possibility of environmental sustainability is inextricably linked with First Nation Sovereignty?

5. Given how far Australia seems to be from both, how do you think these two pressing situations can be addressed?

References

Anderson, M. (2012). *Where we are coming from, moving into a new and exciting future.* http://nationalunitygovernment.org/node/21

Anderson, M. (2014). *First nations sovereignty new way.* http://www.youtube.com/watch?v=ZBz7GLP0vs8

Anderson, M. (2015). *About sovereign union.* http://nationalunitygovernment.org/content/about-sovereign-union

Anderson, M. (2020). *First Nations: Historic resources and activism links.* http://nationalunitygovernment.org/content/first-australians-historic-resources-and-activism-links

Australian Government. (1993). *Native Title Act 1993.* https://aiatsis.gov.au/explore/articles/land-rights

Bell-James, J. (2020). *These young Queenslanders are taking on Clive Palmer's coal company and making history for human rights.* https://theconversation.com/these-young-queenslanders-are-taking-on-clive-palmers-coal-company-and-making-history-for-human-rights-138732

Bennett, B. (2019). The importance of Aboriginal history for practitioners. In B. Bennett & S. Green (Eds.), *Our voices: Aboriginal social work* (2nd ed., pp. 3–30). London: Red Globe Press.

Bennett, B., & Green, S. (2019). *Our voices: Aboriginal social work* (2nd ed.). London: Red Globe Press.

Boetto, H. (2019). Advancing transformative eco-social change: Shifting from modernist to holistic foundations. *Australian Social Work, 72*(2), 139–152.

Brueckner, M., & Ross, D. (2020). Eco-activism and social work: In the public interest. In D. Ross, M. Brueckner, M. Palmer, & W. Eaglehawk (Eds.), *Eco-activism & social work: New directions in leadership and group work* (pp. 3–25). London: Routledge.

Cleary, P. (2012). *Mine-field: The dark side of Australia's resources rush.* Collingwood, VIC: Black Inc.

Environmental Defenders Office, Queensland (2020a). Clive Palmer's Galilee coal project faces human rights challenge. https://www.edo.org.au/2020/05/13/clivepalmers-galilee-coal-project-faceshuman-rights-challenge/

Environmental Defenders Office, Queensland (2020b). Young people and landholders unite to challenge Clive Palmer's coal mine. https://www.edo.org.au/young-people-andlandholders-unite-to-challenge-clivepalmers-coal-mine/

Cleary, P. (2017). *Title fight: The great philanthropist vs the people of the Pilbara.* https://www.themonthly.com.au/issue/2017/september/1504188000/paul-cleary/title-fight

Gaard, G. (2011). Ecofeminism revisited: Rejecting essentialism and re-placing species in a material feminist environmentalism. *Feminist Formulations, 23*, 26–53.

Geia, J. (2013). *Goomeroi people call for a mining freeze on sacred lands.* http://nationalunitygovernment.org/content/goomeroi-people-call-mining-freeze-sacred-lands

Godden, N. (2017). The love ethic: A radical theory for social work practice. *Australian Social Work, 70*(4), 405–416.

Green, S. (2018). Aboriginal People and caring within a colonised society. In B. Pease, A. Vreugdenhil, & S. Stanford (Eds.), *Critical ethics of care in social work: Transforming the politics and practices of caring* (pp. 139–147). London: Routledge.

hooks, b. (2000). All about love. London: New Visions.

Hooper, F. (2012). *Sovereignty claims over Murray-Darling rivers.* http://nationalunitygovernment.org/content/sovereignty-claimed-over-murray-darling-rivers

International Federation of Social Workers. (2018). *Global social work statement of ethical principles.* https://www.ifsw.org/global-social-work-statement-of-ethical-principles/

Jones, P. (2013). Transforming the curriculum: Social work education and ecological consciousness. In M. Gray, J. Coates, & T. Hetherington (Eds.), *Environmental social work* (pp. 213–230). London: Routledge.

Juluwarlu Group Aboriginal Corporation. (2016). *Juluwarlu: Documenting and archiving our Yindjibarndi language, law and culture.* https://www.facebook.com/watch/?v=916069595224142

O'Faircheallaigh, C., & Saleem, A. (2017). *Earth matters: Indigenous peoples, the extractive industries and corporate social responsibility.* London: Routledge.

Pilger, J. (2011). *How the Murdoch press keeps Australia's dirty secret.* http://nationalunitygovernment.org/content/john-pilger-how-murdoch-press-keeps-australia%E2%80%99s-dirty-secret

Poelina, A. (2020a). Foreward. First Law is the natural law of the land. In D. Ross, M. Brueckner, M. Palmer, & W. Eaglehawk (Eds.), *Eco-activism & social work: New directions in leadership and group work* (pp. viii–xii). London: Routledge.

Poelina, A. (2020b). A coalition of hope! A regional governance approach to Indigenous Australian cultural wellbeing. In A. Campbell, M. Duffy, & B. Edmondson (Eds.), *Located research* (pp. 153–180). London: Palgrave Macmillan.

Queensland Government. (2019). *Human Rights Act 2019.* https://www.legislation.qld.gov.au/view/html/asmade/act-2019-005

Ransan-Cooper, H., Ercan, S., & Duus, S. (2018). *Getting to the heart of coal seam gas protests – It's not just the technical risks.* https://theconversation.com/getting-to-the-heart-of-coal-seam-gas-protests-its-not-just-the-technical-risks-107086

Referendum Council. (2017). *Uluru statement from the heart.* https://www.referendumcouncil.org.au/sites/default/files/201705/Uluru_Statement_From_The_Heart_0.PDF

Ross, D. (2015). Social sustainability. In S. Idowu (Ed.), *Dictionary of corporate social responsibility* (p. 466). Cologne: Springer.

Ross, D. (2020). The love ethic practice model. In D. Ross, M. Brueckner, M. Palmer, & W. Eaglehawk (Eds.), *Eco-activism & social work: New directions in leadership and group work* (pp. 125–142). London: Routledge.

Slezak, M. (2016). Coalmines could wipeout threatened black-throated finch-habitat - study. https://www.theguardian.com/australianews/2016/mar/03/coalmines-couldwipe-out-threatened-black-throatedfinch-habitat-study.

Smee, B. (2020). *Access to Adani's Carmichael coalmine in Queensland blocked by traditional owners.* https://www.theguardian.com/environment/2020/

aug/24/adanis-carmichael-coalmine-in-queensland-blocked-by-traditional-owners?fbclid=IwAR3aihH0tVLF99WHFUzMLe10fFfVdnFpe9pBZqOsz5cpMO0xOOUHIcncykk

Stop Adani. (2020). *Fuels global warming.* https://www.stopadani.com/wrecks_our_climate

Wangan Jagalingou. (2019a). *Queensland government wipes out W&J native title for Adani.* https://wanganjagalingou.com.au/qld-govt-wipes-out-wj-native-title-for-adani/

Wangan Jagalingou. (2019b). *We are not just on the frontline, we are the front line.* https://wanganjagalingou.com.au/we-are-not-just-on-the-frontline-we-are-the-frontline/

Wangan Jagalingou. (2020a, February 6). *If they destroy our country, they will destroy us as a people.* https://wanganjagalingou.com.au/if-they-destroy-our-country-they-will-destroy-us-as-a-people/

Wangan Jagalingou. (2020b, April 25). *Adani relies on draconian laws to deny Aboriginal rights.* https://wanganjagalingou.com.au/adani-relies-on-draconian-laws-to-deny-aboriginal-rights/

Wangan Jagalingou. (2020c, May 14). *W&J support for human rights and climate change case against Palmer's coal plans.* https://wanganjagalingou.com.au/wj-support-for-human-rights-and-climate-change-case-against-palmers-coal-plans/

White, R. (2009). Environmental victims and resistance to state crime through transnational activism. *Social Justice, 36*(3), 46–60.

Winter, C. (2017). *Post-hegemonic futures: Decolonising intergenerational environmental justice.* http://sydney.edu.au/environment-institute/opinion/ej-series-part-1-post-hegemonic-futures-decolonising-intergenerational-environmental-justice/

Woodley, M. (2020). The wrong side of Native title, the right side of mining. In D. Ross, M. Brueckner, M. Palmer, & W. Eaglehawk (Eds.), *Eco-activism and social work: New directions in leadership and group work* (pp. 61–73). London: Routledge.

Yellow Bird, M., Coates, J., & Gray, M. (2013). *Decolonising social work.* Burlington: Routledge.

Youth Verdict. (2020). *Young people using the law to fight for justice.* https://www.youthverdict.org.au/

12 Resilience-Based Therapeutic Interventions to Address Intergenerational Trauma

Amy Kennedy

Cultural standpoint

I am a proud Wiradjuri Kalare (river) woman from a small town in the Riverina, New South Wales. In 2018, I graduated from the University of New South Wales with a Bachelor of Social Work and a Bachelor of Sociology and Anthropology. Since then, I have been working in the child protection sector, primarily with Aboriginal out-of-home care agencies. I feel very privileged to work alongside strong and driven Aboriginal sisters and brothers as colleagues and feel even more privileged to work for, protect, and learn from our *galingabangbur*, our future leaders.

Introduction

The process of healing is second nature to Aboriginal[1] people. We have been perpetually healing physically, emotionally, and spiritually since Cook stepped foot onto our lands in 1788. Australia is a colonially scarred country. The invasion was long-lasting and a deliberate attempt to eradicate Aboriginal people and sever ties to Country[2] to gain financial bounty from the land, minerals, and waters originally owned and protected by the first custodians of Australia. The trauma inflicted upon Aboriginal individuals, communities, and families by the colonisers has become personified and now flows through our veins, within our bodies and is passed from our *balumbambal*[3] onto our *galingabangbur*.[4] Initial trauma and subsequent healing go hand in hand. If there is no acknowledgment and no understanding of trauma, it will be both knowingly and unknowingly passed onto the next generation. How do we, Aboriginal people, heal? We draw upon our collective resilience.

This chapter will outline intergenerational trauma, describe resilience in the context of Aboriginal Australians, highlight the importance of feminist theory when working with Aboriginal women, and will emphasise the immense value of Aboriginal specific therapeutic interventions.

The infliction of trauma on Aboriginal communities began with the invasion of the British. Colonisation ensured the spread of trauma not only throughout Aboriginal land but also throughout Aboriginal families and across generations. The engraining of trauma and the motion of perpetual healing coincide with each other. The colonisation of Australia began with the displacement and dispossession of Aboriginal communities from their land, culture, and families. The history of Aboriginal Australia is wrought with anguish, stress, and torture imposed through unjust legislation. From 1788, Aboriginal land was stolen, and frontier wars erupted, resulting in colonial violence (The Law Reform Commission, 1986). From the 1820s, martial law was declared, and more punitive expeditions such as devastating massacres and further colonial violence was common (The Law Reform Commission, 1986). From the 1830s, the House of Commons Select Committee on Aborigines enforced various 'protection' policies, including the establishment of religious missions and government settlements where Aboriginal people were forced to reside; the enactment of special laws prohibiting the consumption of alcohol, restricting the movement of Aboriginal peoples; the regulation of Aboriginal employment and the establishment of boarding houses to remove half-caste[5] Aboriginal children from their parents to educate them in European ways (The Law Reform Commission, 1986). From the 1930s, policies of assimilation ensued, which meant 'all Aborigines and part-Aborigines are expected to attain the same manner of living as other Australians, enjoying the same rights and privileges, accepting the same customs and influenced by the same beliefs as other Australians' (Reynolds, 1972, p. 175); however, this 'equality' came at the forced disposal of Aboriginal identity, language, and customs (The Law Reform Commission, 1986). Since the 1970s, policies of integration and self-determination have been implemented recognising the value of Aboriginal knowledge and practices. However, to speak curtly, the damage has been done. The history and legacy of paternalistic and controlling methods have caused entrenched trauma for Aboriginal Australians. The past trauma of attempted genocide, colonial wars, the theft of Aboriginal children, and the destruction of culture and language has resulted in vast gaps between Aboriginal and non-Aboriginal people that are now reflected within current statistics.

Intergenerational trauma

Intergenerational trauma is the long-lasting pain of colonisation that has been etched into the families and communities of Aboriginal people and communities. It is the effect of previous unresolved traumas that are passed onto the successive generations of an individual's family, community, and culture (Hoffart & Jones, 2018, p. 27). The invasion and colonisation of Australia were executed with the weapons of genocide, cultural degradation, and violence. Aboriginal traditions, language, connection to land, spirituality, and rights were denied and destroyed in an attempt to eradicate Aboriginal culture and Aboriginal people. And the then Australian Government enforced policies of 'protection' and assimilation that has resulted in an enduring and transmissible trauma for Aboriginal people and families.

Intergenerational trauma has been researched and illuminated by many scholars from many fields, but none have explained this concept as eloquently as First Nations Native American social worker and scholar Maria Yellow Horse Brave Heart. Brave Heart coined the concept of historical trauma in the 1990s, mirroring the concept of intergenerational trauma. Brave Heart (2003, p. 7) notes that historical trauma or intergenerational trauma is the 'cumulative emotional and psychological wounding, over the lifespan and across generations, emanating from massive group trauma experiences'. Much like Aboriginal Australians, the Lakota peoples of North and South Dakota also fought in a colonial war which resulted in suffering and bereavement from community and culture that affects the Lakota communities to the present day. One component of Brave Heart's (2003) description of historical trauma is *group trauma experiences*. Aboriginal Australian Blak[6] history highlights a timeline of group trauma experiences incorporating massacres, acts of displacement from Country, the heartless and deliberate removal of children to orphanages and schools (the Stolen Generations), and are culminated by an ongoing loss of language, cultural practices, and kin. It is group trauma experiences like these that result in *historical trauma responses*. Historical trauma responses are the constellations of features in reaction to group trauma experiences (Brave Heart, 2003, p. 7). To understand the responses to trauma, we must first consider the cycle of intergenerational trauma (refer to Figure 12.1).

First, the individual, family, group, or an entire race of people are exposed to a trauma or ongoing traumas; then coping mechanisms, both beneficial and detrimental, take over as those traumas are left unaddressed and looming deep in the genetic make-up of the trauma survivor; then the effects of these traumas are transmitted to the next generation; then the next generation experiences the residual traumas and draws upon the same coping mechanisms; then the next generation does the same and so on the cycle continues and becomes normalised.

Intergenerational or historical trauma is a complex, unrelenting cycle, and until something or someone makes a fracture within that cycle, it will not cease. But how does this fracture occur?

Trauma is incredibly complicated and intricate as it exists in an intangible form that cannot be physically formulated; however, the trauma effects and trauma symptoms are tangible, can be witnessed, are exhibited in DNA (Youssef, Lockwood, Su, Hao, & Rutten, 2018) and have contributed over time to the current statistics that plague Aboriginal communities within Australia. Brave Heart (2003, p. 7) notes that historical trauma responses include coping mechanisms such as drug and alcohol abuse, other types of self-destructive behaviour, emotional dysregulation, rejection of cultural healing, and, personal and family violence. These reactions occur in

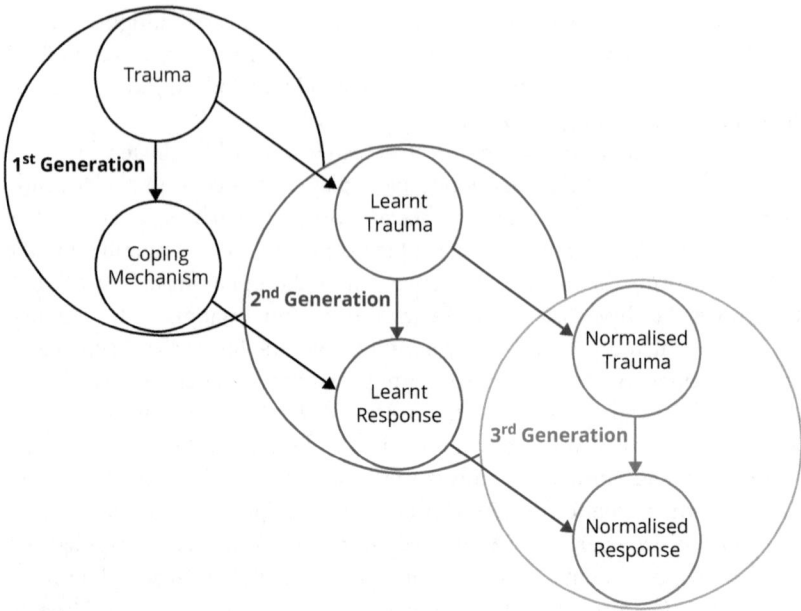

Figure 12.1 The transmission of trauma

individuals and families and causes further displacement and destruction of Aboriginal communities and culture. However, it is imperative to note that these types of trauma responses are not specific to Aboriginal communities and can and do occur elsewhere. Currently, in Australia, detrimental inter-generational adaptions result in very real and very disproportionate gaps between Aboriginal and non-Aboriginal people. Aboriginal children are five times more likely than non-Aboriginal children to be reported to child pro-tective services and ten times more likely to be removed from family and culture and placed in out-of-home care (SNAICC, 2017; Bennett, 2019, p. 3); removal causes trauma. In 2015, it was reported that only 1 in 4 Aboriginal adults live on their Country; the majority are separated and sepa-ration from traditional lands causes trauma (AIHW, 2015). Aboriginal youth are 14 times more likely than non-Aboriginal youth to be under justice supervision and Aboriginal adults are 11 times more likely than non-Aboriginal adults to be under justice supervision; institutionalisation causes trauma (Victorian Aboriginal Justice Agreement, 2018). Aboriginal adults are three times more likely to experience psychological distress than non-Aboriginal adults; stress causes maladaptive coping mechanisms to trauma (AIHW, 2015). Overall, Aboriginal people are less likely to drink alcohol than non-Aboriginal people, however Aboriginal people are three times more likely to consume alcohol at a risky consumption level; alcohol misuse causes maladaptive coping mechanisms to trauma (AIHW, 2020). Aboriginal females and males are, respectively, 35 and 22 times more likely to be hospitalised due to family-related assaults than other non-Aboriginal females and males; family violence causes maladaptive coping mechanisms to trauma (AIHW et al., 2006). Kirmayer, Brass, and Tait (2000, p. 611) note that intergenerational trauma is exacerbated for Aboriginal peoples as shared traumas have become ingrained in the policies, practices, and institutions surrounding them. The forced assimilation of Aboriginal peoples and ongoing losses of language, culture, and spirituality has contributed to the breakdown of family kinship networks and social structures (Brave Heart, 2003, p. 8). This breakdown of social and family connections adds further to the historical legacy and current conditions of ongoing intergenerational trauma.

Jacobs and Davis (2017, p. 201) describe intergenerational trauma as having two components: experiences of race-based traumatic stress and the intergenerational transmission of behaviours learned as adaptations to traumatic experiences. Brave Heart (2003), Kirmayer, Dandeneau, Marshall, Phillips, and Williamson (2012), and Jacobs and Davis (2017) have shared similar concepts of trauma; concepts shrouded in maladaptations and responses to pain and distress. Duran, Duran, Brave Heart, and Yellow Horse-Davis (1998) suggest that trauma responses become normalised within a culture because it becomes embedded in the collective, cultural memory of a people and is transmitted and learned through the same means as culture itself. It could be further argued that detrimental trauma responses have also become embedded in the prejudiced perceptions that surround Aboriginal peoples and communities within Australia. Perceptions such as stereotypes about the way an Aboriginal person should look or act, traditional child-rearing practices, use and misuse of drugs and alcohol, Aboriginal participation in the workforce, welfare dependency, and proclivity to engage in domestic violence and other crimes; the list of prejudices could go on. Some intergenerational and historical trauma responses may appear to look like Aboriginal people's inability to cope appropriately according to white Australia; however, some trauma responses are learnt behaviours of adaptation and survival caused by the fallout of colonial warfare and injustices. And too often are the detrimental trauma responses remembered and not the strength of community and cultural resilience practices. Therefore, to break the cycle of trauma, coping mechanisms that are based on resilience and cultural knowledge are required to limit and eventually prevent detrimental historical trauma responses from occurring. And, to further challenge entrenched negative stereotypes and racist opinions of Aboriginal healing.

Aboriginal resilience

Trauma is the 'cumulative emotional and psychological wounding' (Brave Heart, 2003, p. 7) individuals and communities experience over their lifetimes. Trauma results in lasting and intergenerational impressions upon communities and cultures. Trauma manifests itself in various ways and attacks individuals' psychological and spiritual strengths. Research shows that trauma experienced in childhood becomes embedded in the personality and development of the child through observed social learnings (Bringing Them Home, 1997, p. 170) and is then observed by the next generation. Research also shows that trauma can lead to a change in an individual's biological make-up. Youssef et al. (2018) found that exposure to trauma can result in epigenetic modifications that can be passed to offspring transgenerationally via the inheritance mechanism of DNA. So not only is trauma passed on through the social learnings of the adaptations of one generation to the next; it is also passed on through inheriting traumatised DNA. This evidence was found upon examination of the surviving children of the Tutsi genocide (Perroud et al., 2014) and upon examination of Holocaust survivors (Yehuda et al., 2016). Unresolved trauma leaves open wounds. For Aboriginal people, unresolved grief and trauma can impede the development of resilience and healing. However, the Bringing Them Home report (1997, p. 169) noted that post-trauma effects can be mitigated for Aboriginal people who have a strong self-concept and strong social supports. Therefore, Aboriginal people must be given the therapeutic tools to build a strong concept of self and build strong social supports through resilience-based healing.

Resilience is a thoroughly researched concept. In Western literature, resilience is commonly defined as the ability of individuals to adapt to and flourish successfully in the face of significant adversity (Reid, Stewart, & Mangham, 1996). This ability to adapt is then viewed as an intrinsic personal quality or characteristic (Berkes & Ross, 2013, p. 6) and viewed as a good outcome for people who have experienced adversity (Olsson, Bond, Burns, Vella-Brodrick, & Sawyer, 2003, p. 2). According to Western literature, resilience only occurs when individuals demonstrate good functioning following significant adversities; however, it is important to note that individuals can also demonstrate resilience and adequate coping whilst remaining in the presence of distressing emotions (Olsson et al., 2003, p. 3). This resilience is evident in Aboriginal people living through the effects of intergenerational trauma. Moenkemeyer, Hoegl, and Weiss (2012, p. 632) describe instances of post-traumatic thriving whereby the individual's level of functioning following trauma exceeds the individual's level of functioning prior to the trauma, thus suggesting individuals can learn from trauma situations and can, therefore, exhibit a higher degree of resilience (Kennedy, 2019). This is also evident in Aboriginal people's survival following ongoing traumas. History has not been kind to Aboriginal communities. It has sought to eradicate an entire culture; however, it did not succeed. Aboriginal people, communities, and culture continue to overcome the initial warfare colonisation brought, the laws that were enacted to prevent cultural learnings, the children they stole, and the trauma they rooted into generation after generation. These trauma effects do live on and they are passed from grandmother to mother to daughter; so too is resilience.

Resilience is defined differently by Aboriginal people. The Aboriginal concept of resilience includes a social-ecological framework (Ungar, 2008, p. 225), expressed through narratives (Kirmayer et al., 2012, p. 401), and is solely inclusive of the community (Kennedy, 2019, p. 120). This multi-dimensional definition shifts the understanding of resilience from an individual concept as understood in Western communities to a holistic definition that is embedded within Aboriginal communities (Kennedy, 2019, p. 120). A social-ecological definition draws attention to resilience at levels greater than the individual and, notably, draws attention to family interactions, community, social systems, and culture (Kennedy, 2019, p. 120; Kirmayer et al., 2012). Aboriginal resilience is expressed through narratives; this allows individuals and groups to assert their identities, maintain shared cultural values, become self-determined and confident, and produce new strategies to overcome adversity (Kirmayer et al., 2012, p. 401; Kennedy, 2019, p. 123), and further ensures cultural power and authority is derived from sharing specific Aboriginal narratives and histories (Kennedy, 2019, p. 123). Within the concept of Aboriginal resilience is community resilience. Berkes and Ross (2013, p. 13) note how community resilience exists specifically within communities that have a 'historical intimacy' with their land. Likewise, Clauss-Ehlers, Yang, and Chen (2006) suggest community resilience is a process ingrained in cultural values and relationships with the land. This illustrates that individuals can directly utilise their environments, communities, and cultural knowledge as a resource to promote healing (Kennedy, 2019, p. 124). Aboriginal communities demonstrate resilience by drawing upon social resources (Blackstock & Trocme, 2005, p. 29) and cultural knowledge that is found within the community setting and achieving a balance within changing contexts (Kennedy, 2019, p. 124). Connection to cultural knowledge and relationships with the community and the environment allows protective factors to be produced which ensures adaptations to adversity. So, what does Aboriginal resilience look like?

Aboriginal people draw upon resilience in order to grieve and heal. Williamson, Weir, and Cavanagh (2020) noted that Aboriginal people live with a sense of perpetual grief due to the unresolved and unaddressed trauma of invasion and colonisation. The decimation of culture deeply impacts upon the existence of Aboriginal culture and, by extension, Aboriginal people (Williamson et al., 2020). The long-term effects of colonisation have meant Aboriginal people have become accustomed to living with disastrous impacts upon their communities and over time has continually adjusted and adapted to keep surviving and functioning. I propose it is not perpetual grief, but perpetual healing that allows Aboriginal people to continue to survive. Healing refers to securing and sustaining hope, a sense of identity and belonging, wellbeing, empowerment, control, and renewal (The Healing Foundation, 2016, p. 18). Healing is not an outcome, it is a process, a journey and it involves self-determination and a sense of control for those who are healing. For Aboriginal people, connection and reconnection to culture is central to the healing process as it unlocks knowledge systems, tools to heal, and the safety to do so (The Healing Foundation, 2016, p. 19). Aboriginal communities do grieve for the loss experienced since colonisation and grieve for the losses to come if changes are not made. However, Aboriginal people heal too. And it is through healing and empowerment of the youth that intergenerational trauma will slow its transmission. Trauma causes adversities; adversities are needed to develop resilience; and resilience is developed through connection to culture. Value must be placed on working with cultural knowledge and using cultural practices to aid Aboriginal communities to heal.

Indigenous[7] feminism theory and empowerment

Our society; our modern patriarchal society was designed by men and is designed to ensure men make the majority of the political, economic, and cultural decisions (Lewis & Hemmings, 2019). Feminism challenges the design of our society as it stands. Feminism is a powerful, social, and political tool women have used for decades and across generations to achieve an influential position within this patriarchy. Feminism is a complex ideology that promotes changes in society to end systems and structures that have continually disadvantaged women (Lewis, 2020). Historically, however, feminism did not include all-female populations and often excluded women of colour. The first wave of feminism focused on overcoming political, sexual, and class oppression and is often associated with urban, middle-class women (Castillo, 2010, p. 541) who historically were involved in the marginalisation of Black women. This wave did not consider discrimination through racial bias; further, it did not consider that Black women experience a different and more intense kind of oppression from that of white women. Since the first wave in the mid-nineteenth century, two more waves have come, and many facets of feminism are now recognised that include and consider many different intersectionalities. This chapter will explore one facet of feminism that is inherent to myself and, I believe, to all Blak women; Indigenous feminism.

Indigenous feminism is an intersectional theory and practice of feminism that focuses on decolonisation, Indigenous sovereignty, and Indigenous cultural values (Liddle, 2014), but also shares a commonality with other feminist priorities. Scholars have noted there are many facets of feminism that address Indigenous populations, such as intersectional feminism and transnational feminism (Smith, 2011). However, Indigenous feminism is particular in the sense that it acknowledges the devastating realities of colonisation on Indigenous communities and lands and further highlights the importance of decolonising the oppressive systems that have been constructed within society (Smith, 2011). Most of the literature on this facet of feminism is authored by scholars from Canada and the United States; however, there is a recent rise in contributions from Australian scholars (Fredericks, 2010; Moreton-Robinson, 2002). As Indigenous Australian feminist Aileen Moreton-Robinson (2002) notes, '*all* Indigenous women experience living in a society that casts them aside'; thus, this common experience warrants a common approach and that approach is the implementation of Indigenous feminist theory and practices. Dulfano (2015, p. 46) notes that Indigenous feminism presents strategies that empower women, assume responsibilities, circulate a collective consciousness, and promote tribal sovereignty for Indigenous peoples. Such strategies are vital in healing and preventing further transmission of intergenerational trauma. The direct practice of Indigenous feminism is evident within our communities (Moreton-Robinson, 2002) and varies from the traditional actions of feminists. For example, the second wave of feminism, which occurred approximately in the 1960s and 1970s, viewed motherhood and homemaking as oppressive practices to a modern-day woman. However, within Aboriginal culture, traditionally and even in today's modern time, Aboriginal women often take on the roles of community mothers, caretakers, and creators and view such roles as empowerment and not oppression (Nickel, 2017, p. 302). Grandmothers, mothers, aunties, and sisters are a force to be reckoned with in Aboriginal Australian communities and are often at the forefront of healing and empowerment practices. This does not mean that Blak men, our brothers, fathers, uncles, and Elders are not at the forefront or a force unto themselves. It means historically women have played a quiet, small, and at times, unacknowledged role behind men; Blak women have experienced not only racism and classism but also sexism. Indigenous feminism is all about the empowerment of Indigenous females and being an Indigenous feminist means supporting your sisters and educating your brothers about how they too can support other Blak women. Being an Indigenous feminist means recognising the systems white men and society have created and knowing that we can change them, especially when we are amplified by our Blak male allies – but only when their energy is directed towards giving Indigenous women a voice and a space to be heard.

Aboriginal communities must rebuild and revive their spiritual and cultural practices in order to overcome colonisation (Fredericks, 2010, p. 548). Drawing upon Indigenous feminist theory and implementing therapeutic healing practices led by women and supported by men is a way to ensure resilience and revival within Indigenous communities worldwide and Australia. Aboriginal communities need to reclaim and reconstruct our identities to heal the deep wounds of colonisation and intergenerational trauma (Fredericks, 2010, p. 548). Indigenous feminism is a source of healing and a process to reaffirm, reinstate, and re-empower Aboriginal women (Fredericks, 2010, p. 549) and cannot be progressed without the support and care of our Blak brothers. Healing through Indigenous feminism will be explored further with the practices of yarning circles and *dadirri*.

What can we do now, as social work professionals?

From its conception, social work was developed from the roots of nineteenth-century Christian charity (Hughes, 2010, p. 33) in the United Kingdom and the United States. It was viewed as philanthropic work and was informed by attitudes towards the causes of poverty and social problems at the time (Hughes, 2010, p. 32). Social work in Australia, by comparison, is relatively new and began with the commencement of welfare in Australia (Green, 2019, p. 87). Social workers have been participants in the removal and dis-possession of Aboriginal women, men, and children from communities (Fredericks, 2010, p. 546). Social workers were partly responsible for removing *half-caste* Aboriginal children and placing them with white families to aid the breeding out of Aboriginal culture. Social workers upheld the welfare policies and practices that caused many injustices to the Aboriginal community (Bennett, 2019, p. 23). Social workers held a part of the knife, alongside other professionals, that severed the tie between Aboriginal people and their culture and spirit, and played a part in perpetuating intergenerational trauma. Now, it is vital and necessary for all social workers, irrespective of their background, to take a proactive and genuine stance *with* Aboriginal individuals and communities (Bennett, 2019, p. 23).

In 2010, the Australian Association of Social Workers formally stated within the *Code of Ethics* that 'social workers are responsible for ensuring that their practice is culturally competent, safe and sensitive' (AASW, 2010, p. 5). This responsibility includes decolonising social work practice. The process of decolonising social work practice begins firstly with acknowledging that colonisation has occurred; this, as highlighted by Young (2004, p. 104), may be difficult for the social work profession as it is yet to 'fully engage with an understanding of itself as racialized'. Following the acknowledgment of colo-nisation, the process of decolonising social work practice involves developing strategies that liberate oppressive systems and restoring cultural practices, beliefs, worldviews, and values (Walter & Baltra-Ulloa, 2019, p. 75). Social workers now have an obligation to work alongside and aid Aboriginal indi-viduals, families, and communities with their perpetual healing. Drawing upon Indigenous feminism and decolonising theory and implementing community-led therapeutic interventions is a way for social workers to help break the cycle of intergenerational trauma.

Jones, an African-American feminist scholar from the University of Albany, highlights that the field of social work has increasingly shone a light on the needs of diverse groups through cross-cultural practice literature, reconsidering practice frameworks and adjusting existing practice models to better serve women and people of colour (2015, p. 247). This ensures social work practitioners are equipped with cultural literacy and further ensures the women of colour they are servicing can have safe spaces to heal within. Jones (2015, p. 246) further postulates that Black feminist-centred, therapeutic models are such a space to heal. Black feminism is akin to Indigenous feminism, as both explore the effect of compounding life stressors such as race, gender, culture, and class upon Black women (Jones, 2015, p. 249) and both incorporate support and promotion from Black men. Jones (2015, p. 250) recommends three steps social work practitioners can take to become allies in using the Black feminist perspective. I propose the same steps that can be taken by social work practitioners in becoming an ally of the Indigenous feminist perspective. Jones (2015, p. 250) recommends social work feminists must have the bravery to discuss and document their work on Black feminisms within practice literature and within public forums. In the Indigenous context, social work feminists must work to develop education programs (through University curricula and professional development) that seek to understand the Indigenous feminist perspective to further develop competencies and practice skills for non-Indigenous social workers. This is valuable in ensuring the Indigenous feminist perspective is validated in the sphere of social work practice and further ensures social workers can practice genuinely. Jones (2015, p. 250) further recommends social work practitioners must acknowledge their value systems and its potential impact upon practice. In the Indigenous context, social work feminists must challenge their values and be attuned to diversity in order to maintain empathetic and therapeutic relationships with Indigenous women and colleagues. Lastly, Jones (2015, p. 250) notes that social work practitioners must work to validate the perceptions of racism and discrimination that Black women experience. In the Indigenous context, this involves providing a safe place where Indigenous women can tell their stories without feeling dismissed or judged. The use of Indigenous feminism by Indigenous and non-Indigenous female and male social work practitioners ensures therapeutic interventions such as yarning circles and *dadirri* will foster resilience, empower Indigenous women, and promote positive coping strategies (Jones, 2015, p. 250) that will be passed on to the succeeding generations.

Therapeutic interventions: Yarning circles and *dadirri*

Therapeutic interventions are a means of healing from historical and intergenerational trauma and oppression. Indigenous communities are seeking to transcend experiences of trauma and loss by revitalising cultural practices informed by evidence (Garrett et al., 2014, p. 482). Therapeutic interventions seek to alter an individual's maladaptive coping mechanisms and trauma responses and encourage sensitive and constructive resilience-based responses. Therapeutic interventions are constant; they can be implemented within a crisis situation or built into an ongoing established program. Therapeutic interventions include a number of social work practices that are grounded and restorative for the client. These interventions include:

narrative therapy, active listening, motivational interviewing, psychoeducation, and family group work. Such interventions are interpersonal, relational, and ensure empathetic attunement with the specific intention to establish a truly helpful relationship (Rosenberger, 2014, p. 14) between client and practitioner. Garrett et al. (2014, p. 178) call for interventions that recognise and address historical trauma and further consider the contemporary social and political issues facing Indigenous communities today. All therapeutic interventions are culturally appropriate for Indigenous communities if practitioners can be responsive to the cultural needs of the client. This may include fostering cultural connections, examining the historical context, promoting positive cultural identity, and recognising Indigenous resilience models and coping mechanisms (Garrett et al., 2014, pp. 484–485) in addition to drawing upon the functions of the therapeutic intervention. For example, when working closely with an Aboriginal woman who has experienced trauma, practitioners may wish to implement narrative therapy with the acknowledgment that examining the historical context of the client is necessary to genuinely build and continue a therapeutic relationship.

Although therapeutic interventions can be culturally appropriate for many populations, some interventions exist that are grounded in Indigenous cultural knowledge, tradition, and practice. Such interventions restore cultural integrity, respect historical context, build community trust, develop self-determination and empowerment, and foster ongoing resilience and responsibility for Indigenous people and communities (Garrett et al., 2014, p. 482). Yarning circles and *dadirri* are two different and unique therapeutic interventions that are shrouded in Indigenous ways of knowing.

Yarning circles

Yarning circles have been used by Indigenous communities all around the world for centuries. They are an invaluable process of the continuation of culture and healing. Yarning and storytelling are important components of Indigenous societies where oral traditions were the main form of preserving and sharing knowledge with individuals and between groups (Bessarab & Ng'andu, 2010, p. 38). Yarning circles ensure learning from within a collective group, building respectful relationships, and preserving cultural knowledge (Bessarab & Ng'andu, 2010). Yarning is the process of sharing dialogue; a process that promotes connection, encourages respectful and honest interactions, and ensures cultural safety. Yarning is a conversation style that prioritises Indigenous ways of communicating, where information is shared within the yarn and the listener has the responsibility of dissecting the information (Williams, 2019, p. 148). According to Bessarab and Ng'andu (2010), there are three types of yarning: social yarning, collaborative yarning, and therapeutic yarning. All three types intersect during the process of therapeutic intervention (Williams, 2019, pp. 148–149). Social yarning is informal and unstructured. It is a mindfulness technique that encourages diverse perspectives (McKenzie-Kirkbright, 2019) and ensures developing a connection and building a relationship between participants. Collaborative yarning involves exploring similar ideas or experiences to lead to new understandings (Bessarab & Ng'andu, 2010, p. 40). In practice, a yarning circle occurs when a group of people collaboratively share dialogue, sitting in a circular, non-hierarchical setting with assumed or agreed-upon cultural protocols to ensure a safe and open conversation (McKenzie-Kirkbright, 2019). This leads to exploring common insights, increasing each other's awareness, and responding to trauma. Therapeutic yarning can be intensely personal and emotional, but is also an empowering and relational process for women (Williams, 2019, p. 149). When working with Aboriginal women who have experienced trauma, a yarning circle is a culturally appropriate therapeutic intervention that can assist people and communities to heal. Yarning circles are similar to the Western process of narrative therapy. Narrative therapy is a counselling practice used with individuals, families, groups, and communities that is respectful, empowering, and non-blaming (Bacon, 2014, p. 15). Narrative therapy aids individuals to give expression to their experiences and re-author alternative stories; so too does a yarning circle as both assist individuals to work through their problems (Bacon, 2014, p. 140). A key component of narrative therapy is the process externalising the problem; this too is a key component of addressing trauma (Bacon, 2014, p. 140). Externalising that trauma as an identified problem allows for it to become separate from an individual's identity. This ensures trauma is not viewed as internal to the individual and creates a safe and hopeful place for this trauma to be explored (Bacon, 2014, p. 155). Narrative therapy and yarning circles empower Aboriginal people to open up dialogue, share stories, and separate the problem and the person, allowing space to heal and grow.

Dadirri

Dadirri, the word, concept, and spiritual practice is from the Ngangikurunggurr and Ngen'giwumirri languages of the Aboriginal peoples of the Daly River region in the Northern Territory. Miriam-Rose Ungunmerr-Baumann (2002), Ngangiwumirr Elder, the leading expert of *dadirri*, notes that:

> *Dadirri* is inner, deep listening and quiet still awareness. *Dadirri* recognises the deep spring that is inside us. We call on it and it calls to us. This is the gift that Australia is thirsting for. It is something like what you can 'contemplation'.

Ungunmerr-Baumann (2002) further notes that, with *dadirri*, there is no need for words, as the act of learning is all about listening and not asking questions. *Dadirri* is a practice that allows individuals to open wounds and trauma in a sacred and held space (Atkinson). In practice, *dadirri* has been described as 'a process of listening, reflecting, observing the feelings and actions, reflecting and learning, and in the cyclic process, relistening at deeper and deeper levels of understanding and knowledge-building' (Atkinson, 2002, p. 19). Internal reflection is a large component of this therapeutic intervention. It involves consideration of the community and the diversity and uniqueness each individual brings to the community (West, Stewart, Foster, & Usher, 2012, p. 1586). *Dadirri* also refers to a form of group healing that brings the deep presence found in the solo practice of *dadirri* to a group setting (Atkinson, 2002). This process involves group participants engaging in a rich and meaningful communication with each other, which enables them to better understand themselves and each other (West et al., 2012, p. 1584) *Dadirri* is informed by a sense of community, a concept that is integral to Aboriginal culture (Atkinson, 2002, p. 18). When working with Aboriginal women who have experienced trauma, the process of *dadirri* is a spiritually therapeutic intervention that can assist people and communities to heal. The practice of *dadirri* is similar to the Western intervention of active listening. Active listening skills are an extension of basic communication skills and involve both verbal and nonverbal communication (Robertson, 2005, p. 1053). Active listening involves giving free undivided attention to the speaker; to do so allows for validation of the speaker's thought process and validation of the speaker (Robertson, 2005, p. 1053). Within active listening the listener guides the speaker through reflection; listening and exploring, understanding and relating and focusing and assisting (Robertson, 2005, p. 1054). Active listening emphasises on both what is said and what is not said. *Dadirri* is a deep contemplative process; it is a non-intrusive observation and a process of healing with more than just ears (Atkinson, 2002, p. 16). Active listening and *dadirri* further empowers Aboriginal people to share stories with insight to gain a deeper understanding of themselves and each other.

Conclusion

Intergenerational trauma is an emotional and psychological wound (Brave Heart, 2003, p. 7) that is infected, festering, and poisoning the wounded. If this open wound is not addressed and healing measures are not taken, this poisonous wound will infect the next generation and the next and so on. Aboriginal families and communities remain deeply affected by the ripple effects colonisation has caused as it continues to affect every part of life. Aboriginal children are still removed from family and Country at an alarming rate, Aboriginal people are still institutionalised through the criminal justice and mental health systems; Aboriginal health and mental health outcomes have still not improved and maladaptive coping mechanisms, such as misuse of alcohol and drugs and incidents of domestic violence, still plague Aboriginal communities. Trauma transmission is unfortunate; however, it is not unchangeable as experiencing trauma and the motion of perpetual healing are simultaneous. In times of adversity, Aboriginal people can draw upon Aboriginal resilience in order to move forward. Aboriginal resilience differs from the Western understanding of resilience as it emphasises the functioning of the community rather than the individual. Perpetual healing is not an outcome, but a journey, and it involves being connected and reconnected to cultural knowledge and practices.

Aboriginal people have the intrinsic capabilities to overcome trauma; resilience and perpetual healing; however, due to the entrenched systemic barriers that exist, Aboriginal people require therapeutic professionals to assist them in utilising these skills. Social workers are therapeutic professionals who work alongside individuals, families, and communities to highlight the strengths and tools they already possess. In this context, social workers working with Aboriginal communities have an obligation to acknowledge historical wrongdoings and consider drawing upon the principles of Indigenous feminism to ensure self-determination occurs. Indigenous feminism is vital in validating and empowering Blak women. Social workers must draw upon the principles of Indigenous resilience when implementing therapeutic interventions that are relevant to Aboriginal communities. Yarning circles and *dadirri* are two valuable and culturally rich interventions that, when implemented correctly and genuinely, can assist Aboriginal people in healing each other and themselves. Culture, to Aboriginal communities, is the biggest protective factor, and drawing upon culture in times of need will ensure the transmission of trauma is limited.

Aboriginal resilience, perpetual healing, and culturally therapeutic interventions are the tools Aboriginal people internally possess. Colonisation has impacted Aboriginal communities so greatly that they have forgotten these tools exist. With genuine engagement and inclusive practice, these tools can be rediscovered, and Aboriginal people can once again thrive on land that is theirs and within a culture that remains strong and alive.

Discussion Questions

1. Referring to the 'transmission of trauma' model, explain, using your own example, how trauma is transmitted.

2. Discuss the similarities and difference between Aboriginal and Western resilience.

3. Discuss what other sociological theories may be drawn upon when working within Aboriginal communities.

4. Brainstorm other therapeutic interventions that can be employed to develop resilience and empower Aboriginal communities.

Notes

1. As a Wiradjuri woman, I will be referring specifically to Aboriginal people only.
2. Country is capitalised to demonstrate the importance of one's homelands.
3. Wiradjuri word for 'the ancient ones, ancestors, dead ones'.
4. Wiradjuri word for 'children'.
5. Half-caste is the colonial term for a part Aboriginal child, where one parent was of European descent.
6. 'Blak' is a term used by some Aboriginal people to reclaim historical, representational, symbolical, stereotypical, and romanticised notions of Black or Blackness. It was coined by Destiny Deacon in 1991.
7. For the purposes of this explanation, Indigenous refers to all Indigenous populations within the world.

References

Atkinson, J. (2002). *Trauma trails: Recreating song lines*. North Melbourne, VIC: Spinifex Press.

Australian Association of Social Workers (AASW). (2010). *Code of Ethics*. Canberra, ACT: AASW.

Australian Institute of Health and Welfare (AIHW). (2015). *The health and welfare of Australia's Aboriginal and Torres Strait Islander peoples* (AIHW 147). Canberra, ACT: AASW.

Australian Institute of Health and Welfare (AIHW). (2020). *Alcohol, tobacco and other drugs in Australia* (AIHW 221). Canberra, ACT: AASW.

Australian Institute of Health and Welfare (AIHW), Al-Yaman, F., & Van Doeland, M. (2006). *Family violence among Aboriginal and Torres Strait Islander peoples*. Canberra, ACT: AIHW.

Bacon, V. (2014). Yarning and listening: Yarning and learning through stories. In B. Bennett, S. Green, S. Gilbert, & D. Bessarab (Eds.), *Our voices: Aboriginal and Torres Strait Islander social work* (pp. 136–165). South Yarra, VIC: Palgrave Macmillan.

Bennett, B. (2019). The importance of Aboriginal history for practitioners. In B. Bennett & S. Green (Eds.), *Our voices: Aboriginal social work* (2nd ed., pp. 3–31). London: Red Globe Press.

Berkes, F., & Ross, H. (2013). Community resilience: Toward an integrated approach. *Society and Natural Resources: An International Journal, 26*(1), 5–20.

Bessarab, D., & Ng'andu, B. (2010). Yarning about yarning as a legitimate method in Indigenous research. *International Journal of Critical Indigenous Studies, 3*(1), 37–50.

Blackstock, C., & Trocme, N. (2005). Community-based Child Welfare for Aboriginal children: Supporting resilience through structural change. *Social Policy Journal of New Zealand, 24*, 12–33.

Brave Heart, M. Y. H. (2003). The historical trauma response among natives and its relationship with substance abuse: A Lakota illustration. *Journal of Psychoactive Drugs, 35*(1), 7–13.

Castillo, R. A. H. (2010). The emergence of Indigenous feminism in Latin America. *Signs, 35*(3), 539–541. The University of Chicago Press.

Clauss-Ehlers, C. S., Yang, Y. T., & Chen, W. J. (2006). Resilience from childhood stressors: The role of cultural resilience, ethnic identity and gender identity. *Journal of Infant, Child and Adolescent Psychotherapy, 5*(1), 124–138.

Dulfano, I. (2015). Notes on Indigenous feminism post-testimonial. *Indigenous feminist narratives.* London: Palgrave Pivot.

Duran, E., Duran, B., Brave Heart, M. Y. H., & Yellow Horse-Davis, S. (1998). 'Healing the American Indian Soul Wound' Chapter 21 in Meichenbaum. In Y. Danieli (Ed.), *International handbook of multigenerational legacies of trauma.* Boston, MA: Springer.

Fredericks, B. (2010). Reempowering ourselves: Australian Aboriginal women. *Signs, 35*(3), 546–550.

Garrett, M. T., Parrish, M., Williams, C., Grayshield, L., Awe Agahe Portman, T., Torres Rivera, E., & Maynard, E. (2014). Invited commentary: Fostering resilience among Native American youth through therapeutic intervention. *Journal of Youth and Adolescence, 43*(3), 470–490.

Green, S. (2019). Indigenising social work. In B. Bennett & S. Green (Eds.), *Our voices: Aboriginal social work* (pp. 86–100). London: Red Globe Press.

Healing Foundation. (2016). *Restoring our spirits – Reshaping our futures: Creating a trauma aware, healing informed response to the impacts of institutional child sexual abuse for Aboriginal and Torres Strait Islander people.* Canberra, ACT.

Hoffart, R., & Jones, N. A. (2018). Intimate partner violence and intergenerational trauma among Indigenous women. *International Criminal Justice Review, 28*(1), 25–44.

Hughes, L. (2010). Catholic sisters and Australian social welfare history. *The Australasian Catholic Record, 87*(1), 30–46.

Jacobs, S., & Davis, C. (2017). Challenging the myths of Black women – A short-term, structured, art experience group: Exploring the intersections of race, gender, and intergenerational trauma. *Smith College Studies in Social Work, 87*(2–3), 200–219.

Jones, L. V. (2015). Black feminisms: Renewing sacred healing spaces. *Affilia, 30*(2), 246–252.

Kennedy, A. (2019). Resilience: An Aboriginal perspective. In B. Bennett & S. Green (Eds.), *Our voices: Aboriginal social work* (2nd ed., pp. 117–147). London: Red Globe Press.

Kirmayer, L., Brass, G., & Tait, C. (2000). The mental health of Aboriginal peoples: Transformations of identity and community. *Canadian Journal of Psychology, 45*, 607–616.

Kirmayer, L. J., Dandeneau, S., Marshall, E., Phillips, M. K., & Williamson, K. J. (2012). Chapter 31: Toward an ecology of stories: Indigenous perspective on resilience. In Ungar (Ed.), *The social ecology of resilience: A handbook or theory and practice* (pp. 399–414). New York, NY: Springer.

Lewis, G., & Hemmings, C. (2019). 'Where might we go if we dare': Moving beyond the 'thick, suffocating fog of whiteness' in feminism. *Feminist Theory, 20*(4), 405–421.

Lewis, J. J. (2020). *The core ideas and beliefs of feminism*. Retrieved from https://www.thoughtco.com/what-is-feminism-3528958

Liddle, C. (2014). Intersectionality and Indigenous feminism: An Aboriginal woman's perspective. *The Postcolonialist*.

McKenzie-Kirkbright, L. (2019). *Mindfulness and Aboriginal culture*. Youth Affairs Council Victoria, Victoria. Retrieved from https://www.yacvic.org.au/blog/mindfulness-aboriginal-culture/

Moenkemeyer, G., Hoegl, M., & Weiss, M. (2012). Innovator resilience potential: A process perspective of individual resilience as influenced by innovation project termination. *Human Relations, 65*(5), 627–655.

Moreton-Robinson, A. (2002). *Talkin' up to the White woman: Indigenous women and feminism*. Brisbane, QLD: University of Queensland Press.

National Inquiry into the Separation of Aboriginal and Torres Strait Islander Children from Their Families (Australia). (1997). *Bringing them home: Report of the National Inquiry into the Separation of Aboriginal and Torres Strait Islander Children from their Families*. Sydney, NSW: Human Rights and Equal Opportunity Commission.

Nickel, S. A. (2017). I am not a women's libber although sometimes I sound like one: Indigenous feminism and politicized feminism. *American Indian Quarterly, 41*(4), 299–335.

Olsson, C. A., Bond, L., Burns, J. M., Vella-Brodrick, D. A., & Sawyer, S. M. (2003). Adolescent resilience: A concept analysis. *Journal of Adolescence, 26*, 1–11.

Perroud, N., Rutembesa, E., Paoloni-Giacobinco, A., Mutabaruka, J., Mutesa, L., Stenz, L., Malafosse, A., & Karege, F. (2014). The Tutsi genocide and the transgenerational transmission of maternal stress: Epigenetics and biology of the HPA axis. *World Journal of Biological Psychiatry, 15*(4), 334–345.

Reid, G., Stewart, M., & Mangham, P. (1996). Resiliency: Implications for health promotion. *Health and Canadian Society, 4*(1), 83.

Reynolds, H. (1972). *Aborigines and Settlers: The Australian experience 1788–1939*. Sydney, NSW: Cassell Australia.

Robertson, K. (2005). Active listening: More than just paying attention. *Australian Family Physician, 34*(12), 1053–1055.

Rosenberger, J. B. (2014). Orientation to and validation of relational diversity practice. In J. Rosenberger (Ed.), *Relational social work practice with diverse populations* (Essential clinical social work series). New York, NY: Springer.

Smith, A. (2011). Decolonising anti-rape law and strategizing accountability in native American communities. *Social Justice, 37*(4), 36–43.

SNAICC. (2017). *The family matters report 2017*.

The Law Reform Commission. (1986). *Recognition of Aboriginal Customary Laws* (ALRC Report 31). Australian Law Reform Commission, The Australian Government.

Ungar, M. (2008). Resilience across cultures. *The British Journal of Social Work, 38*(2), 218–235.

Ungunmerr-Baumann, M. (2002). *Dadirri: A reflection by Miriam-Rose Ungunmerr Baumann*.

Victorian Aboriginal Justice Agreement. (2018). *Burra Lotjpa Dunguludja Victorian Aboriginal Justice Agreement Phase 4: A partnership between the Victorian Government and Aboriginal Community*. Victoria Government.

Walter, M., & Baltra-Ulloa, J. (2019). Australian social work is white. In B. Bennett & S. Green (Eds.), *Our voices: Aboriginal social work* (2nd ed., pp. 65–86). London: Red Globe Press.

West, R., Stewart, L., Foster, K., & Usher, K. (2012). Through a critical lens: Indigenist research and the Dadirri method. *Qualitative Health Research, 22*(11), 1582–1590.

Williams, M. (2019). Aboriginal people in a hospital setting. In B. Bennett & S. Green (Eds.), *Our voices: Aboriginal social work* (2nd ed., pp. 65–86). London: Red Globe Press.

Williamson, B., Weir, J., & Cavanagh, V. (2020). Strength from perpetual grief: How Aboriginal people experience the bushfire crisis. *The Conversation*. Retrieved from: https://theconversation.com/strength-from-perpetual-grief-how-aboriginal-people-experience-the-bushfire-crisis-129448

Yehuda, R., Daskalakis, N. P., Bierer, L. M., Bader, H. N., Klengel, T., Holsboer, F., & Binder, E. B. (2016). Holocaust exposure induced intergenerational effects of FKBP5 methylation. *Biological Psychiatry, 80*(5), 372–380.

Young, S. M. (2004). Social work theory and practice: The invisibility of whiteness. In A. Moreton-Robinson (Ed.), *Whitening race* (pp. 104–118). Canberra, ACT: Aboriginal Studies Press.

Youssef, N. A., Lockwood, L., Su, S., Hao, G., & Rutten, B. P. F. (2018). The effects of trauma, with or without PTSD, on the transgenerational DNA methylation alterations in human offsprings. *Brain Sciences, 8*(5), 83.

13 An Ethics Framework Embedded in an Indigenous Epistemology: Implications for Social Work Research and Practice

Maggie Walter and Joselynn Baltra-Ulloa

Introduction

Ethical research with Indigenous peoples, like ethical practice, is not neutral territory. Aboriginal and Torres Strait Islander Peoples[1] are a disproportionately vulnerable group over-represented on negative indicators of social, economic, and cultural wellbeing. Combining this socio-cultural positioning with our relative powerlessness equates to an over-representation of research subjects. Being a young, poor, socially and culturally marginalised population not only makes Indigenous groups 'interesting' but ensures that we have few resources to resist the research gaze. The ethics of research are further complicated by the valid and deep Indigenous suspicion of research and researchers, who mostly are not us. Long awash with racialised assumptions, the Indigenous research agenda has served as a self-referencing evidence source for those assumptions. The distribution of benefits and possible harms are also uneven, with the ledger almost always disproportionately balanced toward the researcher and the dominant socio-cultural group. Again, not us.

More critically, standard ethics codes and approval processes do not reflect Indigenous values or needs. Instead, the ethical principles articulated by Indigenous Peoples and the worldviews of researchers, including Indigenous researchers, are frequently incompatible. Ethics through the Indigenous lens challenges Eurocentric constructs and ways of knowing. What is required as a base for ethical Indigenous research are ethical principles framed by the way Indigenous peoples see the world and organise within it (Tuhiwai Smith, 1999). Such principles recognise, respect, and prioritise Indigenous values, norms, and knowledges and privilege the Indigenous voice, making 'intellectual space for cultural knowledge systems that were denied in the past' (Rigney, 2001, p. 9).

The focus of this chapter is how we might reconceptualise research ethics to reflect Indigenous ways of knowing and being (Porsanger, 2004) and that has, at its core, Indigenous sovereign rights, inclusive of Indigenous data sovereignty rights. We do this via a review of the emergence of Indigenous ethical guidelines in Australia and a critical unpacking of how the new AIATSIS Code of Ethics for Aboriginal and Torres Strait Islander Research, written from an Indigenous worldview, might, or possibly might not, disrupt the Western epistemology that dominates Indigenous research. We then examine the implications of such analysis to social work practice and social work research.

The history of Aboriginal and Torres Strait Islander ethical guidelines

In Australia, Indigenous research concerns have only been recognised as a discrete ethical issue since the 1980s, with two sets of guidelines developed between 1990 and 2019. The earliest, *Interim Guidelines on Ethical Matters in Aboriginal and Torres Strait Islander Health Research,* were initiated by the National Health and Medical Research Council (NHMRC) in the late 1980s and released in 1991. Developed through a series of meetings of Aboriginal and Torres Strait Islander health researchers and community members, these guidelines were a response to Indigenous claims that the mainstream *National Statement of Ethical Conduct in Research Involving Humans* (National Statement) did not adequately address the ethical concerns of Aboriginal and Torres Strait Islander peoples. The response, a set of Indigenous guidelines, to operate alongside the National Statement, was seen as emphasising to researchers that Indigenous ethical concerns are their domain, not a subset of mainstream ethics. The current guidelines, updated twice since 1991, is *Values and Ethics: Guidelines for Ethical Conduct in Aboriginal and Torres Strait Islander Health Research.* The guidelines revolve around six key ethical values (NHMRC, 2003, p.8), which we expand upon below:

1. **Spirit and Integrity** – The overarching value demands that research respect the integrity of Indigenous cultural inheritance and exhibit credibility in negotiations.
2. **Reciprocity** – research is inclusive, demonstrates an equitable and respectful engagement, and advances Indigenous interests.
3. **Respect** – research acknowledges individual and collective contributions, the right to different values, norms, and aspirations, and the consequences of research.
4. **Equality** – research recognises the equality of and values Aboriginal Torres Strait Islander knowledge and there is an equal distribution of the benefit.
5. **Responsibility** – research does no harm to individuals/communities or things they value and is accountable, especially in relation to cultural and social dimensions.

6. **Survival and Protection** – research recognises and values the importance of the personal and collective bond, and cultural distinctiveness.

The other set of ethical guidelines are those developed in 1999 by the Australian Institute of Aboriginal and Torres Strait Islander Studies (AIATSIS). Originally developed for research within AIATSIS these were soon used more widely with the 2012 revised version, *Guidelines for Ethical Research in Australian Indigenous Studies* (GERAIS) included 14 principles divided between six overarching themes: Rights, respect, recognition; Negotiation, consultation, agreement, and mutual understanding; Participation, collaboration, and partnership; Benefits, outcomes, and giving back; Managing research: Use, storage, and access; and Reporting and compliance (AIATSIS, 2012). These principles share attributes with the NHMRC's six values, but are expressed in terms of rights and are more prescriptive. While the NHMRC guidelines were originally the most widely used, in more recent times, the AIATSIS guidelines have become more prominent. With its own Ethics Committee, many government departments and other bodies undertaking Indigenous research outside a university environment have turned to AIATSIS for the granting of ethical approval.

The critical point for this chapter is that both sets of guidelines are just that: guidelines. While Human Research Ethics Committees (HRECs) might ask researchers to comply with the principles and values expressed, neither the NHMRC nor the GERAIS guidelines have the authority of the National Statement. Not complying with the guidelines is not a formal breach of ethics unless non-compliance also breaches some aspect of the National Statement. Thus, under either set of guidelines Aboriginal and Torres Strait Islander peoples and communities are reliant on researchers' goodwill and voluntary commitments; this is not an encouraging position given the high levels of Indigenous mistrust of research and researchers.

The AIATSIS Code of Ethics and Ethics from an Indigenous worldview

This status quo was disrupted in 2019/2020 with the emergence of the AIATSIS Code of Ethics for Aboriginal and Torres Strait Islander Research (the Code). As demonstrated in the following sections, the Code contains some of the previous Indigenous ethical dimensions reflected in both GERAIS and the NHMRC guidelines, such as respect, recognition, and collaborative engagement. The Code also contains new dimensions and responsibilities. The background to the development of the Code is a comprehensive review of the GERAIS 2012. More than an update or a revision, the published Code (2020, p. 4) states: "To mark the twentieth anniversary of the guidelines, we have undertaken a comprehensive review to ensure that AIATSIS continues to set the highest standards of ethical research and human rights in Aboriginal and

Torres Strait Islander research." Throughout 2019 and early 2020 the draft Code, informed and guided by consultation with key stakeholders, was released for comment. Submissions were received from key Indigenous organisations, government departments, universities, human ethics committees, and others, debating issues such as how this Code would be monitored and enforced and how it would facilitate an ongoing successful integration of an Indigenous perspective within the National Statement on Ethical Conduct in Human Research and the Australian Code for the Responsible Conduct of Research (AIATSIS, 2020, p. 6). This process is now complete. The Code was released in October 2020.

The Code diverges in many significant ways from the previous NHRMC or GERAIS guidelines. More critically, this divergence will likely reset the Indigenous researcher–researched relationship to privilege Indigenous worldviews, values, and priorities. As shown in Figure 13.1, the Code is built around an Indigenous understanding of integrity defined by four key principles: Indigenous self-determination; Indigenous leadership; sustainability and accountability; and impact and value.

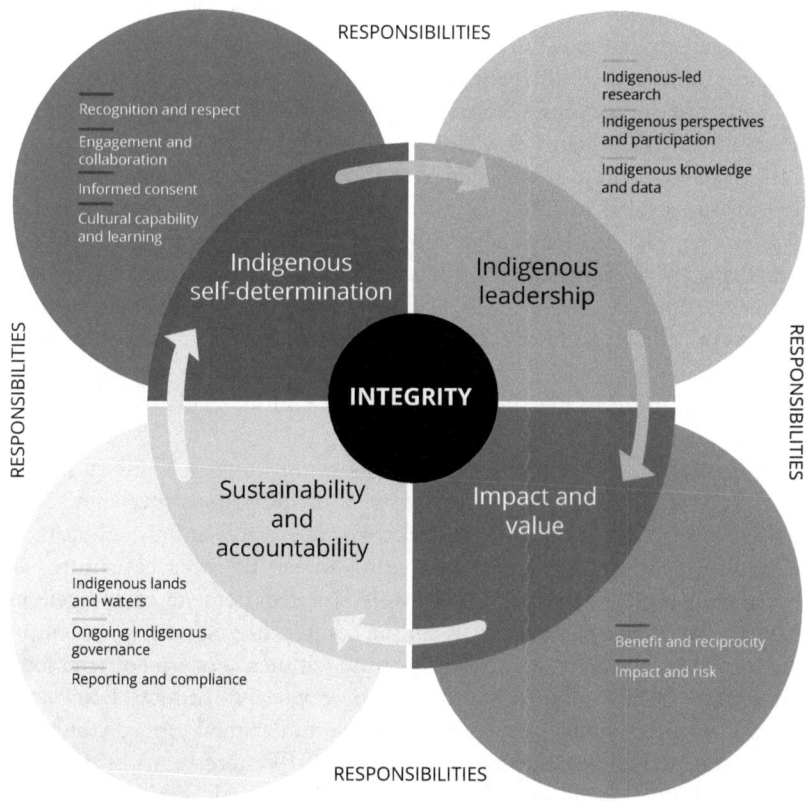

Figure 13.1 AIATSIS Code of Ethics Principles and Responsibilities. (Source: AIATSIS, 2020, p. 10)

Each ethics principle is aligned with a set of ethical responsibilities. As per Figure 13.1, for example, the principle of Indigenous leadership includes the responsibilities of research being Indigenous-led, that it be framed from Indigenous perspectives and participation priorities and that it reflects Indigenous knowledge and data protocols (AIATSIS, 2020).

We aim to critically unpack how a code of ethics embedded in an Indigenous worldview will intersect with the dominant Western values, epistemology, and ontology, especially as it relates to social work research. We explore this conundrum by examining three of the fundamental truths that inform the new AIATSIS Code of Ethics: *Relational Accountability, Connection to Culture, and Indigenous sovereignty*, theorising them as guiding principles for an Indigenous ethics framework embedded in Indigenous worldviews and ways of being (Porsanger, 2004).

The principles of an Indigenous ethics framework

Education scholar Margaret Kovach (2009) iterates that to engage in Indigenous ethics discussions requires those engaging to overtly explain their position to make clear the genesis of their assumptions. We are both social work-trained Indigenous scholars. Maggie is a palawa Aboriginal woman from Lutruwita/Tasmania descended from the Pairrebenne People of North East Tasmania, whose scholarship is framed from an Indigenous lifeworld and an Indigenous methodological frame. Jos is a Mapuche First Nation woman from the Americas, now living and working in Lutruwita Tasmania who brings her Mapuche framed perspectives, worldviews, and relationality to her teaching and research. This context allows us to talk about our peoples' ways with an authority drawn from our reciprocal relationships with our communities; something Western academics and social workers do not, and cannot, bring to the theorising of ethics and its relationship to social work practice.

For us as Indigenous scholars, to speak of an Indigenous ethics framework is to speak of the unfinished business of Indigenous sovereignty and Indigenous recognition within Australia. For many, this unfinished business means there is no singular perspective to present on what constitutes an Indigenous ethics framework. Rather, it is a requirement of Indigenous scholars like us to open a dialogue on the complexities inherent in attempting to articulate Indigenous knowledge from within a Western epistemological terrain. While colonial dominance over what constitutes knowledge continues, Indigenous perspectives will be understood outside of their Indigenous world view. Ethics is understood in Western terms as the 'conscience of our moral values' (Hinman, 2008, p. 5). Ethics within an Indigenous worldview is framed around relationships and of mutual responsibility, acknowledging our interconnectedness with, and responsibility for, the care of all living things in relationships of mutual responsibility (AIATSIS, 2020). This is explained in the Code in the following way: 'For many Indigenous cultures, the land and waters not only sustain life, but are themselves alive and in relationship with people – to harm Country is to harm people' (AIATSIS, 2020, p. 21). Accountability, therefore, acts to close the circle (ibid.) of relationship between peoples and the land. We've termed this truth *relational accountability*.

The principle of relational accountability

Relational accountability is at the heart of an Indigenous epistemology. This core value is reflected in the AIATSIS Code's principle of sustainability and accountability. What is reflected here is that nothing is ever understood or developed or done outside of a deep knowing that we are interconnected; that ways of knowing, being, and doing derive from, and impact upon, the personal and the collective. These understandings are inseparable to the Country. Country defines identity; like a compass it directs the interplay of individual and collective connectedness. Maddison (2009) explains that in the colonised nation-state the Indigenous individual and the Indigenous collective have become separate entities in constant tension with one another, often pulled in opposite direction by the insidious legacy of colonisation and the ongoing pattern of policies that prolong the fight for legitimacy, recognition, and land rights. Much is lost in this way. For example, the complexity and diversity of Indigenous societies being dismissed in favour of the conventional notion of one static Indigenous community. The fact that the collective often extends beyond family ties along with reciprocity is so much more than the exchange of material goods and resources is also often misinterpreted. Rather, the wellbeing and thriving of whole communities, kin, and Country are fundamental to the operationalisation of an Indigenous ethic (Walter, 2007). Relational accountability, as the mechanism by which an Indigenous ethic is upheld, also depends and is measured by how much whole communities, kin, and Country can thrive and prosper. Therefore, any formulation of an Indigenous ethics framework must first grapple with its epistemological roots.

The principle of connection to culture

Another core ethic present in the new AIATSIS Code is the centrality of culture to Indigenous life. Connection to culture is a guiding principle within an Indigenous ethics framework as an intangible feature of Indigenous identity. Culture is a connection to Country, kin, and community. Before the colonial encounter, there was no Indigenous identity (Maddison, 2009); there was no need to identify a culture, a way of life, language, Country, traditions, ceremonies, lore, and kin because the culture was life. Being Indigenous was a necessity created after colonisation as a response to dispossession and as a means of highlighting the invasion of a peoples that were here before the white man invaded (Bodkin-Andrews, Bodkin, Andrews, & Evans, 2017). Under an Indigenous epistemology, there is no singular way to explain what culture is, it grows, changes, and becomes more and more able to change as people are returned their rights to their culture and their land. This idea is particularly important for Indigenous people who live in cities. Urbanisation doesn't deplete Indigenous culture, as Morgan (2006, p. 63) so aptly put it: urbanisation facilitated the 'combination of the old with the new, the traditional with the modern'. Nor does it deplete connection to Country. As King (2012, p. 218) so apply notes, for Indigenous peoples in Australia and elsewhere, the Country is much more than land. It encompasses the 'languages, the stories, and the histories of a people. It provides water, air, shelter, and food. [County] participates in the ceremonies. And [Country] is home' (ibid). Urbanisation also has its cultural contribution. It provides access to political power and leverage, ways to activate, and give voice to Indigenous discontent, facilitating an activist identity and the connection to allies with whom the fight for justice can be shared and advanced. An Indigenous ethics framework is built on an Indigenous epistemology of connection to Country, that is inclusive of the right to define identity and culture, to self-govern, and the right to land.

The principle of sovereignty

The new AIATSIS Code uses the word self-determination regularly, naming it as the number one principle guiding respectful interactions with Indigenous peoples. We contend that self-determination is founded on the core truth that Indigenous peoples were/are sovereign peoples. Sovereignty isn't just about recognition, at a national scale, of Indigenous rights and Indigenous peoples as rights-bearing peoples, although this is a significant aspect. It is also about the complex interplay of identification and the proving of Indigeneity under a Western-defined ideal. In Australia, for example, the discourse that frames who is and who isn't Aboriginal reinforces the homogenisation of Aboriginal identity, a process driven by colonial assimilatory intentions (Russ-Smith, 2019). An Indigenous ethics framework shifts definitions of what it means to be Indigenous, Aboriginal, or First Nation and how we articulate Indigenous ways of knowing, being, and doing, away from Western constructs and towards an Indigenous paradigm.

Sovereignty over Indigenous identity is about privileging Indigenous notions of connection to Country, Indigenous connections to relationships with others, and with the land. The land speaks, tells stories of connection, of culture and identity, land holds meaning that colonisation muted (Grant & Rudder, 2014). As Russ-Smith (2019) posits sovereignty is embodied by Country, language, and lore for Aboriginal people. She says 'When we look and listen to Country, we see and hear sovereignty. Language is not just words. Language is our way of expressing our sovereignty. Within language are our stories.' Russ Smith (2019) goes on to position Lore as transcending law, arguing that lore was and continues to be lived as a way of respecting all things, identities, and relationships in the past, present and future... 'Lore is sovereign and the land, animals, and people are embodiments of this sovereignty' (pp. 239–241). The task is, therefore, to decolonise the definition and process of sovereignty so Indigenous knowledges can once again be the foundations upon which we achieve self-determination. The consideration and implementation of an Indigenous ethics framework are fundamentally about sovereignty as a mechanism of achieving self-determination. Sovereignty that is not guided or facilitated solely by land ownership, or language acquisition or lore that governs only behaviour. Sovereignty is a way of being that no colonial ethic can ever fully articulate.

The principle of Indigenous data sovereignty and data governance

The AIATIS Code also includes the principle of Indigenous leadership, inclusive of Indigenous knowledge and data. Here we relate that principle to Indigenous data sovereignty. Indigenous data sovereignty is the right of Indigenous peoples to determine the means of collection, access, analysis, interpretation, management, dissemination, and reuse of data pertaining to the Indigenous peoples from whom it has been derived, or to whom it relates. Indigenous data sovereignty centres on Indigenous collective rights to data about our peoples, territories, lifeways, and natural resources (Kukutai & Taylor, 2016; Snipp, 2016). Indigenous data sovereignty is operationalised via Indigenous data governance, which harnesses Indigenous decision-making across data lifecycles and ecosystems to assert Indigenous rights and interests (Smith, 2016; Walter & Suina, 2018). Research is the primary generator of data on Indigenous peoples, whether it be collecting new data or utilising existing datasets of the type held by government agencies such as the Australian Bureau of Statistics (ABS).

At the core of Indigenous data, governance is Indigenous leadership. Indigenous-led and controlled research and research decision-making ensures that Indigenous values, priorities, cultures, and ways of knowing are coherent with Indigenous data, making such data relevant, contextualised, and aligned with the aspirations of Indigenous peoples (Walter & Suina, 2018; Rainie et al., 2019). It is research that generates data and while Aboriginal and Torres Strait Islander peoples have frequently had data collected from us we have rarely drawn value from those data. We need sovereignty and governance of data to disrupt the Indigenous data paradox. In this paradox, we have both too much data generated by official statistics that focus almost exclusively, and pejoratively, on our various dire socio-economic and health inequalities. These have been summarised as the 5D's: difference, disparity, disadvantage, dysfunction, and deprivation data (Walter, 2016). We also have too little data. There are little or no data at all that fits Aboriginal and Torres Strait Islander development objectives, or alternatively it is not available or amenable to our needs. Yet there is an overwhelming need for data that reflect our lived realities and our innate differences (Lovett, 2016). More pragmatically, we need data for development and nation rebuilding. First Nations leadership structures need data to carry out the multitude of tasks that make up governance (Cornell, Curtis, & Jorgensen, 2004); to make decisions about citizens, communities, and resources. Indigenous governments, in whatever format, also need ways to honour, protect, and control their data both internally and externally via Indigenous data governance (Carroll et al., 2019). Aboriginal and Torres Strait Islander peoples, therefore, require not just governance of existing data, but access and control of data for governance (Smith, 2016). At its core, the Indigenous data sovereignty movement seeks to transform the data landscape to the benefit of Indigenous peoples (Lovett, Lee, Kukutai, Rainie, & Walker, 2019).

By 2017, Indigenous peoples in three Anglo-colonised societies had created Indigenous data sovereignty networks to advance Indigenous data rights and interests. The Te Mana Raraunga Māori Data Sovereignty Network (temanararaunga.maori.nz) in Aotearoa New Zealand; the United States Indigenous Data Sovereignty Network (USIDSN; usIndigenousdata.org); and in Australia the Maiam nayri Wingara Aboriginal and Torres Strait Islander Data Sovereignty Collective (maiamnayriwingara.org). A 2018 summit, facilitated the Maiam nayri Wingara and the Indigenous Governance Institute, determined that Aboriginal and Torres Strait Islander peoples had the right to exercise control of the Indigenous data ecosystem inclusive of data creation, development, stewardship, analysis, dissemination, and infrastructure to ensure that such data are contextual and disaggregated, relevant and empowering of sustainable self-determination and effective self-governance, accountable to Indigenous peoples, and protective of Indigenous individual and collective interests (Indigenous Data Sovereignty Summit Communique, 2018).

Implications for social work practice

We reiterate here our core tenet that to discuss Indigenous requires an overt explanation of our positionality as Indigenous scholars, social workers writing from the Western academy. There can be no exception here; as we move towards theorising the impact of an Indigenous ethics framework on social work practice, we do not detach or de-moor our perspectives from that of our Indigenous First Nations roots. Therefore, when we talk about social work's primary function as a caring profession invested in social change and we blend that with the principles of an Indigenous ethics framework we are creating an epistemological conundrum for social work.

Care, informed by Indigenous ethics, is no longer about bestowing care on people as a responsibility or obligation the social worker solely holds. Nor is social change the product of empowering social work practice. Care and social change, from an Indigenous ethics perspective, are relational, experiential, and contextual, as elements and products of an approach to a way of life. In the Indigenous worldview, this approach is deeply embedded in an interbeing between humans and non-humans. Beyond Western understandings of empowering social work practice, culturally relevant practice, anti-oppressiveness, anti-racists, ally-ship, an Indigenous worldview challenges and reinterprets our relationship with each other, with our practice as a product of Western know-how and thus with our 'clients'.

Green (2018), in her elaboration of the Yindyamarra and Wirrimbirragu Ngurambanggu concepts from the Wiradyuri people of western New South Wales, discusses how an Indigenous worldview never sees a disconnection between people and nature. Caring, in this context, happens slowly in active gentle relational steps where your surroundings (both human and non-human) provide the how, the why, and the when of the caring. Green (2018, p. 140) goes on to explain that Yindyamarra asks for gentleness as a means of conscious awareness, and integration of how a caring practice is caring for one another and our impact on our surroundings, both human and non-human. Attending to care incorporates the impact of caring for each other and for the planet (Green, 2019, p. 140). The Wiradyuri people acknowledge this process happens also within and because of Buyaa lore (Green, 2019). Buyaa dictates a way of life where no one element exists independently or can be attended to in isolation of the rest. If caring is to happen, it will only happen in this circle of relationships situated in and embodied by Country, involving all human and non-human beings consciously aware of one another and their collective impact on each other.

The epistemological conundrum then occurs when the practice is forced to be formulated from a Western code of ethics only, guided only by Western understandings of human rights and social justice. Pragmatically analysed, right now, Australian social work cannot embrace an Indigenous ethics framework from an Indigenous epistemological perspective. The profession needs to move towards a new de-colonised paradigm. We stress here that decolonising is a concept that applies to non-Indigenous frameworks and systems, not to Indigenous values or ways of being. We explore these initial decolonising steps next, mindful that ultimately what is required is social work reimagined from an Indigenous worldview.

First step: Addressing Western superiority

The unfinished business of Indigenous sovereignty is the product of the coloniser's ongoing arrogance; an unchallenged, self-proclaimed superiority over what counts as a valid way of life. Western epistemologies have a direct investment in maintaining whiteness, in maintaining the advantage of the dominant group (mostly white Euro-Australians) who see their way of life as the norm and all other ways of life as deviations from this norm (Diangelo, 2018, p. 25). Whiteness in colonised nation-states like Australia is not skin colour; it is a socio-political, cultural, and economic standpoint of advantage, a state of being that propels and sustains a Western worldview as superior to all others and in particular that of Indigenous and First Nations peoples. This suppression is unacknowledged as white privilege relies on societal invisibility for its power. Whiteness bestows, on the dominant group, a unique individualism, a state of being in the world that allows for a fluid self-defined identity. This identity is believed to function autonomously, void of any outside influences. Therefore to the dominant group success and failure in life are seen as an individual endeavour, the product of either hard work or simply not enough hard work (Bonilla-Silva, 2009). In what Bonilla-Silva (2009) describes as colour-blind racism, the (white) individual is perceived as the most important social unit, this individual is 'just a human' outside or innocent of race and socio-political-cultural stratification (Diangelo, 2018, p. 27). Western supremacy sits inside these conceptualisations of whiteness and individualism and is a useful way to think about the larger socio-political, cultural, and economic systems that are a product of, and simultaneously support and propel, whiteness and individualism. Thus, what we are referring to here is not the actions and intentions of most individual people advantaged by Western superiority, but rather the overarching political, social, and cultural systems that exist to dominate and suppress other world views (Mills, 1997).

Unsettling Western superiority is where social work can become a decolonising practice informed by an Indigenous ethics framework. The tenets for an unsettling of Western supremacy in social work practice would include:

1. *Contextualising oppression* – making overt links in practice to the structural contexts that give way to inequality. Social workers recognising and acting from the fact that there is an overarching political, social, and cultural system that advantages the dominant group is how social work practice becomes about contextualising oppression.

2. *No one is neutral or apolitical in social work* – there is a need to problematise and critically examine the standpoint from which spring the actions both of social work as a profession and of every individual social worker. Whether willingly or not, aware or otherwise, the social work standpoint is predominantly the product of whiteness. Practice is thus always a political act and needs to be named up as political intervention. Allowing 'clients' to respond to this overt assertion creates a more level playing field from which clients and social workers can more realistically examine their relationship and the work they will do together.

3. *Connecting the head, heart, and hand* – such a connection in the work social workers do goes a long way to unsettling Western professional superiority. In the context of an Indigenous ethic, we also need spiritual connection, connection with the Country, connection with nature. These are important parts of the Indigenous worldview and critical parts of how Indigenous peoples do sorry business and heal.

4. *Facilitating Indigenous leadership* – social workers aren't always the answer; it helps to know they are there as allies, as resources and as conduits and connectors but sometimes (in fact most of the time) there is a need for things to be done by Indigenous people for Indigenous people. Knowing when to step aside, and stepping aside when asked to, are two key steps towards unsettling Western superiority in social work practice.

5. *Be prepared to be wrong, irrelevant, challenged, and offended* – a key part of unsettling Western superiority in practice is to accept not knowing, accept you will offend and be offended, and accept you are not an expert or the holder of the right answer. An Indigenous ethic embedded in an Indigenous epistemology values time in deep questioning, time in developing good questions like these are often believed to evolve out of relationships with and in between self, others, kin, community, and Country.

6. *Challenging the immobility triggered by white fragility* (Diangelo, 2018) – this is probably one of the most challenging and invisible by-products of unsettling Western supremacy. Often when the members of the dominant group are asked to be prepared to be wrong and accept offending and being offended, the default responses tend to be 'this is unfair', 'I'm being targeted', 'Tell me what to do'. These are defensive responses that paralyse direct action and short-circuit the opportunity to step up to learning and/or unlearning in practice. They are missed chances to enter uncertainty and be in someone else's world. They are also a white power play to regain control. A social work practice invested in unsettling Western supremacy pushes beyond this paralysis and embraces ethically the constant discomfort of having one's world view challenged.

Second step: Addressing the disconnection from nature

To truly enact an Indigenous ethic from an Indigenous epistemology is to create a viable social work practice informed by the partnership between humans and nature. The basis of a Western epistemology is objectivity (Wahl, 2016, p. 93). This means that even when thinking takes a whole-systems approach, seeing life as a web of interconnected systems, Western know-how leans heavily (if not solely) on seeking one pure objective way to explain life (Bortoft, 1996).

The Indigenous worldview differs; for Indigenous people, there is a dynamic way of seeing the world where knowledge comes into being relationally. There is no objective one system out there waiting to be discovered, Indigenous epistemology relies on the wholeness of many systems created from the same parts as truth. This wholeness is never one tangible objective truth, this wholeness is not the sum of its parts either; this wholeness is nature and humans as one part of that intangible collection of multiple ever-evolving interconnected parts.

For Indigenous and First Nation peoples, nature is everywhere and in everything, mutual reciprocal relationships of all the parts that make up nature are what creates and maintains ways of knowing, being, and doing. Green (2018) explains: 'we are not just interconnected and dependent for our survival; we are created from the same elements' (p. 145). From this perspective, it is impossible to disconnect from nature and seek to care for humans outside of a caring for nature. This is the great challenge for ethical social work practice. The epistemological pitfall of a purely analytical objectifying approach to life dislocates how Indigenous ethics are enacted and embodied in and within nature.

Addressing a disconnection from nature through social work practice requires a reconceptualising of what social work practice is. If social work practice is about social justice and human rights in nature then nature is theory, practice, and thus praxis. Learning to see nature in all that we do as social workers are how an Indigenous ethic comes to be in social work. Nature is the blueprint for healing and for restoring balance.

Third step: Harnessing decolonisation

An Indigenous ethics framework from an Indigenous epistemology is an act of decolonisation. But what does decolonisation offer social work? Decolonisation is a process that recognises we have all been colonised into believing that there is only one normal, civilised, a preferred way of life – that of the Western individualised capitalist neo liberal settler. Decolonisation is a process that recognises we need a way of life that values the wisdom of many ways of knowing, being, and doing in the world. Decolonisation as a process recognises that Indigenous ways of life hold much wisdom and science that has been ignored and suppressed and could offer a much-needed new perspective in twenty-first-century social work. Not long ago, as Indigenous scholars we had to do so much work to convince the settler society that decolonisation was a worthwhile consideration, a process worth investing in. Today, during a pandemic, we can see that the Western neo liberal project is collapsing and, with its collapse, there is a disruption to the 'business as usual'. Social work has a huge opportunity in this moment in history to harness the potential of decolonisation and in doing so embrace an Indigenous ethic.

How do we, as social workers, harness the potential of decolonisation? To begin with, by embracing whole systems thinking, shifting how we think, and thus how we respond as social workers, to integrate the wellbeing and good health of the planet with that of human beings. Humans cannot be well, socially, culturally, physically, and emotionally if the planet isn't doing well. This is a fundamental truth for Indigenous peoples around the world. A truth they lived by for millennia, a truth that allowed them to thrive and live in balance with their surroundings, a truth that is the Indigenous ethic. We are one interdependent eco-system, so addressing the wellbeing and health of one organism like humans is undeniably also about addressing the health and wellbeing of all other organisms that co-exist within this one loop we call Earth. Health and wellbeing are inextricably linked across ecological and societal health as one system-wide emergent property (Wahl, 2016, p. 98).

Harnessing the potential of decolonisation is also about harnessing the potential of a different kind of collaboration with Indigenous peoples. Robert Steele (2012) describes the collaboration as a method for unleashing human ingenuity, creativity, and an abundance of potential. A decolonising collaboration would mean that social workers learn to see Indigeneity not as a sign of paralysis in development, but rather as a source of great wisdom on how to live an ethical life of adaptability and responsiveness to change. Indigenous peoples were stripped of everything they held important through colonisation; this loss is insurmountable and yet they survive and thrive. In collaborating with them, there is a space created to learn and unlearn for social work from a group of people who know how to take account of our interconnection and interdependence both with each other and with the planet. They know how to relinquish; they know how to restore; and they know about resilience, reconciliation, and regeneration. In this time in the history of great disruptiveness to the 'business as usual', of sensing the inevitable loss of a way of life, Indigenous peoples are the people to look for in learning to transition to a new paradigm.

Implications to social work research

An Indigenous ethics framework embedded in an Indigenous epistemology radically changes the how and the why of social work research. Research is a relational activity for Indigenous peoples; an act of service, an opportunity to honour culture and Country, a political act to name up injustices, and to evoke collective responsibility. We examine these below.

Research as relational

Indigenous epistemology is intrinsically relational in nature. Nothing is ever understood nor developed or done outside of a deep knowing that we are interconnected and as such we are in an eternal relationship with one another and nature. This worldview has consequences for how to research, as a knowledge-seeking activity, is viewed and carried out. It is explicitly built upon the respect that is owed to those the research involves and to those the research will impact, and this includes non-human participants (Kovach, 2009). Owing respect is about relational accountability, research activity does not sit outside the responsibility of caring for all those who participate and stand to be affected by the research activity itself. For this reason, when a social worker researches this way she has to demonstrate how her activity will give back to individuals and communities (Kovach, 2009).

Relational accountability is, therefore, the foundational truth of Indigenous epistemology and a feature of the new AIATSIS Code of Ethics' *Impact and Value* principle. Research activity conducted from an Indigenous epistemology and with and/for the Aboriginal and Torres Strait Islander peoples must be accountable to, and demonstrate benefits for, the individual and the collective. In demonstrating benefit and being accountable to the individual and the collective, then nature is always included. Social work research conducted under this framework is never removed from social and ecological inquiry (Bodkin-Andrews et al., 2017). If social and ecological inquiry are intrinsically connected in the Indigenous paradigm, then social work research can become a decolonising act that seeks to reconnect the human and the natural world.

Research as service

Research as a relational enterprise naturally to the idea of research in the service of humans and non-humans. This understanding disrupts individualistic Western understandings of research value. Research under an Indigenous ethic involves giving and receiving, it's a form of reciprocity that acknowledges and honours knowledge sharing. Research as service challenges notions of a deficit, the binaries of expert versus novice, the hierarchy of researcher and participant. What is meant here is that, when research is the product of relationships and is conducted relationally as a form of service for the betterment of the collective, such processes inevitably transform. They bring the researcher into the Indigenous world, their lived experience, their stories as told by them, challenging much of the story of Indigenous people as told by the coloniser. There is no idealised proposition here, doing research in this way brings many challenges least of which is how to reciprocate in ways that are genuine, relevant, that doesn't disturb the balance of relationships or reinstate colonisation.

The challenges for social work research of this nature are many, the answers are nuanced, contextual, and Green (2019) summarises them well in the following quote:

> Social Work in Australia does recognise that it needs to work with and develop knowledge regarding the First Peoples of this Country. It has started upon the journey of decolonising by recognising that it needs to decolonise. However, it also needs to find a way to move beyond that recognition into transforming social work from being embedded within colonialism to a social work that is unique to the Australian context... The answer to all those issues and problems are contained with the local First Nations, and this is how social work can heal itself, transform its relationship with First peoples and also to commence the journey of decolonisation. The richness of this Country, its people, its lands and its diversity are its greatest resources. (97)

Research that localises knowledge

Social work research embedded in an Indigenous ethic framework would always be seeking to name up where it is conducted from, whom it represents, what nation, group, or community it speaks about and whose interests it serves. This is because an Indigenous epistemology upholds the importance of Country, what place are the stories from, and where knowledge is grounded. This is an important aspect of respecting culture and of honouring relationships. Localising knowledge means moving beyond Western analytical explanations, 'this is about the kinetic, the affective and spiritual' (Kovach, 2009, p. 176). For Indigenous peoples, knowledge is born in place, knowledge is of place, it speaks distinctly about a place and its peoples and it shapes each place and its peoples distinctly.

For social work, this approach to localising knowledge challenges the need to prescribe methods and apply one recipe to research activity in the same way everywhere research is conducted. Localising knowledge, as per the Indigenous epistemological requirement, urges social workers to be flexible, to contextualise their research practice, to name up their place of reference, name the places and the peoples from which the knowledge is generated, for which the knowledge will be relevant. The Western construct that evidence-based knowledge can be generated from one place and then be applied across others becomes unworkable in an Indigenous world. Knowledge is local, of Country, by Country, and for Country. Knowledge is the product of relationships of place and in place. In the same light, as an Indigenous worldview seeks to unify when knowledge is produced and is the product of one place and it meets knowledge from another the point is to identify the distinct qualities that each offers. In an interconnected world, then all knowledges can contribute to an understanding of the world. Ultimately, the purpose of an Indigenous ethic embedded in an Indigenous epistemology is to seek respect and any research activity conducted under such ethics, in a settler society, then seeks equal validity alongside all other knowledge production mechanisms (Kovach, 2009).

Conclusions

The AIATSIS Code of Ethics promises greater alignment with the Indigenous worldview, it is a much-anticipated document that will also present a great opportunity for social work's decolonisation. We face ever-increasing disruption to the business as usual, not just as a profession but as a species living on this planet. An Indigenous ethics framework embedded in an Indigenous epistemology promotes key fundamental truths; that humans and non-humans are interconnected; that knowledge production is a relational process that seeks to honour and respect Country and culture; and that sovereignty over how Indigeneity is defined, how knowledge is produced, shared, and owned is paramount to the Indigenous ethic. If social work is to genuinely engage and enact an Indigenous ethic, it will need to address the legacy of its colonial roots. Unmasking and unsettling its white superiority, reconnecting practice to nature, and harnessing the potential of decolonisation. The road is long, but such is the path of transformation.

 Discussion Questions

1. What would need to change in your social work practice to incorporate what an Indigenous ethic calls for?

2. How would an Indigenous ethics framework impact the designing of social work research projects?

3. What changes would you make to the AASW's Code of Ethics to align with the AIATSIS Code of Ethics?

Note

1. The term Indigenous is used interchangeably with the term Aboriginal and Torres Strait Islander. Unless otherwise specified, the term Indigenous means Aboriginal and Torres Strait Islander.

References

Australian Institute of Aboriginal and Torres Strait Islander Studies (AIATSIS). (2020). *AIATSIS Code of Ethics for Aboriginal and Torres Strait Islander Research.* Canberra, ACT: Australian Institute of Aboriginal and Torres Strait Islander Studies. Available at: https://aiatsis.gov.au/sites/default/files/2020-10/aiatsis-code-ethics.pdf

AIATSIS. (2012). *Guidelines for ethical research in Australian Indigenous studies*. Canberra, ACT: Australian Institute of Aboriginal and Torres Strait Islander Studies.

Bodkin-Andrews, G., Bodkin, A. F., Andrews, U. G., & Evans, U. R. (2017). Aboriginal identity, world views, research and the story of the Burra'gorang. In C. Kickectt-Tucker, D. Bessarab, J. Coffin, & M. Wright (Eds.), *Mia Mia Aboriginal community development. Fostering cultural security* (pp. 19–33). London: Cambridge University Press.

Bonilla-Silva, E. (2009). Are the Americas "sick with racism" or is it a problem at the poles? *Ethnic and Racial Studies, 32*, 1071–1082.

Bortoft, H. (1996). *The wholeness of nature – Goethe's way of science*. Edinburgh: Floris Books.

Carroll, S. R., Rodriguez-Lonebear, D., & Martinez, A. (2019). Indigenous data governance: Strategies from United States native nations. *Data Science Journal, 18*(1), 31.

Communique Indigenous Data Sovereignty Summit. (2018, June 20). Canberra, ACT Maiam nayri Wingara Aboriginal and Torres Strait Islander Data Sovereignty Collective and Australian Institute for Indigenous Governance. Canberra. Available at: 25e9cabf4a6/1533808545167/Communique%2B-%2BIndigenous%2BData%2BSovereignty%2BSummit.pdf, https://static1.squarespace.com/static/5b3043afb40b9d20411f3512/t/5b6c0f9a0e2e7

Cornell, S., Curtis, C., & Jorgensen, M. (2004, February). *The concept of governance and its implications for first nations*. Available at: https://hpaied.org/sites/default/files/publications/The%20Concept%20of%20Governance%20and%20its%

DiAngelo, R. J. (2018). *White fragility: Why it's so hard for White people to talk about racism*. Boston, MA: Beacon Press.

Grant Snr, S., & Rudder, J. (2014). *A new Wiradjuri dictionary*. Wagga Wagga, NSW: Restoration House.

Green, S. (2018). Aboriginal people and caring within a colonised society. In B. Pease, A. Vreugdenhil, & S. Stanford (Eds.), *Critical ethics of care in social work. Transforming the politics and practices of caring* (pp. 139–147). Oxon: Routledge.

Green, S. (2019). Indigenising social work. In B. Bennett & S. Green (Eds.), *Our voices Aboriginal social work* (2nd ed., pp. 86–100). London: Red Globe Press.

Hinman, L. M. (2008). *Ethics: A pluralistic approach to moral theory* (4th ed.). Belmont, CA: Thomson Higher Education.

Indigenous Data Sovereignty Summit Communique. (2018, June 20). Canberra, ACT Maiam nayri Wingara Aboriginal and Torres Strait Islander Data Sovereignty Collective and Australian Institute for Indigenous Governance. Canberra. Available at: https://www.aigi.com.au/wp-content/uploads/2019/10/Communique-Indigenous-Data-Sovereignty-Summit-1.pdf

King, T. (2012). *The inconvenient Indian: A curious account of the native people of North America*. Toronto, ON: DoubleDay Canada.

Kovach, M. (2009). *Indigenous methodologies. Characteristics, conversations, and contexts*. Toronto, ON: University of Toronto Press.

Kukutai, T., & Taylor, J. (2016). Data sovereignty for Indigenous peoples: Current practice and future needs. In T. Kukutai & J. Taylor (Eds.), *Indigenous data sovereignty: Towards an agenda* (CAEPR Research Monograph, 2016/34) (pp. 1–24). Canberra, ACT: ANU Press.

Lovett, R. (2016). Aboriginal and Torres Strait Islander community well-being: Identified needs for statistical capacity. In T. Kukutai & J. Taylor (Eds.), *Indigenous Data Sovereignty: Towards an Agenda* (CAEPR Research Monograph, 2016/34) (pp. 213–232). Canberra, ACT: ANU Press.

Lovett, R., Lee, V., Kukutai, T., Rainie, S. C., & Walker, J. (2019). Good data practices for Indigenous data sovereignty. In A. Daly, K. Devitt, & M. Mann (Eds.), *Good data* (pp. 26–36). Amsterdam: Institute of Network Cultures Inc.

Maddison, S. (2009). *Black politics. Inside the complexity of Aboriginal political culture*. Crows Nest, NSW: Allen and Unwin.

Maiam nayri Wingara Maiam nayri Wingara Aboriginal and Torres Strait Islander data sovereignty collective: About us. Available at: https://www.maiamnayriwingara.org/about-us

Mills, C. (1997). *The racial contract*. Cornell University Press. Retrieved March 20, 2020. www.jstor.org/stable/10.7591/j.ctt5hh1wj

Morgan, G. (2006). Aboriginal politics, self-determination and the rhetoric of community. *Dialogue, 25*, 19–29.

National Health and Medical Research Council. (2003). *Values and ethics: Guidelines for ethical conduct in Aboriginal and Torres Strait Islander heath research*. Available at: https://www.nhmrc.gov.au/about-us/publications/values-and-ethics-guidelines-ethical-conduct-aboriginal-and-torres-strait-islander-health-research

Porsanger, J. (2004). An essay about Indigenous methodology. *Nordlit, 8*. doi: https://doi.org/10.7557/13.1910.

Rainie, S. C., Kukutai, T., Walter, M., Figueroa-Rodriguez, O. L., Walker, J., & Axelsson, P. (2019). Issues in open data: Indigenous data sovereignty. In T. Davies, S. Walker, M. Rubinstein, & F. Perini (Eds.), *The state of open data: Histories and horizons* (pp. 300–319). Cape Town/Ottawa: African Minds and International Development Research Centre.

Rigney, L. (2001). *A first perspective of Indigenous Australian Participation in Science: Framing Indigenous research towards Indigenous Australian Intellectual Sovereignty*. Available at: https://www.semanticscholar.org/paper/A-FIRST-PERSPECTIVE-OF-INDIGENOUS-AUSTRALIAN-IN-Rigney/d2928e856fc39aee3821c70b67c06701788c9405

Russ-Smith, J. (2019). Embodiment of sovereignty. In B. Bennett & S. Green (Eds.), *Our voices Aboriginal social work* (2nd ed., pp. 238–243). London: Red Globe Press.

Smith, D. E. (2016). Governing data and data for governance: The everyday practice of Indigenous sovereignty. In T. Kukutai & J. Taylor (Eds.), *Indigenous data sovereignty: Towards an agenda* (CAEPR Research Monograph, 2016/34) (pp. 117–138). Canberra, ACT: ANU Press.

Snipp, M. (2016). What does data sovereignty imply: What does it look like? In T. Kukutai & J. Taylor (Eds.), *Indigenous data sovereignty: Towards an agenda* (CAEPR Research Monograph, 2016/34) (pp. 39–56). Canberra, ACT: ANU Press.

Steele, R. (2012). *The open-source manifesto: Transparency, truth, and trust.* Berkeley, CA: Evolver Editions.

Te Mana Raraunga Maori Data Sovereignty Network. (2018). *About us.* Available at: https://www.temanararaunga.maori.nz/

Tuhawai Smith, L. (1999). *Decolonizing methodologies.* London: Zed Books.

US Indigenous Data Sovereignty Network. (2018). *About us.* Available at: https://usindigenousdata.org/

Wahl, D. C. (2016). *Designing regenerative cultures.* Axminster: Triarchy Press.

Walter, M. (2007). Indigenous sovereignty and the Australian state: Relations in a globalizing era. In A. Moreton-Robinson (Ed.), *Sovereign Subjects: Indigenous sovereignty matters* (pp. 155–167). Sydney, NSW: Allen and Unwin.

Walter, M. (2016). Data politics and Indigenous representation in Australian statistics. In T. Kukutai & J. Taylor (Eds.), *Indigenous data sovereignty: Towards an agenda* (CAEPR Research Monograph, 2016/34) (pp. 79–98). Canberra, ACT: ANU Press.

Walter, M., & Suina, M. (2018). Indigenous data, Indigenous methodologies and indigenous data sovereignty. *International Journal of Social Research Methodology, 22*, 233–243.

14 Policy: Agendas and Actions. Analysing Policy Effects on First Australian Peoples

Jennie Briese and Jodie Satour

Introduction

Social policy concerns studying the causes of social 'problems' and how governments can intervene to affect change. Dominant social, political, and cultural values are reflected in policy; therefore, policy cannot be value-free nor void of dominant ideologies promoting particular forms of governmentality.

Post-World War II, the Australian state began provisioning important welfare services under an economic system known as the Keynesian Welfare State (KWS) (Mendes, 2008). This included publicly provided universal benefits such as healthcare and a social wage for vulnerable people. By 1980, neoliberalists argued that welfare provisions under the KWS created passive welfare recipients, and was not economically viable in the new global economy (Mishra, 1999). Neoliberal ideologies are a resurgence of classic liberalism, where competition drove the market, and peoples' life chances. While many social policies are thought to 'help' vulnerable people, within the contemporary global neoliberal climate policy instead usually targets increased the degree of citizen responsibilisation. That is, forcing citizens to actively participate in their own life chances and contribute to the state and global market economies (Williams, 2000). Neoliberal governmentality is therefore political rationality of 'practical' governance; a cultural change reformulating relationships between citizens and the state by shifting welfare risk management from the state to the individual. This ideology heavily influences contemporary policy-making and how social 'problems' are 'managed'.

Neoliberal governmentality also heightens class struggles and further marginalises those who are already disadvantaged, marginalised, or unable to compete in a capitalist market (Mendes, 2008). This chapter discusses historical government policies and practices that segregated, disenfranchised, and marginalised First Australian peoples, creating massive disparities in contemporary life outcomes between First Australian and non-First Australian peoples. Policies designed to address these ongoing structural barriers faced by First Australian peoples is scrutinised through a policy analysis lens that highlights neoliberal ideologies of responsibilisation and undertones of neocolonial assimilation agendas. Further, we discuss how social workers and students can engage in policy to create effective change. Finally, we highlight Bacchi's (2009) 'problematisation' framework for policy analysis. For the purposes of this chapter, we have used the terminology First Australian peoples to respectfully include all Aboriginal and Torres Strait Islander peoples.

Positionality statements

We acknowledge the Ancestors, Elders, Traditional Custodians, and Indigenous peoples from other nations, and follow our protocols by introducing ourselves culturally before introducing our professional selves.

I am Jennie Briese, a First Australian woman. I was born on Yugerra Country (Qld, Australia) and have a strong placial connection to Giabal Country (Darling Downs, Qld) where I feel connected, nurtured, and cared for. I have not always known who I am, yet have been Ancestrally guided throughout my life journey. My Ancestors speak to me in various ways, directing all that I do. As someone who was raised in a white adoptive family, I have experienced great privilege in access to Western education and other areas of social 'advantage'. It is this privilege I share now, as a social worker and new academic. I am grateful for the Ancestors and Elders who have and continue to guide me in how I contribute to the advancement of First Australian people and our voices in decision-making about our lives.

I am Jodie Satour, an Eastern Aranda woman from the Northern Territory. My skin name is Angale linked to kin and my social and cultural relationships, including responsibilities, roles, obligations, land, ceremony, and our songlines. Through kin and my language, we recognise our relations by bloodlines and not by the colour of skin. I am also an Australian social worker, where I have worked in unique landscapes with vast distances in many positions not necessarily bearing this title. These positions include mental health, alcohol and other drugs, child protection, juvenile justice, disability, community development, research, and policy. I was raised to believe that *honesty is the best policy*. However, not all parties or organisations I have worked for or with have engaged with my people honestly, transparently, or genuinely in their consultations when it comes to policies affecting us. It is for this reason I have participated in bringing about change through the process of policy-making.

Historical

Entangled threads of Australia's colonial histories are producing and reproducing colonial knowledge and practices. Social and public policies discursively work to ensure control over First Australian peoples. As early as the

British invasion, policies were imported to Australia and over seventy policies enacted on First Australian peoples (Dow & Gardiner-Garden, 2011). These also arose out of racial conflicts that have predominantly featured in policies to primarily secure our lands and included, but are not limited to, disqualifying the right to vote and the denial of citizenship and welfare rights (ALRC, 2010; Bennett, 1999). This colonial power was also used in policies to 'civilise' and control First Australian peoples, with the provision of our welfare in being 'protected', segregated, and assimilated. Such policies reflect paternalistic colonial assumptions of First Australian peoples needing to be 'managed'. In part, this is often attributed to the invaders' belief that First Australian peoples were a 'dying race' (Hollinsworth, 2006) who needed to be managed until we died out. However, rather than 'protecting' First Australian people, these policies left us as fringe-dwellers on our own Country (Dodson, 2018), and served political and social agendas founded on white supremacy and racism (Bennett, 1999; Hollinsworth, 2006), leading to many human rights atrocities being committed against First Australian peoples.

Practices such as the forced removals of First Australian children from their families and communities between the mid-1800s and early 1970s were supposedly for our own good, but resulted in extreme and ongoing trauma for many First Australian people, families, and communities (HREOC, 1997). This trauma is often framed as 'dysfunction' within the Australian political arena, thereby facilitating governmentality of disconnect between historical practices and contemporary outcomes. Government policy decisions have also had a substantial impact on the over-representation of First Australian peoples within statutory welfare and criminal justice systems, and also contributed to ongoing disparities in health, education, housing, and employment outcomes (Briese & Menzel, 2020) between First Australian and non-First Australian people. Ongoing systemic inequality can be attributed to the relegation of First Australian peoples as supposedly racially inferior (non-)citizens (we were once considered alongside flora and fauna after all) and remains deeply entrenched within the social, political, legal, and institutional structures of Australia.

Contemporary

Contemporaneously positioned within a colonising society, First Australian peoples collectively experience how policy discourses are often used through statistics and over-representation to characterise us as a 'problem' resulting from our own dysfunction (Askew, Brady, Mukandi, Singh, Sinha, Brough, & Bond, 2020; Bacchi, 2009). According to Australian law, we are all humanised to be treated as equals (EQBB, 2020). However, in policy terms, we know this not to be true. Being historically considered alongside flora and fauna dehumanised us, and this dehumanisation remains an embedded undertone in most contemporary policy. Additionally, between invasion and the present day, policy emphatically reflects undertones of paternalistically 'managing' the assimilation of First Australian peoples into Western ideologies, with individual 'responsibilisation' emerging as a key policy driver over recent decades.

Paternalistic ideology is evident in the pattern of policies that moved between 'segregation and protection (from *settlement* to early-twentieth-century); assimilation (from 1937); integration and self-determination (1972)… and self-management (1976)' (Bacchi, 2009, p. 117, emphasis added) and now supposedly sits within the realms of evidence-based policy-making. However, Newman (2017, p. 214) notes that evidence is often ignored and 'in many countries, governments continue to enact policies that are counter to the best available and most widely accepted evidence'. Bacchi (2009) highlights how representing social 'problems' in a particular way enables the government to set an agenda in centralised policy creation to gain a particular result. Dodson (2018, p. 126) describes this 'centralized decision-making…' about First Australian peoples' needs, without our voices informing policy, as a new era of fringe-dwelling; that of the 'policy fringe-dweller'. For First Australian peoples, being represented as a social 'problem' by policy-makers reinforces an assimilationist agenda, continues to dehumanise us and silences First Australian peoples' voices; the very voices that could contribute to policy formation around their identified needs.

Current policy and examples

A plethora of policy and legislation specific to First Australian peoples currently exists in Australia, some representing significant and hard-fought achievements. For example, land rights acts paved the way for First Australian peoples to once again occupy traditional lands after being dispossessed of them by colonisers. However, land rights were not merely handed to First Australian peoples. This was an arduous journey requiring immense cultural strength. A constant and prolonged protest against the colonial structural and systemic domination was required to gain legal rights around caring for Country and other cultural practices; rights that should never have been taken. In the Northern Territory, a defining moment in land rights occurred in December 1976 when the Whitlam Labour government passed the *Aboriginal Land Rights (Northern Territory) Act*. The process began in 1966 when the Gurindji people, working on Wave Hill station, walked off in protest of unfair wages (HRLC, 2017). During the first year of the walk-off, a journey to traditional Country at Daguragu was made, and the movement shifted focus from unfair wages to include advocating for control of Country. The years between the walk-off in 1966 and the passage of the *1976 Act* included nation-wide campaigning that placed First Australian land rights in the public spotlight. While legal processes may seem irrelevant in policy considerations, it is imperative that advocates for policy change are aware of significant histories and how those histories are reflected (or omitted) in how policy 'managing' First Australian peoples emerges. We include this to highlight how as First Australian peoples we can 'manage' our own affairs, as this is rarely reflected in policies; particularly those that aim to 'close the gap' in disparities between First Australian and non-First Australian peoples' life outcomes. Rather, First Australian peoples are predominantly represented as 'dysfunctional problems' in need of 'management'.

In Australia, each state and territory has implemented health plans for First Australian people, with some geographically localised plans also actioned. These then sit under and/or within the *National Aboriginal and Torres Strait Islander Health Plan 2013–2023* (NATSIHP), which provides an overarching framework targeting equality in health outcomes between First Australian and non-First Australian people. The overarching goal of the NATSIHP framework is stated as 'Targeted, evidence-based action that will contribute to achieving equality of health status and life-expectancy between Aboriginal and Torres Strait Islander people and non-Indigenous Australians by 2031 (one of the six Closing The Gap [CTG] targets)' (p. 8). Additionally, NATSIHP's vision states:

> The Australian health system is free of racism and inequality and all Aboriginal and Torres Strait Islander people have access to health services that are effective, high quality, appropriate, and affordable. Together with strategies to address social inequalities and determinants of health, this provides the necessary platform to realise health equality by 2031. (p. 7)

Ironically, this is the first time in Australian policy that racism has been explicitly highlighted as a social determinant of health, yet no mention is noted within the document around how a racism-free health system will be realised. This poses uncertainty around the actual intent of the original plan. That is, one may ponder whether the underlying assumption is that First Australian peoples cannot take responsibility for our health and it needs to be 'managed', or if perhaps this was a genuine oversight. Bacchi (2009) highlights the need for policy advocates to question any underlying 'tones' in policy language, and how that language constructs people as the 'problem'. However, Bacchi (2009) also encourages policy advocates to explore further, looking for silenced voices and possible political agendas. This means ensuring a careful exploration of amendments or enhancements to policy is conducted.

The *Implementation Plan for the National Aboriginal and Torres Strait Islander Health Plan 2013–2023* (the Plan) was created in 2013 and released in 2015. It emphasises partnerships between government and First Australian-led organisations. The Plan contains significant information around actions required for addressing systemic racism (as highlighted in NATSIHP) within health settings and other intersectional priority areas. Responsibility for the implementation of the plan's goals, such as mechanisms to address racism and measuring cultural safety outcomes, falls jointly between First Australian-led organisations and mainstream services. This could certainly be viewed as potentially being a genuine partnership recognising the cultural and human rights, and voices of First Australian peoples. However, a strong problematising tone is reflected in the implementation plan within comments such as 'good health enables participation in the labour force, which models good behaviour for children to go to school' (p. 4). Statements such as this imply that we do not already participate in 'good' health practices and the labour force, or encourage our children to attend school. Additionally, the language throughout implies the 'need' for First Australian peoples to assimilate to the Western neoliberal ideologies of competition and individual participation in the market. This in itself is contradictory to the espousing of culturally safe and competent practices mentioned elsewhere throughout the plan. Altman and Klein (2017) describes the depth of control inherent within the contemporary policy as neo-paternalism.

The neo-paternalistic and assimilative nature of policy direction are also evident in the Closing The Gap [CTG] Strategy, which seeks to achieve equality against targeted performance measures, and the Northern Territory Emergency Response [NTER] (mis)use of political power and media to perpetuate racism and force Western ideological conformity on First Australian peoples. Both are discussed as examples of how First Australian people are often 'problematised' (Bacchi, 2009) as being a result of our own dysfunction.

The CTG initiatives launched in 2008 provide a broad policy framework to reduce systemic inequality and disadvantages experienced by many First Australian peoples with regard to child mortality, early childhood, schooling, health, economic participation, healthy homes, safe communities' and governance and leadership. A *National Indigenous Reform Agreement* was established for federal, state, and territory governments' commitment to working with First Australian peoples on the CTG objectives, including performance measures, outputs and inputs, and delivery of programs and services. Already, neoliberal ideologies inherent within the language of measurement poses significant questions, such as 'who' we are being measured against. If we are to be measured against Western 'norms', there lies the potential for CTG alignment against previous assimilation policies. Education outcomes of EAL/ESL learners being taught a Eurocentric curriculum in remote communities cannot possibly be measured or compared accurately against Western education outcomes. According to Bacchi (2009), analysing how the 'problem' of education outcomes is represented can highlight strengths and inadequacies of policy. In this instance, the policy does not reflect language as a barrier to gaining equity in education outcomes. Rather, non-attendance at school by First Australian children is highlighted as 'the problem'. Therefore, the policy expectations potentially align with a need for remote First Australian school-children to speak English as a first language before education equity can be achieved.

In assessing the Indigenous expenditure and progress of the initiatives four years from its inception, the Steering Committee for the Review of Government Service Provision (Productivity Commission, 2012) reported there were a number of problems with the data; that many outcomes were not improving or were worse. Altman (2012) elaborated, stating no clarity on spending was evident, nor the effectiveness of services delivered in meeting First Australian targets. The Steering Committee (Productivity Commission, 2012) further acknowledged limited expenditure information on programs existed; however, some service cost issues were associated with geographical locations and the complexities related to culture and language but did not further elaborate. The framework makes no concession for diversity. A further issue with statistics presented in CTG reporting is that it created a problem of what is not produced, where victim-blaming can occur at the individual level and not of the structural conditions and relationships between First Australian and non-First Australian people, who remain vastly unequal (Pholi, Black, & Richards, 2009, p. 4). Within Western industrialised communities, there is a reliance on individuals to participate in a society where neoliberalism defines people as subjects rather than citizens, who are responsible for their own health (Lewis, 2014). Neoliberal reforms can then curtail the basic access rights to services by those most vulnerable in society (Howard-Wagner, Bargh, & Altamirano-Jimenez, 2018) and increase systemic inequality and disadvantage. This reinforces the problematisation of First Australian peoples being dysfunctional.

Prior, in assessing the progress of the CTG initiatives in 2010, then Prime Minister Julia Gillard presented an annual report favouring a discourse of reductive narratives in framing First Australian peoples. Subsequent reports mirrored similar deficit language. With no government policy success stories, and politicians framing us within reductive narratives, many Australian people see us as 'the problem' (Bacchi, 2009; Paradies, 2006). However, CTG indicators are based on comparative Western performance measures to 'fix and change us for the better', towards a normalisation that is not far removed from previous assimilationist policies (Pholi, Black, & Richards, 2009, pp. 9–10). This message, that it is we who are dysfunctional and need responsibilising, is reinforced through the many government officials and politicians who perpetuate negative discourses excluding narratives on the structural barriers and geographical disadvantages with regard to accessibility to appropriate services for many First Australian peoples (Fogarty, Bulloch, McDonnell, & Davis, 2018). It is therefore unsurprising that targets are often not met and First Australian peoples may be reluctant to engage in western institutions.

The National Aboriginal Community Controlled Health Organisation (NACCHO), a national peak body responsible for providing advice and guidance on the CTG policy, argued health services performed poorly and created further barriers where First Australian peoples often experienced feeling racialised and unwelcome (NACCHO, 2018). Furthermore, accessibility to services continues to be linked to institutional racism, where within the health system there has been an underutilisation of services by First Australian peoples (Paradies, 2014). First Australian peoples participating in a study of the Victorian health system also identified racism in having been treated unfairly or experiencing discrimination because of their racial or cultural background (Markwick, Ansari, Clinch, & McNeil, 2019, p. 2). A discursive pattern of contemporary racist beliefs in political and parliamentary discussions was highlighted within the study. These discussions openly express how racist beliefs have led to negative views of minority groups (Markwick et al., 2019, p. 2).

In racial and cultural terms, othering is normalised in Australia (Peters, 2017, p. 64; Moreton-Robinson, 2004). Said (1978) describes cultural othering as involving one group viewing themselves as more powerful 'over' another. Cultural othering in politics is evident in Pauline Hanson's publicly expressed distaste of Migration and Aboriginal Affairs, and John Howard's language choices towards First Australian people with regard to government speeches and reports on accountability and promoting economic independence, alongside erasing social justice and self-determination in favour of self-management to 'normalise' cultural difference (Howard-Wagner, Bargh, & Altamirano-Jimenez, 2018; Peters, 2017). Peters (2017, p. 80) defines these actions as 'colonial attitudes of paternalism and racial superiority to view racism as someone else's problem'.

To change the way policy-makers and government interacts with First Australian people, NACCHO petitioned for the implementation of a formal agreement on the CTG initiatives. With the continual failure of government in meeting the CTG targets, and the absence of First Australian people in its design, language, and determining of targets and frameworks, 13 peak bodies across Australia collaborated with NACCHO to write to address the Prime Minister (ANAO, 2019). This resulted in a genuine formal partnership whereby a coalition of peak bodies works with the Council of Australian Governments (COAG), giving voice to First Australian peoples on issues that affect their communities.

A refresh of CTG was announced in 2016, eight years after its inception, with the development and implementation of the next phase to commence by mid-2019 (ANAO, 2019). When the 2020 report was released, NACCHO announced work was still needed as the majority of targets were not met. The peak bodies have put forward structural priority reforms on which government and other agencies should work with and deliver services to First Australian people. In his 2020 February parliament address on CTG, Prime Minister Scott Morrison admits that the initiative from the start was the wrong approach, with a 'top-down, one size fits all approach', and should include 'stories of success and hope' and partnerships led by First Australian peoples (Morrison, 2020). It is too early to predict if these reforms will make a difference. However, it is encouraging to imagine policy-makers and government interacting genuinely with First Australian peoples around how the CTG might be redesigned using a bottom-up approach. What is not encouraging is the potential for further explicitly racist policies, such as those linked to the 2007 NTER to emanate from the echelons of government policy-making in the future.

Further policies affecting First Australian people were evident by the catalyst of the NTER measures with the release of the *Ampe Akelyernemane Meke Mekarle: 'Little Children are Sacred'* report (Wild & Anderson, 2007). Then Prime Minister John Howard had a strained history with First Australian peoples during his leadership. Howard had abolished, without consultation, the Aboriginal and Torres Strait Islander Commission, formally involved in the processes of government affecting Indigenous lives. He also refused to apologise sorry for First Australian peoples being removed from their families. Howard publicly denounced the findings from the National Inquiry and release of the *Bringing Them Home Report*, that genocide had taken place in Australia's history (Davidson, 2014; Howard, 2007). The *Bringing Them Home Report*, among its findings, stated that

> When a child was forcibly removed that child's entire community lost, often permanently, its chance to perpetuate itself in that child. The inquiry has concluded that this was a primary objective of forcible removals and is the reason they amount to genocide. (HREOC, 1997, p. 218)

Negative constructions of First Australian peoples continued when Howard implemented policies for the NTER that required suspending the *Racial Discrimination Act 1975* (AHRC, n.d.). This meant no protection against racial discrimination, thereby allowing further production of policies and legislation targeting First Australian peoples. Changes included the quarantining of First Australian peoples' welfare payments and amendments to the *Aboriginal Land Rights (Northern Territory) Act 1976,* which gave government 'control of Aboriginal townships' (Bacchi, 2009, p. 117). There was also discursive language framing First Australian men as paedophiles, which was combined with media platforms that perpetuated various levels of racism (Fogarty, Bulloch, McDonnell, & Davis, 2018). Howard provided a narrative that a civilised society did not exist in First Australian communities and the government needed to protect Aboriginal children (Altman, 2013), making further use of the language of 'normalisation' (Altman, 2013) to justify why the Commonwealth were intervening. The Coalition government, led by Howard, deployed the Army and Federal Police to ensure there was no resistance to any of the compulsory measures, including child health checks. The abuse of power inherent in the handling of this 'intervention' included refusing consultation with First Australian peoples, and punitive measures for a public health campaign facilitating social control (Bielefeld, 2017). Howard justified the lack of community consultation by framing community Elders as part of the problem (Bacchi, 2009). Media represented the communities as dysfunctional and reported that paedophile rings *had* been operating in First Australian communities (Fogarty et al., 2018; Bielefeld, 2017). Subsequently, the Australian Crime Commission conducted an independent investigation and found there was no truth in what was reported as fact (NTERT, 2008).

Bacchi (2009, p. xii) recommends identifying what effects are potentially (or actually) produced and what is left 'unproblematised' by a particular representation of the 'problem'. This is crucial to presenting factual and strong arguments in policy advocacy work. Within the NTER, initiatives designed to 'protect vulnerable children' created fear amongst the communities of children once again being removed from their families (potential/actual effects). Changes to the *Aboriginal Land Rights (Northern Territory) Act 1976* were left unproblematised in the process, raising questions around the correlation between 'protecting vulnerable children' and land acquisition (Altman & Klein, 2017; Bacchi, 2009). This highlights the potential underlying agenda. The 'problem' was represented as child sexual abuse; however, the agenda appears to be land acquisition. The Coalition, taking a public position of being a 'neo-protector', used assimilationist policies within the NTER legislation to promote socially responsible behaviour with colonising views of shaping First Australian peoples to fit in with mainstream Australia (Fogarty et al., 2018; Altman & Klein, 2017). To do so, a higher level of control over First Australian lands was required. Therefore, within the NTER measures, First Australian peoples were yet again dehumanised, and represented as dysfunctional, and hard-fought battles for land rights were discredited to enable government control. In this, policy can be seen as an instrument of power within particular political and ideological governmentalities.

Rolling back the intervention, parliament member Barbara Shaw, who was also a citizen living under these conditions, publicly campaigned against the draconian discriminatory laws. Participating as a member of the action group, Shaw wrote to the Standing Commission on Indigenous Affairs. Community members had also taken their complaints to the United Nations Committee. The government ignored the many concerns and recommendations raised by the international United Nations bodies, whose narrative explicitly reflected Australia was not complying with their international human rights obligations under this policy (AHRC, 2017).

Repealing the NTER legislation in 2012, the Labor Party made amendments and renamed it Stronger Futures. Their approach was to close the gap between First Australian people and mainstream Australia. Again, the policy adopted the ideology of 'norms' similar to that of their predecessor. The government did agree to consult with 73 communities in the Northern Territory. However, Bielefeld (2017, pp. 151–152) argues that there is no public evidence of how the government involved the community in the decision-making process, or if consultations were led by First Australian peoples on what measures were remaining. The Labor Party did reinstate the RDA 1975 (Cth), however, the Stronger Futures policy retained many of the NTER's discriminatory and disempowering measures; including managing people's income through Centrelink basic cards, payments for school attendance and criminalisation of the consumption of alcohol on prohibited areas (Bielefeld, 2017). Concerns were again raised by the United Nations Special Rapporteur regarding the Stronger Futures policy (AHRC). Despite this, in 2014, then Prime Minister for Indigenous Affairs Tony Abbott supported the continuation of the legislation due to expire in 2022, but redirected funds to the Closing the Gap National Partnership Agreement delivered by departments from Prime Minister and Cabinet. The Commonwealth had also moved funds, making the state responsible to provide services to remote communities. The Productivity Commission also showed that under Abbott over 80 percent of services for First Australian peoples had been moved to non-First Australian organisations (Productivity Commission, 2015).

Neoliberal ideologies are highly visible in policies regarding the recentralisation of services from remote and rural to urban settings. The technical and social context contributed to how power had been disseminated through policies differently in the participation of austerity policy measures. Abbott used technology (the media) in attempting to change human behaviour through negative reinforcement that taxpayers should not be subsiding First Australian people's 'choice' of living in remote communities in not accessing adequate services and fully participating in society to close the gap (ABC, 2015). Yet these same groups of First Australian peoples are disproportionately represented in poverty statistics in Australia, where median incomes in household families are below average compared with non-First Australian families (Davidson, Saunders, Bradbury, & Wong, 2018). The Coalition was criticised by the Greens (Greens, 2016) for their paternalistic measures and lack of impact being made through the Stronger Futures policy of a 'one size fits all' approach, thereby further disadvantaging First Australian peoples. Policies that continue to exclude First Australian peoples from meaningful participation and self-determination usually have long-term and far-reaching negative impacts on people's perceptions of their value and dignity as human beings.

Engaging with policy and creating effective change

Discussion around genuine engagement, consultation, and respect from government policy-makers has sparked varying responses from First Australian leaders and communities (Hunt, 2013). Policies reflect values, ideologies, and discourses that often perpetuate privilege and oppression amongst groups (Bacchi, 2009). Australia's policy-making process has bolstered a neo-protectionist regime, where power has been exerted over First Australian peoples (Dow & Gardiner-Garden, 2011). Therefore, First Australian voices in future policy-making are crucial.

Power provokes many approaches and can include certain outcomes at the expense of others, particularly in social policy areas that look at the redistribution of resources creating powerlessness and inequality in society. Economic precedence over emancipatory policies has occurred, with successive governments tightening eligibility for welfare assistance, and promoting individual participation (Carson & Kerr, 2017, p. 82). Government intentions in 2020 are purported to reset the relationships with First Australian people seeking active participation in the policy-making process. Practitioners can use their power positively by engaging these opportunities to influence policy. For effective policy practice, efforts are required in legislative, agency, and community settings that work toward social and economic justice (Bessant, Watts, Dalton, & Smyth, 2006; Jamrozik, 2005). To facilitate change, students and practitioners can share insights with top-down policy-makers, who are often gatekeepers for Indigenous Affairs on what happens on the ground. This is not an exhaustive list, but practitioners can and should attempt to influence policy-making at the local, national, and international levels through the media, politicians, and local members of parliament and councils. Engagement can transpire by advocating against repressive laws such as bans on, for example, marriage equality and climate change, or on accessibility to basic public transport, finances, health services, and access to lands and natural resources.

Policy can be influenced at both formal and informal practice levels. This section is not intended to prescribe the only engagement techniques, but provides examples on how to engage at these different policy practice levels. It should be noted that the process in policy should always suit the issue being addressed with the stakeholders who are most affected (Bacchi, 2009; Bessant et al., 2006). Stakeholders are those who are interested in the outcomes of the policy practice initiative, such as the ability to participate in social and cultural practices that are of significant benefit for that person, family, and/or community. Policy operates in cycles and usually has a variety of key players involved at different stages (Bacchi, 2009; Bessant et al., 2006; Jamrozik, 2005). Key players include the public, interest groups, media, government employees (including administration workers), politicians, and the legal system representatives who might interpret the law. The National Disability Incentive Scheme care plan based on necessary needs is one example of policy created through the involvement of a variety of key players, including clients, family, community, service providers, and departments (The Lowitja Institute, 2019).

Knowing who and how to engage in policy practicing skills can create changes in both law and social conditions affecting First Australian peoples. Engagement therefore might include a hand-in-hand bottom-up approach involving discussions facilitated by the community on a particular issue (Ife, 2016). Practitioners need awareness that understanding community is also influenced by the community's own history and identity. This brings into light the importance of widening perspectives to understand the community from a non-Indigenous perspective and requires 'genuine' engagement (Ife, 2016). The aforementioned rolling back of the Intervention Action Group on the NTER is another example. Membership included those from the health, law, and community sectors led by local First Australian peoples on issues affecting them as a direct implementation of the NTER policy. The voice of the people was imperative, and practitioners needed to consider the local history as experienced by community members within the local agency and government settings. The Action Group had presented people's lived experiences in their discussion with the Federal government and Amnesty International. The Action Group wrote a submission to the Human Rights Commission. On such matters, practitioners can write to the United Nations Special Rapporteur. This involves completing an online form on the alleged violations with regard to any rights; civil, economic, political, cultural, and social. A practitioner can help in this process by providing information on the lived experiences from stakeholders, individual community members, and specific legislation, institutional or policy affecting those concerned. The Special Rapporteur will elicit information, including content from legislation, policy, and practices not deemed compliant with international human rights conventions (UNHRC, 2020). This was the outcome of the NTER policy. Practitioners can assist in the policy process by lobbying to government and through media campaigns (Althaus, Bridgman, & Davis, 2017).

Media releases can be an effective tool in raising interest on a particular issue. Some of the basic rules are the timing of when to release the key issue to maximise the attention the community and or practitioner is seeking. A media release is one page in length and the written style is direct, concise, and active language. Use of a punchy heading, an introductory paragraph with the key message with the 'five W's': who, why, what, where, and when. The first sentence should also set the tone (Brenner, 2018). The agency, community, and/or individual may also include an embargo date of when the issue can be released. Good practice areas when dealing with media also include stating the goal, position statement, clear objectives, research (collect evidence), identify a target audience, and, if community participation will be involved, types of stakeholders (DPMC, 2013). Good media relations are about preparation and development with media professionals in agencies and within government departments.

Within a Westminster model, human service practitioners are located in departments and can advise ministers for the Cabinet. The Cabinet, chaired by the Prime Minister, is the epicentre of the executive government who coordinate policy. Each government decides how the Cabinet will operate (Althaus et al., 2017; Young, 2012). The Prime Minister's role includes presenting bills, proposed laws, and policy statements from the government departments under designated portfolios. Policy statements, different from policy procedures, can appear in a number of documents, including ministerial statements, bills, and papers (Althaus et al., 2017; Healy & Mulholland, 2007). The Prime Minister's role is to also inform parliament and the public about any action taken by themselves or office officials. It is important to note representation in parliament. In Australia's Upper and Lower house, there are no dedicated parliamentary seats for Indigenous representation, and whilst numbers have increased these numbers are still low in making a change on First Nation issues (Appleby, 2015).

Practitioners may also need to engage with the local council members due to by-laws and state or territory laws affecting a community group. Community and lobby groups can approach their local members of parliament with suggestions for bills (Healy & Mulholland, 2007). A green paper is prepared at the direction of a Minister, often labelled discussion paper (Young, 2012). This paper is a preliminary report that the government wishes to stimulate from the public to find out if what is proposed will be popular and/or if existing legislation may need revamping. This is often the first step in changing a law. Encouraging social action can empower communities to rally together around situations affecting their local area (Young, 2012). Non-government organisations are particularly good at informing the community on papers that might be affecting them. These documents invite ideas, feedback on issues, and proposals that can be used to prepare a white paper. A white paper is usually on a specific topic presented as a Cabinet submission. This is an authoritative document that presents the government policy on an issue. The green paper forms part of the coalescing process by inviting the public to both discuss and write on specific public policy issues as aforementioned (Young, 2012; Healy & Mulholland, 2007). The discussion and policy papers, once cleared by the Cabinet, are tabled in Parliament. Government and political parties may also call for policy submissions as part of public consultation.

Similar to the media release practitioners can also use the same techniques for a Ministerial briefing note. This document is short in length and informs the decision maker on an issue. There are also briefing papers that are lengthier. These documents are mainly used in government departments between managers, senior officials, and ministers (Healy & Mulholland, 2007). Good characteristics include clear and concise points and purpose. The briefing must be accurate, factual, and logical. It can also be presented with background on how a situation arose and previous decisions. Actions are presented as a brief summary of the history of the topic. Current situation might include who is involved and what is happening now, key considerations are presented as a summary of the facts substantiated by any evidence. Appendices can be added if needed. Options are concise with descriptions of their pros and cons of what will happen next and a conclusion and/or recommendations that should not introduce anything new, but cover the points you most want the reader to be clear about (Wu, Ramesh, Howlett, & Fritzen, 2010; Bacchi, 2009).

Bacchi's (2009) framework for policy analysis

Analysing existing policy and identifying strengths and weaknesses opens opportunities to then advocate for change. This may seem daunting; however, many policy analysis frameworks exist. In our discussion, we have referred to Bacchi's (2009) stepped framework throughout. Bacchi (2009, p. xii) offers a six-step process that asks us to first identify the 'problem' and how it is represented within a policy, scrutinise any assumptions and/or values underpinning how the 'problem' is represented, and explore how this particular 'problem' representation has emerged. From there, we can then discover what might have been ignored within the 'problem' representation (for example, whose voice is 'silenced' and how could we think differently about the 'problem'). We then need to consider potential effects arising from the representation of the 'problem'. Finally, we need to consider 'How/where has this representation of the 'problem' been produced, disseminated, and defended? How could it be questioned, disrupted, and replaced?' (Bacchi, 2009, p. xii). Bacchi's (2009) framework is used widely within various university settings and provides students and practitioners alike with a line of questioning for interrogating policy. We have interwoven threads of Bacchi's work throughout to provide context around how the framework highlights key areas within a policy that might otherwise be overlooked or left unproblematised.

Conclusion

Whilst we acknowledge that this chapter has not addressed every single policy, it is the beginning of a discussion. Further work needs to be done in linking policy and its ramifications to social work practice, particularly with First Australian peoples. This chapter has used two of the more prominent contemporary policies to highlight how policy continues to problematise and stereotype First Australian peoples. It is our hope that, in reading this, social workers begin to be more critically reflexive and aware of the implications of the policies and procedures they and the organisations they work for are complicit to. For the status to change for us, we need social workers to be more powerful advocates in the policy space.

Discussion Questions

1. How does historical policy link to contemporary policies?

2. How do social workers look for underlying government agendas in policy?

3. How can social workers contribute to (and force) policy changes in Australia?

4. Can you find any policies currently in Australia that may be deficit focused? How do you know?

References

Althaus, C., Bridgman, P., & Davis, G. (2017). *The Australian policy handbook* (6th ed.). Crows Nest, NSW: Allen and Unwin Book Publishers.

Altman, J. (2012). Tracking Indigenous policy 2011–2014. *Journal of Indigenous Policy, 15,* 77–82. Retrieved from https://www.uts.edu.au/sites/default/files/article/downloads/JIP_15_2014.pdf

Altman, J. (2013). Arguing the intervention. *Journal of Indigenous Policy, 14,* 1–156.

Altman, J., & Klein, E. (2017). Lessons from a basic income Programme for Indigenous Australians. *Oxford Development Studies.* doi: https://doi.org/10.1080/13600818.2017.1329413.

Appleby, G. (2015, June 12). Constitutionalising an Indigenous voice in Australian law making: Some institutional design challenges. *Symposium on Indigenous Recognition* (pp. 1–17). Sydney Law School. Retrieved from https://www.sydney.edu.au/content/dam/corporate/documents/sydney-law-school/research/centres-institutes/CRU-Conf-Indigenous-Recognition-Appleby.pdf

Askew, D., Brady, K., Mukandi, B., Singh, D., Sinha, T., Brough, M., & Bond, C. (2020). Closing the gap between rhetoric and practice in strengths-based approaches to Indigenous public health: A qualitative study. *Australian and New Zealand Journal of Public Health, 44*(2), 102–105. Retrieved from https://onlinelibrary.wiley.com/doi/pdf/10.1111/1753-6405.12953

Australian Broadcasting Commission. (2015). *7.30 report with Leigh Sales, PM'S lifestyle choice comments wrong but highlight important debate, says chief adviser,* Wed 11 March. Retrieved from https://www.abc.net.au/7.30/pms-lifestyle-choice-comments-wrong-but-highlight/6304964?nw=0

AHRC. *See* Australian Human Rights Commission.

Australian Human Rights Commission. (n.d.). *The suspension and rein-statement of the RDA and special measures in the NTER.* Retrieved from https://humanrights.gov.au/our-work/suspension-and-reinstatement-rda-and-special-measures-nter-0

Australian Human Rights Commission. (2017). *Report of The Special Rapporteur on the rights of indigenous peoples on her visit to Australia* (36th session) (pp. 1–21). United Nations General Assembly.

Australian Law Reform Commission (ALRC). (2010). *Changing policies towards Aboriginal people.* Retrieved from https://www.alrc.gov.au/publication/recognition-of-aboriginal-customary-laws-alrc-report-31/3-aboriginal-societies-the-experience-of-contact/changing-policies-towards-aboriginal-people/

Australian National Audit Office (ANAO). (2019). *Closing the gap, performance audit report.* Retrieved https://www.anao.gov.au/work/performance-audit/closing-the-gap

Bacchi, C. (2009). *Analysing policy: What's the problem represented to be?* Frenchs Forest: NSW: Pearson.

Bessant, J., Watts, R., Dalton, T., & Smyth, P. (2006). *Talking policy: How social policy is made.* Crows Nest, NSW: Allen & Unwin.

Bennett, S. (1999). *White politics and Black Australians*. St. Leonards, NSW: Allen & Unwin.

Bielefeld, S. (2017). The intervention, stronger futures and racial discrimination: Placing the Australian Government under scrutiny. In E. Baehr & Schmidt-Haberkamp (Eds.), *And there'll be no dancing. Perspectives on policies impacting Indigenous Australia since 2007* (9th ed., pp. 145–166). Cambridge: Scholars Publishing.

Brenner, C. (2018). *How to write a press release in 2020* (+7 Press Release Format Examples). Learning Hub. Retrieved from https://learn.g2.com/how-to-write-a-press-release

Briese, J., & Menzel, K. (2020). No more 'Blacks in the Back': Adding more than a splash of black into social work education and practice by drawing on the works of Aileen Moreton-Robinson and others who contribute to Indigenous Standpoint Theory. In C. Morley, P. Ablett, C. Noble, & S. Cowden (Eds.), *The Routledge handbook of critical pedagogies for social work* (pp. 375–87). Abingdon: Routledge.

Carson, E., & Kerr, L. (2017). *Australian social policy and the human services* (2nd ed.). Cambridge: Cambridge University Press.

Davidson, H. (2014, September 22). John Howard: There was no genocide against Indigenous Australians. *The Guardian*. Retrieved from https://www.theguardian.com/world/2014/sep/22/john-howard-there-was-no-genocide-against-indigenous-australians

Davidson, P., Saunders, P., Bradbury, B., & Wong, M. (2018). *Poverty in Australia, 2018* (ACOSS/UNSW Poverty and Inequality Partnership Report No. 2). Sydney, NSW: ACOSS.

DPMC. *See* Department of Prime Minister and Cabinet.

Department of Prime Minister and Cabinet. (2013). *Cabinet implementation unit toolkit, engaging stakeholders*. Australian Government. Retrieved from https://www.pmc.gov.au/sites/default/files/files/pmc/implementation-toolkit-3-engaging-stakeholders.pdf

Dodson, P. (2018). Constitutional recognition. *International Journal of Applied Science, 15*, 124–127.

Dow, C., & Gardiner-Garden, J. (2011). *Overview of Indigenous Affairs; Part 1: 1901 to 1991*. Parliament of Australia. Retrieved from https://www.aph.gov.au/about_parliament/parliamentary_departments/parliamentary_library/pubs/bn/1011/indigenousaffairs1

Equality before the Law Bench Book (EQBB). (2020). *Equality before the law and discrimination*. Judicial Commission of New South Wales 2020. Retrieved from https://www.judcom.nsw.gov.au/publications/benchbks/equality/currency.html#EQBB_16

Fogarty, W., Bulloch, H., McDonnell, S., & Davis, M. (2018). *Deficit discourse and Indigenous health: How narrative framings of Aboriginal and Torres Strait Islander people are reproduced in policy*. Melbourne, VIC: The Lowitja Institute.

Greens. (2016). *Report finds NT intervention to Close the Gap and meet international human rights obligations*. https://greens.org.au/wa/news/media-release/report-finds-nt-intervention-failed-close-gap-and-meet-international-human

Healy, K. D., & Mulholland, J. D. (2007). *Writing skills for social workers* (pp. 173–188). SAGE Publications PDF. Retrieved from http://ebookcentral.proquest.com

Hollinsworth, D. (2006). *Race and racism* (3rd ed.). South Melbourne, VIC: Cengage Learning.

Howard-Wagner, D., Bargh, M., & Altamirano-Jimenez, I. (2018). *The neoliberal state, recognition and Indigenous rights, new paternalism and new imaginings.* Centre for Aboriginal Economic Policy Research, Australian National University Monograph No. 40, Canberra.

Howard, J. (2007). To stabilise and protect: Little children are sacred. *The Sydney Papers, 19*(Winter 3), 68–76. Retrieved from https://search.informit.com.au/documentSummary;dn=018440362568649;res=IELHSS

HREOC. *See* Human Rights and Equal Opportunities Commission.

Human Rights and Equal Opportunities Commission (HREOC). (1997). *Bringing them home: National inquiry into the separation of Aboriginal and Torres Strait Islander children from their families.* Australian Government, Canberra, Australian Capital Territory.

Human Rights Law Centre (HRLC). (2017). *Why Aboriginal Australians are still having their wages 'stolen' 50 years after the Wave Hill Walk-off.* November 30. Retrieved from https://www.hrlc.org.au/opinion/2017/11/30/why-aboriginal-australians-are-still-having-their-wages-stolen

Hunt, J. (2013). *Engaging with Indigenous Australia- exploring the conditions for effective relationships with Aboriginal and Torres Strait Islander communities* (Issues Paper 5) (pp. 1–53). Closing the Gap Clearinghouse. Australian Institute of Health and Welfare. Retrieved from https://www.aihw.gov.au/getmedia/7d54eac8-4c95-4de1-91bb-0d6b1cf348e2/ctgc-ip05.pdf.aspx?inline=true

Ife, J. (2016). *Community development in an uncertain world.* Cambridge: Cambridge University Press.

Implementation Plan for the National Aboriginal and Torres Strait Islander Health Plan 2013–2023. (2013). *Commonwealth of Australia.* Retrieved from https://www1.health.gov.au/internet/main/publishing.nsf/Content/AC51639D3C8CD4ECCA257E8B00007AC5/$File/DOH_ImplementationPlan_v3.pdf

Jamrozik, A. (2005). *Social policy in the post-welfare state* (2nd ed., pp. 304–310). Frenchs Forest, NSW: Pearson Education.

Lewis, J. M. (2014). Health policy in Australia change and continuity. In A. McClelland & P. Smyth (Eds.), *Social policy in Australia understanding for action* (4th ed., pp. 190–203). South Melbourne, VIC: Open University Press.

Markwick, A., Ansari, Z., Clinch, D., & McNeil, J. (2019). Experiences of racism among Aboriginal and Torres Strait Islander adults living in the Australian state of Victoria: A cross-sectional population-based study. *BMC Public Health, 19*(309), 1–14. doi: https://doi.org/10.1186/s12889-019-6614-7.

Mendes, P. (2008). Leading the backlash: The neoliberal critique of the welfare state. In *Australia's welfare wars revisited* (pp. 42–65). Sydney, NSW: UNSW.

Mishra, R. (1999). The logic of globalization: The changing context of the welfare state. In *Globalisation and the welfare state* (pp. 1–16). Cheltenham: Edward Elgar.

Moreton-Robinson, A. (Ed.). (2004). *Whitening race: Essays in social and cultural criticism*. Canberra, ACT: Aboriginal Studies Press.

Morrison, S. (2020). *Prime Minster Australia, address, closing the gap statement to parliament*. Canberra, ACT: Parliament House. Retrieved from https://www.pm.gov.au/media/address-closing-gap-statement-parliament

NACCHO. *See* National Aboriginal Community Controlled Health Organisation.

NATSIHIP. *See* National Aboriginal and Torres Strait Islander Health Plan.

National Aboriginal Community Controlled Health Organisation (NACCHO). (2018). *Close The Gap Reflections – 10 years on*. Retrieved from https://www.naccho.org.au/close-the-gap-reflections/

National Aboriginal and Torres Strait Islander Health Plan 2013–2023 (NATSIHP). (2013). *Commonwealth of Australia*. Retrieved from https://www1.health.gov.au/internet/main/publishing.nsf/content/B92E980680486C3BCA257BF0001BAF01/$File/health-plan.pdf

Newman, J. (2017). Deconstructing the debate over evidence-based policy. *Critical Policy Studies, 11*(2), 211–26. Retrieved from https://www.tandfonline.com/loi/rcps20

Northern Territory Emergency Response Taskforce. (2008). *Final report to Government Canberra: Department of Families, Housing, Community Services and Indigenous Affairs at 1 July 2010*. Retrieved from https://www.dss.gov.au/sites/default/files/documents/05_2012/nter_taskforce_report.pdf

Paradies, Y. (2006). A systematic review of empirical research on self-reported racism and health. *International Journal of Epidemiology, 35*, 888–901. Retrieved from https://doi.org/10.1093/ije/dyl056

Paradies, Y. (2014). *Racism as a determinant of indigenous health and wellbeing*. Retrieved from http://www.sanyas.ca/downloads/racism-as-a-determinant-of-indigenous-health-and-wellbeing.pdf

Peters, A. (2017). *Moondani Yulenj, an examination of Aboriginal culture, identity and education artefact and exegesis*. Doctoral dissertation. Retrieved from https://researchbank.swinburne.edu.au/file/da96e93e-1731-4a09-86e1-4c2cea5cd665/1/Andrew%20John%20Peters%20Thesis%20pdfa.pdf

Pholi, K., Black, D., & Richards, C. (2009). Is close the Gap a useful approach to improving the health and wellbeing of Indigenous Australians? *Australian Review of Public Affairs, 9*(2), 1–14.

Productivity Commission. (2012). *Steering Committee for the review of government service provision, Report on government services 2012*. Melbourne, VIC: Productivity Commission.

Productivity Commission. (2015). *National Indigenous Reform Agreement: Performance Assessment 2013–14*. Canberra, ACT: Australian Government. Retrieved from http://www.pc.gov.au/research/supporting/indigenous-reform-assessment/indigenous-reform-assessment.pdf

Said, E. W. (1978). *Orientalism*. New York, NY: Random House.

The Lowitja Institute. (2019). *Understanding disability through the lens of Aboriginal and/or Torres Strait Islander people – challenges and opportunities*.

Australia's National Institute for Aboriginal and Torres Strait Islander Health Research Policy Brief October 2019 (PDF). Victoria, Australia.

United Nations Human Rights Office of the High Commissioner (UNHRC). (2020). *Submission of information to the special procedures.* Retrieved from https://spsubmission.ohchr.org/

Wild, R., & Anderson, P. (2007). *Ampe Akelyernemane Meke Mekarle: Little children are sacred. Report of the Northern Territory Board of Inquiry into the Protection of Aboriginal Children from Sexual Abuse.* Darwin, NT: Human Rights. Retrieved from https://humanrights.gov.au/sites/default/files/57.4%20 %E2%80%9CLittle%20Children%20are%20Sacred%E2%80%9D%20 report.pdf

Williams, C. (2000). "Reinventing" the welfare state: Neo-liberalism and beyond. In A. McMahon, J. Thomson, & C. Williams (Eds.), *Understanding the Australian Welfare State: Key documents and themes* (pp. 248–256). Croyden, VIC: Macmillan.

Wu, X., Ramesh, M., Howlett, M., & Fritzen, S. A. (2010). *Policy formulation.* London: Routledge.

Young, J. (2012). *Approaches for community decision making and collective reasoning: Knowledge technology support.* Sydney, NSW: IGI Global.

15 Aboriginal Activism and Embodying Activism in Social Work

Jessica Russ-Smith and Amelia Wheeler

Introduction

Diverse standpoints, dialogues, and enactments of activism regarding Aboriginal sovereignty and rights have existed (and continue to exist) across Australia. This chapter does not aim to describe or analyse these diverse ways of knowing, being, and doing activism; rather, it aims to learn from these diverse ways to engage with a critical discussion into what these actions of strength and power can teach social work practice.

As authors, we continue to be guided by the Ancestors, Elders, and leaders around us. These learnings continue to be significant in transforming our practice to embody a critical and decolonising approach in our ways of knowing, being, and doing. We honour and acknowledge that we stand on the shoulders of giants and aim to enact this honour through this chapter as a space of reflection and learning from Aboriginal activism. Furthermore, as an Indigenous and a non-Indigenous/white social worker, we acknowledge the importance and power of our relationship in our profession to embody and live decolonising and critical ways of practice. As such, we see our role as learners and listeners to and of sovereign action and hold a responsibility to reflect critically upon how these lessons can transform social work practice in its fight for social justice. We want to make the everyday actions of Aboriginal activism visible and celebrate them in a way that centres the power and honours the legacy of Aboriginal activists and the sovereignty of the land we work upon as social workers. Within this chapter and discussions of Aboriginal activism, we privilege and are guided by Aboriginal understandings of sovereignty and we call upon social workers, especially white social workers, to reflect critically on how they view Aboriginal sovereignty and therefore how they perceive Aboriginal activism.

Initially, we proposed to look at the criminalisation and demonisation of dominant Aboriginal activism spaces and practices. As we reflected within the writing process, concerns emerged about how this exploration could be problematic as it may feed classification systems of what activism is and is not, and what it looks like, or should look like. This discussion can keep activism in the 'out there' space as it frames it as a radical act, but we believe as social workers we are activists and need to draw attention to how we enact and embody activism in our practice. Therefore, this chapter is about stepping back and looking critically at activism and social change in social work and what this means, rather than what it can or should *look like*.

In this chapter, we discuss how Aboriginal activism demonstrates the ways in which justice is about both process and outcome. The process is the doing of activism, and this is important for us as social workers. Furthermore, we consider the importance of reconceptualising activism in social work and how we can learn from Aboriginal activism, knowing, being, and doing as to how we can embody this activism.

Aboriginal activism: Refusal, resistance, and sovereignty

Aboriginal activism has existed and continues to exist across various times and spaces in Australia. From a strong tradition of public marches, protest, and industrial action (see Scrimgeour, 2012), Aboriginal activists stand firm in power, resistance, and sovereignty. Ginsburg and Myers (2006, p. 31) frame Aboriginal policy activism from the 1960s onwards as being organised around three key themes:

(1) the lack of recognition of Aboriginal land rights;
(2) the limitation of Aboriginal civil rights; and
(3) the practice of removing 'part-Aboriginal' children for their imagined improvement.

From the 1965 Freedom Rides to present-day grassroots movements such as Grandmothers Against Removals (GMAR) and protests that often combine public gatherings and social media campaigns, these forms of activism can be seen as 'ritualised, embod[ied] display[s] [which] stand as a form of evidentiary truth' (Ginsburg & Myers, 2006, p. 32). These activist movements build and continually engage strong relational networks of both Aboriginal and non-Aboriginal people (see Petray, 2010). Tent embassies, such as the Aboriginal Tent Embassy (established in 1972) and the Nyoongar Tent Embassy (established in 2012), exist as 'spatial intervention[s] and assertion[s] of sovereignty, claiming space and disrupting the settler state's reconciliation narrative' (Cox & Jones, 2018, p. 363).

Walter's (2010) account of Aboriginal activism emerging from the mid-1990s onwards is a powerful example of sovereign expression and resistance to the neoliberal nation-state. Walter sees the initial act of 100 Indigenous leaders standing and turning their backs on then Prime Minister John Howard as he addressed the 1997 Australian Reconciliation Council as marking a new phase in resistance: 'one where Indigenous people were confident enough to meet disrespect with disrespect' (Walter, 2010, p. 124):

> We are no longer as naïve or as willing to believe in incremental or evolutionary change, or that good intentions are enough, or that being patient will work in our best interests. Surviving has also led to new ways of seeing things, less orthodoxy, more voices, less trust, and more determination. Neither are we willing to go back to the way it was. (Walter, 2010, p. 135)

Aboriginal activists continue to challenge the neoliberal notion that equity between Aboriginal and non-Aboriginal people has been achieved. The neoliberal state ignores history and frames attendance to the rights of Aboriginal people as 'special treatment that is inequitable and unethical' (Weaver, 2016, p. 133). This connects with Western approaches to sovereignty, which are further explored and critiqued below. The continued presence of Aboriginal people, despite centuries of attempts by the state and its actors to exterminate them, can in and of itself be seen as an act of resistance and a strong statement of sovereignty.

Yet resistance is found not only in these spaces conceived as traditionally 'activist'. Aboriginal scholars and academics embody activism in their writing, teaching, and multidimensional contributions across many spaces. Aboriginal Elders embody activism in the community and relationships with others. Aboriginal people embody activism in their survival. Aboriginal activism is a dynamic, living being of sovereignty and resistance, which is acted and enacted across time and space.

When we see activism through Aboriginal ways of knowing, being, and doing, we see that activism *is* the embodied, everyday, lived experience of Aboriginal people in connection to Country, through which sovereignty is seen, felt, and heard (Russ-Smith, 2019b, p. 239). Aboriginal activism, whilst existing and acting in diverse ways, shares a commonality of resistance to colonial power. This is Aboriginal activism beyond the gaze of whiteness, which can frame activism as 'authentic' only when overt or performative in expression. This whiteness lens can demand Aboriginal performativity, while at the same time criminalising those who engage in it. Aboriginal activism disrupts the myth of white superiority and demonstrates sovereignty and therefore activism in dynamic and multifaceted ways. This is activism as both process *and* outcome, as relational, and as a refusal to be subject to white sovereignty.

Sovereignty *as* activism

Core to Aboriginal activism in Australia is the active refusal and resistance to white sovereignty and the celebration and embodiment of Aboriginal sovereignty. We begin this section by examining the difference between white sovereignty and Aboriginal sovereignty, as 'understandings of sovereignty encompass epistemological and ontological views of ownership, land and power' (Russ-Smith, 2019a, p. 106), and are thus relevant to all discussions on activism and social justice. White understandings of sovereignty reflect white possessive logics that relate to ideas of ownership and authority over land and people (Moreton-Robinson, 2015; Russ-Smith, 2019a). White sovereignty justifies its power through narratives of terra nullius and white superiority:

> The nation-state's legitimacy is based on the legal assumption that its claim to sovereignty is necessarily superior, stronger, and deeper than any assertions of Indigenous people because underlying title – the real 'bedrock' title – belongs to the Crown. (Mackey, 2016, p. 10)

In contrast to these possessive logics, Aboriginal sovereignty grounds itself in relationship with Country, emphasising deep respect for all living and non-living things, and deep care for future generations (Russ-Smith, 2019a; Moreton-Robinson, 2015). Within this chapter and discussions of Aboriginal activism, we privilege and are guided by Aboriginal understandings of sovereignty and we call upon social workers, especially white social workers, to critically reflect on how they view Aboriginal sovereignty, and therefore how they perceive Aboriginal activism. This is important as debates and dialogues regarding sovereignty predominantly frame sovereignty as a legal matter linked to the power of nation-states:

> One obstacle in the debate has been confusion that surrounds the use of the word 'sovereignty'. It is a term that has become a catch-phrase for Indigenous people in expressing their vision for the future but a phrase that is met with confusion and suspicion from non-Indigenous people who understand the word only in its context under international law. They see the claim as radical, subversive, and dangerous and they therefore strongly oppose it. (Behrendt, 2003, pp. 94–95)

In contrast, sovereignty has been widely adopted within Aboriginal activists' dialogues and debates as it reflects a powerful, political, social, and cultural symbol of resistance and refusal to colonialism. Sovereignty was never ceded and is not an object to obtain or own; rather, it is a movement, symbol, and cultural power that has always existed for Aboriginal peoples. Sovereignty is embodied in the everyday, in the knowing, being, and doing of Aboriginal peoples and culture (Russ-Smith, 2019b). Therefore, activism and sovereignty exist within a relationship that expands beyond time and space, across the past, present, and future.

We need to look at activism and sovereignty through Aboriginal ways of knowing, being, and doing. This means understanding white possessive logics and how we need to decolonise constructions of activism and reconstruct these in ways that respect and pay tribute to Aboriginal ways of knowing, being, and doing:

> *Furthermore, framing Indigenous sovereignty within colonial systems, such as [Western] law, is in fact contradictory to our sovereignty. Sovereign ways of knowing and being are key in shifting colonial discourse and power from law to lore.* (Russ-Smith, 2019b, pp. 238–239)

Aboriginal sovereignty and the embodiment of sovereignty are grounded within Country:

> Country is not just a place or space that holds meaning. Country is our sovereignty. Country is a 'field of self' (Elsey, 2013, p. 58). It is past, present, future, life, death, story, dreaming, all at once. Country existed long before, and will exist long after, the duration of our human lifespan. It is greater than us, it is our anchor to all things, then, now and always. When we look and listen to Country, we see and hear sovereignty. (Russ-Smith, 2019b, p. 239)

Aboriginal sovereignty is *always* in relationship to Country, and this is embodied by Aboriginal activists. The expression of Aboriginal sovereignty in activist spaces is also multifaceted. Behrendt (2003, p. 99) draws upon Kerry Reed-Gilbert's vision of sovereignty as 'a *starting point* for recognition of rights and inclusion in democratic processes.' This views sovereignty not only as the goal of Aboriginal activism, but as the very point from which activism begins. Therefore, Aboriginal activism is an embodiment of sovereignty as it is asserted in and through various day-to-day actions, in personal, cultural, and political spaces (Behrendt, 2003, pp. 100–101). Aboriginal activism is thus an act *of* sovereignty, as well as guided *by* sovereignty. Activism is *for* sovereignty, and activism *is* sovereignty.

Refusal and resistance *as* activism

As Aboriginal sovereignty is embodied and expressed in many ways within Aboriginal activism, the embodiment of refusal and resistance must also be explored. Refusal and resistance to colonial power *is* activism, and this refusal *is* sovereignty. Refusal and resistance, especially in the face of colonisation, oppression, genocide, and systemic racism, strongly and powerfully declare that Aboriginal sovereignty and culture is here and will not be erased (Behrendt, 2003; Foster, 2000). Central to these processes of refusal and resistance is Aboriginal peoples' survival. Survivance in the face of colonisation is itself resistance and therefore *is* activism. By simply surviving Aboriginal people represent a weapon of refusal and resistance (Goodyear-Ka'opua, 2017, p. 187), as 'survivance is not just survival but also resistance' to colonial domination (Vizenor, 1999, p. 93 as cited in Tuck & McKenzie, 2015, p. 129). Survivance is the resistance of Aboriginal people and their refusal to be erased by colonialism and whiteness (Cox & Jones, 2018), as their mere existence creates a tension within colonial societal norms, destabilising the power of those norms to silence Aboriginal sovereignty (Wood & Rossiter, 2017, p. 168).

Survivance does not just relate to Aboriginal people existing but additionally embodies the survivance of language and story. Through language and story, Aboriginal sovereignty continues (Russ-Smith, 2019b). Here, the embodiment of sovereignty by Aboriginal people weaves together to reflect the diverse and endless ways Aboriginal activism exists across time and space. Through the embodiment of sovereignty, especially story, 'Indigenous peoples resist colonial erasure and violence, living out the stories of the ancestors in ways that sustain, resist, and create anew' (Sium & Ritskes, 2013, p. VI). Moreover, Aboriginal survivance and the continuation of lore and the role of Elders in the community is an act of activism as the importance of storytellers continues to thrive in Aboriginal communities. Story and storytelling are foundational to Aboriginal sovereignty, and they are simultaneously embodying activism in their existence and their actions:

> Storytellers have never been silent in the face of colonial violence that subverted and neutralized various other forms of resistance; the storytellers and griots have never been idle, working through participatory mediums to maintain and sustain Indigenous ways of being and living. Here, the role of the storyteller is central to the exercise of agency and renewal. (Sium & Ritskes, 2013, p. v)

Furthermore, survival and activism relate to resistance and refusal of Western/white ways within other spaces, such as academic institutions and universities. This is evidenced by the various publications, courses, teachings, and programs by Indigenous peoples regarding Indigenous methodologies, Indigenous research, and Indigenous knowledges (Tuck & Yang, 2012; Tuck & Gaztambide-Fernandez, 2013; Smith, 2012) that continue to emerge.

Aboriginal survivance, refusal, and resistance *are* activism, as they are ways Aboriginal people assert their sovereignty:

> Refusal turns the gaze back upon power, specifically the colonial modalities of knowing persons as bodies to be differentially counted, violated, saved, and put to work. It makes transparent the metanarrative of knowledge production—its spectatorship for pain and its preoccupation for documenting and ruling over racial difference. Refusal generates, expands, champions representational territories that colonial knowledge endeavours to settle, enclose, domesticate. (Tuck and Yang, 2014, p. 817)

Aboriginal activism, sovereignty, resistance, and refusal provide invaluable teachings for social work practice. We now apply these learnings through a discussion and reconceptualisation of the meaning of activism in social work practice.

Reconceptualising activism in social work

Current constructions of activism within social work vary greatly from previous discussions of Aboriginal activism. We believe there is a need for the reconceptualisation of activism in social work that is informed by Aboriginal activism and social work values. We propose a shift to embodying activism within social work practice. This transformation requires a critical exploration of how activism is constructed and used/not used in practice. Historically and internationally, social work has actively engaged in social movements (Jeyapal, 2017). However, in Australia engagement in social and activist movements by social workers can align strongly with the white status quo, in that issues that reflect covert activism often align with some causes more than others, for example, women's rights in comparison to Aboriginal rights.

The Australian Association of Social Workers (AASW) Code of Ethics (2010) does not mention 'activism' or 'activist'. The code of ethics highlights the role of advocacy as a core aspect of social work practice (AASW, 2010); however, it often refers to advocacy in relation to individual working relationships. The code of ethics (AASW, 2010) generally presents the role of core values and ethics concerning individual and micro settings of social work practice. This creates a dissonance with one of the core values: social justice. Regarding social justice and social change, the profession 'promotes justice and social fairness, by acting to reduce barriers and to expand choice and potential for all persons, with special regard for those who are disadvantaged, vulnerable, oppressed or have exceptional needs' (AASW, 2010, p. 13). Whilst such values and commitments are articulated within the code of ethics (AASW, 2010), the ongoing integration and upholding of these values of social change and justice in practice face diverse challenges within organisations and agencies.

Managerial and neoliberal approaches dominate practice spaces, inundating social workers with bureaucratic processes, auditing, paperwork, the management of risk, and an emphasis on indicators. This has been met with the accompanying loss of critical activist social workers (Morley, 2016, p. 54; Greenslade, McAuliffe, & Chenoweth, 2015, p. 423). Furthermore, fear has played a key role in the minimisation and loss of activism in social work practice. This fear relates to concerns of repercussions of enacting 'overt' activism in the workplace, for example, reprisal from organisations and agencies (Gair, 2017; Greenslade et al., 2015). In response to these fears, Greenslade et al. (2015) found that social workers employed in statutory settings adopted 'covert' forms of activism within their practice:

> Not content to accept the loss of the social work role, nor inclined to give up and resign, participants instead found ways to push back against the system and in doing so challenge the underlying ideology of contemporary practice. They believed in the aims and values of the social work role and despite the fractures at the frontier, they remained committed to what they believe delivering on the job of social work was supposed to be about. (Greenslade et al., 2015, p. 427)

Moreover, a similar adaptation of covert activism is argued by Gair (2017) in a study regarding social work students' perceptions and challenges of activism in practice:

> An increased emphasis on quieter, micro, everyday resistance and small, accessible acts of 'doing activism' rather than 'being [an] activist' seems relevant to these findings and future social work education and practice. (Gair, 2017, p. 173)

Whilst these adaptations to covert activism in practice highlight social worker's commitments to upholding ethics and values, they simultaneously highlight an important issue regarding the construction of activism in the field. This construction echoes negative connotations of 'being an activist' or being perceived as 'an activist', drawing associations of radical and disruptive behaviour. This fear of being perceived in this way further perpetuates a dichotomy of covert and overt activism, which produces two key issues. Firstly, the claims of 'covert' activism can create space for practitioners to 'justify' their practice as critical and ethical. Covert actions can be difficult to assess and hold accountable as they are less visible. This creates space for arguments around intention over the impact to emerge, in effect creating a shield towards accountability, critical reflection, and the transformation of practice. Secondly, this dichotomy negatively frames overt activism as aggressive and therefore frames covert activism as a preferred way of 'being an activist' as it minimises disruption to the status quo.

This is not a critique of social work practitioners who face this dilemma: rather, it is a point from which to reflect on the privilege and power embedded within experiences and challenges of embodying critical activist social work (Jeyapal, 2017; Reisch, 2016). Critically reconceptualising activism in social work is necessary as it emphasises shifting divisive dichotomies of activism and re-grounding as a collective, which is a key lesson from Aboriginal activism. This is why a critical reconstruction of activism in social work needs to be informed by Aboriginal activism as it does not focus on fears of 'being an activist', but rather on the importance of responsibility and care to the wider community. For Aboriginal people, 'being an activist' does not demonise the actions; instead, it celebrates and demonstrates a commitment to social change and social justice, even in the face of fear.

Additionally, this dichotomy issue and shielding of covert activism are further complicated by individualist approaches to social work practice. These approaches de-centre professional commitments to social change and social justice, in effect re-emphasising dominant issues of whiteness, privilege, and power present in social work practice:

> Arguably, 'by not taking an active part in genocide or a pogrom one may claim to avoid being party to unequal treatment: however, it does nothing to promote equality' (Solas, 2008, p. 820)... The intrinsic paradox of social work practice that envisions structural issues as peripheral, rather than central, to social work ethics requires critical rethinking. (Jeyapal, 2017, p. 47)

In relation to critical activist social work, this critical rethinking aims to embody activism in practice as it relates to both process *and* outcome. It is about going above 'not doing harm' or having 'good intentions', but actively embedding activism into our individual and collective identity and practice of social work (Weaver, 2016, p. 139). In this, we are directly informed and inspired by Aboriginal activism. Generations of Aboriginal people and activists have sacrificed their lives, bodies, and wellbeing in the fight for social justice. To negate the importance of social change and to frame overt activism negatively, consciously or not, nonetheless disrespects the legacies of activists who have come before us. Hence, an embodied approach to critical activist social work is ethically, and politically, necessary.

Embodying critical activist social work

We conclude this chapter with some thoughts about what an embodied, critical activist social work approach might look like, as informed by Aboriginal activism. We offer these thoughts not as definitive ideas about what practice 'should' look like, but rather as a means to foster critical reflection and transformation of both professional and profession. Embodying critical activist social work is not a transformation that can happen in isolation, but calls for a reflective process that considers power, privilege, responsibilities, and roles, especially by non-Aboriginal and white social workers:

> Non-Aboriginal Social Workers hold a unique position in Aboriginal sovereignty. As agents of social change, you hold a responsibility to enact this duty in all aspects of social injustice, one aspect being social work pedagogy and practice within Australia. In order to respect and honour Indigenous sovereignty, you must critically reflect on your positions, locations and views of Aboriginal people, culture and sovereignty. (Russ-Smith, 2019b, p. 243)

Critical activist social work, informed by Aboriginal activism, involves a commitment to 'showing up' in every sense of this phrase. For non-Indigenous and especially white social workers, this involves a commitment to personal anti-racist work (Dominelli, 2008) and 'decolonising our minds' (see Green & Baldry, 2008). This is a lifelong journey in which we continually commit and recommit to deconstructing systems of oppression, and where we hold ourselves accountable for both our intentions and our impact. 'Showing up' also entails a commitment to consistent, meaningful engagement with the causes and concerns of Aboriginal people across various spaces. 'Showing up' looks like an active resistance to dominant deficit-saturated discourses so often directed towards Aboriginal people and communities. Being able to integrate our profession's values and commitments necessitates an attendance to personal integrity and the development of a social and moral conscience (Hugman & Carter, 2016, p. 218). Aboriginal activism teaches us the importance of practice *as* ethics, where our ways of being, knowing, and doing are aligned.

From Aboriginal activism, we learn the importance of our individual and collective responsibilities to actively advocate for social change and social justice. Moreover, Aboriginal activism teaches us the importance of embodying these values and ethics in all aspects of life. Activism takes place in 'the personal and social domains; work places, political areas; economy; and interpersonal interactions' (Dominelli, 2008, p. 221), highlighting the vast ways and spaces we can embark on our commitment to social change and social justice. As opposed to conceptualising activism as overt or covert, Aboriginal activism emphasises activism as a *way of being*. Therefore, embodying critical activist social work is a way of being that embeds activism into all aspects of practice.

Critical activist social work acknowledges that process and outcome exist in a relationship and are of equal importance in the pursuit of social justice (Dominelli, 2008; Fook, 2016), and this understanding is embedded in practice. Critical activist social work requires critical consciousness, a consistent act of critical self-reflection that examines the self and society (Gair, 2017), and how these interplay in relation to social justice. Aboriginal activism, ways of being, knowing, and doing value the importance and care of the collective and the community, alongside the importance of each member. An embodiment of activism in social work celebrates the diverse spaces we practice within. We are individual workers who have a variety of strengths and exist in a variety of spaces, and therefore have a variety of opportunities to embody activism. However, we are also part of a collective community that shares a commitment to the pursuit of social justice and therefore our activism must extend beyond our organisational and agency contexts. Russ-Smith (2019b) argues for this activism in relation to Country:

> Your advocacy must go beyond speaking on behalf of Aboriginal people, to creating space for this voice to speak for itself. You need to advocate for Country informed social work practices, and resist generalised culturally competent frameworks attached to practice. In the way you advocate for children's rights or women's rights, you must advocate for the rights of Country, for sovereignty. This is not to say that we are unable to specialise or focus our capacities on our passions, but rather a reminder that to enact our values of respect, justice and integrity is to embody these against all systems of oppression. (Russ-Smith, 2019b, p. 243)

Aboriginal activism teaches us to ground our ways of being, knowing, and doing in relation to the rights and social justice of the collective and individuals. Aboriginal activism embodies solidarity and care in its diverse ways of enacting activism. Within social work practice, Banks (2012, p. 154) refers to collaborative collective action between the social worker and client as 'a more radical version of empowerment', as it emerges from a space of community to collaboratively challenge systems of injustice. Furthermore, this collective movement aids the embodiment of activism as it creates a sense of community that shares a common purpose for social justice. This sense of solidarity, belonging, and connection supports individual practitioners to embody activism in their various contexts, especially in the face of fear. Through this individual and collective embodiment of activism, the fight for social justice is actioned across micro and macro spaces, displaying courage and integrity in doing so (Reisch, 2016, pp. 42–43). Again, the importance of the collective is emphasised in our learnings from Aboriginal activism, as it is through community and solidarity we can ensure ethical practice that commits to social justice and social change:

> We need to remember our collective community as social workers, our collective aims, goals, and most importantly, values. We must resist neo-liberal and colonial structures of society and ensure the wellbeing of all things is prioritised. We must have unity and connection, through listening and caring. (Russ-Smith, 2019b, p. 243)

These are just some of the many ways we can embody critical activist social work within our practice. This is by no means an exhaustive list, and we invite you to consider the relationship of process and outcome again and continue this reflection in your practice.

Conclusion

Aboriginal activism, its history, present, and future, provides insightful and invaluable lessons for social work practice. Aboriginal activism fuels a sense of courage for social workers to stand strong in our values and commitments to social justice. Aboriginal activism, the survivance of Aboriginal people, sovereignty, resistance, and refusal inspires us to harness our power and positionality as political agents and embody critical activist social work in our practice. Reconceptualising and embodying critical activist social work is a part of a process that aims to shift understandings of activism and enhance commitment in practice to social justice and social change. As social workers, we are political agents who hold power, a positioning that enables us to be activists and embody activism. This involves reconceptualising our understanding of activism as a collective community of political agents who have a shared commitment to social justice, as opposed to individuals siloed in organisations or fields of practice. As a profession, we need to draw upon the knowledge and power shared by Aboriginal activism to guide and fuel us in our practice for social change and social justice. To honour these teachings, we must embody activism in all aspects of our practice.

Discussion Questions

1. How do you personally 'activism'? Does this definition differ from the ways of understanding activism discussed in this chapter?

2. In what ways do you see 'activism' as a part of social work practice?

3. In what ways can you embody activism in your field of practice or workplace?

References

Australian Association of Social Workers. (2010). *Code of Ethics*. Canberra, ACT: Australian Association of Social Workers.

Banks, S. (2012). *Ethics and values in social work*. London: Palgrave Macmillan.

Behrendt, L. (2003). *Achieving social justice: Indigenous rights and Australia's future*. Alexandria: The Federation Press.

Cox, S., & Jones, T. (2018). Native title and the politics of rejection: Beyond post-political binary of consensus and dissensus in urban Aboriginal activism. *Geographical Research, 56*(4), 358–367. doi:https://doi.org/10.1111/1745-5871.12319.

Dominelli, L. (2008). *Anti-racist social work* (3rd ed.). New York, NY: Palgrave Macmillan.

Elsey, C. J. (2013). *The poetics of land & identity among British Columbia Indigenous peoples*. Winnipeg: Fernwood Publishing.

Fook, J. (2016). *Social work: A critical approach to practice* (3rd ed.). London: Sage.

Foster, R. (2000). 'Endless trouble and agitation': Aboriginal activism in the protectionist era. *Journal of the Historical Society of South Australia, 28*, 15–27.

Gair, S. (2017). Pondering the colour of empathy: Social work students' reasoning on activism, empathy and racism. *British Journal of Social Work, 47*, 162–180.

Ginsburg, F., & Myers, F. (2006). A history of Aboriginal futures. *Critique of Anthropology, 26*(1), 27–45. doi:https://doi.org/10.1177/0308275X06061482.

Goodyear-Ka'Opua, N. (2017). Protectors of the future, not protestors of the past: Indigenous Pacific activism and Mauna a Wakea. *The South Atlantic Quarterly*, 116(1), 184–194.

Green, S., & Baldry, E. (2008). Building Indigenous Australian social work. *Australian Social Work, 61*(4), 389–402.

Greenslade, L., McAuliffe, D., & Chenoweth, L. (2015). Social workers' experiences of covert workplace activism. *Australian Social Work, 68*(4), 422–437. doi: https://doi.org/10.1080/0312407X.2014.940360.

Hugman, R., & Carter, J. (2016). Rethinking values and ethics in social work: The way forward. In R. Hugman & J. Carter (Eds.), *Rethinking values and ethics in social work* (pp. 210–224). London: Palgrave Macmillan.

Jeyapal, D. (2017). The evolving politics of race and social work activism: A call across borders. *Social Work, 62*(1), 45–52.

Mackey, E. (2016). *Unsettled expectations: Uncertainty, land and settler decolonization*. Nova Scotia: Fernwood Publishing.

Moreton-Robinson, A. (2015). *White possessive logic, property and Indigenous sovereignty*. Minneapolis, MN/London: University of Minnesota Press.

Morley, C. (2016). Promoting activism through critical social work education: The impact of global capitalism and neoliberalism on social work and social work education. *Critical and Radical Social Work, 4*(1), 39–57.

Petray, T. (2010). 'This isn't a black issue': Homophily and diversity in Aboriginal activism. *Social Movement Studies, 9*(4), 411–424. doi: https://doi.org/10.1080/14742837.2010.522309.

Reisch, M. (2016). Social justice. In R. Hugman & J. Carter (Eds.), *Rethinking values and ethics in social work* (pp. 33–48). London: Palgrave Macmillan.

Russ-Smith, J. (2019a). Indigenous social work and a Wiradyuri framework to practice. In B. Bennett & S. Green (Eds.), *Our voices: Aboriginal social work* (2nd ed., pp. 103–116). London: Red Globe Press.

Russ-Smith, J. (2019b). Embodiment of sovereignty. In B. Bennett & S. Green (Eds.), *Our voices: Aboriginal social work* (2nd ed., pp. 238–243). London: Red Globe Press.

Scrimgeour, A. (2012). 'Battlin' for their rights': Aboriginal activism and the leper line. *Aboriginal History, 36*, 43–65.

Sium, A., & Ritskes, E. (2013). Speaking truth to power: Indigenous storytelling as an act of living resistance. *Decolonization: Indigeneity, Education and Society, 2*(1), I–X.

Smith, L. T. (2012). *Decolonizing methodologies: Research and Indigenous peoples* (2nd ed.). London: Zed Books.

Solas, J. (2008). What kind of social justice does social work seek? *International Social Work, 51*(6), 813–822.

Tuck, E., & Gaztambide-Fernandez, R. A. (2013). Curriculum, replacement and settler futurity. *Journal of Curriculum Theorizing, 29*(1), 72–89.

Tuck, E., & McKenzie, M. (2015). *Place in research: Theory methodology and methods*. New York, NY: Routledge.

Tuck, E., & Yang, K. W. (2012). Decolonization is not a metaphor. *Decolonization: Indigeneity, Education & Society, 1*(1), 1–40.

Tuck, E., & Yang, K. W. (2014). Unbecoming claims: Pedagogies of refusal in qualitative research. *Qualitative Inquiry, 20*(6), 811–818.

Walter, M. (2010). Market forces and Indigenous resistance paradigms. *Social Movement Studies, 9*(2), 121–137.

Weaver, H. (2016). Ethics and settler societies: Reflections on social work and Indigenous peoples. In R. Hugman & J. Carter (Eds.), *Rethinking values and ethics in social work* (pp. 129–145). London: Palgrave Macmillan.

Wood, P. B., & Rossiter, D. A. (2017). The politics of refusal: Aboriginal sovereignty and the Northern Gateway pipeline. *The Canadian Geographer, 61*(2), 165–177.

16 Mistakes and Misunderstandings: Why are Social Workers Still Not Getting it Right?

Bindi Bennett, Stuart McMinn, Nigel Millgate, and Claire Morse

We acknowledge the Traditional Custodians of where we work and live and we pay our respects to the Elders both past, present, and emerging. This chapter is a collaboration between an Aboriginal Kamilaroi social worker; an Aboriginal Dharug and Gubbi Gubbi social worker; an Aboriginal Karulkiylu social worker; and a non-Indigenous social worker. Two of the authors were part of an Australian Research Council (ARC) grant exploring the cultural responsiveness, understanding and practice within Australian social work. The other two writers were involved in the research as stakeholders and to added their professional and personal expertise to the project.

For stage one of the research, we surveyed and interviewed 37 Aboriginal and Torres Strait Islander stakeholders from across Australia. As a result of this survey it became clear that, despite the conscientious undertakings of the Australian Association of Social Workers (AASW) to prepare social workers to work in culturally responsive and inclusive ways, in some instances social workers were causing irrevocable harm to Aboriginal and Torres Strait Islander individuals, communities, and organisations. Despite many social workers expressing well-meaning intentions, there is a proportion of social workers that have a general unwillingness, apathy, or perhaps fear to engage effectively with cultural responsiveness. A lack of cultural knowledge regarding Aboriginal and Torres Strait Islander protocols, coupled with ignorance and an inability to foster reciprocal respectful relationships, give rise to cultural mistakes and misunderstandings that social workers find difficult to navigate. This chapter examines these issues and suggests productive improvements to the training of social workers.

Cultural responsiveness

Cultural Responsiveness is defined as the capacity of social workers to develop collaborative and respectful relationships with Aboriginal and Torres Strait Islander peoples in order to respond to their issues and needs in ways that promote social justice and uphold human rights. (Zubrzycki et al., 2014, p. 21)

As social workers, we are ethically and professionally bound to become more culturally responsive and inclusive within our practice. The AASW state: 'Social workers are responsible for ensuring that their practice is culturally responsive, safe and sensitive' (AASW, 2016, p. 1). The AASW clearly outlines the professional commitment to valuing Aboriginal and Torres Strait Islander people's valuing, 'continuing and enduring cultures which deepen and enrich the lives of our nation and communities' (AASW, 2010, p. 5). Incorporating Aboriginal ways of knowing, doing, and being into the social work curriculum has become a core component of AASW accredited programs. Social workers must make a professional commitment to acknowledging 'the strengths, capacities, abilities, and contributions that Aboriginal peoples make to wider society' (AASW, 2016, p. 1).

Downing and Kowal (2011) highlighted five predominant approaches that would inform Indigenous training in Australia, and these demand building cultural awareness, competence, respect, security, and safety. These approaches vary in two fundamental ways: (i) placing the emphasis on changing the behaviour of the individual worker as opposed to promoting more systemic behavioural change (for example, changing processes and service structures to be more considerate of cultural needs); and (ii) focusing on training workers to develop an understanding of their own culture and processes of identity as opposed to teaching them to 'understand' the culture of others. Culture is central to how all individuals and successful organisations operate. Therefore, cultural responsiveness is not just a matter of goodwill, but fundamental to the work of individuals and agencies as it implies both action and accountability in order to create better and safer practices (Stewart, 2006).

Research exploring the beliefs and attitudes of non-Aboriginal and Torres Strait Islander Australian social workers and social science graduates towards working with Aboriginal and Torres Strait Islander communities revealed that a resounding majority of those interviewed felt daunted, ill-prepared and anxious with regard to their abilities to engage with Aboriginal and Torres Strait Islander peoples in collaborative and culturally respectful ways (Bennett, Redfern, & Zubrzycki, 2017; Bennett, Zubrzycki, & Bacon, 2011). Concerningly, and coupled with this finding, non-Indigenous educators who are fundamentally responsible for embedding Aboriginal and Torres Strait Islander content and perspectives in the curriculum responded with uncertainty when asked about their abilities to be culturally responsive (Zubrzycki et al., 2014). Consequently, it is not surprising that there remains a proportion of social workers that persist with a general unwillingness, apathy, or perhaps fear in engaging effectively with cultural responsiveness. Our Aboriginal and Torres Strait Islander stakeholders, who were interviewed from across Country, echoed these concerns.

> The majority of Australians, you know, there's a lot of ignorance around. And I don't think that's anyone's fault that comes from intergenerational stuff. You only know what, you know, if your

mom tells you not to cross the road when cars are coming, you probably don't cross the road when cars are coming. Mom tells you to avoid black people, you probably avoid black people. I believe strongly this might be cliché, but there is an inherent distrust from service providers. You know you look at people around the Stolen Generation, I'm pretty sure the numbers now say that that's skyrocketed. Children are being removed more now. So obviously you've got a service provider coming to your house. There's some issues there, on the scale and magnitude of what they are. So straight away a bit of, hey, can I get your name right. Your address? Oh, we just need to take this back to the office, put it onto our servers – then the front doors shut. I get asked a lot of times, how do I build a relationship with my Aboriginal community? (Stakeholder 1)

Developing cultural responsiveness fosters healthy reciprocal respectful relationships and requires social workers to become both aware of and skilful in cross-cultural knowledge, cultural differences, and cultural humility. Developing micro-, mezzo-, and macro-cultural responsiveness skills (such as communication, critical empathy, self-reflection, and personal/professional positionality) are learning attributes that all social workers must strive for. Bennett et al. (2011) discussed the need to develop deep, respectful listening whilst respecting, understanding, and valuing Aboriginal and Torres Strait Islander peoples and the knowledge that they possess. In this way, social workers can develop trusting relationships that have both respect and authenticity (Bennett et al., 2011).

When you think about it, and I'm preaching to the choir, relationship is everything, its universal. (Stakeholder 1)

Non-Indigenous social workers are encouraged to refrain from internalising and personalising Aboriginal and Torres Strait Islander resistance or anger and instead develop cultural courage (Zubrzycki & Bennett, 2006) and to respond with humility. Bennett et al. (2011) highlighted a need for a broader understanding of the concepts of 'whiteness' and 'white privilege' (AASW, 2016, p. 7.) and the importance of making a commitment to engage in 'decolonising practices' (Bennett et al., 2011). The need for equality with our Aboriginal and Torres Strait Islander stakeholders demonstrates that it is essential for social workers to engage in an open and receptive way when working in community.

I think there has been a bit of generalisation about Aboriginal and Torres Strait Islanders and what that meant. I think just having an understanding and awareness that there is difference and there is a lot of stuff that won't be the same. You must be open to not knowing and open to being educated. Being aware and mindful that you don't know everything and that you won't know everything. You need to be there and be willing to understand and be able to take on that information and hold onto that. That is a gift in itself, having that information and knowing as well. (Stakeholder 2)

Cultural responsiveness, it's valuing someone's culture and making sure that you don't do the wrong things when you see people especially children and youth,... you have a responsibility as a non-cultural person to actually get the right values, principles, and practices in place. (Stakeholder 3)

One such cultural responsiveness action framework has been that presented by Indigenous Allied Health Australia (IAHA) (2015). Their framework comprises six capabilities divided under their respective subcategories of Aboriginal and Torres Strait Islander 'being' (attitudes and values), 'doing' (actions) and 'knowing' (skills, knowledge, and experiences) with the expected outcome. These capabilities are detailed below;

1. *Respect for centrality of culture.* This capability identifies culture at the centre of Aboriginal and Torres Strait Islander people's health, wellbeing, and prosperity.

2. *Self-awareness.* In this component, the onus is on the individual for continuous development of self-knowledge, including their personal beliefs, assumptions, values, perceptions, attitudes, and expectations. From this positionality, they need to reflect critically on how these facets may impact upon Aboriginal and Torres Strait Islander peoples moving forward. This capacity requires an individual to be self-motivated, self-directed, and self-evaluating.

3. *Proactivity.* This capacity is the ability to plan for and anticipate any adverse concerns, issues, and unanticipated fewer desirable outcomes. It involves preparing for action in advance of possible situations and aims to reduce reactionary responses with methodical and decisive decision pre-planning.

4. *Inclusive engagement.* This is about providing earnest and transparent opportunities for Aboriginal and Torres Strait Islander individuals, communities, and organisations to promote engagement in meaningful and supportive ways with social workers and their service providers.

5. *Leadership.* This capacity addresses the need for social workers to be at the forefront, to inspire, influence, and lead others when contributing to support the positive wellbeing of Aboriginal and Torres Strait Islander individuals, families, and communities.

6. *Responsibility and accountability*. This is the process of making sure that as social workers, we are owning our actions and decisions whilst being truly committed to social justice and human rights principles of our professional guidelines (IAHA, 2015).

According to Williams (2007), there are four distinct phases of cultural responsiveness.

Phase 1 is resistance and denial. This phase includes attitudes such as 'this happened a long time ago and is not relevant today', 'I wasn't here so I shouldn't be made to feel guilty or have to say sorry', and 'I treat all my clients the same'. These general and insensitive statements lessen the responsibility of the individual and minimise the impacts for Aboriginal and Torres Strait Islander peoples (Zubrzycki et al., 2014).

Phase 2 is stereotyping. These attitudes include conversations around 'real' and 'traditional' Aboriginal and Torres Strait Islander person versus 'fake' or 'non-traditional'. Often it involves individuals claiming they do not have the specialised knowledge for skills to practice in the area of Aboriginal and Torres Strait Islander people, and in this way devolve themselves of responsibility and duty of care. Sometimes stereotyping can lead to an acceptance of poor behaviour and attitudes as the cultural norm and, for this reason alone, must be challenged (Zubrzycki et al., 2014).

> I think to be culturally responsive you must have an awareness and acknowledgement of our history. Depending on where you live and work, you need to know a little bit about the people you are servicing. The people that you work with, the history of their country, the nation that you are on. This is foundational. You need to be able to sit there and look and listen rather than come in like a bull in the bloody china shop. You need to be able to sit down with our mob and listen and understand. So, for you to be culturally responsive, you need to learn and listen. I think once you can do that, you'll have an appreciation. (Stakeholder 4)

Phase 3 is glorification. This stage can lead to ideas that Aboriginal culture is exotic and lacks the recognition of how culture evolves and changes over time. It can lead to a tendency to avoid challenging or engaging with attitudes and practices that require change and development (Zubrzycki et al., 2014).

> I hear all the time 'Oh you are Aboriginal; you don't look Aboriginal.' So, you really must challenge what is Aboriginal. And what are you being sold, what are you being taught? Cause our media our school our education is all about this is what an Aboriginal person looks and acts and relates. Often you must challenge those

stereotypes and the stigma and those assumptions that are made. If you look at the east coast and then you look at the Kimberley's our mobs look very different. Everyone looks, speaks, and behaves differently. I think they are all important things to be aware of when you are working in the community. (Stakeholder 4)

Phase 4 is cultural responsiveness. Attitudes and values in this phase include a good understanding of the diversity of Aboriginal and Torres Strait Islander people. It includes acknowledgements at meetings and being aware of protocols. It shows the individual being aware of their responsibilities in self-education and continually reflecting on practice. It shows a lifelong commitment to building capacity and to being open. Significantly cultural responsiveness shows the importance of relationship building and gaining trust from Aboriginal and Torres Strait Islander peoples (Zubrzycki et al., 2014).

If you can't share a little bit about yourself and give a little bit of your journey how are you going to expect someone to share or create that safe place for people to go 'Oh this who I am and why I am here'. (Stakeholder 4)

Social workers must reflect upon each phase as it relates to their individual practice and circumstances. It is important to note that social workers should be asking themselves critically self-reflective questions: am I moving forwards or backward along the continuum of cultural responsiveness?; am I being an ally to Aboriginal and Torres Strait Islander people and, if not, why might this be?; and how can I move further along the continuum to become more culturally responsive? These processes require a social worker to articulate their knowledge, skill, and experience and become critically self-aware of their assumptions and values.

Social workers require self-awareness as well as the development of Aboriginal ways of knowing (skills, knowledge, and experiences), doing (actions), and being (attitudes and values) (Martin & Mirraboopa, 2003). They also need to encompass the core values of being a social worker, namely respect for all persons, social justice and professional integrity, as well as the AASW commitment to valuing 'the different cultural knowledge systems, unique lived experience and histories of Aboriginal and Torres Strait Islander peoples' (AASW, 2016, p. 8) which, since 2010, are the core components of AASW-accredited social work programs. Culturally responsive practice is an affirmation of diversity, valuing groups, identities, and cultures within Australia. It is being truly sensitive to other cultures, customs, beliefs, values, and behaviours (Williams, 2007) that continue and expand throughout the social worker's career.

Why might we be missing the mark within social work?

Have social workers grown tired of learning about and discussing the concepts of race and racism? It is true that once a social worker has graduated from their university course there is no professional requirement to continue to learn about issues that affect cultural responsiveness, such as racism and white privilege. And is not a core aspect of re-registration at this stage. Currently, there is no continuing education course requiring social workers to ascertain their level of cultural responsiveness and perhaps this situates social workers in a precarious position, unable to comprehend the complexity of racism and how it permeates within society and through organisations. We also believe that fatigue contributes significantly to the challenge of understanding, challenging, and changing individual and systemic racism which affects cultural responsiveness.

Fatigue

'White fatigue occurs for White students who have grown tired of learning and discussing race and racism, despite an understanding of the moral imperative of anti-racist and anti-oppressive practices' (Flynn, 2015, p. 115). White fatigue is related to, but distinct from other concepts such as white resistance (Goodman, 2011), white guilt (Tatum, 1994; Leonardo, 2004), and white fragility (DiAngelo, 2011). Unlike these concepts, white fatigue is brought about by the intellectual and emotional challenges and complexities of learning about racism. There is a specific dynamic that seems to occur when explicitly teaching racism and the structures which encourage it. For some white students, this involves stressors that arise as they attempt to shift their thinking from focusing on individual racism (i.e. prejudice and discrimination) towards understanding institutional and systemic racism, they become overwhelmed. This might also be the first time they have encountered anti-racist and multicultural educators or challenged discussions and opinions expressed in the media and popular culture. For some students, this can be confronting (Flynn, 2015).

White fatigue can be a temporary state; it can also be the imperative that causes individuals to disengage from or assume they no longer need to continue learning about how racism and/or white privilege function (Flynn, 2015). This outcome will leave individuals with a simplistic understanding of racism that is often accompanied by impatience, flippancy, sarcasm, frustration, or resignation (Flynn, 2015). White fatigue arises from the suspension of critical thinking about the complex nature of systemic and institutional racism. It can cause harm as individuals do not necessarily feel guilty about their whiteness or the role white people have played in shaping historic, institutional, and systemically racist policies and practice; this ignorance or avoidance may lead to them further damaging relationships, attitudes, and practices (Flynn, 2015).

In contrast, white guilt is associated with the negative or uncomfortable feelings that arise from initial exposure to the ill actions of previous generations and the unearned assets accumulated through racial privilege (Hitchcock, 2002). White guilt emerges from the feelings that arise when trying to come to grips with the weight and repercussions of historic events (which can involve the student's ancestors), and the crippling feeling that one has no idea of what to do to make it all better. We argue that this guilt is also expressed by non-white Australians in society with conversations that disregard the assumed characteristic that Australia is the 'lucky' country where everyone gets a 'fair go'. White guilt can generate/result in/give rise to white resistance which is the outright rejection of the principles of anti-racism (Flynn, 2015).

When confronted with the behaviours generally associated with guilt or resistance, many social workers (and people in general) become angry or distressed. This has been termed white fragility and defined as 'a state in which even a minimum amount of racial stress becomes intolerable, triggering a range of defensive moves (DiAngelo, 2011). These moves include the outward display of emotions such as anger, fear, and guilt, and behaviours such as silence, and leaving/ignoring the stress-inducing situation. These behaviours, in turn, function to reinstate and reinforce white racial equilibrium' (p. 54). White fragility is an automatic, uncritical response to the introduction of critical conversations about race and racism. To a certain degree, it is a manifestation of resistance (DiAngelo, 2018).

Discomfort or anxiety about making a cultural *faux pas* may be the reason why some social workers are still sitting ambivalent with regard to acknowledging and eliminating racism. Hooks (1992) noted that white people who conceptualise themselves as the least racist often become the angriest when confronted with people viewing them as white. Hooks states 'often their rage erupts because they believe that all ways of looking that highlight difference subvert the liberal belief in a universal subjectivity that they think will make racism disappear. They have a deep emotional investment in the myth of "sameness," even as their actions reflect the primacy of Whiteness as a sign informing who they are and how they think' (1992, p. 167).

Difficult emotions, such as anger, hostility, frustration, and emotional pain, must be used to engage in a process that is creative enough to establish new forms of social existence where both parties are transformed and benefit (Leonardo & Porter, 2010). It is important that social workers, even with the limited time that they have, are not rushing through tasks without pausing and considering. In this way, gently and thoughtfully engaging with the issues of racism and colonisation are essential steps in recognising and rectifying the mistakes of the past that continue to resonate and oppress in the twentieth century.

Racial battle fatigue and white people fatigue syndromes arise in Aboriginal and Torres Strait Islander peoples from having to constantly address and teach white people how and why particular actions and microaggressions are not trivial, but inherently racist. Racial battle fatigue (Smith, 2004; Smith, Hung, & Franklin, 2011a; Smith, Yosso, & Solorzano, 2006) includes the increased levels of psychosocial stressors and subsequent psychological (e.g. frustration, shock, anger, disappointment, resentment, hopelessness), physiological (e.g. headache, backache, 'butterflies', teeth grinding, high blood pressure, insomnia) and behavioural responses (e.g. social withdrawal, self-doubt, and a dramatic change in diet) of fighting continual racial microaggressions. The Feminist Griote (2013), a Black queer feminist activist, stated 'I am tired of always having to prove to whites that racism exists ... I am tired of whites trying to prove to me that they aren't racist, but as soon as it is time for them to interrupt oppression on my behalf, I am on my own' (para. 1).

Microaggressions are subtle and often subconscious verbal and non-verbal insults based on one's race, gender, class, sexuality, language, immigration status, which cause unnecessary stress to people of colour while endorsing the historical privilege of white people. The accumulative stress from racial microaggressions produces racial battle fatigue. The stress of unavoidable racial talks leads to minorities feeling mental, emotionally, and physically exhausted. The stress from racial microaggressions can even lead to self-harm and suicide when the accumulation of physiological symptoms of racial battle fatigue are left untreated, unnoticed, misdiagnosed, or personally dismissed (Smith, Yosso, & Solórzano, 2011b).

One of the stakeholders had this to say:

> I think it is so important to create spaces for these types of conversations, it is so important that instead of our people getting angry and shutting it down we stand our ground. We can do this by educating ourselves well enough to stand our ground but to do that without losing our shit you know for want of a better word, without losing it and stand our ground intelligently.
>
> I can't fix this all myself, I didn't create all the issues myself and so I need people walking with me in that and part of healing is sometimes working with the very thing that was the trauma in the first place, creating space and creating opportunity for conversation and growth and welcoming people in so they feel like they can be a part of the journey but then also being harsh when you need to be, being up front and saying that is not appropriate for this reason and you need to rethink the way that you do that.
>
> For me it is about finding tangible ways to assist people to feel where you are at. We can academically tell people a whole range

of different knowledge all the time but unless someone feels it, then change isn't going to come. People need to feel it internally and feel empowered enough to do something about it for real change to happen so the processes that I use is education, through tangible activities that assist people to develop an understanding, a range of activities such as taking them on a journey and inviting them into my culture and showing them different cultural practices but then also helping people to understand that sometimes it is not their space to work in and they need to sit back and understand that we need to guide this part of the process and helping them understand that they are going to be uncomfortable, they are going to sit and be uncomfortable and that is very much part of the journey as anyone else and they are not going to understand everything at that point. They will see it enough and build their own understanding that some things just take time; they say it took three generations to break culture for Aboriginal people and it is going to take a hell of a lot longer to put back, it is a generational process.

You need the broad support; you need every layer of the organisation supporting the movement and then you can start moving forward together but that takes time. It takes conversations, it takes uncomfortable conversations but the relationship there is huge and that is a journey, that is a huge journey that you need to take people on. (Stakeholder 5)

Racism is, and has been, painful for all of us. Friere (1970) reminded us that under regimes of oppression both the oppressed and the oppressor are dehumanised. Through the process of liberation, both must be humanised and, if the oppressed continues to perpetuate the practices of the oppressor, no one is truly liberated. Now is not the time for privileged peoples to ignore these issues because they want to avoid conflict or to take neutral stances on Aboriginal and Torres Strait Islander issues. Now is the time for all to become culturally responsive and to help those who are being marginalised. The following case studies discuss how cultural misunderstanding and mistakes are continuing to be made and what can be done to address and avoid this from occurring.

Case study discussion

Despite social workers stating they want to become more culturally responsive, discussions with stakeholders identified that there are still frequent cultural misunderstandings and mistakes being made and these make the relationship and trusting process complicated and may even break them. What exactly is occurring, and how can we prevent it? One of the things the Aboriginal authors have identified is that there seems to be a lack of honest discussion about the real cultural protocols surrounding interactions with an Aboriginal community. This, coupled with good-natured, well-intentioned but still ignorant, white privileging, leads to major mistakes.

The information used in this chapter were gathered from a series of interviews undertaken as part of an Australian Research Council grant (ARC). We focused on interviewing several Aboriginal and Torres Strait Islander peoples across Australia who, over the course of their personal or professional life, had interacted with social workers. They were asked what made culturally responsive behaviour and to give examples or comment on behaviour that they had observed that was not culturally responsive or inclusive. There were nine males and nine females and two Torres Strait Islander stakeholder responses. These discussions made clear to the authors that, although social workers were trying to engage, something was still going wrong and it was creating defensiveness and unwillingness to engage for both parties. To understand what was occurring, one of the Aboriginal authors posted on twitter asking Aboriginal people – 'what are the common mistakes social workers are making when they are trying to engage with us?' These case studies are based on both the ARC responses and social media responses and the Aboriginal authors' personal experiences.

Box 16:1 Case study 1

I have a question for you. (no culturally appropriate introduction) I am wanting to (source a name using Aboriginal and Torres Strait Islander words, get a piece of Aboriginal artwork) for my professional or personal space (to be more culturally responsive?) I am wondering if you can help me with how you would do this. I want words that I can pronounce and artwork/names that I like. Would you be able to suggest something or send me to someone who can help me?

Common mistakes in social work – 1

Creating a space that is given an Aboriginal name or displays a piece of artwork is not necessarily representing the community/ies in which you live. These examples can be taken out of context or seen as tokenistic. It makes the Aboriginal person responsible for the tasks of finding, sourcing, and referring to the artist/Traditional Custodians and takes the accountability of reciprocal relationship away from the non-Indigenous person. For many Aboriginal and Torres Strait Islander people, requests for this kind of recognition are never-ending but,

---

even after engaging with the name/artwork, the organisation/people/ service doesn't seem to change their cultural responsiveness – which may become exhausting.

Aboriginal stakeholder comments: Stakeholder 6 stated that social workers need an understanding of the Aboriginal communities that they live in and work with. This means spending time with the community and becoming accepted by the community. This would mean having the connections to be able to know how to make an organisational space more culturally responsive (which may *then* include naming a space or artwork), but it should involve the community from the outset. Stakeholders also suggested that it was important to be respectful and listen to the needs of the community and to engage with genuine intent rather than treating the relationship as 'just a job'.

Box 16.2 Case study 2

I am are interested in Aboriginal and Torres Strait Islander (insert topics here) and am keen to learn as much as possible. During our placement/work/volunteer, I have had many challenges, both personally and professionally. I would like to speak to you for guidance on how to navigate Aboriginal (issues) work in Australia. Any advice you may have to offer would be incredibly valued.

Common mistakes in social work – 2

Approaching Aboriginal and Torres Strait Islander persons without a prior relationship or without another Aboriginal person to vouch for your appropriateness and safety is rude and can be considered unsafe by the Aboriginal person. As well as this, it may seem to be treating Aboriginal persons as a Google source, expecting them to give time and provide cultural information for free and with no obvious social benefit. Non-Indigenous people wouldn't ask a privileged white person to give their expertise for free. Aboriginal and Torres Strait Islander knowledge is culturally specific and could be considered unique and specialised. It should never be assumed that an Aboriginal person will performs unpaid labour or give cultural knowledge for free. For the Aboriginal and Torres Strait Islander people, they do not know what will happen with the shared knowledge and this could be considered unsafe. It is also considered polite if you don't already have any relationship, to give a culturally appropriate introduction so that the Aboriginal and Torres Strait Islander persons can make choices about the nature of the interactions. The worker could use paid cultural supervision or create a relationship with an Aboriginal worker/s for a support system.

Aboriginal stakeholder comments: '*I often get the question from people if they are not culturally aware tell us your story. It's like to tell us your own story. Everyone has a story about where they come from and what happened to them, their journey. It is frustrating sometimes in that way. Especially when you are trying to build a mutual sharing relationship. It is not about us always telling. It has to be equal. It has to be reciprocal*' (Stakeholder 4).

Box 16.3 Case study 3

We are piloting a (research study, program,). We have put together the attached description which still needs some work to be culturally responsive. If you have a minute, as an Aboriginal person can you cast your eye on the brief document, it would be great to get your thoughts. We hope to start the pilot in the next few months. It is also possible that we might apply for a small research grant. **xxx** is keen to be mentored in this work.

Common mistakes in social work – 3

To 'cast your eye over' means read not only a lengthy document but also give 60,000 years of cultural expertise for free. Being asked to be on any project when it has already begun, and the objectives established, is very rude. We often say: 'if we are not at the table then we are on the menu'. Giving free cultural knowledge without reward, kudos, or not having your name attached to any output is a form of cultural appropriation and is not responsive behaviour. Asking to provide mentorship with no conversation about how the Aboriginal person will be recognised and recompensed is also rude (and possibly abusive). Aboriginal and Torres Strait Islander people who are approached about mentoring should have the power to decide whether that person is suitable, to decide if the individual is an ally in their space, and respectfully decline if they aren't the right fit.

Aboriginal stakeholder comments: Stakeholder 5 states '*I know for our people it is really hard to say no. So Aboriginal people might say it in numerous other ways. But if someone is not truly listening, they miss the no*'.

Box 16.4 Case study 4

My name is xxx and I am writing to introduce myself. I am currently the chair of the inclusivity and diversity group (insert other such names here). We were wondering if you would come and meet with us to discuss XX and how it affects Aboriginal people (insert all kinds of topics requested in here).

Common mistakes in social work – 4

Is this example a non-Indigenous, able-bodied, straight person employed is in a role that demands skills, attitudes, and responsibilities for which they are unsuited. If so, these shortcomings will be obvious to an Aboriginal onlooker. The Aboriginal authors say that if a white person is sitting in our chair, we are too polite to ask you to stand up so that we can sit down. This metaphor demands that you ask yourself: Am I or the committee that I am currently sitting on making excuses for the lack of representation and saying, 'we can't find anyone Aboriginal or Torres Strait Islander' or 'no one Aboriginal or Torres Strait Islander applied'? Currently there are over 500 Aboriginal and Torres Strait Islander social workers in Australia, so their absence for decision making groups is inexcusable. The truth is more likely that the organisation is not culturally safe enough and this discourages us from applying for membership. Ask yourself this: Is the chair that you are currently occupying getting hot and uncomfortable? If so, you should stand up and wait a while to check whether an Aboriginal could sit down? Ideally, you should be more proactive and looking for someone Aboriginal to replace you. Don't talk about enabling us and then disempower us by making no effort to install us in a position of influence. In the unlikely event that there is no Indigenous persons trained to occupy the position, you must co-run the group until the appointed Aboriginal person is skilled enough to assume sole control.

Aboriginal stakeholders' comments:

Be guided by rather than listen and guide others. (Stakeholder 5)

Hold on you don't know me and I don't know you. Who are you? For me, it is that gut reaction where you feel safe and I am going to tell you about what is really going on or I am just going to oh I don't want to be here, and I am not going to come back. And I might not tell you that. (Stakeholder 4)

That's a big thing when you are working with people you know from a different culture or a different place, you got to think about how your interaction is impacting other people, you've got to always be critically reflecting. (Stakeholder 7)

> **Box 16.5 Case study 5**
>
> I was training Aboriginal 'at risk' teenagers. After the first morning, everyone went to lunch and half of them didn't come back. I rang the Elders annoyed. They told me to take them to lunch. Many cafes wouldn't let us in, and the police constantly stopped and searched the young boys. My lack of understanding was shameful.
>
> This is not an example of a mistake, but it does highlight the need to be critically reflexive of your privilege and your own experiences before you go into any Aboriginal and Torres Strait Islander communities to do social work practice.
>   Aboriginal stakeholder comments:
>
> > Everything in a mainstream service tailors to a mainstream service. It tailors to whiteness. (Stakeholder 5)
> >   To work with people, you have to be self-reflective and understand your privilege regardless of where you are from and what your history is. (Stakeholder 4)

Discussion

'Once we presume to "know" another we appropriate that person's culture and reinforce our own dominant, egocentric position. I am proposing that we distrust the experience of "competence" and replace it with a state of mind in which are interested and open but always tentative about we understand' (Dean, 2001, p. 629). From the case studies, it is obvious that it is in the very first interaction and what you do or say that can determine whether you engage or disengage Aboriginal and Torres Strait Islander peoples. Successful engagement may just be that little extra step before or making sure you are following respectful cultural protocols. Some advice from our Aboriginal stakeholders includes:

> Tell them who you are and where you are from and what's brought you here. So if they don't get a good vibe from you Aboriginal people are not going to want to engage with you; they are not going to want to see you, they are not going to disclose what they need to disclose to you for you to be able to do best practice. That it is going to be hard especially I find a lot of people are afraid to open up about themselves for them they got to think if you are unwilling to do it how are they going to do it with you? (Stakeholder 8)

> It is vital to have community input, control, and choice if you want to improve your cultural responsiveness and that of the services you offer as a social worker. As noted above, it will be considered rude or inappropriate to approach an Aboriginal person unless you plan to have an ongoing and consistent relationship that is based on equity, trust, and mutual respect. (Stakeholder 7)

Non-Indigenous people trying to be of assistance to Aboriginal people need to make sure that they are not being patronising. Aboriginal people may not have the same conventional educational outcomes or skills but, as Stakeholder 5 stated, *'this does not mean they are less human or any less sharp than what someone else might be'*. It is very important when starting to be culturally responsive that non-Indigenous people do not try to come across as saviours, appear to fake concern, or are even apologetic concerning past and present discrimination. Aboriginal people do not want special treatment; they just want to be treated with respect as valuable members of society. Culturally responsive practice will not happen overnight and it demands commitment and frequent self-analysis before it eventually becomes an integral part of your personality.

Discussion Questions

1. Have you reviewed IAHA's cultural responsiveness framework? What has it taught you?

2. How might you react differently now you have read this chapter? (e.g. you might read a document on language or protocols)

3. How might you explain to another social worker a better approach based on this chapter and the knowledge you now have?

References

AASW. (2010). *Code of ethics*. Canberra, ACT: Australian Association of Social Workers.

AASW. (2016). *Preparing for culturally responsive and inclusive social work practice in Australia: Working with Aboriginal and Torres Strait Islander peoples*. Canberra, ACT: Australian Association of Social Workers.

Bennett, B., Redfern, H., & Zubrzycki, J. (2017). Cultural responsiveness in action: Co-constructing social work curriculum resources with Aboriginal communities. *British Journal of Social Work, 48*(3), 808–825.

Bennett, B., Zubrzycki, J., & Bacon, V. (2011). What do we know? The experiences of social workers working alongside Aboriginal people. *Australian social work, 64*(1), 20–37.

Dean, R. G. (2001). The myth of cross-cultural competence. *Families in Society, 82*(6), 623–630.

DiAngelo, R. (2011). White fragility. *International Journal of Critical Pedagogy, 3*(3), 54–70.

DiAngelo, R. (2018). *White fragility: Why it's so hard for white people to talk about racism*. Boston, MA: Beacon Press.

Downing, R., & Kowal, E. (2011). A postcolonial analysis of Indigenous cultural awareness training for health workers. *Health Sociology Review, 20*(1), 5–15.

Flynn Jr., J. E. (2015). White fatigue: Naming the challenge in moving from an individual to a systemic understanding of racism. *Multicultural Perspectives, 17*(3), 115–124.

Friere, P. (1970). *Pedagogy of the oppressed*. [Translated by Myra Bergman Ramos]. New York, NY: Continuum.

Goodman, D. J. (2011). *Promoting diversity and social justice: Educating people from privileged groups*. London: Routledge.

Hitchcock, J. (2002). *Lifting the white veil: An exploration of White American culture in a multi-racial context*. Roselle, NJ: Crandall, Dostie & Douglass Books.

Hooks, B. (1992). *Black looks: Race and representation*. Boston, MA: South End Press.

Indigenous Allied Health Australia (IAHA). (2015). *Cultural responsiveness in action: An IAHA framework*. Deakin, ACT: IAHA.

Leonardo, Z. (2004). The color of supremacy: Beyond the discourse of 'white privilege'. *Educational Philosophy and Theory, 36*(2), 137–152.

Leonardo, Z., & Porter, R. K. (2010). Pedagogy of fear: Toward a Fanonian theory of 'safety' in race dialogue. *Race Ethnicity and Education, 13*(2), 139–157.

Martin, K., & Mirraboopa, B. (2003). Ways of knowing, being and doing: A theoretical framework and methods for Indigenous and Indigenist re-search. *Journal of Australian Studies, 27*(76), 203–214.

Smith, W. A. (2004). Black faculty coping with racial battle fatigue: The campus racial climate in a post-civil rights era. In D. Cleveland (Ed.), *A long way to go: Conversations about race by African American faculty and graduate students* (pp. 171–190). Thousand Oaks, CA: Sage.

Smith, W. A., Hung, M., & Franklin, J. D. (2011a). Racial battle fatigue and the miseducation of Black men: Racial microaggressions, societal problems, and environmental stress. *The Journal of Negro Education, 80*, 63–82.

Smith, W. A., Yosso, T. J., & Solorzano, D. G. (2006). Challenging racial battle fatigue on historically White campuses: A critical race examination of race-related stress. In C. A. Stanley (Ed.), *Faculty of color teaching in predominantly White colleges and universities* (pp. 299–327). Bolton, MA: Anker.

Smith, W. A., Yosso, T. J., & Solórzano, D. G. (2011b). Challenging racial battle fatigue on historically White campuses: A critical race examination of race-related stress. In *Covert racism* (pp. 211–237). Boston, MA: Brill.

Stewart, S. (2006). *Cultural competence in health care*. Sydney, NSW: Diversity Health Institute.

Tatum, B. D. (1994). Teaching White students about racism: The search for White allies and the restoration of hope. *Teachers College Record, 95*, 462–467.

The Feminist Griote. (2013, April 23). *White people fatigue syndrome.* (Web log comment). Retrieved from http://thefeministgriote.com/white-peoplefatigue-syndrome/

Williams, O. (2007). *Concepts in creating culturally responsive services for supervised visitation centers.* Institute on Domestic Violence in the African American Community. http://www.idvaac.org/media/pubs/SuperVisitBook.pdf. Accessed 27 June 2016.

Zubrzycki, J., & Bennett, B. (2006). Aboriginal Australians. In W. Hong Chui & J. Wilson (Eds.), *Social work and human services best practice* (pp. 192–210). Leichhardt, NSW: The Federation Press.

Zubrzycki, J., Green, S., Jones, V., Stratton, K., Young, S., & Bessarab, D. (2014). *Getting it right: Creating partnerships for change. Integrating Aboriginal and Torres Strait Islander knowledges in social work education and practice.* Sydney, NSW: Office for Learning and Teaching (OLT).

INDEX